M

L
C

D1325685

Invoice : 07/1400 Price EUR45.79
Title: Children's illustrate
Class:

032

# DORLING KINDERSLEY
# CHILDREN'S ILLUSTRATED ENCYCLOPEDIA

## NEW EDITION

# DORLING KINDERSLEY
# CHILDREN'S
# ILLUSTRATED
# ENCYCLOPEDIA

DK

LONDON, NEW YORK,
MELBOURNE, MUNICH, AND DELHI

### FIRST EDITION 1991

**Senior Editor** Ann Kramer
**Senior Art Editor** Miranda Kennedy
**Editors** Christiane Gunzi, Susan McKeever, Richard Platt, Clifford Rosney
**Art Editors** Muffy Dodson, Debra Lee, Christian Sévigny, Val Wright
**Picture Research** Anne Lyons
**Additional Research** Anna Kunst, Deborah Murrell
**Picture Manager** Kate Fox
**Production Manager** Teresa Solomon
**Editorial Director** Sue Unstead

### SIXTH EDITION 2006

**Editors** Jenny Finch, Aekta Jerath
**Designers** Sheila Collins, Romi Chakraborty
**Senior Editor** Fran Baines
**Managing Editor** Linda Esposito
**Managing Art Editor** Diane Thistlethwaite
**Publishing Managers** Caroline Buckingham, Andrew Macintyre
**Category Publisher** Laura Buller
**Picture Researcher** Bridget Tily
**DK Picture Library** Martin Copeland
**Senior Cartographic Editor** Simon Mumford
**Cartographer** Ed Merritt
**Production Controller** Erica Rosen
**DTP Designers** Siu Chan, Harish Aggarwal
**DTP Coordinator** Pankaj Sharma
**Jacket Designer** Phil Letsu
**Jacket Editor** Mariza O'Keeffe

First published in Great Britain in 1991
by Dorling Kindersley Limited,
9 Henrietta Street, London WC2E 8PS
Reprinted 1991, 1992 (twice), 1993
Reprinted with revisions 1992
Second edition 1993
Third edition 1995
Fourth edition 1996, reprinted 1997
1998, 1999
Fifth edition 2000
Sixth edition 2006

Copyright © 1991, 1993, 1995, 1996, 2000, 2006 Dorling Kindersley Limited
A Penguin Company

2 4 6 8 10 9 7 5 3 1

All rights reserved. No part of this publication may be reproduced, stored
in a retrieval system, or transmitted in any form or by any means, electronic,
mechanical, photocopying, recording, or otherwise, without the prior
written permission of the copyright owner.

A CIP catalogue record for this book is available from the British Library.

ISBN-13: 978-1-40531-497-8
ISBN-10: 1-4053-1497-4

Colour reproduction by Colourscan, Singapore
Printed and bound by Toppan, China

Discover more at
**www.dk.com**

# CONTENTS

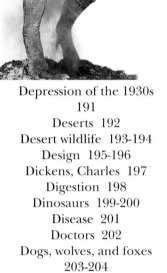

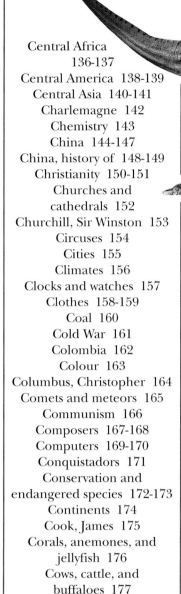

# HOW TO USE THIS BOOK

IT IS EASY TO FIND in-depth information on a wide range of subjects in the *Dorling Kindersley Children's Illustrated Encyclopedia*. The next three pages will show you how. Main entries are in alphabetical order, beginning with Aboriginal Australians and ending with Zoos. Each main entry has either one or more pages to itself. To find your chosen topic, look through the main headings at the top of the pages alphabetically. If you can't find the topic you are looking for, then it is not a main entry and does not have its own page. In that case, turn to the index at the back, which will tell you what page to look at for information about your topic.

**ILLUSTRATIONS**
Detailed illustrations bring subjects to life. This illustration shows people bringing gifts for the king of Persia to the royal palace on New Year's Day.

**ANNOTATION**
Every illustration or photograph is clearly explained using annotation.

**MAPS**
Some pages include a map to show the location of the relevant area in the world. This map shows the location and extent of the Persian Empire.

**TIMELINE**
Many historical entry pages include a timeline, which is like a calendar of history on a scroll. Timelines give you all the dates you need, at a glance. This timeline guides you through the rise of the Ancient Persians to the collapse of the Persian Empire.

**INTRODUCTION**
Each main entry page begins with an introduction, which provides general information and key facts about a subject. You will be able to gain a basic knowledge of a subject before reading on.

**SUB-ENTRIES**
Further information on a subject is given in sub-entries, such as this one describing the city of Persepolis, the royal capital of Ancient Persia.

**PHOTOGRAPHS**
Photographs appear on most pages and show all kinds of subjects. This photograph is of a carved horse's head from the Ancient Persian city of Persepolis.

**FIND OUT MORE**
The Find Out More box at the lower right-hand corner of the page at the end of every entry directs you to other main entries on related subjects. For example, the Ancient Persians' Find Out More box lists five related entries: Alexander the Great, Assyrians, Babylonians, Ancient Greece, and Middle East. By turning to these you will discover more about the world of the Ancient Persians.

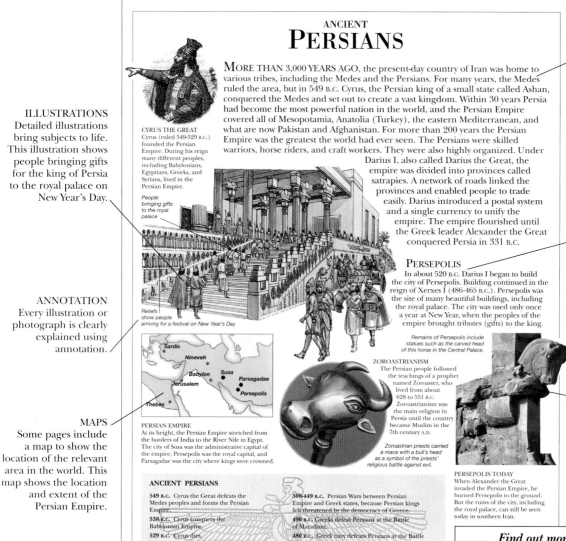

ANCIENT
## PERSIANS

MORE THAN 3,000 YEARS AGO, the present-day country of Iran was home to various tribes, including the Medes and the Persians. For many years, the Medes ruled the area, but in 549 B.C. Cyrus, the Persian king of a small state called Ashan, conquered the Medes and set out to create a vast kingdom. Within 30 years Persia had become the most powerful nation in the world, and the Persian Empire covered all of Mesopotamia, Anatolia (Turkey), the eastern Mediterranean, and what are now Pakistan and Afghanistan. For more than 200 years the Persian Empire was the greatest the world had ever seen. The Persians were skilled warriors, horse riders, and craft workers. They were also highly organized. Under Darius I, also called Darius the Great, the empire was divided into provinces called satrapies. A network of roads linked the provinces and enabled people to trade easily. Darius introduced a postal system and a single currency to unify the empire. The empire flourished until the Greek leader Alexander the Great conquered Persia in 331 B.C.

**CYRUS THE GREAT**
Cyrus (ruled 549-529 B.C.) founded the Persian Empire. During his reign many different peoples, including Babylonians, Egyptians, Greeks, and Syrians, lived in the Persian Empire.

*People bringing gifts to the royal palace*

*Reliefs show people arriving for a festival on New Year's Day*

**PERSEPOLIS**
In about 520 B.C. Darius I began to build the city of Persepolis. Building continued in the reign of Xerxes I (486-465 B.C.). Persepolis was the site of many beautiful buildings, including the royal palace. The city was used only once a year at New Year, when the peoples of the empire brought tributes (gifts) to the king.

*Remains of Persepolis include statues such as the carved head of this horse in the Central Palace.*

**ZOROASTRIANISM**
The Persian people followed the teachings of a prophet named Zoroaster, who lived from about 628 to 551 B.C. Zoroastrianism was the main religion in Persia until the country became Muslim in the 7th century A.D.

*Zoroastrian priests carried a mace with a bull's head as a symbol of the priests' religious battle against evil.*

**PERSIAN EMPIRE**
At its height, the Persian Empire stretched from the borders of India to the River Nile in Egypt. The city of Susa was the administrative capital of the empire, Persepolis was the royal capital, and Parsagadae was the city where kings were crowned.

*Sardis · Nineveh · Babylon · Susa · Parsagadae · Jerusalem · Persepolis · Thebes*

**PERSEPOLIS TODAY**
When Alexander the Great invaded the Persian Empire, he burned Persepolis to the ground. But the ruins of the city, including the royal palace, can still be seen today in southern Iran.

### ANCIENT PERSIANS

**549 B.C.** Cyrus the Great defeats the Medes peoples and forms the Persian Empire.

**538 B.C.** Cyrus conquers the Babylonian Empire.

**529 B.C.** Cyrus dies.

**525 B.C.** Persians conquer Egypt.

**521-486 B.C.** Reign of Darius the Great.

**510 B.C.** Persians invade southeast Europe and central Asia.

**500-449 B.C.** Persian Wars between Persian Empire and Greek states, because Persian kings felt threatened by the democracy of Greece.

**490 B.C.** Greeks defeat Persians at the Battle of Marathon.

**480 B.C.** Greek navy defeats Persians at the Battle of Salamis.

**334 B.C.** Alexander the Great invades Persia.

**331 B.C.** Alexander defeats Persians at the Battle of Gaugamela. Persian Empire collapses.

509

*Find out more*
ALEXANDER THE GREAT
ASSYRIANS
BABYLONIANS
GREECE, ANCIENT
MIDDLE EAST

## SYMBOLS

| Volcano | Mountain | Ancient monument | Capital city | Large city/ town | Small city/ town |
|---|---|---|---|---|---|

**SYMBOLS**
Each map has symbols to indicate features of interest. These include capital cities, major cities and towns, tallest mountains or highest points, volcanoes, ancient monuments and places of historical importance.

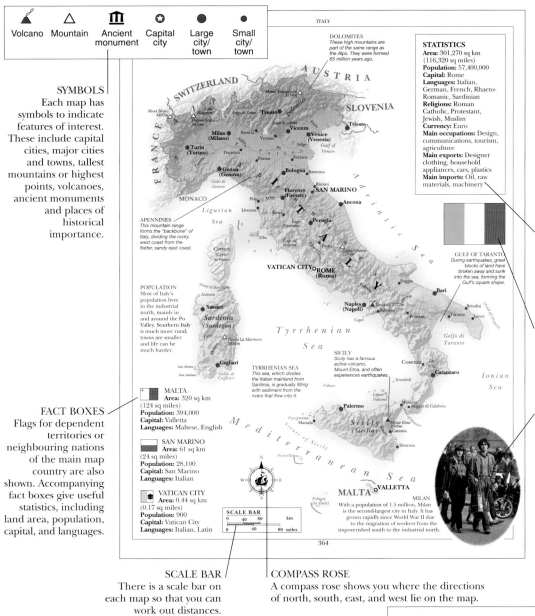

ITALY

**DOLOMITES**
These high mountains are part of the same range as the Alps. They were formed 65 million years ago.

**STATISTICS**
**Area:** 301,270 sq km (116,320 sq miles)
**Population:** 57,400,000
**Capital:** Rome
**Languages:** Italian, German, French, Rhaeto-Romanic, Sardinian
**Religions:** Roman Catholic, Protestant, Jewish, Muslim
**Currency:** Euro
**Main occupations:** Design, communications, tourism, agriculture
**Main exports:** Designer clothing, household appliances, cars, plastics
**Main imports:** Oil, raw materials, machinery

**APENNINES**
This mountain range forms the "backbone" of Italy, dividing the rocky west coast from the flatter, sandy east coast.

**GULF OF TARANTO**
During earthquakes, great blocks of land have broken away and sunk into the sea, forming the Gulf's square shape.

**POPULATION**
Most of Italy's population lives in the industrial north, mainly in and around the Po Valley. Southern Italy is much more rural; towns are smaller and life can be much harder.

**TYRRHENIAN SEA**
This sea, which divides the Italian mainland from Sardinia, is gradually filling with sediment from the rivers that flow into it.

**SICILY**
Sicily has a famous active volcano, Mount Etna, and often experiences earthquakes.

**MALTA**
**Area:** 320 sq km (124 sq miles)
**Population:** 394,000
**Capital:** Valletta
**Languages:** Maltese, English

**SAN MARINO**
**Area:** 61 sq km (24 sq miles)
**Population:** 28,100
**Capital:** San Marino
**Languages:** Italian

**VATICAN CITY**
**Area:** 0.44 sq km (0.17 sq miles)
**Population:** 900
**Capital:** Vatican City
**Languages:** Italian, Latin

**MILAN**
With a population of 1.5 million, Milan is the second-largest city in Italy. It has grown rapidly since World War II due to the migration of workers from the impoverished south to the industrial north.

364

**FACT BOXES**
Flags for dependent territories or neighbouring nations of the main map country are also shown. Accompanying fact boxes give useful statistics, including land area, population, capital, and languages.

**MAPS**
There are maps for all the continents and major countries of the world. Each map shows main regions, physical features, large cities, and some important historical sites. On every map page is a fact box containing flags and information about the region. Photographs show subjects of interest.

**STATISTICS BOX**
Every map is accompanied by a statistics box giving information on factors such as land area, population, languages, religions, currency, and main occupations.

**FLAG**
The flag of the major country on the map is always shown. This is the Italian flag.

**SUBJECTS OF INTEREST**
Photographs show characteristic views of different regions. This one shows a scene in Milan, the fashion centre of Italy.

**BIG BANG**
NEARLY FOURTEEN BILLION YEARS AGO, the universe exploded out of virtually nothing. The first scientist to propose this astonishing theory, now known as the Big Bang, was George Lemaître (1894-1966). His idea was supported by the work of Edwin Hubble (1889-1953), which showed that the universe is expanding. If this is so, the entire cosmos must have originated from a single point of explosion. But what was that single point? Scientists call it a "singularity" – a tiny, infinitely dense dot that once contained all the matter of the universe. Such a thing is impossible to imagine, and even astronomers do not really understand it. Yet within a few minutes of the Big Bang, the single point would have been converted into an immense, expanding cloud of gas. Over millions of years this became the galaxies, stars, and planets of the universe.

**SCALE BAR**
There is a scale bar on each map so that you can work out distances.

**COMPASS ROSE**
A compass rose shows you where the directions of north, south, east, and west lie on the map.

**SWIMMING**
FROM CROWDS ON A BEACH TO BATHERS by a pool, most people enjoy swimming. It is one of the most popular sports for people of all ages. Swimming – using your arms and legs to move through water – exercises every part of the body, encouraging health and fitness. It is also an important international sport. Competitive swimmers need to be very strong and fit. They train for hours, swimming huge distances every week. For swimmers such as these, an Olympic gold medal is the ultimate goal. But almost anyone can learn to swim, whether taking a fast-moving crawl, slower breaststroke, or even a doggy paddle. Learning to swim well is an important safety measure, and it can save lives.

**Diagrams explain scientific theories clearly and simply.**

**Sports pages show the type of equipment used for specific activities.**

A biography box gives at-a-glance facts and dates about a person.

**CHARLES DARWIN**

1809 Born in Shrewsbury, Shropshire, England.
1825-27 Studies medicine at Edinburgh University.
1827 Studies divinity at Cambridge, but spends more time on biology, zoology, and geology.
1831-36 HMS Beagle voyage.
1858 Evolutionary theory first explained to the world.
1859 Publishes On the Origin of Species – it is a best-seller.
1882 Dies; buried at Westminster Abbey, London.

ON 27 DECEMBER 1831, HMS Beagle sailed from Plymouth, England to survey the east and west coasts of South America. On board was the ship's naturalist, Charles Darwin. The ship sailed beyond the Americas to the Pacific Ocean, where Darwin made many scientific discoveries, especially on the Galapagos and Keeling Islands. As a schoolboy, Darwin had often been in trouble with his headmaster for spending time on chemistry experiments and collecting specimens instead of studying Greek and Latin. But his boyhood interest in the natural world led him to make startling discoveries about life on Earth and the development of the planet. When he returned from sea in 1836, he married, settled in London, and wrote up the results of his discoveries. They formed the basis of his famous theory of evolution.

**VOYAGE OF THE BEAGLE**

**DEEP-SEA WILDLIFE**

THE DEPTHS OF THE SEA form the largest wildlife habitat on Earth. In waters below about 1,000 m (3,000 ft) no plants can grow because there is no sunlight. Yet here, in the vast blackness, many extraordinary creatures live. These animals are found nowhere else. They have adapted to survive where the water pressure is up to 1,000 times that at the surface. Some deep-sea fish feed on the bodies and remains of plants and animals that sink down from the water above. Some other fish have enormous mouths and long, back-curved teeth for grabbing and swallowing anything that swims by. These fish have huge stomachs which stretch to hold prey that is even bigger than themselves. On the deep-sea floor, sea anemones, worms, a cucumbers, brittlestars, crabs, prawns, and other cliffish serve the mud searching for tiny particles of old. Many kinds of deep-sea squid, shrimps, and flyfish are also found here.

**Nature pages include maps that show the main regions of the world where particular types of wildlife live.**

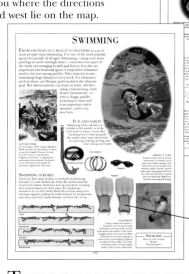

## TYPES OF MAIN ENTRY PAGES

There are main entry pages on a comprehensive range of subject matter, including biography and history, sports, natural history, science, and technology. All main entries appear in alphabetical order to make it easy to find the topic you are looking for.

# FACT FINDER

At the back of the encyclopedia is the Fact Finder, which provides an at-a-glance, fact-packed guide to history, geography, nature, science, and world facts. The Fact Finder provides instant information – clearly arranged in tables and charts – that will help you with school projects. It also acts as a reference source to support the subjects in the main entry pages.

*A timeline runs across the top of all the history pages so you can compare what happened in each continent on a certain date.*

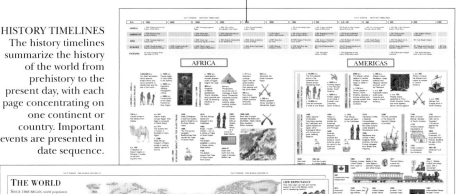

## HISTORY TIMELINES
The history timelines summarize the history of the world from prehistory to the present day, with each page concentrating on one continent or country. Important events are presented in date sequence.

## THE WORLD AROUND US
Within this section are three world maps showing different aspects of the current world situation: political boundaries and population growth, energy production and consumption, and the development of global communications. Introduction text describes current trends and how they affect the world we live in. Comparative statistics are shown in accessible charts and graphs.

*Charts make complex subjects easy to understand.*

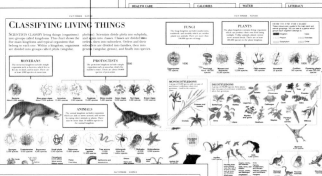

*Three-dimensional bar charts give comparative statistics for different countries.*

## NATURE
This section includes a comprehensive chart classifying plants and animals, a list of endangered species, and many other facts about the natural world.

*Star maps show the different constellations.*

*Many types of plant and animal life are illustrated.*

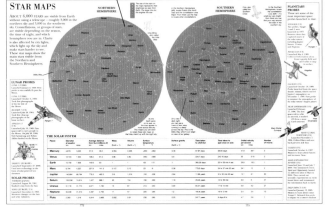

## STAR MAPS

## SCIENCE
In the science section you will find star maps, measurement and conversion charts, mathematical formulas, and a periodic table. Useful world facts, such as time zones, weather records, and lists of noteable geographic features, are also included.

# SIZE COMPARISONS AND ABBREVIATIONS

## SIZE COMPARISONS
Occasionally you will find this girl and boy. They are about 1.2 m (4 ft) tall and are there to give you an idea of the comparative sizes of objects or animals in relation to human beings.

## ABBREVIATIONS
Some words are abbreviated, or shortened, in the encyclopedia. The list below explains what the abbreviations stand for:

°C = degrees Celsius
°F = degrees Fahrenheit
mm = millimetre
cm = centimetre
m = metre
km = kilometre
sq km = square kilometre
km/h = kilometres per hour
in = inch
ft = foot
yd = yard
sq mile = square mile
mph = miles per hour
g = gram
kg = kilogram
oz = ounce
lb = pound
l = litre
c. before a date = "about"
B.C. = before Christ
A.D. = anno Domini, which refers to any time after the birth of Christ

## INDEX
There is an index at the back of the book in which you can find any subject mentioned in the encyclopedia. The numbers in the index refer to page numbers.
• Numbers in **bold** type refer to main A–Z entries.
• Numbers in *italic* type refer to pages in the Fact Finder, the reference section at the back of the encyclopedia.
• Numbers in normal type refer to general references within the encyclopedia.

*The number **101** tells you that there is a main entry about bridges on page 101.*

*The number 763 tells you that there is more information about bridges in the Fact Finder.*

*The number 709 tells you that the British Empire is mentioned on page 709.*

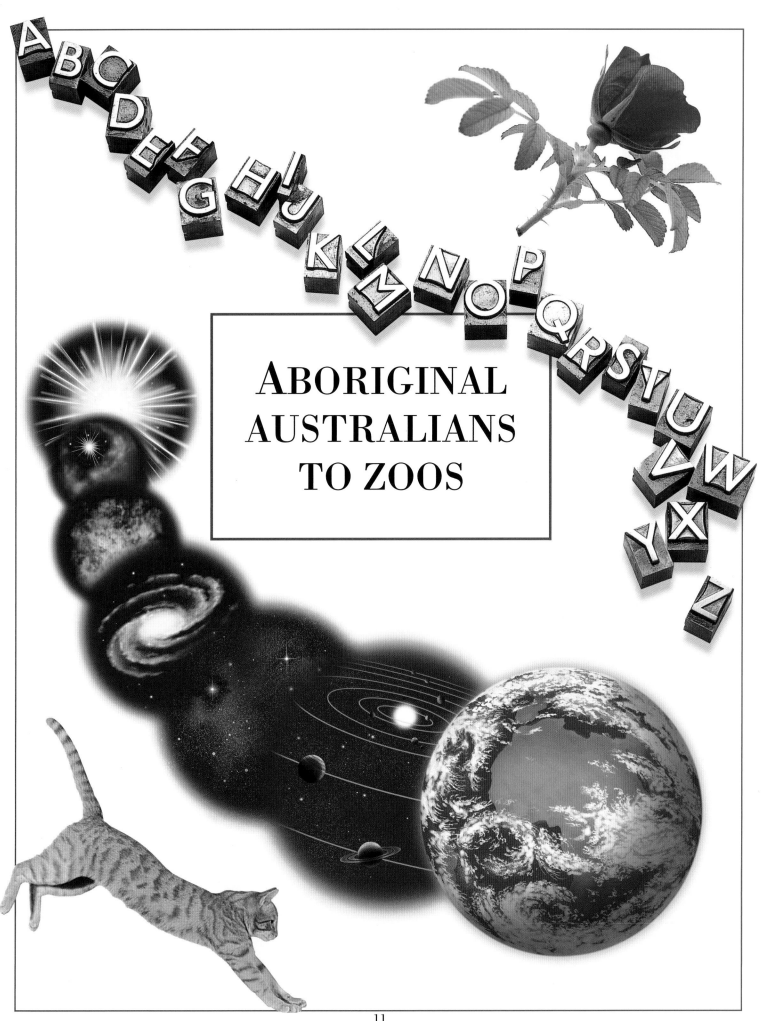

ABORIGINAL
AUSTRALIANS
TO ZOOS

# ABORIGINAL AUSTRALIANS

THE FIRST INHABITANTS of Australia were nomadic (wandering) people who reached the continent from Southeast Asia about 40,000 years ago. When Europeans settled in Australia at the end of the 18th century, they called these native inhabitants "aboriginals", meaning people who had lived there since the earliest times. Today there are about 410,000 aboriginals in Australia. Most live in cities, but a few thousand still try to follow a traditional way of life. They travel through the bush, hunting with spears and boomerangs (throwing sticks) and searching for food such as plants, grubs, and insects. They have few possessions and make everything they need from natural materials. This way of life does not change or harm the fragile environment of the Australian outback (the interior). The well-being of the land, and its plants and animals are vital and sacred to the aboriginal people.

**ART**
Aboriginal art is mostly about Dreamtime and is made as part of the ceremonies celebrating Dreamtime. Paintings of the people, spirits, and animals of Dreamtime cover sacred cliffs and rocks in tribal territories. The pictures are made in red and yellow ochre and white clay, and some are thousands of years old.

Private ceremonies and secret rituals are an important part of aboriginal life. Through dancing, singing, and chanting, young aboriginal people learn about Dreamtime.

Dancers, singers, and musicians paint their bodies with elaborate patterns.

The didjeridu, a wooden wind instrument, is used to play basic rhythms in aboriginal music.

## DREAMTIME
Aboriginal Australians believe that they have animal, plant, and human ancestors who created the world and everything in it. This process of creation is called Dreamtime. There are many songs and myths about Dreamtime, which generations of aboriginal people have passed down to their children.

**URBAN LIFE**
The majority of aboriginal Australians live in cities and towns. Some have benefitted from government education and aid programmes and have careers as teachers, doctors, and lawyers. Many, though, are poor and isolated from white society. They have lost touch with traditional aboriginal tribal ways, and because they do not fit neatly into white Australian society, they cannot always share its benefits. However, there are now campaigns among urban aboriginal people to revive interest in the tribal culture of their ancestors.

**LAND CLAIMS**
When British settlers arrived in Australia, they seized sacred sites and other land which belonged to aboriginal people. With the help of aboriginal lawyers, aboriginal Australians campaigned to get the land back. In 1976, the Australian government agreed that aboriginal people have rights to their tribal territories, and some land was returned.

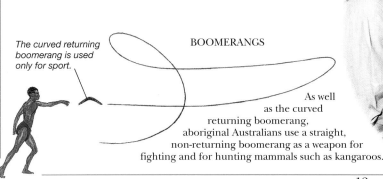

The curved returning boomerang is used only for sport.

BOOMERANGS

As well as the curved returning boomerang, aboriginal Australians use a straight, non-returning boomerang as a weapon for fighting and for hunting mammals such as kangaroos.

**Find out more**
AUSTRALIA
AUSTRALIA, HISTORY OF
AUSTRALIAN WILDLIFE
FESTIVALS
MYTHS AND LEGENDS

# ADVERTISING

GIANT HOARDINGS by the side of the road serve the same purpose as tiny classified newspaper advertisements. They tell us what products are available, and try to persuade us to choose one brand instead of another. Today's television commercials reach millions of people, but the first forms of advertising were much more local. Market traders shouted out what they had for sale, and shops displayed large signs to indicate their trade. Modern advertising began about 150 years ago when factories first produced goods in large quantities. Newspapers carried advertisements for everything from hats to patent medicines. Nowadays, advertising forms part of the business of marketing, which also includes product design, competitive pricing, packaging, and shop displays. Advertisements appear everywhere, not just on television and radio. They are also broadcast through in-store music, and painted on vehicle sides and in smoke trails in the sky. These advertising messages often amuse us, but not all advertisements are welcome. Strict laws protect the shopper from misleading advertising, and there are restrictions on the advertising of certain harmful products, such as tobacco and alcohol.

## COCA-COLA

Successful advertising makes a product so familiar that shoppers ask for it by name. Well-known goods are called brands. Some brands are sold worldwide. Coca-Cola is one of the most famous brand names. It was invented in the United States in 1886. From the beginning the makers of Coca-Cola advertised the drink widely, using a distinctive symbol, or trademark, of elegantly interlocking red letters. Within 10 years people in every state drank Coca-Cola. Today, the trademark is so well-known that it is recognizable in any alphabet.

© The Coca-Cola Company

*Market research questionnaire*

*Sample packaging material*

*Storyboard*

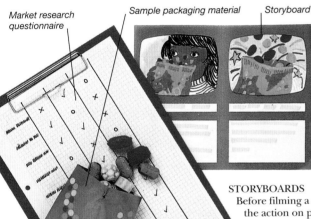

## LAUNCHING NEW PRODUCTS

Advertising is very expensive, so before launching a new bar, the chocolate company must be sure that it has created an appealing product that people will want to buy.

### STORYBOARDS
Before filming a commercial, a designer must draw the action on paper scene by scene, like a comic strip. A copywriter makes up the script and slogans to go with the pictures.

### MARKET RESEARCH
Hundreds of people taste the chocolate bar before it goes on sale, and answer questions about it. This process is called market research. They give their opinions on price, name, and size of the bar, and may look at plans for the wrapper.

### CAMPAIGNS
No manufacturer has an unlimited budget, so most advertising is concentrated into campaigns – short, intense bursts of advertising. During the campaign, advertisements appear in very carefully chosen spots. For example, commercials for a chocolate bar might appear during children's television programmes, not late at night. Similarly, press ads might appear in magazines aimed at young people.

## PROPAGANDA

Government advertisements which inform or advise the public are called propaganda. This poster, for instance, encourages Chinese people to work for a better society. Other campaigns persuade people to stop smoking, or to drive safely.

*Press advertisement*

*Television advertising is very costly, but reaches the biggest audience.*

*Displays in shops are called point-of-sale advertising.*

*Catchy tunes feature in much radio advertising.*

***Find out more***
SHOPS AND SHOPPING
TELEVISION AND VIDEO
TRADE AND INDUSTRY

# AFRICA

FEW REGIONS OF THE WORLD are as varied as Africa. On this vast continent there are 53 independent nations and many times this number of peoples and ancient cultures. There are mountains, valleys, plains, and swamps on a scale not seen elsewhere. The northern coast is rich and fertile; below it lies the dry Sahara Desert. South of the Sahara, lush rainforest grows. Most of southern and eastern Africa is savanna, a form of dry plain dotted with trees and bushes. The nations of Africa are generally poor, though some, such as Nigeria, have rich natural resources. Many governments are unstable, and rebellions and civil wars are common. There are few large cities; most are near the coast. The rest of the continent is open countryside where people follow traditional lifestyles.

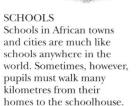

## SCHOOLS
Schools in African towns and cities are much like schools anywhere in the world. Sometimes, however, pupils must walk many kilometres from their homes to the schoolhouse.

Africa is roughly triangular in shape. The Atlantic Ocean lies to the west and the Indian Ocean to the east. In the northwest only a few kilometres of sea separate the African continent from Europe.

*The Tuareg peoples, who inhabit the Sahara, are pastoralists.*

*The Ashanti peoples of West Africa are mainly farmers.*

*The tall Masai of Kenya herd cattle on the open plains.*

## PEOPLE
In the African countryside many people live in tribal villages. Some, such as the Kikuyu of East Africa, are descended from tribes that have lived in the same place for many centuries. Others are recent immigrants from other parts of Africa or from other continents. Borders between countries take little account of these varied cultures. People of one culture may live in two different countries, and in one nation may be found more than a dozen different tribal groupings.

*Few pygmies are taller than 1.5 m (5 ft). They live in the dense Congo rainforest.*

*The towers of mosques dominate Cairo's skyline.*

*The Bushmen roam the deserts of southern Africa and gather wild food from the harsh environment.*

## KILIMANJARO
The tallest and most beautiful mountain in Africa is Kilimanjaro, in Tanzania. Its highest peak, which rises 5,895 m (19,340 ft), is an extinct volcano. Although the mountain is only a few kilometres from the equator, the top is always covered in snow. A footpath leads to the top, which can be reached in three days from the nearest road. Many people live on the lower slopes, where they farm tropical fruit.

## CAIRO
Cairo is the capital city of Egypt and the largest city in Africa, with a population of 15 million. It sits on the River Nile near the head of the river's delta. The older part of the city contains narrow, winding streets. The new city has wider streets and many modern office buildings and flats. The people of Cairo are mostly Egyptian, although some come from all over North Africa, as well as from Europe and the Middle East.

# SAHARA DESERT

The Sahara is the largest desert in the world and covers nearly one third of Africa. In recent years the desert has spread, destroying farmland and causing famine. In some areas irrigation has stopped the spread of the desert, but long-term irrigation can make the soil salty and infertile. Temperatures have been known to exceed 50°C (120°F) in this inhospitable environment.

## MUSIC AND CULTURE

Africa has a rich and varied culture. North Africa shares the Islamic traditions of the Middle East, producing beautiful mosques and palaces. West African music has a strong rhythm, and there are many interesting dances from this region. The area is also home to a flourishing wood-carving industry. Eastern and southern Africa have become famous for beautiful beadwork and colourful festive costumes.

*In West Africa, drumming is a highly developed art. People once used drum beats to pass on messages.*

## MEDICINE AND HEALING

When seeking a cure for sickness, some Africans consult Western-style doctors. Others consult a traditional healer (above). Healers are respected members of a community, with vast knowledge of local herbs and plants and the ways in which they can be used as medicines. To identify the source of an illness, the healer might contact good or evil spirits by going into a trance. Treatment may include animal sacrifice.

## WAR AND FAMINE

Civil wars and famines are common in Africa. Many are caused by political disagreements, and some are the result of tribal conflicts. In Chad a civil war lasting many years was fought between the desert Tuaregs, backed by Libya, and the farmers of the wetter areas. In Rwanda and Burundi fighting between the Tutsi and Hutu tribes has led to thousands of deaths. Other misery is caused by famine. Traditionally, most people grew enough food each year to last until the next harvest. However, African countries increasingly produce export crops and rely on imported food. If food distribution breaks down or drought ruins crops, thousands of people may starve.

# RURAL LIFE

Although African cities have been growing fast, most Africans still live in the countryside. They grow their own food and only rarely have a surplus to sell or exchange for other goods. Many tribes have farmed the same land for generations, living in villages with all of their relatives. Sometimes the young men go to live in cities for a few years to earn money in mines or factories. Then they return to the village to marry and settle down. The types of crops grown vary widely. Yams, cassava, and bananas are produced in the lush tropical regions; farmers in drier areas concentrate on cattle and corn.

*Road building in Nigeria*

## DEVELOPMENT

Poor infrastructure, including unreliable roads, railways, and electricity supplies, holds back the economic growth of many African nations. Most countries rely on loans from Western governments and international banks to pay for their development programmes.

### Find out more

AFRICA, HISTORY OF
CENTRAL AFRICA
EAST AFRICA
SOUTH AFRICA
WEST AFRICA

AFRICA

## POLITICAL AFRICA
Independent African states, with few exceptions, are territorially identical to the colonies they replaced. Until the 1960s, most of Africa was controlled by European countries as part of their overseas empires. By the late 1980s, nearly every country had gained its independence. In many cases, hasty attempts were made to set up European-style governments. Leaders often became dictators, or the army seized power. However, in recent years, there has been a shift towards multiparty democracy.

 **ALGERIA**
**Area:** 2,381,740 sq km (919,590 sq miles)
**Population:** 31,800,000
**Capital:** Algiers

 **ANGOLA**
**Area:** 1,246,700 sq km (481,551 sq miles)
**Population:** 13,600,000
**Capital:** Luanda

 **BENIN**
**Area:** 112,620 sq km (43,480 sq miles)
**Population:** 6,700,000
**Capital:** Porto-Novo

 **BOTSWANA**
**Area:** 581,730 sq km (224,600 sq miles)
**Population:** 1,800,000
**Capital:** Gaborone

 **BURKINA**
**Area:** 274,200 sq km (105,870 sq miles)
**Population:** 13,000,000
**Capital:** Ouagadougou

 **BURUNDI**
**Area:** 27,830 sq km (10,750 sq miles)
**Population:** 6,800,000
**Capital:** Bujumbura

 **CAMEROON**
**Area:** 475,440 sq km (183,570 sq miles)
**Population:** 16,000,000
**Capital:** Yaoundé

 **CAPE VERDE**
**Area:** 4,030 sq km (1,556 sq miles)
**Population:** 463,000
**Capital:** Praia

 **CENTRAL AFRICAN REPUBLIC**
**Area:** 622,980 sq km (240,530 sq miles)
**Population:** 3,900,000
**Capital:** Bangui

 **CHAD**
**Area:** 1,284,000 sq km (495,752 sq miles)
**Population:** 8,600,000
**Capital:** N'Djamena

 **COMOROS**
**Area:** 2,230 sq km (861 sq miles)
**Population:** 768,000
**Capital:** Moroni

 **CONGO**
**Area:** 342,000 sq km (132,040 sq miles)
**Population:** 3,700,000
**Capital:** Brazzaville

 **DEMOCRATIC REPUBLIC OF CONGO**
**Area:** 2,345,410 sq km (905,563 sq miles)
**Population:** 52,800,000
**Capital:** Kinshasa

 **DJIBOUTI**
**Area:** 23,200 sq km (8,958 sq miles)
**Population:** 703,000
**Capital:** Djibouti

 **EGYPT**
**Area:** 1,001,450 sq km (386,660 sq miles)
**Population:** 71,900,000
**Capital:** Cairo

 **EQUATORIAL GUINEA**
**Area:** 28,050 sq km (10,830 sq miles)
**Population:** 494,000
**Capital:** Malabo

 **ERITREA**
**Area:** 93,680 sq km (36,170 sq miles)
**Population:** 4,100,000
**Capital:** Asmara

 **ETHIOPIA**
**Area:** 1,128,221 sq km (435,605 sq miles)
**Population:** 70,700,000
**Capital:** Addis Ababa

 **GABON**
**Area:** 267,670 sq km (103,347 sq miles)
**Population:** 1,300,000
**Capital:** Libreville

 **GAMBIA**
**Area:** 11,300 sq km (4,363 sq miles)
**Population:** 1,400,000
**Capital:** Banjul

 **GHANA**
**Area:** 238,540 sq km (92,100 sq miles)
**POPULATION:** 20,900,000
**Capital:** Accra

 **GUINEA**
**Area:** 245,860 sq km (94,926 sq miles)
**Population:** 8,500,000
**Capital:** Conakry

 **GUINEA-BISSAU**
**Area:** 36,120 sq km (13,940 sq miles)
**Population:** 1,500,000
**Capital:** Bissau

 **IVORY COAST**
**Area:** 322,463 sq km (124,503 sq miles)
**Population:** 16,600,000
**Capital:** Yamoussoukro

 **KENYA**
**Area:** 580,370 sq km (224,081 sq miles)
**Population:** 32,000,000
**Capital:** Nairobi

 **LESOTHO**
**Area:** 30,350 sq km (11,718 sq miles)
**Population:** 1,800,000
**Capital:** Maseru

 **LIBERIA**
**Area:** 111,370 sq km (43,000 sq miles)
**Population:** 3,400,000
**Capital:** Monrovia

 **LIBYA**
**Area:** 1,759,540 sq km (679,358 sq miles)
**Population:** 5,600,000
**Capital:** Tripoli

 **MADAGASCAR**
**Area:** 587,040 sq km (226,660 sq miles)
**Population:** 17,400,000
**Capital:** Antananarivo

 **MALAWI**
**Area:** 118,480 sq km (45,745 sq miles)
**Population:** 12,100,000
**Capital:** Lilongwe

 **MALI**
**Area:** 1,240,190 sq km (478,837 sq miles)
**Population:** 13,000,000
**Capital:** Bamako

 **MAURITANIA**
**Area:** 1,025,520 sq km (395,953 sq miles)
**Population:** 2,900,000
**Capital:** Nouakchott

 **MAURITIUS**
**Area:** 1,860 sq km (718 sq miles)
**Population:** 1,200,000
**Capital:** Port Louis

 **MOROCCO**
**Area:** 698,670 sq km (269,757 sq miles)
**Population:** 30,600,000
**Capital:** Rabat

 **MOZAMBIQUE**
**Area:** 801,590 sq km (309,493 sq miles)
**Population:** 18,900,000
**Capital:** Maputo

 **NAMIBIA**
**Area:** 824,290 sq km (318,260 sq miles)
**Population:** 2,000,000
**Capital:** Windhoek

 **NIGER**
**Area:** 1,267,000 sq km (489,188 sq miles)
**Population:** 12,000,000
**Capital:** Niamey

 **NIGERIA**
**Area:** 923,770 sq km (356,668 sq miles)
**Population:** 124,000,000
**Capital:** Abuja

 **RWANDA**
**Area:** 26,340 sq km (10,170 sq miles)
**Population:** 8,400,000
**Capital:** Kigali

 **SAO TOME AND PRINCIPE**
**Area:** 964 sq km (372 sq miles)
**Population:** 175,900
**Capital:** São Tomé

 **SENEGAL**
**Area:** 196,720 sq km (75,950 sq miles)
**Population:** 10,100,000
**Capital:** Dakar

 **SEYCHELLES**
**Area:** 280 sq km (108 sq miles)
**Population:** 80,500
**Capital:** Victoria

 **SIERRA LEONE**
**Area:** 71,740 sq km (27,699 sq miles)
**Population:** 5,000,000
**Capital:** Freetown

 **SOMALIA**
**Area:** 637,660 sq km (246,200 sq miles)
**Population:** 9,900,000
**Capital:** Mogadishu

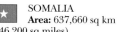 **SOUTH AFRICA**
**Area:** 1,221,040 sq km (471,443 sq miles)
**Population:** 45,000,000
**Capital:** Pretoria

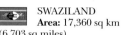 **SUDAN**
**Area:** 2,505,815 sq km (967,493 sq miles)
**Population:** 33,600,000
**Capital:** Khartoum

 **SWAZILAND**
**Area:** 17,360 sq km (6,703 sq miles)
**Population:** 1,000,000
**Capital:** Mbabane

 **TANZANIA**
**Area:** 945,090 sq km (364,900 sq miles)
**Population:** 37,000,000
**Capital:** Dodoma

 **TOGO**
**Area:** 56,790 sq km (21,927 sq miles)
**Population:** 4,900,000
**Capital:** Lomé

 **TUNISIA**
**Area:** 163,610 sq km (63,170 sq miles)
**Population:** 9,800,000
**Capital:** Tunis

 **UGANDA**
**Area:** 235,880 sq km (91,073 sq miles)
**Population:** 25,800,000
**Capital:** Kampala

 **ZAMBIA**
**Area:** 740,720 sq km (285,992 sq miles)
**Population:** 10,800,000
**Capital:** Lusaka

 **ZIMBABWE**
**Area:** 390,580 sq km (150,800 sq miles)
**Population:** 12,900,000
**Capital:** Harare

| Volcano | Mountain | Ancient monument | Capital city | Large city/ town | Small city/ town |
|---------|----------|------------------|--------------|------------------|------------------|

## STATISTICS
**Area:** 30,278,093 sq km (11,690,481 sq miles)
**Population:** 849,384,400
**Number of independent countries:** 53
**Highest point:** Kilimanjaro (Tanzania) 5,895 m (19,340 ft)
**Longest river:** Nile, 6,695 km (4,160 miles)
**Largest lake:** Lake Victoria: 69,484 sq km (26,828 sq miles)
**Main occupation:** Agriculture

## MINING

Africans have been mining and processing minerals, including iron ore, copper, and gold, for more than two thousand years. Gold mined in the forest country of western Africa was carried across the Sahara by African traders and exported to Europe and Asia. During the colonial period mining was intensified. Today, South Africa, Zimbabwe, Zambia, and Democratic Republic of Congo possess heavily industrialized mining areas. These areas have yielded minerals such as gold, diamond, copper, and uranium.

*Large-scale drilling equipment (above) is used in the gold mining industry.*

*Dogon dancers (right) from Mali perform a funeral dance.*

### MASKS AND DANCE
Masked dance is performed in many communities in west and central Africa and plays an important part in social events. Once inside the costume, the person takes on the character represented by the mask. Often parts of the body are exaggerated with padding or pieces of wood (left). The dance steps, songs, and sounds complete the costume and energetically represent both the spirit world and the world of humans.

### CAPE VERDE
*The independent republic of the Cape Verde islands lies 620 km (385 miles) off the coast of Senegal, in the Atlantic Ocean. The islands have a population of 463,000, but almost twice this number of Cape Verdeans live abroad.*

### HORN OF AFRICA
*Because of its shape, the easternmost point of the African continent is called the Horn of Africa. It is one of the poorest regions on Earth, with few natural resources. Recent droughts and civil wars have killed thousands of people and made many more homeless.*

### SAO TOME AND PRINCIPE
*The volcanic islands of São Tomé and Príncipe form a republic with a population of 175,900. São Tomé, the larger island, lies just north of the equator.*

### GAME PARKS AND CONSERVATION
The animal life of Africa is rich and varied. However in the last century, numerous animal and plant species have been lost forever. As the land has been turned into farms and industrial sites, many animals have been driven from their habitats. Their numbers have also been severely reduced by hunters. To protect animals from extermination, several African governments have set aside large game reserves where hunting is prohibited.

### Map labels

EUROPE
Mediterranean Sea
ALGIERS
Madeira (to Portugal)
RABAT
TUNIS
TUNISIA
MOROCCO
TRIPOLI
Atlas Mountains
Canary Islands (to Spain)
Nile Delta
LAÂYOUNE
ALGERIA
LIBYA
EGYPT
Giza CAIRO
Thebes
Western Sahara (Occupied by Morocco)
Tropic of Cancer
Sahara
Ahaggar
Tibesti
Libyan Desert
Red Sea
ASIA
Tropic of Cancer
MAURITANIA
NOUAKCHOTT
MALI
NIGER
CHAD
KHARTOUM
ERITREA
ASMARA
Niger
Sahel
CAPE VERDE
PRAIA
SENEGAL
DAKAR
GAMBIA
BANJUL
BAMAKO
BURKINA
NIAMEY
OUAGADOUGOU
NIGERIA
Lake Chad
SUDAN
NDJAMENA
White Nile
Blue Nile
DJIBOUTI
DJIBOUTI
Gulf of Aden
Horn of Africa
GUINEA-BISSAU
BISSAU
CONAKRY
GUINEA
GHANA
BENIN
TOGO
ABUJA
ADDIS ABABA
FREETOWN
SIERRA LEONE
YAMOUSSOUKRO
IVORY COAST
Niger
Benue
PORTO-NOVO
CENTRAL AFRICAN REPUBLIC
ETHIOPIA
MONROVIA
LIBERIA
ACCRA
LOMÉ
CAMEROON
YAOUNDÉ
BANGUI
Ubangi
MALABO
EQUATORIAL GUINEA
SAO TOME & PRINCIPE
SAO TOMÉ
GABON
LIBREVILLE
CONGO
Congo Basin
UGANDA
KAMPALA
Lake Turkana
SOMALIA
MOGADISHU
Equator
Equator
BRAZZAVILLE
KINSHASA
DEM REP CONGO
RWANDA
KIGALI
BUJUMBURA
BURUNDI
Lake Victoria
KENYA
NAIROBI
Kilimanjaro 5895m
Cabinda (to Angola)
DODOMA
Zanzibar
LUANDA
Lake Tanganyika
TANZANIA
ATLANTIC OCEAN
ANGOLA
Lake Nyasa
COMOROS
MORONI
MAYOTTE (to France)
Comoro Islands
Mamoudzou
ZAMBIA
LUSAKA
MALAWI
LILONGWE
Zambezi
HARARE
MOZAMBIQUE
MADAGASCAR
ANTANANARIVO
NAMIBIA
Victoria Falls
ZIMBABWE
INDIAN OCEAN
WINDHOEK
BOTSWANA
Tropic of Capricorn
GABORONE
Kalahari Desert
TSHWANE (PRETORIA)
MAPUTO
MBABANE
SWAZILAND
BLOEMFONTEIN
MASERU
LESOTHO
SOUTH AFRICA
CAPE TOWN
Cape of Good Hope

### SCALE BAR
| 0 | 400 | 800 | km |

| 0 | 400 | 800 | miles |

# HISTORY OF
# AFRICA

FOR MUCH OF ITS HISTORY, Africa has been hidden from outsiders' eyes. The Sahara Desert cuts off communication from north to south for all but the hardiest traveller. The peoples of Africa have therefore developed largely by themselves. By about 1200 B.C., rich and powerful empires such as Ancient Egypt had arisen. The empires have disappeared, but they left behind buildings and other clues to their existence. Other African peoples left records of their history in songs that have been passed down from parent to child through countless generations. Europeans remained ignorant of this rich history until, during the 1400s, they explored the west coast. Soon they were shipping thousands of Africans to Europe and the Americas as slaves, a "trade" that destroyed many traditional societies. During the late 1800s, Europeans penetrated the interior of Africa and, within 20 years, had carved up the continent between them. Almost all of Africa remained under European control until the 1950s, when the colonies began to gain their independence. Today, the peoples of Africa are free of foreign control.

**BANTUS**
Most of the peoples of southern Africa are related to the Bantus, who originated in the western part of the continent between 3000 and 2000 B.C. They had moved south by A.D. 400.

*Ivory traders*

## GREAT ZIMBABWE

The stone city of Great Zimbabwe was a major religious, political, and trading centre in southern Africa during the 14th century. It grew rich on the proceeds of herding cattle and mining gold, copper, and iron. The peoples of Great Zimbabwe exported their produce to the coastal port of Sofala in what is now Mozambique, and then up the coast of Africa to Arabia.

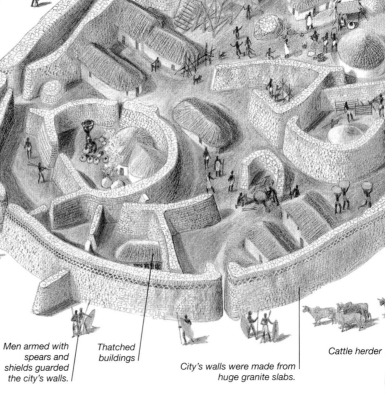

*Men armed with spears and shields guarded the city's walls.*

*Thatched buildings*

*City's walls were made from huge granite slabs.*

*Cattle herder*

Great enclosure at Great Zimbabwe

## BENIN

The West African kingdom of Benin reached the height of its power between the 14th and 17th centuries. Its people traded ivory, pepper, palm oil, and slaves with the Portuguese. They also excelled in casting realistic figures in bronze. On the left is a Benin bronze mask.

**SOAPSTONE BIRDS**
Soapstone carvings of local birds on columns stood in an enclosure outside Great Zimbabwe. One of these birds has been the national symbol of Zimbabwe since the country gained its independence in 1980.

# SCRAMBLE FOR AFRICA

Until the 1880s, European conquest in Africa was restricted to the coastal regions and the main river valleys. But European powers wanted overseas colonies (settlements). Throughout the 1880s and 1890s, European nations competed for land in Africa. By 1900, almost all of Africa was in European hands. The only independent states left were the ancient kingdom of Ethiopia in the east, and the free slave state of Liberia in the west. The cartoon (left) shows Germany as a bird "swooping" onto Africa.

ON THE SWOOP!

ZULU WARS
Some African peoples managed to resist the Europeans for a time. After 1838, the Zulus of southern Africa fought first the Boers (Dutch settlers) and then the British. In 1879, however, Britain finally defeated the Zulus. In 1887, Zululand became a British colony. Above is a picture of the British trying to break through Zulu lines.

INDEPENDENCE
The coming of independence to much of Africa after 1956 did not always bring peace or prosperity to the new nations. Many were weakened by famines and droughts or torn apart by civil wars. Few have managed to maintain civilian governments without periods of military dictatorships. In 1964 Malawi (formerly Nyasaland) became Africa's 35th independent state. Above is the celebration scene.

## APARTHEID

In 1948 the National Party came to power in South Africa. Years of segregation, known as apartheid, followed. This policy gave white people power but denied black people many rights, including the vote. In 1990 the African National Congress (ANC), a banned black nationalist movement led by Nelson Mandela, was legalized, and the apartheid laws began to be dismantled. In 1994, the first-ever free elections were held.

ORGANIZATION
OF AFRICAN UNITY
Despite the many political differences that exist between the individual African states, they all share problems of poverty, poor health, and lack of schools. In 1963, the Organization of African Unity (OAU) was founded to promote unity in the continent and to co-ordinate economic, health, and other policies among its 51 member nations. Above are two members of the OAU medical unit treating civil war victims.

NELSON MANDELA
In 1994, Nelson Mandela (left), a leader of the ANC, became the President of South Africa.

**AFRICA
700-1200**
Kingdom of Ghana in West Africa grows rich on cross-Saharan trade with the Arabs.

**c. 800-1800** Kanem-Bornu kingdom.

**1200s** Trading cities flourish on east coast.

**1235-1500** Kingdom of Mali.

**1300-1600** Kingdom of Benin.

**1300s** Great Zimbabwe flourishes.

**1350-1591** Kingdom of Songhai.

**1500-1800s** Europeans take Africans as slaves to America.

**1838-79** Zulus fight against Boers and British.

**1880s** Europeans take almost total control of Africa.

**1957-75** Most of Africa independent.

**1990** Namibia independent.

---

*Find out more*
AFRICA
BENIN EMPIRE
EGYPT, ANCIENT
PREHISTORIC PEOPLES
SLAVERY

# AFRICAN WILDLIFE

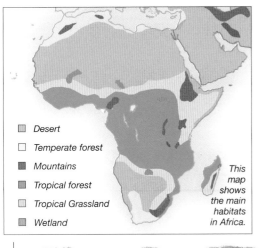

Desert
Temperate forest
Mountains
Tropical forest
Tropical Grassland
Wetland

This map shows the main habitats in Africa.

AFRICA HAS AN INCREDIBLE variety of wildlife. The cheetah, the world's fastest runner, lives in Africa, sprinting after its prey in the scrubland and grassland. The huge Nile crocodile lurks in the River Nile. Vast herds of wildebeest, zebra, and buffalo wander the grassy plains, together with the biggest land animal, the elephant, and the largest bird, the ostrich. In Africa's central rain forests are gorillas and chimpanzees. In the Kalahari and Namib deserts, which are among the driest areas on Earth, sand skinks shelter in the shade of giant euphorbia plants, watching out for the poisonous Namibian sidewinder snake. Although humans have turned many regions into farmland, there are still plenty of wild places in Africa.

### NATIONAL PARKS
Many wild places in Africa are being destroyed for timber, firewood, and farmland. The Korup National Park in Cameroon is one of Africa's least spoiled rain forest areas. It is now protected as a national reserve.

Egyptian vulture has a bald head and neck. It feeds on carrion (remains of dead animals).

### SAVANNA
The grassy African plains are called savannas. They are home to many spectacular large mammals, including elephants, rhinoceroses, zebras, and lions. The African savannas cover almost a quarter of Africa, mainly in the east and south.

The secretary bird is a snake killer found in grassland areas.

### GIRAFFE
The giraffe is the tallest animal on Earth. A large male can measure 5 m (17 ft) to its horn tips. Its long legs and long neck enable it to reach higher into the trees to feed than any other hoofed mammal. The giraffe's long tail, with its coarse hairs, is an effective fly swatter to flick away flies and other insects.

### HYENA
This hunter-scavenger hunts at night and consumes whatever it can, including goats and other mammals, birds, snakes, fruit, but mainly the remains of other animals' prey. Despite its dog-like shape, the hyena is more closely related to the mongoose family.

### MEERKAT
The meerkat is a kind of mongoose. It forages for insects, lizards, and other small creatures, moving around a fixed area to look for food. Meerkats live in groups and dig burrows for shelter and for raising young.

Meerkats stand near the burrow entrances to watch for predators.

### AFRICAN WETLANDS
The African wetlands consist of swamps and lakes and are inhabited by a great number of herons, pelicans, flamingos, and other water birds, as well as lungfishes and huge shoals of cichlids and other fish. In the Kalahari Desert, crocodiles and hippopotamuses live in the water among vast beds of papyrus stems in the Okovango Basin – the largest oasis on Earth.

Two male hippos fighting each other for their territory

### HIPPOPOTAMUS
An adult hippopotamus can weigh more than 2.7 tonnes (2.7 tons), making it one of the heaviest animals on land. During the day, hippopotamuses wallow in mud or bathe in rivers and lakes, almost submerged, with only their ears, eyes, and nostrils showing. At night they come onto land to feed on grass near the riverbank.

### PANGOLIN
There are seven kinds of pangolins in Africa and in Asia. They live in savanna and forest areas, where they lick up ants and termites with their long, sticky tongues. A pangolin can roll itself into a ball for defence; its overlapping scales help protect it against predators.

Countless beetles and other creatures scavenge and recycle nutrients in the soil.

---

*Find out more*
ELEPHANTS
LIONS, TIGERS, and other big cats
MARSH AND SWAMP WILDLIFE

---

# AIR

A MIXTURE OF GASES makes up the air that all plants and animals need for life. We give the name wind to moving air. When air moves, it presses against everything in its path, rustling leaves and lifting kites high above the treetops. Still air presses too. There is a blanket of air roughly 650 km (400 miles) deep that surrounds the Earth. Although air is light, this layer of air is so thick that it presses down on everything it engulfs. At ground level its force is equal to 10.4 m (34 ft) of water. We do not notice the weight of air pressing down on us, because it presses equally from all sides and because the liquids in our body press outwards against the pressure of the air. Atmospheric pressure is lower at high altitudes; in an aeroplane at a height of about 16,000 m (52,000 ft) above the ground, air pressure is only one tenth the pressure on the ground.

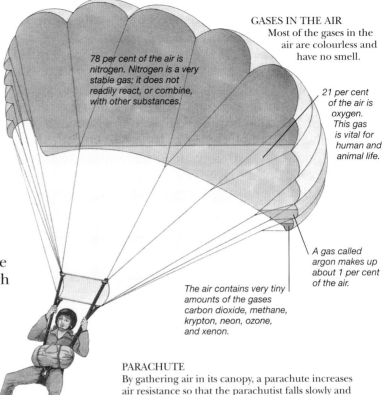

*78 per cent of the air is nitrogen. Nitrogen is a very stable gas; it does not readily react, or combine, with other substances.*

### GASES IN THE AIR
Most of the gases in the air are colourless and have no smell.

*21 per cent of the air is oxygen. This gas is vital for human and animal life.*

*A gas called argon makes up about 1 per cent of the air.*

*The air contains very tiny amounts of the gases carbon dioxide, methane, krypton, neon, ozone, and xenon.*

### PARACHUTE
By gathering air in its canopy, a parachute increases air resistance so that the parachutist falls slowly and safely to the ground. Skydivers also use air resistance to control their speed before opening the parachute. They spread their arms and legs to slow the fall.

### AIR RESISTANCE
Like any other substance, air occupies space. So when a car moves along, it has to push the air out of the way. This produces a force called air resistance, or drag, which slows down the car. Modern vehicles are designed with sleek, streamlined shapes that make way for the air to move out smoothly. New designs are tested in wind tunnels which blow air at high speed over a model of the car.

### SUCTION
Differences in air pressure provide a useful way of moving liquids and solid objects. For example, when you suck on a drinking straw, you use your lungs as a pump to reduce the air pressure above the liquid in the straw. The higher pressure of the air outside the straw pushes the drink up the straw and into your mouth.

## AIR PRESSURE
Air pressure can help with everyday tasks. For example, a siphon uses the push of atmospheric pressure to empty a fish tank that is too heavy to lift when full. Many machines work using air pressure. Pumping air under pressure into car tyres keeps them solid yet flexible, cushioning passengers from bumps in the road. Many tools, such as pneumatic screwdrivers and drills, are powered by air at high pressure which is produced by mechanical pumps.

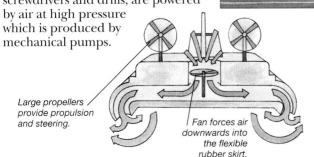

*Large propellers provide propulsion and steering.*

*Fan forces air downwards into the flexible rubber skirt.*

### HOVERCRAFT
A layer of pressurized air keeps a hovercraft, or air-cushion vehicle, floating a little distance off the ground and distributes the vehicle's weight evenly. This means the hovercraft can travel over swamps, deep snow, or water without sinking in. A large fan creates the cushion of air which lifts the craft off the ground.

---
***Find out more***
ATMOSPHERE
EARTH
OXYGEN
POLLUTION
WEATHER
---

# AIRCRAFT

LESS THAN 100 YEARS AGO, even the fastest ship took more than a week to cross the Atlantic Ocean. Today, most jet airliners (large passenger planes) can make this 4,800-km (3,000-mile) journey in less than seven hours. Aircraft are the fastest way to travel because they can soar straight over obstacles such as mountains and oceans. Powerful jet engines enable the fastest combat aircraft to reach speeds of 3,200 km/h (2,000 mph) – three times faster than sound. Even ordinary jet airliners fly at more than 850 km/h (530 mph). Modern aircraft are packed with advanced technology to help them fly safely and economically at great speed. Sophisticated electronic control and navigation systems keep the aeroplane on course. Computer-designed wings help cut fuel costs. And airframes (aircraft bodies) are made of metal alloys and plastic composites that are lightweight and strong.

## JET AIRLINER
Like all jet airliners, the *Boeing 747-400* flies high above the clouds to avoid bad weather. Its airtight cabin is pressurized – supplied with air at a suitable pressure. This protects passengers and crew from the drop in air pressure and lack of oxygen at high altitudes.

## FLIGHT DECK
The captain and crew control the aircraft from the flight deck. In the past, the flight deck of an aeroplane was a mass of dials and switches. New jet airliners are packed with electronics, and computer screens have replaced the dials. Other new features include computer-controlled autopilot systems that enable the plane to take off and land when bad weather obscures the pilot's vision.

*The undercarriage (landing wheels) folds up inside the aeroplane during flight to reduce drag (air resistance).*

*The* Boeing 747-400 *airliner can carry 412 people and fly non-stop for more than 13,600 km (8,470 miles). Seats are arranged on two decks.*

*The aircraft's radar shows the crew the weather conditions up to 320 km (200 miles) ahead so that they can avoid storms.*

## FLYING AN AEROPLANE
Every aeroplane has three main controls: the throttle to control speed; rudder pedals for steering to the left or right (yawing); and a control column that tilts the aircraft to either side (rolling), or up and down (pitching). The pilot usually operates all three to guide the plane through the air.

*To roll, the pilot moves the control column to the left or right, which raises the ailerons on one wing and lowers them on the other.*

*Aileron*

*Elevator*

*To pitch up or down, the pilot pushes or pulls on the control column, raising or lowering the elevator flaps on the tail wing.*

*To yaw left or right, the pilot's feet swivel the rudder bar, turning the upright rudder on the tail of the aeroplane.*

*Rudder*

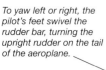

*Like a bicycle going around a curve, an aircraft has to bank into a turn. To do this, the pilot uses the control column and the rudder pedals together so that the aircraft rolls and yaws at the same time.*

## AEROPLANES
Aeroplanes are powered aircraft that have wings. The word aircraft describes all flying machines including helicopters, gliders, hang gliders, and aeroplanes. Most large airliners and combat aeroplanes have jet engines enabling them to fly fast and high. But jets are expensive and use a lot of fuel, so many smaller planes are driven by propeller, just like the first aeroplanes.

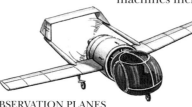

### OBSERVATION PLANES
Specially designed aircraft give a clear view of everything from traffic jams to diseased crops.

### JET AIRCRAFT
Each year jet airliners enable billions of people to take long journeys. A jet engine called a turbofan drives most jet airliners. Turbofans are powerful and relatively quiet.

### SEAPLANES
Aircraft are ideal for getting in and out of remote places. Seaplanes have floats instead of landing wheels to land and take off on water.

### CONCORDE
The airliner *Concorde* is supersonic, which means it can fly faster than sound. Indeed, it streaks over the Atlantic in less than four hours, twice as fast as any other airliner. But its engines are noisy and use a lot of fuel.

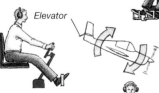

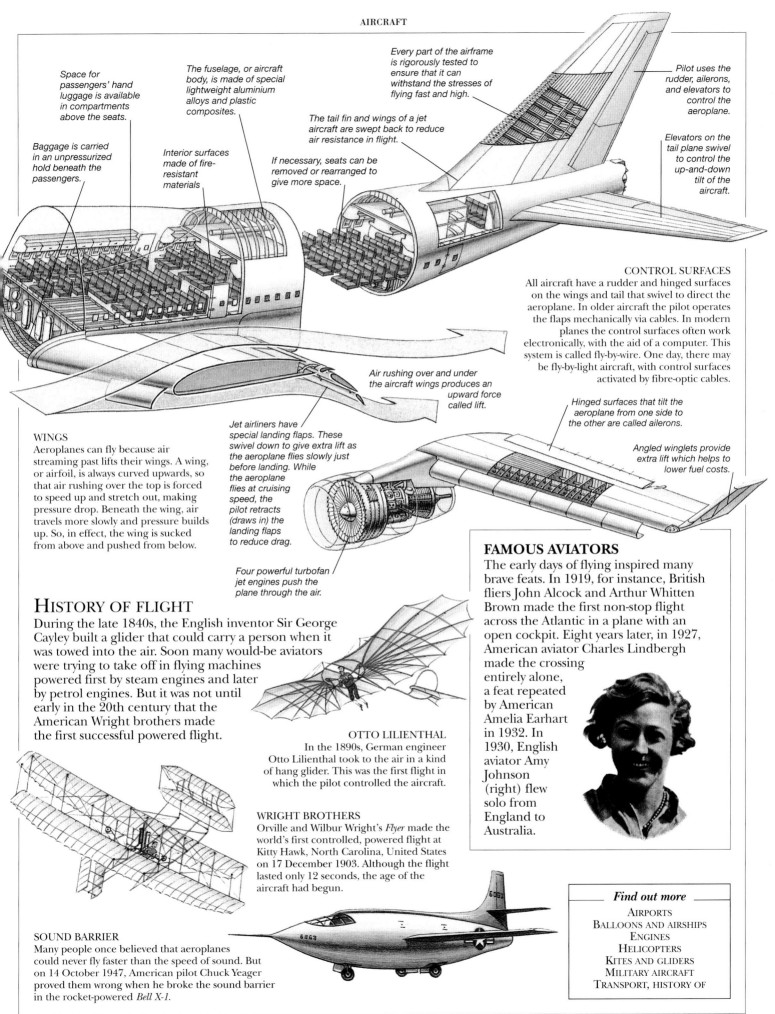

Space for passengers' hand luggage is available in compartments above the seats.

Baggage is carried in an unpressurized hold beneath the passengers.

The fuselage, or aircraft body, is made of special lightweight aluminium alloys and plastic composites.

Interior surfaces made of fire-resistant materials

Every part of the airframe is rigorously tested to ensure that it can withstand the stresses of flying fast and high.

The tail fin and wings of a jet aircraft are swept back to reduce air resistance in flight.

If necessary, seats can be removed or rearranged to give more space.

Pilot uses the rudder, ailerons, and elevators to control the aeroplane.

Elevators on the tail plane swivel to control the up-and-down tilt of the aircraft.

## CONTROL SURFACES
All aircraft have a rudder and hinged surfaces on the wings and tail that swivel to direct the aeroplane. In older aircraft the pilot operates the flaps mechanically via cables. In modern planes the control surfaces often work electronically, with the aid of a computer. This system is called fly-by-wire. One day, there may be fly-by-light aircraft, with control surfaces activated by fibre-optic cables.

Air rushing over and under the aircraft wings produces an upward force called lift.

Hinged surfaces that tilt the aeroplane from one side to the other are called ailerons.

Angled winglets provide extra lift which helps to lower fuel costs.

## WINGS
Aeroplanes can fly because air streaming past lifts their wings. A wing, or airfoil, is always curved upwards, so that air rushing over the top is forced to speed up and stretch out, making pressure drop. Beneath the wing, air travels more slowly and pressure builds up. So, in effect, the wing is sucked from above and pushed from below.

Jet airliners have special landing flaps. These swivel down to give extra lift as the aeroplane flies slowly just before landing. While the aeroplane flies at cruising speed, the pilot retracts (draws in) the landing flaps to reduce drag.

Four powerful turbofan jet engines push the plane through the air.

## HISTORY OF FLIGHT
During the late 1840s, the English inventor Sir George Cayley built a glider that could carry a person when it was towed into the air. Soon many would-be aviators were trying to take off in flying machines powered first by steam engines and later by petrol engines. But it was not until early in the 20th century that the American Wright brothers made the first successful powered flight.

### OTTO LILIENTHAL
In the 1890s, German engineer Otto Lilienthal took to the air in a kind of hang glider. This was the first flight in which the pilot controlled the aircraft.

### WRIGHT BROTHERS
Orville and Wilbur Wright's *Flyer* made the world's first controlled, powered flight at Kitty Hawk, North Carolina, United States on 17 December 1903. Although the flight lasted only 12 seconds, the age of the aircraft had begun.

## FAMOUS AVIATORS
The early days of flying inspired many brave feats. In 1919, for instance, British fliers John Alcock and Arthur Whitten Brown made the first non-stop flight across the Atlantic in a plane with an open cockpit. Eight years later, in 1927, American aviator Charles Lindbergh made the crossing entirely alone, a feat repeated by American Amelia Earhart in 1932. In 1930, English aviator Amy Johnson (right) flew solo from England to Australia.

## SOUND BARRIER
Many people once believed that aeroplanes could never fly faster than the speed of sound. But on 14 October 1947, American pilot Chuck Yeager proved them wrong when he broke the sound barrier in the rocket-powered *Bell X-1*.

*Find out more*
AIRPORTS
BALLOONS AND AIRSHIPS
ENGINES
HELICOPTERS
KITES AND GLIDERS
MILITARY AIRCRAFT
TRANSPORT, HISTORY OF

# AIR FORCES

**FIRST AIR FORCES**
Before the invention of aeroplanes, armies used balloons and kites to watch and attack their enemies. The first air force pilots flew in aircraft made of wood, canvas, and wire. They fought with machine guns and dropped small bombs out of the cockpit by hand.

HELICOPTERS, JET FIGHTERS, AND BOMBERS play a vital role in modern warfare. As part of an air force, these aircraft support and defend armies and navies. They can also attack targets that are impossible to approach by land or sea. Armies first used aeroplanes in battle during World War I (1914-18), and by World War II (1939-45) modern air forces had been established. People serving in the air force perform a variety of jobs. The crew of an aircraft includes a pilot, a navigator, and a gunner to operate the weapons. Many more people work on the ground. Radar crews find out where enemy and friendly aircraft are flying. Surface-to-air missile crews try to shoot down enemy aircraft. Rescue crews go to the aid of pilots whose aircraft have crashed in the sea or on land.

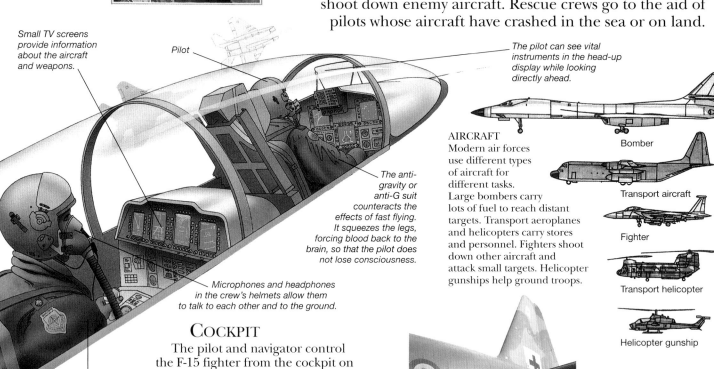

Small TV screens provide information about the aircraft and weapons.

Pilot

The pilot can see vital instruments in the head-up display while looking directly ahead.

The anti-gravity or anti-G suit counteracts the effects of fast flying. It squeezes the legs, forcing blood back to the brain, so that the pilot does not lose consciousness.

Microphones and headphones in the crew's helmets allow them to talk to each other and to the ground.

Navigator

**AIRCRAFT**
Modern air forces use different types of aircraft for different tasks. Large bombers carry lots of fuel to reach distant targets. Transport aeroplanes and helicopters carry stores and personnel. Fighters shoot down other aircraft and attack small targets. Helicopter gunships help ground troops.

Bomber

Transport aircraft

Fighter

Transport helicopter

Helicopter gunship

## COCKPIT
The pilot and navigator control the F-15 fighter from the cockpit on top of the aircraft's fuselage. The instruments and controls that surround the two airmen help them fly the aircraft, locate the enemy, and fire weapons. If enemy weapons hit the F-15, crew members fire explosive charges under their seats to eject them from the cockpit. They land by parachute.

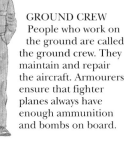

**RELIEF SUPPLIES**
In peacetime air forces do not fight. Instead they patrol the air to monitor other air forces and discourage them from attacking. During emergencies such as famines and earthquakes, transport planes carry food and supplies to the victims.

**AIRCREW**
Personnel who fly in aircraft are called the aircrew. They include pilots, navigators, who tell the pilot which course to fly, and loaders, who work in transport planes.

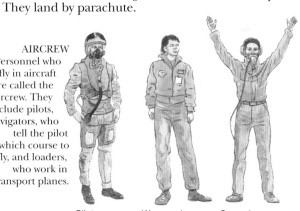

**GROUND CREW**
People who work on the ground are called the ground crew. They maintain and repair the aircraft. Armourers ensure that fighter planes always have enough ammunition and bombs on board.

Pilots carry flight plans in pads on their knees.

Women aircrew do not usually fly aircraft in battle.

Ground crew uses hand signals to show pilots where to park their aircraft.

Engineers check aircraft carefully after every flight.

> *Find out more*
> AIRCRAFT
> BALLOONS AND AIRSHIPS
> HELICOPTERS
> NAVIGATION
> RADAR
> WORLD WAR I
> WORLD WAR II

# AIRPORTS

EVERY YEAR MORE THAN 100 MILLION PEOPLE pass through the world's airports. Freight terminals handle the millions of tonnes of cargo carried by aircraft. Whenever people or goods travel by air, they must pass through an airport. Some airports are extremely large. At John F. Kennedy International Airport in New York City, in the United States, nearly 1,000 aeroplanes take off every day. Some huge international aircraft fly thousands of kilometres to other continents. Smaller planes make internal flights, taking passengers to other parts of the country. They may land at tiny airports which serve towns or islands. All airports have runways for aircraft to pick up speed and take off. They also have facilities for refuelling and making repairs. In larger airports there are restaurants and lounges where passengers can wait to board their flights.

**PASSPORTS**
International travellers use passports to prove their identity. Officials at the airport often stamp the passport to show that the traveller entered the country legally. The use of passports began in the 16th century but has only become widespread in the last 50 years.

*The whole airport can be seen from the control tower.*

*Catering staff supplies food and drink to the galleys, or kitchens.*

*Cleaners vacuum the cabin and remove rubbish.*

*Engineers make careful checks on all the aeroplane's functions.*

*Ground crew refuels the aircraft from tankers or hydrants.*

*Fire fighters stand by while the aircraft refuels.*

*Ramp for boarding*

## PASSENGER TERMINAL
A large modern airport employs thousands of people. As soon as an aircraft lands, air traffic controllers direct it towards a disembarkation point, where it stops. Passengers leave the aircraft by means of a ramp or steps from the aircraft to the ground. Baggage handlers remove the suitcases from the aircraft and take them to the terminal for collection. When passengers have their luggage they go through customs, then take connecting flights or travel onwards by bus, car, or train.

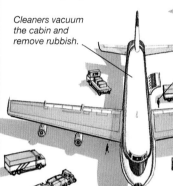

**CUSTOMS**
Passengers on incoming flights pass through customs. Officials there search baggage and clothing for drugs and other illegal substances, and check for goods on which travellers should pay import or export tax. Smugglers try to trick customs officers by hiding illegal or taxable goods.

*Smugglers hide drugs in hollow ornaments and other objects.*

**SECURITY**
Airport authorities carry out security checks to protect aircraft from bombs and armed terrorists. X-ray machines scan hand luggage for bombs and guns. Passengers walk through an arch that detects metal; a heavy lump of metal such as a gun triggers an alarm.

**AIR TRAFFIC CONTROL**
At a busy airport, as many as 50 aircraft take off and land every hour. Air traffic controllers in the control tower decide when each plane can take off. They also radio instructions to the aircraft that are circling in the sky above, waiting to land.

| *Find out more* |
| :---: |
| AIRCRAFT |
| AIR FORCES |
| TRANSPORT, HISTORY OF |
| X-RAYS |

# ALEXANDER THE GREAT

BY 323 B.C. ONE MAN HAD CONQUERED most of the known world and set up an empire that extended from Asia Minor (now Turkey) to India. The name of the general was Alexander, today known as Alexander the Great. He was the son of King Philip II, ruler of Macedonia, a small but powerful Greek kingdom. In 336 B.C. Philip was murdered and Alexander became king, although he was only 20 years old. Alexander was an ambitious and brilliant general. In 334 he invaded the great Persian Empire ruled by Darius III. By a series of remarkable victories, Alexander then went on to conquer a vast empire running from Egypt in the west to India in the east. When Alexander died, aged only 33, he had led his armies at least 19,000 km (12,000 miles) and had encouraged the spread of Greek culture throughout the known world. After he died, his empire was divided. But he is still considered one of the greatest generals who ever lived.

**ALEXANDER**
As a young man Alexander (356-323 B.C.) was brave and intelligent. He was taught by the Greek philosopher Aristotle, from whom he developed a lifelong interest in Greek culture.

**PHALANX**
The army that Alexander led into Persia (Iran) consisted mostly of infantry, or foot soldiers, armed with long spears. The infantry fought in a formation called a phalanx. The men were packed closely together with their spears pointing towards the enemy.

## BUCEPHALUS
Alexander rode into battle on a beautiful horse called Bucephalus. According to legend, Bucephalus was completely wild and responded only to Alexander. When Bucephalus died, Alexander built a monument and town, called Bucephala, in honour of him. The city still exists in India today.

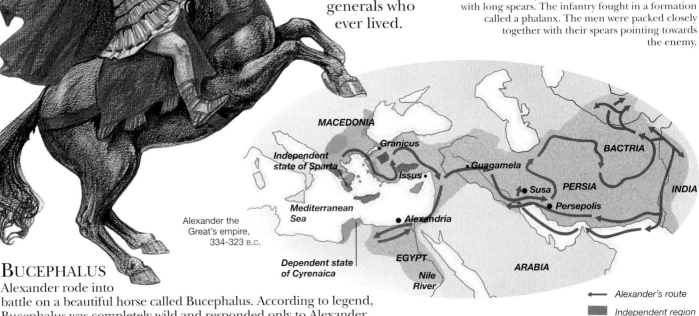

MACEDONIA
Granicus
Independent state of Sparta
Issus
Guagamela
BACTRIA
PERSIA
Susa
Persepolis
INDIA
Mediterranean Sea
Alexandria
Alexander the Great's empire, 334-323 B.C.
Dependent state of Cyrenaica
EGYPT
Nile River
ARABIA

← Alexander's route
Independent region
Dependent region
Alexander's empire

### ALEXANDRIA
In 332 B.C. Alexander founded the city of Alexandria (named after himself) on the Mediterranean coast. It soon became a great port and a centre of Greek culture and learning, attracting poets and scientists from all over the world. Today, Alexandria is the second largest city in Egypt.

*After Alexander's death, Ptolemy Soter, commander of Egypt, created a huge library at Alexandria. It was said to have contained more than 500,000 books; today only ruins remain.*

BATTLES
Alexander fought many battles. Usually he had fewer men than his enemy, but he won because his men were well trained and equipped. At the Battle of Issus in 333 B.C. Alexander, with 36,000 men, defeated Darius and his 110,000 troops. Two years later, with a force of 45,000 men, Alexander again overwhelmed Darius and his 100,000 soldiers at the Battle of Guagamela.

*Find out more*
ARMIES
GREECE, ANCIENT

# ALFRED THE GREAT

THE YOUNGEST OF FIVE ROYAL BROTHERS, Alfred had to wait his turn to become King of Wessex, the land of the West Saxons, one of seven Anglo-Saxon kingdoms of England. He was born in Wantage, Berkshire, and as a child travelled to Italy to meet Pope Leo IV. In A.D. 871 Alfred became king, and set about defeating the Danes who had been at war with the Anglo-Saxons for many years. He finally beat them at the Battle of Edington in A.D. 878, and all the Anglo-Saxon kingdoms recognized him as their king. A fearless warrior and a great leader, Alfred established the Navy and built defensive forts on land. He brought teachers and scholars from Europe and England to Wessex, and introduced a code of laws to improve government. Alfred's achievements were so important that he became known as "the Great".

The Alfred Jewel, thought to contain a likeness of the king, was made in his lifetime.

## BURNING CAKES

There are many stories about Alfred. One takes place during the war with the Danes. Alfred hid in a peasant's hut. The owner, who did not recognize the king, asked him to watch her cakes while she went out, but Alfred fell asleep, and the cakes burned.

Alfred lets the cakes burn.

## DANELAW

From about A.D. 800, Danish Vikings constantly attacked the Anglo-Saxon kingdoms, and took over much of the country. There were many battles. A few years after the Battle of Edington, Alfred forced the Danes to withdraw to the eastern part of England. This area was known as the Danelaw.

Anglo-Saxons

Danelaw

The Danes were confined to the eastern part of England.

## THE NAVY

Alfred is often called "the father of the English Navy". When the Vikings began to attack his country, he ordered ships to be built that could outrun and outfight the Viking longships. By the A.D. 900s, fleets of these ships were stationed along the English coast and at ports, to guard against invasion.

Alfred's ships copied the design of Viking longships, but were wider and chunkier.

Main ports and cities were fortified against attack.

WINCHESTER
Alfred made his capital at Winchester, Hampshire, which the Anglo-Saxons called Wintecaester. The king fortified the town with thick walls. When he died on 28 October, A.D. 901, Alfred was buried in Hyde Abbey. King Canute is also buried in Winchester.

### Find out more
ANGLO-SAXONS
ENGLAND
VIKINGS

# ALPHABETS

WHEN PEOPLE FIRST BEGAN TO WRITE, they did not use an alphabet. Instead, they drew small pictures to represent the objects they were writing about. This is called picture writing, and it was very slow because there was a different picture for every word. An alphabet does not contain pictures. Instead, it is a collection of letters or symbols which represent sounds. Each sound is just part of one word. Joining the letters together forms a whole word. The human voice can make about 35 different sounds in speech. So alphabets need at most 35 letters to write any word, and most alphabets manage with fewer. The Phoenicians, who lived about 3,000 years ago in the Middle Eastern country now called Syria, developed the first modern alphabet. The ancient Greeks adapted the Phoenician alphabet, and later the Romans improved it. The Roman alphabet is now used widely throughout the world.

*The ancient Romans used the letters of the alphabet for numbers. For example, C is 100.*

## abcdefghi jklmnopqr stuvwxyz

### CAPITAL AND SMALL LETTERS
The first Roman alphabet had only capital letters. Small letters started to appear after the 8th century. In English, capital letters are used at the beginning of a sentence, and for the first letter of a name. Capital letters are also used when words are abbreviated, or shortened, to their first letters, such as UN for United Nations.

## .,;?!éäêç

### SYMBOLS AND ACCENTS
In addition to letters, writers use punctuation marks such as a full stop to show where a sentence ends. Some languages, such as French, also use accents – marks which show how to speak the word. The sloping acute accent over the *e* in *café* makes it sound like the *a* in *day*.

*In traditional printing, raised lead letters are used to print the words on paper.*

*In every alphabet, letters have a special order that does not change. Dictionaries, phone books, and many other books are arranged in alphabetical order so that it is easy to find a word or a name.*

*The Romans did not have the letter W. For J they used I, and for U they used V.*

## ROMAN ALPHABET
The alphabet used in English and other European languages is based on the Roman alphabet, which had 23 letters. This alphabet is also used in some Southeast Asian languages, such as Vietnamese and Indonesian.

АБВГДЕЁЖЗИЙКЛМНОПРСТУФХЦЧШЩЪЫЬЭЮЯ
Cyrillic (Russian)

ΑΒΓΔΕΖΗΘΙΚΛΜΝΞΟΠΡΣΤΥΦΧΨΩ
Greek

अ आ इ ई उ ऊ ए ऐ ओ औ ऋ क ख ग घ ङ च छ ज झ ञ ट ठ ड ढ ण त थ
द ध न प फ ब भ म य र ल व श ष स ह क्ष त्र ज्ञ श्र
Hindi (India)

### MODERN ALPHABETS
The Roman alphabet is only one of the world's alphabets. Many other languages use different symbols to represent similar sounds, and the words may be written and read quite differently from the Roman alphabet. Japanese readers start on the right side of the page and read to the left, or start at the top and read down the page.

### ROSETTA STONE
The ancient Egyptians used a system of picture writing called hieroglyphics. The meaning of this writing was forgotten 1,600 years ago, so nobody was able to read Egyptian documents until 1799 when some French soldiers made a remarkable discovery. Near Alexandria, Egypt, they found a stone with an inscription on it. The words were carved in hieroglyphics and in Greek. Using their knowledge of Greek, scholars were able to discover what the hieroglyphics meant.

### CUNEIFORM
About 5,000 years ago in Mesopotamia (now part of Iraq) a form of writing called cuneiform developed. It started off as picture writing, but later letters began to represent sounds. The Mesopotamians did not have paper; instead they wrote on damp clay using wedge-shaped pens. Cuneiform means "wedge-shaped".

### CHINESE PICTOGRAMS
In traditional Chinese writing, symbols called pictograms are used to represent ideas. There is a different character for every word.

Bird

Horse

Tree

Sun

# AMERICAN CIVIL WAR

ONLY 80 YEARS AFTER the states of America had united and won their independence from England, a bitter conflict threatened to destroy the Union. Between 1861 and 1865, civil war raged as the nation fought over several issues, one of which was slavery. Slavery was legal in the South but had been outlawed in the North. The immediate cause of the war was the election in November 1860 of Abraham Lincoln as president. Lincoln wanted to stop the spread of slavery, and he hoped it would die out in the South. The southern states wanted to continue with it, and one by one they left the Union to form their own alliance, called the Confederacy, with Jefferson Davis as president. Fighting broke out in April 1861. General Robert E. Lee, an able military leader, led the Confederate armies. However, the Union army was larger, and the North had many industries which supplied the army, whereas the South's main business was agriculture. The war was brutal, and by the time the Confederacy was defeated in 1865, much of the South was devastated. The Union victory led to the abolition of slavery throughout the United States, but the country remained split between North and South for many years.

Free states · Slave states · Territories

Oregon · Free states · Territories · California · Slave states

**THE DIVIDED NATION**
In 1860 the free states and slave states were divided as shown on the map above.

## A MODERN WAR
The American Civil War was the first conflict in which railways and iron warships played an important part. It was also the first war to be widely photographed and reported in the world's newspapers.

## THE END OF THE WAR
On 9 April 1865, Confederate general Robert E. Lee surrendered to Union general Ulysses S. Grant at Appomattox, Virginia, United States. More than 600,000 Americans were killed in the war, and many more were injured.

Union · Confederacy

**TROOPS**
Most of the American Civil War troops were infantrymen (foot soldiers). Three million people fought in the two opposing armies.

### EVENTS IN CIVIL WAR

**1860** Abraham Lincoln is elected president.

**1860-1861** Eleven southern states leave the Union and join the Confederacy.

**1861** Confederates attack Fort Sumter. Civil War begins.

**1861** Confederate victory at Bull Run.

**1862** Stalemate for months.

**1862** Confederate victory at Fredericksburg.

**1862** Naval battle between battleships *Monitor* and *Merrimack*.

**1862** Battle of Shiloh, Tenn.

**1863** Lincoln's Emancipation Proclamation proclaims freedom of slaves in Confederacy.

**1863** Confederate victory at Chancellorsville.

**1863** Confederate defeat at Gettysburg during invasion of the Union marks turning point in war.

**1863** Confederate defeats at Vicksburg and Chattanooga.

**1864** Union general W.T. Sherman captures Atlanta, Georgia, and begins "march to the sea".

**1865** Confederate general Robert E. Lee surrenders to Union general Ulysses S. Grant; war ends.

**1865** Slavery abolished in U.S.

*Find out more*
LINCOLN, ABRAHAM
SLAVERY
UNITED STATES OF AMERICA, history of

# AMERICAN REVOLUTION

**PAUL REVERE'S RIDE**
On the night of 18 April 1775, silversmith Paul Revere took his now famous ride from Charlestown, Massachusetts, to warn the people that the British army was coming.

EVERY YEAR ON 4 JULY, Americans celebrate the birth of their nation. Independence Day is a reminder of the moment when the 13 American colonies declared that they would no longer be ruled by Britain. The colonists did this because they had to pay British taxes, yet could not elect representatives to the British Parliament. The colonists had tried to make peace with Britain. At the First Continental Congress in 1774, representatives of each colony met to try and arrange fairer taxation. They failed, and fighting broke out between British soldiers and colonists at Lexington, Massachusetts, the following year. The colonists formed an army, led by George Washington. A second Congress again failed to make peace, and on 4 July 1776, the Americans declared their independence. France sent aid to the colonies which helped defeat the British. In 1781, the war ended. Britain recognized the independence of the United States two years later.

## THE BATTLE OF LEXINGTON

British soldiers set out from Boston, Massachusetts, on 19 April 1775, to capture the military stores at Concord. On their way, the British met a group of armed Americans at Lexington. The fighting that followed was the first battle of the war.

## BOSTON TEA PARTY

In 1773, the British government cut the tax on tea in Britain but kept the rate the same in America. The colonists had no legal way of objecting because they did not have a Member of Parliament in Britain. On the night of 16 December a group of colonists dressed as Native Americans boarded three tea ships in Boston harbour and threw all the tea into the water as a protest.

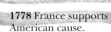

**AMERICAN REVOLUTION**

**1767** Britain imposes high taxes on American colonies.

**1773** Boston Tea Party protests unfair taxation.

**1774-1775** Continental Congress against Britain.

**1775** Battle of Lexington marks start of war.

**1775** Battle of Bunker Hill won by British but strengthens American resistance.

**1776** Declaration of Independence.

**1777** Americans win Saratoga campaign.

**1778** France supports American cause.

**1781** General Cornwallis surrenders at Yorktown to Americans and French.

**1783** Britain recognizes American independence in the Peace of Paris.

A NEW FLAG
The first flag of the new country of the United States consisted of 13 stripes and 13 stars, one for each of the original states.

*Find out more*

EXPLORERS
UNITED STATES, HISTORY OF
WASHINGTON, GEORGE

# ANGLO-SAXONS

IN A.D. 449 KING VORTIGERN of Britain was finding it hard to fight off the invading Picts and Scots. So he invited Germanic tribes (Angles, Saxons, and Jutes) to come and help him. They quarrelled with the British, but joined together to become a powerful nation in their own right – the Anglo-Saxons. By A.D. 600, they had driven out the native British and taken over most of the country. To begin with, there were seven separate kingdoms, but eventually these became three. These kingdoms were known as *Engla land*, or *Angle land*, which is where the name England comes from. Anglo-Saxon rule lasted about 500 years, until 1066. During that time, Anglo-Saxon kings fought many battles and made alliances with the Vikings and Danes. Christianity was brought to England, and people learnt how to read and write. The greatest Anglo-Saxon king was Alfred.

ANGLO-SAXON OCCUPATION
By the end of the 9th century, Anglo-Saxon England was divided into Wessex, Mercia, and Northumbria.

*Wooden building, with thatched roof*

*A minstrel entertains people in the mead hall.*

## ANGLO-SAXONS

**c. 449** Angles, Saxons, and Jutes come to Britain.

**597** Ethelbert, King of Kent, becomes a Christian.

**802-39** King Egbert rules Wessex; unites Anglo-Saxon kingdoms.

**830s** Vikings invade.

**871-899** Alfred reigns; beats Danes at Edington in 878.

**978-1016** Ethelred II the Unready pays money to Vikings to keep the peace.

**1016** Danish king Canute takes the English throne.

**1042** Edward the Confessor becomes king.

**1066** William of Normandy conquers England.

## BATTLE OF MALDON

In A.D. 991, the men of Essex, led by Brihtnoth, fought a battle at Maldon, Essex, against 5,000 Vikings, led by Olaf Tryggvason. The Vikings won. They became more powerful, and, by 1016, England had a Danish king. All we know about the battle comes from *The Battle of Maldon,* a poem from the 10th or 11th century.

Ash spear and shield

## MEAD HALL

Daily life in an Anglo-Saxon village centred around the mead hall. This was a large building where people came to meet and feast. Travelling minstrels would sing or recite long story poems to entertain the people while they drank. The mead hall belonged to the local *eorl*, or lord.

CANUTE
In 1016, the Danes finally overthrew the Anglo-Saxons and took the English throne. The Danish prince Canute, or Cnut (A.D. 994-1035), became King of England. He was popular, ruled wisely, passed laws to restore order and kept up Anglo-Saxon customs. In 1019 he became King of Denmark, and in 1028 took over the Norwegian throne. For a short time England and Scandinavia formed an empire.

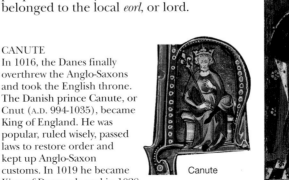

Canute

EDWARD THE CONFESSOR
King Alfred's last descendant, Edward the Confessor (1002-66), founded Westminster Abbey, and was made a saint in 1161. He was not a strong king, and allowed his Norman advisors to rule for him. Edward had no children, and after his death there was a squabble for the throne. William of Normandy claimed that Edward had promised it to him. Edward's brother-in-law, Harold, said the throne was rightly his. Harold was crowned in 1066.

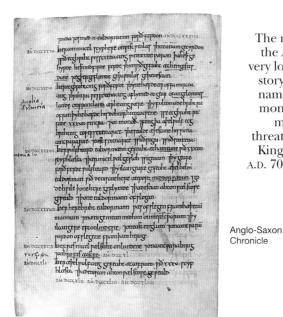

Anglo-Saxon Chronicle

## BEOWULF

The most important piece of literature in the Anglo-Saxon language is *Beowulf* – a very long, epic (heroic) poem. It tells the story of the noble warrior Beowulf (his name means Bee Wolf) who fights the monster Grendel and Grendel's even more terrifying mother, who were threatening the people of the Danish King Hrothgar. It was written in the A.D. 700s, but the author is unknown.

Title page of *Beowulf*

## ANGLO-SAXON CHRONICLE

Started by the Saxon King Alfred the Great, the Anglo-Saxon Chronicle was a kind of early newspaper. It recorded events in England, gave accounts of wars and battles, and included works translated from Latin. Alfred undertook many translations himself. The Chronicle continued until 1154, and is a very important source of information about the history and language of the Anglo-Saxon people.

Monks wrote in ink on specially prepared parchment.

MONKS
Books and manuscripts were produced by monks. They had to copy each book by hand, and so books were very precious. The monks worked in a special room in the monastery called a scriptorium. One monk prepared the parchment, a second copied in the words, and a third illustrated the manuscript (text). Books were written in Latin and Anglo-Saxon.

Illustrations and decorative initials added to the text

Coloured inks made from plants and minerals.

THE VENERABLE BEDE
Known as "The Father of English History", Bede, or Baeda (A.D. 673?-735) was a monk and teacher who lived and worked in a monastery in Jarrow, north-eastern England. He wrote many books on the Bible and scientific subjects. Bede's most famous work is *The Ecclesiastical History of the English Nation*, finished in A.D. 731.

## SUTTON HOO

In 1939, archaeologists unearthed buried treasure at Sutton Hoo in Suffolk, England. They found 11 burial mounds containing Anglo-Saxon coins, weapons, bowls, and ornaments dating from between A.D. 650 and 670. The site was probably a memorial to a great king.

Iron helmet trimmed with bronze and silver

Sompting Church

CHURCH BUILDING
Most of the Anglo-Saxon buildings that can still be seen today are churches. This is because they were built from stone rather than wood. Sompting Church is in West Sussex but most surviving Anglo-Saxon churches are in East Anglia.

### Find out more
ALFRED THE GREAT
MONASTERIES
NORMANS
UNITED KINGDOM, HISTORY OF
VIKINGS

# ANIMALS

THE ANIMAL KINGDOM is one of the largest groups of living things; scientists believe that there are up to 30 million species. Animals range from tiny, simple creatures that look like blobs of jelly, to gigantic blue whales. The huge animal kingdom is divided into many groups. A hedgehog, for example, belongs to the order of insectivores because it eats insects. It also belongs to the class of placental mammals. All mammals are vertebrates (animals with backbones) and belong to a group known as chordates. An animal is a living creature that feeds, moves, and breeds. During its life cycle, an animal is born, grows, matures, reproduces, and eventually dies. It ingests (takes in) food to build and develop its body. Food provides the animal with the energy to move around. Some types of animal do not move at all; the adult sponge, for example, spends its life anchored to a rock. All kinds of animals from dinosaurs to dodos have become extinct; many others, including elephants and tigers, may soon disappear, if their habitat is destroyed, and if they continue to be killed recklessly for their hides and bones.

**FROG**
Like all animals, the common green frog is aware of its surroundings and able to move, feed, and reproduce. Frogs belong to the class of animals called amphibians. All amphibians spend part of their lives in or near water.

## INTERNAL SKELETONS
The animal world can be divided into vertebrate animals and invertebrate animals. Vertebrates have an internal skeleton with a vertebral column or backbone. In most cases, this is made of bone. Some sea-dwelling vertebrates, such as sharks, have a backbone made of tough, rubbery gristle called cartilage.

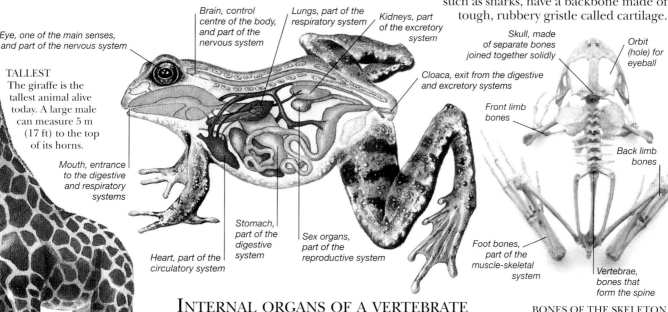

Eye, one of the main senses, and part of the nervous system

Brain, control centre of the body, and part of the nervous system

Lungs, part of the respiratory system

Kidneys, part of the excretory system

Skull, made of separate bones joined together solidly

Orbit (hole) for eyeball

Cloaca, exit from the digestive and excretory systems

Front limb bones

Back limb bones

**TALLEST**
The giraffe is the tallest animal alive today. A large male can measure 5 m (17 ft) to the top of its horns.

Mouth, entrance to the digestive and respiratory systems

Heart, part of the circulatory system

Stomach, part of the digestive system

Sex organs, part of the reproductive system

Foot bones, part of the muscle-skeletal system

Vertebrae, bones that form the spine

## INTERNAL ORGANS OF A VERTEBRATE
Inside an animal, such as the frog above, are many different parts called organs. Organs are all shapes and sizes. Each one has a job to do. Several organs are grouped together to form a body system, such as the digestive system, the circulatory system, and the reproductive system. The nervous system and the hormonal system control and co-ordinate all the internal systems.

**SMALLEST**
The smallest organisms are single-celled creatures called protozoa – so tiny they can hardly be seen by the human eye. The tiniest mammals are the bumblebee bat and Savi's pygmy shrew. This pygmy shrew measures only 6 cm (2.3 in) including its tail.

### BONES OF THE SKELETON
The skeletons of vertebrate animals are similar in design, but each differs in certain details through adaptation to the way the animal lives. A frog, for example, has long, strong back legs for leaping. All vertebrates have a skull that contains the brain and the main sense organs. Vertebrates also have two pairs of limbs. Some bones, such as the skull bones, are fixed firmly together; others are linked by flexible joints, as in the limbs.

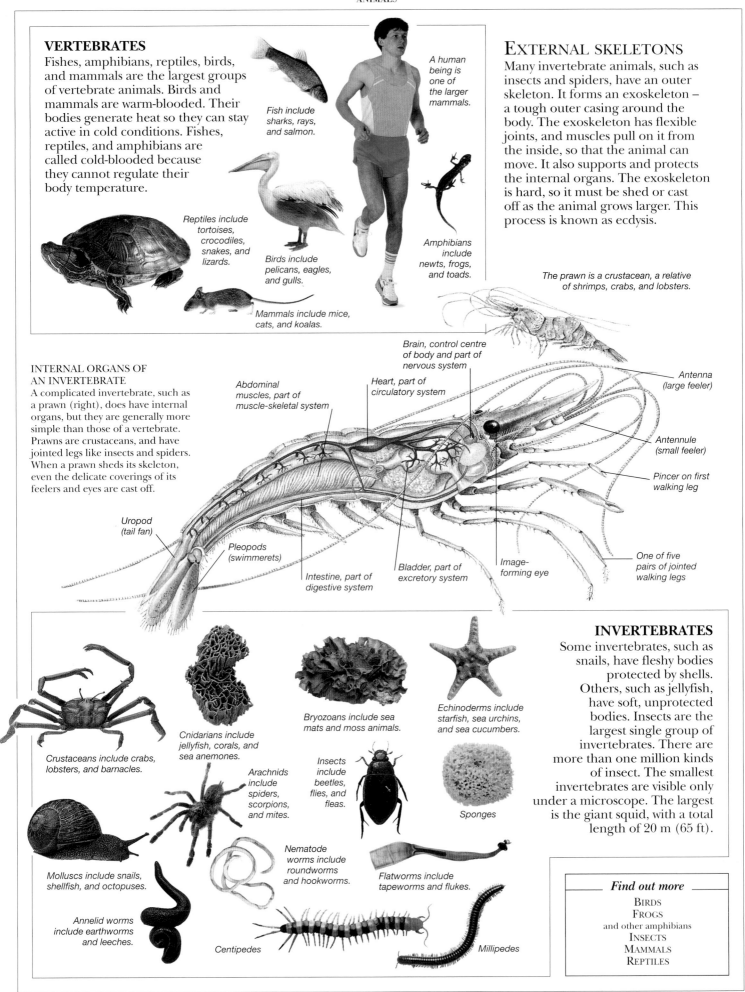

## VERTEBRATES

Fishes, amphibians, reptiles, birds, and mammals are the largest groups of vertebrate animals. Birds and mammals are warm-blooded. Their bodies generate heat so they can stay active in cold conditions. Fishes, reptiles, and amphibians are called cold-blooded because they cannot regulate their body temperature.

A human being is one of the larger mammals.

Fish include sharks, rays, and salmon.

Reptiles include tortoises, crocodiles, snakes, and lizards.

Birds include pelicans, eagles, and gulls.

Amphibians include newts, frogs, and toads.

Mammals include mice, cats, and koalas.

## EXTERNAL SKELETONS

Many invertebrate animals, such as insects and spiders, have an outer skeleton. It forms an exoskeleton – a tough outer casing around the body. The exoskeleton has flexible joints, and muscles pull on it from the inside, so that the animal can move. It also supports and protects the internal organs. The exoskeleton is hard, so it must be shed or cast off as the animal grows larger. This process is known as ecdysis.

The prawn is a crustacean, a relative of shrimps, crabs, and lobsters.

### INTERNAL ORGANS OF AN INVERTEBRATE

A complicated invertebrate, such as a prawn (right), does have internal organs, but they are generally more simple than those of a vertebrate. Prawns are crustaceans, and have jointed legs like insects and spiders. When a prawn sheds its skeleton, even the delicate coverings of its feelers and eyes are cast off.

Brain, control centre of body and part of nervous system

Abdominal muscles, part of muscle-skeletal system

Heart, part of circulatory system

Antenna (large feeler)

Antennule (small feeler)

Pincer on first walking leg

Uropod (tail fan)

Pleopods (swimmerets)

Intestine, part of digestive system

Bladder, part of excretory system

Image-forming eye

One of five pairs of jointed walking legs

## INVERTEBRATES

Some invertebrates, such as snails, have fleshy bodies protected by shells. Others, such as jellyfish, have soft, unprotected bodies. Insects are the largest single group of invertebrates. There are more than one million kinds of insect. The smallest invertebrates are visible only under a microscope. The largest is the giant squid, with a total length of 20 m (65 ft).

Crustaceans include crabs, lobsters, and barnacles.

Cnidarians include jellyfish, corals, and sea anemones.

Bryozoans include sea mats and moss animals.

Echinoderms include starfish, sea urchins, and sea cucumbers.

Arachnids include spiders, scorpions, and mites.

Insects include beetles, flies, and fleas.

Sponges

Molluscs include snails, shellfish, and octopuses.

Nematode worms include roundworms and hookworms.

Flatworms include tapeworms and flukes.

Annelid worms include earthworms and leeches.

Centipedes

Millipedes

*Find out more*

BIRDS
FROGS and other amphibians
INSECTS
MAMMALS
REPTILES

# ANIMAL SENSES

ALL ANIMALS ARE AWARE of their surroundings. Touch, smell, taste, sight, and hearing are the five senses that animals and humans use to detect what is happening around them. Animals, however, have a very different array of senses than humans. A dog's nose is so sensitive to odours that it "sees" the world as a pattern of scents and smells, in the same way that we see light and colour with our eyes. Many creatures, particularly fish, can determine where they are by picking up the tiny amounts of bio-electricity produced by other living things around them. A fish also detects vibrations in the water using a row of sense organs down each side of its body, called the lateral line.

An animal's senses, like its body shape, are a result of evolution and suit the animal's needs. Eyes would be of little use to a creature such as the cave fish, which lives in endless darkness. Instead, these creatures rely on other senses such as smell and touch. Some senses are extremely specialized. Long, feathery antennae enable a male emperor moth to "smell" the odour of a female moth 5 km (3 miles) away.

HUNTING SENSES
A shark can smell blood in the water hundreds of metres away. As this shark closes in for the attack, it makes use of its keen eyesight and electricity-sensing organs.

*A clear lens at the front of the eye focuses rays of light into the back of the eye to produce a sharp image.*

*The otter's scenting organs can detect many scents in the air. These special organs lie inside the nose in the roof of the nasal cavity.*

*Lips detect sharp pieces of shell in food, then spit them out.*

*Sensitive forepaws manipulate food. The otter also uses its paws to crack open shellfish.*

*The skin and hair roots bear sensors that detect vibrations, light touch, heavy pressure, and heat and cold.*

*The otter hears by sensing vibrations when they strike its eardrums. To help the otter balance, tiny fluid-filled canals inside the ear work like miniature levels to register gravity.*

*Whiskers are sensitive to touch. They also respond to vibrations, so they are useful in murky water.*

*Claws and soles of feet are sensitive to touch.*

## OTTER

While the sea otter floats on its back in the water, eating a shellfish, its sense organs continuously send information about its surroundings to the brain. The organs include the eyes, ears, nose, tongue, whiskers, fur, skin, and balance sensors. Stretch receptors in the joints and muscles also convey information about the otter's body position. The smell of a poisoned shellfish or the ripples from a shark's fin instantly alert the otter to possible danger.

## BLOODHOUND

Bloodhounds have been specially bred as tracker dogs. Their sense of smell may be as much as one million times sharper than a human's sense of smell. Bloodhounds can even detect the microscopic pieces of skin that are shed from a person's body.

*The Bloodhound's sense of smell is so sharp that it can even pick up scent that is several days old.*

*Dog follows scent with nose very close to ground.*

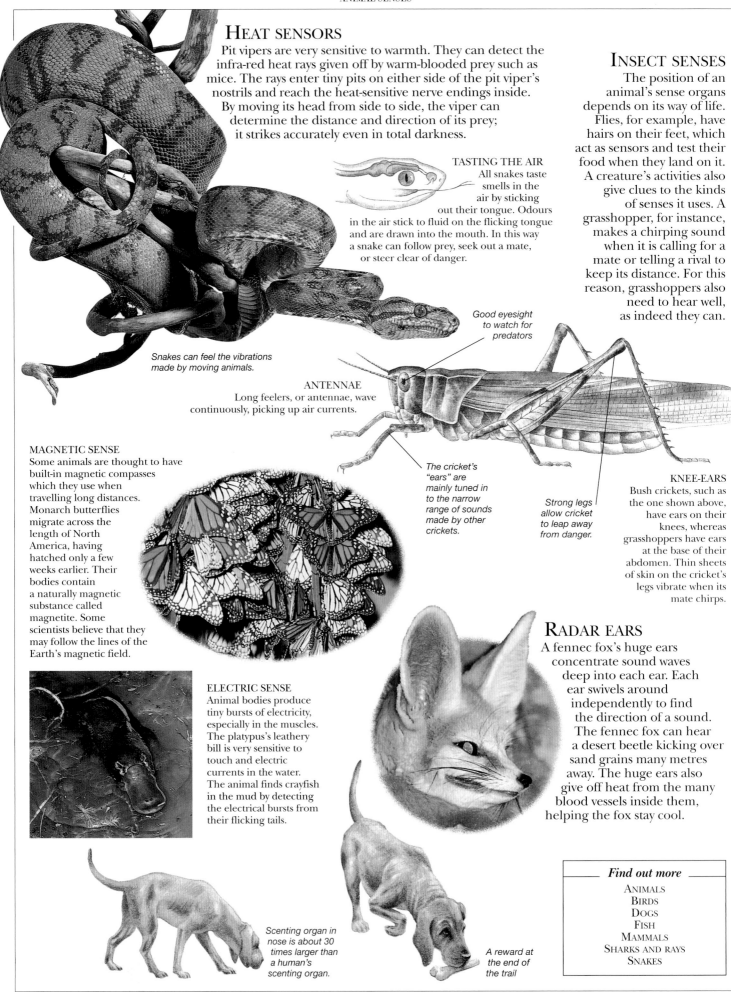

## HEAT SENSORS

Pit vipers are very sensitive to warmth. They can detect the infra-red heat rays given off by warm-blooded prey such as mice. The rays enter tiny pits on either side of the pit viper's nostrils and reach the heat-sensitive nerve endings inside. By moving its head from side to side, the viper can determine the distance and direction of its prey; it strikes accurately even in total darkness.

**TASTING THE AIR**
All snakes taste smells in the air by sticking out their tongue. Odours in the air stick to fluid on the flicking tongue and are drawn into the mouth. In this way a snake can follow prey, seek out a mate, or steer clear of danger.

*Snakes can feel the vibrations made by moving animals.*

## INSECT SENSES

The position of an animal's sense organs depends on its way of life. Flies, for example, have hairs on their feet, which act as sensors and test their food when they land on it. A creature's activities also give clues to the kinds of senses it uses. A grasshopper, for instance, makes a chirping sound when it is calling for a mate or telling a rival to keep its distance. For this reason, grasshoppers also need to hear well, as indeed they can.

*Good eyesight to watch for predators*

**ANTENNAE**
Long feelers, or antennae, wave continuously, picking up air currents.

*The cricket's "ears" are mainly tuned in to the narrow range of sounds made by other crickets.*

*Strong legs allow cricket to leap away from danger.*

### MAGNETIC SENSE
Some animals are thought to have built-in magnetic compasses which they use when travelling long distances. Monarch butterflies migrate across the length of North America, having hatched only a few weeks earlier. Their bodies contain a naturally magnetic substance called magnetite. Some scientists believe that they may follow the lines of the Earth's magnetic field.

**KNEE-EARS**
Bush crickets, such as the one shown above, have ears on their knees, whereas grasshoppers have ears at the base of their abdomen. Thin sheets of skin on the cricket's legs vibrate when its mate chirps.

### ELECTRIC SENSE
Animal bodies produce tiny bursts of electricity, especially in the muscles. The platypus's leathery bill is very sensitive to touch and electric currents in the water. The animal finds crayfish in the mud by detecting the electrical bursts from their flicking tails.

## RADAR EARS

A fennec fox's huge ears concentrate sound waves deep into each ear. Each ear swivels around independently to find the direction of a sound. The fennec fox can hear a desert beetle kicking over sand grains many metres away. The huge ears also give off heat from the many blood vessels inside them, helping the fox stay cool.

*Scenting organ in nose is about 30 times larger than a human's scenting organ.*

*A reward at the end of the trail*

---

*Find out more*

ANIMALS
BIRDS
DOGS
FISH
MAMMALS
SHARKS AND RAYS
SNAKES

---

# ANTARCTICA

STRETCHING ACROSS AN AREA greater than the United States, the continent of Antarctica sits beneath a huge sheet of ice up to 2 km (1.2 miles) thick. Antarctica is centred on the South Pole and is surrounded by the ice-covered Southern Ocean. Powerful winds create a storm belt around the continent, bringing fog and severe blizzards. It is the coldest and windiest place on earth. Even during the short summers the temperature barely climbs above freezing, and the sea ice only partly melts. In winter, temperatures can plummet to -80°C (-112°F). Few animals and plants can survive on land, but the surrounding seas teem with fish and mammals. Due to its harsh climate, there are no permanent residents on Antarctica. The only people on the continent are tourists, and scientists and staff working in research stations. These few people have brought waste and pollution to the region. As a result, the environmental impact of tourism and scientific activities is now carefully monitored. Other environmental concerns include overfishing and the depletion of the ozone layer above the region.

Situated at the southernmost point of the world, Antarctica covers an area of about 14 million sq km (5.5 million sq miles). The nearest land masses are South America and New Zealand. The highest point is Vinson Massif, which rises to 4,897 m (16,067 ft).

Radio transmitters allow scientists to track the movements of penguins.

## ANTARCTIC TEMPERATURES

2°C (28°F) Sea water freezes. On the Antarctic coast, summer temperatures are only a degree or so warmer than this.

-25°C (-13°F) Steel crystallizes and becomes brittle.

-40°C (-40°F) Synthetic rubber becomes brittle, and exposed flesh freezes rapidly.

-89°C (-128.6°F) Lowest temperature ever recorded, at Vostok Research Station, Antarctica, 1983.

## SCIENTIFIC RESEARCH

There are 40 permanent, and as many as 100 temporary, research stations in Antarctica devoted to scientific projects for 15 different nations. Teams of scientists study the wildlife and monitor the ice for changes in the Earth's atmosphere. Antarctic-based research has resulted in a number of scientific breakthroughs, including the discovery of a hole in the ozone layer above the continent.

### TOURISM

Cruise liners have been bringing tourists to the Antarctic region since the 1950s. In 1983, Chileans began to fly to King George Island where an 80-bed hotel has been built for holiday-makers. Antarctica receives several thousand tourists each year. Visitors come to see the dramatic landscape and unique wildlife, such as King penguins.

Platinum

Iron

Gold

### MINERAL WEALTH

Antarctica has deposits of minerals, such as gold, copper, uranium, and nickel. However, extracting them may damage the fragile polar environment.

___ *Find out more* ___

CONTINENTS
GLACIERS AND ICECAPS
INUITS
POLAR EXPLORATION
POLAR WILDLIFE

| Volcano | Mountain | Ancient monument | Capital city | Large city/ town | Small city/ town | Research Station |
|---|---|---|---|---|---|---|

## STATISTICS
**Area:** 13,900,000 sq km
(5,366,790 sq miles)
**Population:** No
permanent residents
**Capital:** None
**Languages:** English,
Spanish, French,
Norwegian, Chinese,
Polish, Russian,
German, Japanese
**Religions:** Not applicable
**Currency:** None
**Main occupation:**
Scientific research
**Main exports:** None
**Main imports:** None

### WHALE PROTECTION
Large-scale whale hunting in Antarctic seas began
in the 20th century. The whale population soon
fell and in 1948 the International Whaling
Commission was set up to monitor the
diminishing numbers. Following an international
agreement in 1994, a whale sanctuary was created
to protect whale feeding grounds from overfishing.

## FOREIGN TERRITORIES
Various nations, including Australia,
France, New Zealand, Norway,
Argentina, Chile, and the UK
claimed territory in Antarctica when
it was first discovered in the 19th
century. However, these claims have
been suspended under the 1959
Antarctic Treaty which came into
force in 1961. Under the treaty,
the continent can be used only for
peaceful purposes. Stations may
be set up for scientific research but
military bases are forbidden.

**FROZEN SEAS**
*During the cold winter months, the seas
surrounding Antarctica freeze, almost
doubling the size of the continent.*

**ANTARCTIC ICE**
Icebergs barricade more than 90 per cent of the Antarctic
coastline. The continent contains over 80 per cent of the world's
fresh water in the form of ice.

**LAMBERT GLACIER**
*The Lambert Glacier is the world's largest
series of glaciers. It is 80 km (50 miles)
wide at the coast and reaches more than
300 km (186 miles) inland.*

**PETER I ISLAND**
(to Norway)

**TRANSANTARCTIC MOUNTAINS**
*The Transantarctic
Mountains run across
the continent, splitting
it into Greater and
Lesser Antarctica.*

**ROSS ICE SHELF**
*Ice shelves are permanent
floating ice sheets that are
attached to land and
are constantly fed by
glaciers. The Ross Ice Shelf
is 183–914 m (600–3,000 ft)
thick and about 966 km
(600 miles) long.*

**SCALE BAR**

# ANTS AND TERMITES

IMAGINE HOW MANY millions of ants and termites live on this planet. There are at least 9,000 different kinds of ants and 2,750 kinds of termites. These tiny creatures are among the most fascinating animals on Earth. Both ants and termites are social insects, living in large groups called colonies where each individual has a specific job to do. The queen (the main female) mates with a male, then spends her life laying eggs. The hordes of workers do such jobs as gathering food and rearing the young. Soldiers and guards protect the nest and the foraging workers. Ants eat a variety of food, including caterpillars, leaves, and fungi. Termites feed mostly on plant matter, and they are among nature's most valuable recyclers.

## ANT HEAD
The Asian tree-living ant has simple jaws for feeding on soft insects. Other ants and termites have strong jaws for chewing wood and hard plant stems.

## TERMITE MOUND
Many termites make small nests in dead trees or underground. A few kinds of termites build a mound which contains a termite city – a home for many millions of termites. In hot areas the mounds have tunnels and ventilation holes, and may be more than 6 m (20 ft) high. The mounds are often occupied for more than 50 years, and the thick walls help to keep out anteaters and other predators. The queen and king termites live in a royal chamber deep inside the mound.

Cooling chimney lets air in and out of the termite mound.

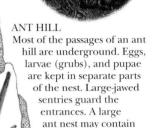

## ANT HILL
Most of the passages of an ant hill are underground. Eggs, larvae (grubs), and pupae are kept in separate parts of the nest. Large-jawed sentries guard the entrances. A large ant nest may contain 100,000 ants.

Courtier workers

Queen termite

Termite mound

Termite mound has many tunnels.

Front leg

Jaws

Antenna can bend like an elbow joint.

Eye

Middle leg

Thorax

Head

Rear leg

Claw

Fungus grows on the termites' dung (waste matter) inside the termite mound. These areas are called fungus gardens. Termites feed on the fungus.

Nursery for termite larvae

Queen lays 20,000 or more eggs daily in royal chamber.

Soldier termite

King termite

Young female termite

Ant squirts formic acid from rear of body in self-defence.

Abdomen

Worker ant

Workers regurgitate (spit out) food for queen, king, and soldier termites. Courtier workers feed and clean queen and king.

## WORKER ANT
All worker ants are female. Their long, claw-tipped legs allow them to run fast and climb well. Workers collect food, regurgitate it to feed the other ants, look after eggs and larvae, and clean the nest. They do not have wings, unlike the queen and male ants.

## TERMITES
The queen and male termites have wings. They take flight and mate, then the queen returns to the nest. The queen does not leave the nest again, and is cared for by the courtier workers. The main male, or king, is larger than the workers and remains with the queen.

## ARMY ANTS
A few ants, such as these army ants of South America, do not make permanent nests and are ever on the move. As the colony marches through the forests, they forage for insects, and sometimes even eat large animals alive.

## LEAF-CUTTING ANTS
Ants can lift objects that weigh more than they do. Leaf-cutting ants bite off pieces of leaves and carry them back to a huge underground nest. Here they chew the leaves and mix them with saliva to make a kind of compost. Fungus – the leaf-cutting ant's only food – grows on this compost.

*Find out more*
AFRICAN WILDLIFE
ANIMALS
ECOLOGY AND FOOD WEBS
INSECTS

# ARCHAEOLOGY

FOR AN ARCHAEOLOGIST, brushing away the soil that hides a broken pot is like brushing away time. Every tiny fragment helps create a more complete picture of the past. Archaeology is the study of the remains of past human societies, but it is not the same as history. Historians use written records as their starting point, whereas archaeologists use objects. They excavate, or dig, in the ground or under water for bones, pots, and anything else created by our ancestors. They also look for seeds, field boundaries, and other signs of how long-dead people made use of the landscape. But archaeology is not just concerned with dead people and buried objects. It also helps us understand what may happen to our own society in the future. Archaeology has shown that human actions and changes in the climate or environment can destroy whole communities.

HEINRICH SCHLIEMANN
In 1870 the pioneer German archaeologist Heinrich Schliemann (1822-90) discovered the site of Troy in Turkey. He also set out basic rules for excavation, such as careful recordkeeping. He did not always follow his own rules. His impatient hunt for treasure sometimes destroyed the objects he was seeking.

*A grid pattern divides the site into squares so that archaeologists can quickly record in which square they made each find.*

*In photographs of the site, the stripes painted on poles make it easy to judge the size of objects.*

*By sketching objects, archaeologists can sometimes record more detail than a camera can.*

*Small trowels allow archaeologists to remove soil carefully.*

## ANALYSIS
The position and location of the objects uncovered in a dig can provide important information. For this reason archaeologists measure, examine, record, and analyze everything they find, and preserve it if possible. Scientific methods such as radioactive dating enable archaeologists to find out the exact age of objects made thousands of years ago.

*Archaeologists sieve the soil they remove to check for objects they may have overlooked.*

*A soft brush removes dry soil without damaging the object.*

## EXCAVATION
Archaeologists gather much of their information about the past by carrying out excavations, or digs. They decide where to dig by looking at aerial photographs, old pictures, maps, documents, or marks on the ground. Then they carefully remove layers of soil, often using trowels and other small tools. The archaeologists keep digging until they reach undisturbed soil with no trace of human occupation.

BRONZE AGE TOOLS
Archaeologists often find tools from ancient times. The axe and arrowhead shown above date from the Bronze Age and are estimated to have been used by humans between 3,000 and 8,000 years ago.

*19th-century drain*

*17th-century floor*

*Brick-lined well, c. 1800*

*16th-century chalk floor*

*14th-century chalk-lined cesspit*

*Roman tiled floor*

## STRATIFICATION
Archaeologists on a dig determine the relative age of each object they find from where it is buried, using the principle of stratification. This principle says that older objects are usually buried deeper in the ground than newer objects.

# TOLLUND MAN

In 1950, archaeologists in Denmark made a dramatic discovery. They found the remarkably well preserved body of a man in a peat bog called Tollund Mose. The man had been hanged and buried about 2,000 years ago. Most dead bodies soon rot underground, but the peat had tanned Tollund man so that his flesh was hard like a leather shoe. Many details remained, and scientists could even tell that his last meal had been a kind of porridge.

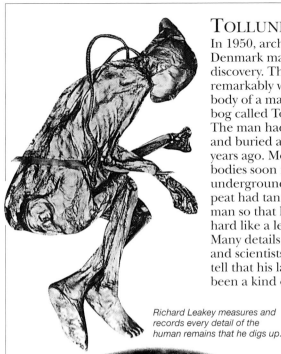

## AERIAL PHOTOGRAPHY

Photography of the ground from aeroplanes began in the 1920s. It made archaeology easier because the high viewpoint reveals traces of buildings, roads, and fields that are invisible from the ground.

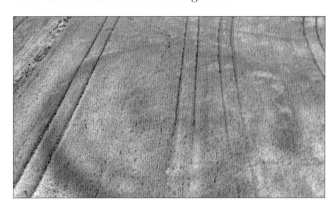

*Richard Leakey measures and records every detail of the human remains that he digs up.*

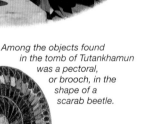

# LEAKEY

The Leakey family has made major discoveries about the origins of human beings. Louis and his wife, Mary, began to work in the Olduvai Gorge in Tanzania (Africa) in the 1930s. There they showed that human life existed 1,750,000 years ago. They found that human evolution began in Africa, not – as people once thought – in Asia. Since the 1960s their son Richard has continued their research, and now believes that the human race may be more than two million years old.

*Among the objects found in the tomb of Tutankhamun was a pectoral, or brooch, in the shape of a scarab beetle.*

*Archaeologists excavating the wreck of the Slava Rossi found Russian icons (religious paintings).*

# SHIPWRECKS

The development of lightweight diving equipment over the last 50 years has enabled archaeologists to excavate sites under water. They use many of the same methods that are used on land. Most underwater archaeologists look for shipwrecks, but they sometimes discover landscapes, buildings, and even towns of ancient civilizations.

## TUTANKHAMUN

The discovery of the tomb of Tutankhamun was one of the most sensational events in the history of archaeology. Tutankhamun was a boy-king who ruled in Egypt 3,500 years ago. In 1922, the British archaeologist Howard Carter (1873-1939) found Tutankhamun's fabulously rich burial place in the Valley of the Kings. Near the boy-king's remains lay gold treasure and beautiful furniture.

*Howard Carter (left) found the sarcophagus, or coffin, of Tutankhamun. It was remarkably well preserved.*

*Find out more*
BRONZE AGE
EGYPT, ANCIENT
EVOLUTION
FOSSILS
GEOLOGY
IRON AGE
PREHISTORIC PEOPLES

# ARCHITECTURE

EVERY BUILDING YOU SEE – home, school, airport – has been planned by an architect. The word architect is Greek for "builder" or "craftsworker" and architects aim to design and construct buildings that are attractive, functional, and comfortable. Architecture means designing a building; it also refers to the building style. Styles of architecture have changed over the centuries and differ from culture to culture, so architecture can tell us a lot about people. The Ancient Greeks, for example, produced simple, balanced buildings that showed their disciplined approach to life. Architects are artists who create buildings. But unlike other artists, they must sell their ideas before they are able to produce their buildings.

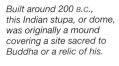

Built around 200 B.C., this Indian stupa, or dome, was originally a mound covering a site sacred to Buddha or a relic of his.

In 447 B.C., the Greek architects Ictinus and Callicrates designed the Parthenon, a temple to the goddess Athena, in Athens, Greece. With its graceful columns, it is a perfect example of classical architecture.

## CLASSICAL ARCHITECTURE

The Ancient Greeks and Romans developed a style that we call classical architecture. Most Greek buildings consisted of columns supporting a triangular roof. The types of columns varied according to the particular classical "order" (style) that was used. Everything was simple and perfectly even. The Romans, who came after the Greeks, developed the arch, dome, and vault.

Elegantly curving skyward in several tiers, pagodas were built as shrines to Buddha. On the right is the pagoda of Yakushi-ji Temple, Japan. Each element in the building's design originally had a religious meaning.

Milan Cathedral in Italy (right) is an example of late Gothic architecture.

## GOTHIC ARCHITECTURE

With their multitudes of pointed arches, finely carved stonework, and intricate windows, Gothic buildings are the opposite of simple classical ones. The Gothic style of architecture began in western Europe in the 12th century. It was used mainly in building cathedrals and churches. Although most Gothic buildings were huge, their thin walls, pointed arches, and large areas of stained-glass windows made them seem light and delicate.

## FRANK LLOYD WRIGHT

American architect Frank Lloyd Wright (1869-1959) influenced many other architects. He tried to blend buildings into their natural surroundings and create a feeling of space, with few walls, so that rooms could "flow" into one another. At Bear Run, Pennsylvania, he built Falling Water, a house over a waterfall.

Following the client's brief, the architect presents a drawing (below) to the client to show how the finished building will look.

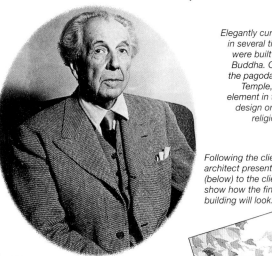

## ARCHITECTS

If you wanted to build a house, you would approach an architect, giving clear and precise details of what you required (a brief). An architect must know from a client what the building is to be used for, how many people will use it, and how much money is available. A good architect will make sure that the new design fits in with existing buildings around it, and is built from suitable material. The architect then presents drawings and plans to the client. When the plans are approved, work on the building can begin.

| Doric column | Ionic column | Corinthian column | Barrel vault | Groin vault | Rib vault | Dome |

## EXTRAORDINARY ARCHITECTURE

Some architects design weird and wonderful buildings which really stand out from the rest. A new town was built outside Paris, France, called Marne-la-Vallée. It has many extraordinary buildings, designed by various adventurous architects. The apartment complex, left, is like a monument that people can live in. Two circular buildings face each other across a central courtyard. It was designed by a Spaniard named Manolo Nunez-Yanowsky.

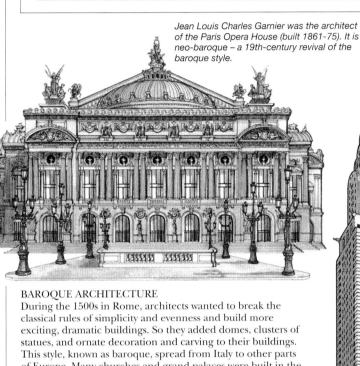

*Jean Louis Charles Garnier was the architect of the Paris Opera House (built 1861-75). It is neo-baroque – a 19th-century revival of the baroque style.*

*The American Chrysler Building, a New York City skyscraper, was completed in 1929.*

*Designed by the British architect Richard Rogers, the Lloyds office building in London, England, has all its services, such as plumbing, on the outside. This means they can be easily replaced.*

### BAROQUE ARCHITECTURE

During the 1500s in Rome, architects wanted to break the classical rules of simplicity and evenness and build more exciting, dramatic buildings. So they added domes, clusters of statues, and ornate decoration and carving to their buildings. This style, known as baroque, spread from Italy to other parts of Europe. Many churches and grand palaces were built in the baroque style.

*The architect draws up detailed plans of the inside of the building to show how the space will be used.*

*Working drawings contain exact measurements, materials, and structures, down to the tiniest detail.*

*The builder works from working drawings (above) when constructing the building.*

### CONTEMPORARY ARCHITECTURE

Glass, steel, and concrete are the building materials of today's architecture. There is little decoration, because a building's purpose is considered more important than its shape or form. The "international" style – glass and concrete suspended on a steel framework – is seen almost everywhere in the world.

Pediment

Gothic arch

Romanesque arch

Cornice

> ### *Find out more*
> BUILDING
> CHURCHES AND CATHEDRALS
> CITIES
> HOUSES
> SCULPTURE

43

# ARCTIC

THE SMALLEST OF THE world's oceans, the Arctic centres on the North Pole. Between the months of December and May, most of the Arctic Ocean is covered by polar sea ice, up to 30 m (98 ft) thick. The ocean is surrounded by the Arctic regions, where much of the ground is permanently frozen to depths of 460–600 m (1,500–2,000 ft). During the long, cold winters in the far north, much of the land is subject to periods of total darkness. This is because of the low angle of the Sun in relation to the ground. Beneath the rocks of the Arctic regions lie rich reserves of iron, nickel, copper, zinc, and oil. Severe weather conditions and very limited transport mean that these reserves are still under-exploited. Yet people such as the Inuit of Canada and Greenland have been known to live in these harsh conditions for at least 3,000 years.

The Arctic Ocean centres on the North Pole, the northern extremity of the Earth's axis. Three of the world's largest rivers, the Ob, Yenisey, and Lena, flow into the frozen waters of the Arctic Ocean. The Arctic regions consist of Alaska, Canada, Greenland and northern Siberia.

## ICE-BREAKING

Although half of the Arctic Ocean is covered by ice in winter, special ships called ice-breakers, can still sail through the ice. During particularly harsh winters, ice can become so dense in harbours and ports that it freezes right down to the sea bed, marooning ships for months at a time. Ice-breakers are designed to crush the ice with their steel hulls, opening up a lane that other ships can pass through. The Russian atomic-powered *Arcticka* is the world's most powerful ice-breaker. It can cut through ice that is 2.1 m (7 ft) thick at 11 km/h (7 mph).

*Teams of hardy husky dogs were traditionally used to pull sleds across the frozen ground.*

## ARCTIC SETTLERS

The Arctic is one of the world's most sparsely populated regions. Today, some 120,000 Inuit (Eskimo) peoples live in Greenland, Alaska, and Canada. Over the past 3,000 years they have adapted to their ice-bound conditions, hunting with kayaks (canoes) and harpoons, and existing on a diet of caribou, seal, whale meat, and fish. They lived in houses made of frozen snow (igloos) or semi-underground stone pit-houses. Today, snowmobiles (above) have replaced sleds, and rifles are used for hunting.

## COAL MINING

The Norwegian island of Spitsbergen, in the Arctic Ocean, has very extensive coal deposits. Its coal-mining towns are isolated and are desolate places. The sea-route to mainland Norway, some 1,000 km (620 miles) away, is frozen for four months of the year. Many Inuit have moved to towns such as these to work in the coal mines.

## POLAR BEARS

Between 25,000 and 40,000 polar bears roam the Arctic. Their white coats provide perfect camouflage, and a 10-cm (4-in) layer of body fat keeps them warm. Bears gorge on seals from April to July – they can survive for eight months without food. They can swim as far as 150 km (93 miles) in search of prey.

### Find out more

INUITS
GLACIERS AND ICECAPS
OCEANS AND SEAS
POLAR EXPLORATION
POLAR WILDLIFE

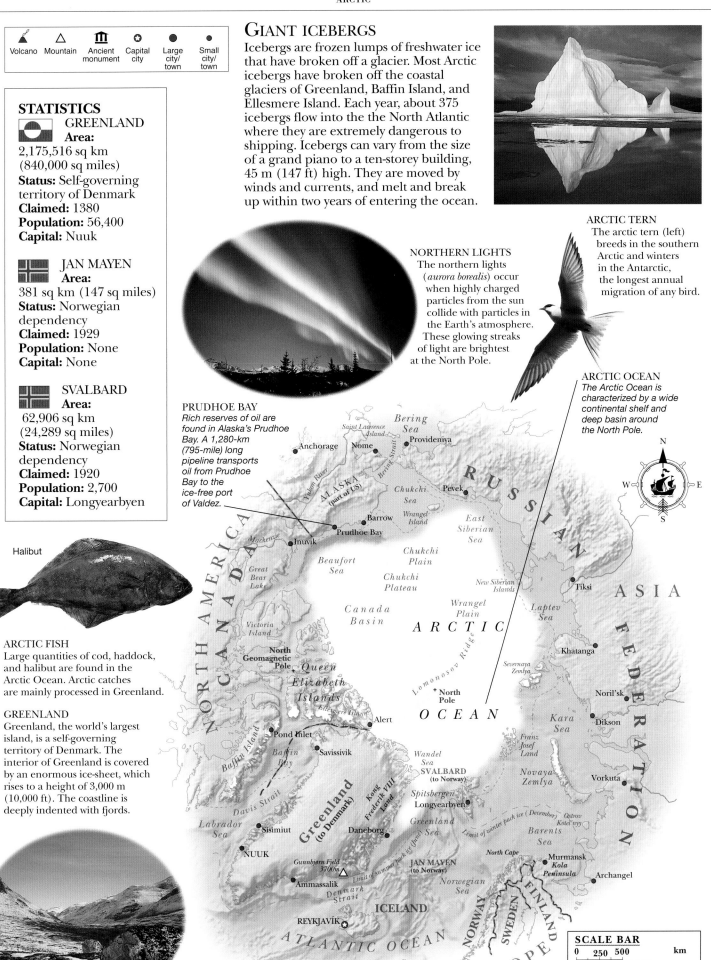

# GIANT ICEBERGS

Icebergs are frozen lumps of freshwater ice that have broken off a glacier. Most Arctic icebergs have broken off the coastal glaciers of Greenland, Baffin Island, and Ellesmere Island. Each year, about 375 icebergs flow into the the North Atlantic where they are extremely dangerous to shipping. Icebergs can vary from the size of a grand piano to a ten-storey building, 45 m (147 ft) high. They are moved by winds and currents, and melt and break up within two years of entering the ocean.

## STATISTICS

### GREENLAND
**Area:**
2,175,516 sq km
(840,000 sq miles)
**Status:** Self-governing territory of Denmark
**Claimed:** 1380
**Population:** 56,400
**Capital:** Nuuk

### JAN MAYEN
**Area:**
381 sq km (147 sq miles)
**Status:** Norwegian dependency
**Claimed:** 1929
**Population:** None
**Capital:** None

### SVALBARD
**Area:**
62,906 sq km
(24,289 sq miles)
**Status:** Norwegian dependency
**Claimed:** 1920
**Population:** 2,700
**Capital:** Longyearbyen

Volcano  Mountain  Ancient monument  Capital city  Large city/town  Small city/town

Halibut

**ARCTIC FISH**
Large quantities of cod, haddock, and halibut are found in the Arctic Ocean. Arctic catches are mainly processed in Greenland.

**GREENLAND**
Greenland, the world's largest island, is a self-governing territory of Denmark. The interior of Greenland is covered by an enormous ice-sheet, which rises to a height of 3,000 m (10,000 ft). The coastline is deeply indented with fjords.

**NORTHERN LIGHTS**
The northern lights (*aurora borealis*) occur when highly charged particles from the sun collide with particles in the Earth's atmosphere. These glowing streaks of light are brightest at the North Pole.

**ARCTIC TERN**
The arctic tern (left) breeds in the southern Arctic and winters in the Antarctic, the longest annual migration of any bird.

**ARCTIC OCEAN**
The Arctic Ocean is characterized by a wide continental shelf and deep basin around the North Pole.

**PRUDHOE BAY**
Rich reserves of oil are found in Alaska's Prudhoe Bay. A 1,280-km (795-mile) long pipeline transports oil from Prudhoe Bay to the ice-free port of Valdez.

## Map labels

Bering Sea
Saint Lawrence Island
Anchorage
Nome
Provideniya
Bering Strait
ALASKA (part of US)
Chukchi Sea
Pevek
RUSSIAN
Yukon River
Barrow
Wrangel Island
East Siberian Sea
Prudhoe Bay
Inuvik
Mackenzie
Chukchi Plain
Chukchi Plateau
New Siberian Islands
Tiksi
ASIA
Great Bear Lake
Beaufort Sea
Wrangel Plain
Laptev Sea
FEDERATION
Canada Basin
A R C T I C
Khatanga
Victoria Island
North Geomagnetic Pole
Lomonosov Ridge
Severnaya Zemlya
Noril'sk
NORTH AMERICA
CANADA
Queen Elizabeth Islands
+ North Pole
O C E A N
Kara Sea
Dikson
Ellesmere Island
Alert
Pond Inlet
Baffin Island
Savissivik
Baffin Bay
Wandel Sea
Franz Josef Land
Novaya Zemlya
Vorkuta
Davis Strait
Greenland (to Denmark)
Kong Frederik VIII Land
SVALBARD (to Norway)
Spitsbergen
Longyearbyen
Greenland Sea
Limit of winter pack ice (December)
Ostrov Kotel'nyy
Barents Sea
Labrador Sea
Sisimiut
Daneborg
NUUK
Gunnbjørn Field 3700m
Limit of summer pack ice (June)
JAN MAYEN (to Norway)
North Cape
Murmansk
Kola Peninsula
Archangel
Ammassalik
Denmark Strait
Norwegian Sea
NORWAY
SWEDEN
FINLAND
ICELAND
REYKJAVÍK
ATLANTIC OCEAN
EUROPE

## SCALE BAR
0  250  500  km
0  250  500  miles

# ARGENTINA

Argentina stretches for 3,460 km (2,150 miles) down the southeastern coast of South America. Its border in the west is defined by the Andes. To the south it straddles the Strait of Magellan.

ARGENTINA CONSISTS OF THREE MAIN REGIONS. In the north lies the hot, humid lands of the Gran Chaco. In the centre, the temperate grasslands of the Pampas provide some of the world's best farming country. Argentina is a world leader in beef exports, and a major producer of wheat, maize, fruit and vegetables. In the far south, the barren semi-desert of Patagonia is rich in reserves of coal, petroleum and natural gas. Argentina was settled by the Spanish in 1543. New European diseases, as well as conflict between the Spanish and Native Americans, considerably reduced Argentina's original population. In the 19th century, many immigrants from southern Europe, especially Spain and Italy, came to Argentina to work on farms and cattle ranches. Although Spanish is the official language today, many other languages are spoken, ranging from Welsh to Basque, reflecting the varied origins of Argentina's many settlers.

## GAUCHOS

These nomadic cowboys of the Argentine Pampas first appeared in the 18th century when they were hired to hunt escaped horses and cattle. Their standard equipment included a lasso, knife and *bolas* (iron balls on leather straps, thrown at the legs of the escaping animals). In the 19th century, they were hired by ranch-owners as skilled cattle-herders. Today, Argentine cow-herders keep their culture alive. They still wear the gaucho costume of a poncho (a woollen cape), high leather boots, and long, pleated trousers.

ARGENTINIAN WINE
European vines were introduced to Argentina by Spanish missionaries, and thrived in the temperate climate and fertile soils of the central regions. Argentina is the fourth-largest wine-producing country in the world – much of the wine is for sale in Argentina only.

A street performance (below) of a tango in Buenos Aires. The South American version of the tango developed from a blend of rhythms brought to South America by African slaves, and rhythms from Spain.

## BUENOS AIRES

Argentina's capital, Buenos Aires, is one of the largest cities in South America. Situated on the Plate river estuary, it is also a major port and thriving industrial centre. It was founded by Spanish settlers in 1580, and some historic buildings survive. The city expanded in the 19th century when European immigrants flooded to Argentina. Its museums, library, opera house, and cafés all give the city a European flavour.

TANGO DANCERS
Tango developed in the 1880s in the poorer districts of Buenos Aires. By 1915 it had become a craze in the fashionable ballrooms of Europe. Today, the sensuous dance, accompanied by melancholy song, is still popular on the streets of the city.

## ANDES

This wall of mountains forms a natural border between Argentina and its western neighbour, Chile. In 1881, the two countries signed a treaty defining this boundary. In western Argentina, the extinct volcano, Cerra Aconcagua, reaches a height of 6,959 m (22,816 ft). It is the highest peak in the South American Andes.

*Find out more*

COAL
DANCE
SOUTH AMERICA

BOLIVIA

PARAGUAY

BRAZIL

URUGUAY

**ARGENTINA**

*Tropic of Capricorn*

*Atacama Desert*

*A n d e s*

Cerro Ojos
del Salado
6880m

Cerro Aconcagua
6959m

San Salvador
de Jujuy
Salta

San Miguel
de Tucumán

Santiago
del Estero

Formosa

Resistencia

Corrientes

Posadas

La Rioja

San Juan

Mendoza

Godoy
Cruz

Santa Fe

**Córdoba**

Paraná

**Rosario**

Concordia

Gualeguaychú

Río Cuarto

San Rafael

*Pampas*

Junín

**BUENOS AIRES**

**La Plata**

Santa Rosa

Olavarría

Azul

Dolores

Tres Arroyos

Mar del Plata

*Colorado*

Bahía
Blanca

Necochea

*Bahía Blanca*

Zapala

Neuquén

*Río Negro*

San Antonio
Oeste

Viedma

*Lago Nahuel Huapí*

*Gulf of San Matías*

San Carlos de Bariloche

**Península
Valdés**

Esquel

*Chubut*

Rawson

*Chico*

Sarmiento

*Patagonia*

Comodoro Rivadavia

Perito
Moreno

*Gulf of San Jorge*

Caleta Olivia

*Deseado*

*Golfo de Penas*

Puerto
Deseado

*Chico*

*Santa Cruz*

El Calafate

*Bahía
Grande*

Río Gallegos

*Strait of Magellan*

Río Grande

*Tierra del Fuego*

*Isla de los Estados*

**Cape Horn**

*Drake Passage*

*Gran Chaco*

*Pilcomayo*

*Bernejo*

*Paraná*

*Salado*

*Laguna Mar
Chiquita*

*Paraná*

*Salado*

*Uruguay*

*River Plate*

*Tropic of Capricorn*

PACIFIC OCEAN

ATLANTIC OCEAN

N
W · E
S

*Volcano* ⚱ *Mountain* △ *Ancient
monument* 🏛 *Capital
city* ✪ *Large
city/
town* ● *Small
city/
town* ●

## STATISTICS
**Area:** 2,766,890 sq km
(1,068,296 sq miles)
**Population:**
38,400,000
**Capital:** Buenos Aires
**Languages:** Spanish,
Italian, Amerindian
languages
**Religions:** Roman
Catholic, Jewish,
Protestant
**Currency:**
Argentine peso
**Main occupation:**
Agriculture
**Main exports:** Beef,
wheat, fruit, wine
**Main imports:**
Designer clothing

TIERRA DEL FUEGO
This string of islands is separated
from the South American mainland
by the Strait of Magellan. They are
divided between Argentina and
Chile. The landscape, with its
mountains, frozen lakes and glaciers,
is bleak and windswept. It is also
barren – only stunted trees and
mosses grow there. Herds of sheep
graze the land. Oil has been
discovered in this remote area.

## FALKLAND ISLANDS
Discovered by the British in
1592, the Falkland Islands are a
self-governing British colony,
some 480 km (300
miles) off the coast
of Argentina. The
cool, windy islands
are only suitable for
grazing sheep, and
meat and wool are
their main resource. In
1982, Argentina claimed
the Falklands as their
territory, and invaded the
islands. They surrendered after
10 weeks, but British troops still
protect the islands.

**FALKLAND
ISLANDS**
(to UK)

*West
Falkland*

*East
Falkland*

**SCALE BAR**

| 0 | 200 | 400 | km |
|---|-----|-----|-----|
| 0 | 200 | 400 | miles |

# ARMIES

EVER SINCE THE ASSYRIAN armies swept across the ancient region of Mesopotamia more than 3,000 years ago, the purpose of armies has been the same: to conquer enemy territory and to defend their country. In Europe, there were no modern-style armies until the 16th century; instead sections of the population were called to arms whenever the country was at war. Today, however, most nations have a full-time army consisting of highly trained soldiers. Armies vary in size but most modern armies contain not only personnel but also the latest technology, including helicopters, guided missiles, and tanks. Technology has changed the role of the army. Previously, soldiers engaged in hand-to-hand combat; today, most armies rely on long-range weaponry.

## RECRUITMENT
In 1917, Uncle Sam, symbol of the United States, called on young men to enlist, or volunteer for fighting, in World War I. Some countries recruit volunteers during peacetime but have conscription – compulsory military service – during wartime.

## TRAINING
Soldiers, such as these Israeli women, are fighters trained for combat on land. In the army men and women learn the techniques of fighting and how to care for their weapons, and they exercise to become fit. They also learn confidence, discipline, and the importance of obeying orders so that they will fight well.

*Pouches on webbing, or harness, hold small equipment.*

*Mask protects against gas attack.*

*Helmet with protective padding*

*Mess kit for cooking and eating*

*Uniform fabric is coloured to look like foliage, so that soldiers are hard to see in battle.*

*Heavy boots for marching*

## UNIFORM
A soldier's fighting uniform must be practical. Strong, heavy clothes and boots provide protection against weather. Uniforms are also designed to provide camouflage so that the soldier can hide from the enemy.

Australia    China

United Kingdom    United States

### UNIFORMS OF THE WORLD
Soldiers of each country wear identifying uniforms, which may be different for war and peace times. Badges or stripes show the rank of the soldier and the regiment or group he or she belongs to.

## GUERRILLA ARMIES
In 1808, France invaded and defeated Spain. But Spanish farmers did not give in. They formed small groups and continued the war. They made surprise attacks on French patrols and supply depots. The Spanish called the campaign *guerrilla*, meaning "little war"; this term is still used today to describe similar methods of fighting wars.

*Modern guerrillas, such as these in Africa, usually belong to a group of people fighting for religious, national, or political beliefs.*

### Find out more
GUNS
NAPOLEONIC WARS
ROCKETS AND MISSILES
VIETNAM WAR
WEAPONS
WORLD WAR I
WORLD WAR II

# ARMOUR

ANCIENT WARRIORS quickly realized that they would survive in battle if they could protect themselves against their enemies. So they made armour – special clothing which was tough enough to stop weapons from injuring the wearer. Prehistoric armour was simple. It was made of leather but was strong enough to provide protection against crude spears and swords. As weapons became sharper, armour too had to improve. A thousand years ago the Roman Empire employed many armourers who made excellent metal armour. But after the fall of Rome in the 5th century, blacksmiths began to make armour and its quality fell. In the 14th century, specially trained armourers invented plate armour to withstand lances, arrows, and swords. But even the thickest armour cannot stop a bullet, so armour became less useful when guns were invented. Today no one uses traditional armour, but people in combat still wear protective clothing made out of modern plastics and tough metals.

### ANIMAL ARMOUR
Soldiers have used animals in warfare, such as dogs for attack and horses for riding into battle. Armour protected these animals when they fought. The most elaborate animal armour was the elephant armour of 17th-century India.

Arrows bounced off the curves of the helmet. Knights often wore mail or padding beneath the helmet.

The breastplate was flared so that enemy sword strokes bounced off.

The vambrace was a cylindrical piece to protect the upper arm.

The cowter protected the elbow, but allowed it to move freely.

The gauntlet was made up of many small pieces so that the hand could move freely.

The cuisse protected only the front of the leg.

Poleyns had to bend easily when the knight rode a horse.

Greaves were among the earliest pieces of body armour to be made of sheet metal.

## HELMETS
A single heavy blow to the head can kill a person, so helmets, or armoured hats, were among the first pieces of armour to be made. They are still widely used today. Different shapes gave protection against different types of weapon.

Bronze Age helmets protected against swords more than 3,000 years ago.

Pikemen of the 16th century

Twelfth-century helm

Modern helmets give protection against shrapnel (metal fragments from bombs).

### BULLETPROOF VEST
Modern police and security forces sometimes wear bulletproof vests to protect themselves from attack by criminals and terrorists. The vests are made of many layers of tough materials such as nylon and are capable of stopping a bullet.

### CHAIN MAIL
Chain mail was easier and cheaper for a blacksmith to make than a complicated suit of plate armour. Mail was very common between the 6th and 13th centuries. It was made of a large number of interlocking rings of steel. It allowed the wearer to move easily, but did not give good protection against heavy swords and axes.

## SUIT OF ARMOUR
Late 15th-century armour provided a knight with a protective metal shell. The armour was very strong, and cleverly jointed so that the knight could move easily. However, the metal suit weighed up to 30 kg (70 lb), so that running, for example, was virtually impossible.

### Find out more
JAPAN, HISTORY OF
KNIGHTS AND HERALDRY
MEDIEVAL EUROPE
ROMAN EMPIRE
WEAPONS

# ASIA

The Ural Mountains form the border between the continents of Asia and Europe. Asia is separated from Africa by the Red Sea. The Bering Strait, only 88 km (55 miles) wide, marks the gap between Asia and North America. Australia lies to the southeast.

THE LARGEST OF THE SEVEN CONTINENTS, Asia occupies one-third of the world's total land area. Much of the continent is uninhabited. The inhospitable north is a cold land of tundra. Parched deserts and towering mountains take up large areas of the central region. Yet Asia is the home of well over half of the world's population, most of whom live around the outer rim. China alone has more than 1,300 million people, and India has more than 1,000 million. Altogether, Asia contains 48 nations, and many times this number of peoples, languages, and cultures. It has five main zones. In the north is the Russian Federation. Part of this is in Europe, but the vast eastern region, from the Ural Mountains to the Pacific Ocean, is in Asia. The Pacific coast, which includes China, Korea, and Japan, is known as the Far East. To the south of this lie the warmer, more humid countries of Southeast Asia. India and Pakistan are the principal countries of the Indian subcontinent in south Asia. One of the world's first civilizations began here, in the Indus Valley. Bordered by the Mediterranean and Arabian seas, the Middle East lies to the west where Europe, Asia, and Africa meet.

## MIDDLE EAST

The hot, dry lands of the Middle East occupy the southwest corner of Asia. Almost the entire Arabian peninsula, between the Red Sea and The Gulf, is desert. To the north, in Iraq and Syria, lie the fertile valleys of the rivers Tigris and Euphrates. Most of the people of the Middle East are Arabs, and speak Arabic.

*The Arabs of the Middle East drank coffee long before it reached other countries.*

*Siberian scientists looking for minerals in north Asia have to work in subzero temperatures, and the cold can freeze their breath.*

### SIBERIA

The northern coast of Asia is fringed by the Arctic Ocean. The sea here is frozen for most of the year. A layer of the land, called permafrost, is also always frozen. This area is part of the vast region of the Russian Federation called Siberia. Despite the cold, Russian people live and work in Siberia because the region is rich in timber, coal, oil, and natural gas.

## ANCIENT TRADE ROUTES

Even 2,000 years ago, there was trade between the Far East and Europe. Traders carried silk, spices, gems, and pottery. They followed overland routes across India and Pakistan, past the Karakoram mountains (above). These trade routes were known as the Silk Road; they are still used today.

### TROPICAL RAIN FORESTS

The warm, damp climate of much of Southeast Asia provides the perfect conditions for tropical rain forests, which thrive in countries such as Burma (Myanmar) and Malaysia. The forests are the habitat for a huge variety of wildlife, and are home to tribes of people whose way of life has not changed for centuries. But because many of the forest trees are beautiful hardwoods, the logging industry is now cutting down the forests at an alarming rate to harvest the valuable timber.

*Sunlight breaks through the dense foliage of the rain forest only where rivers have cut trails through the trees.*

## PROSPERITY

Some Asian countries, such as Japan and Singapore, are among the world's most prosperous nations. The discovery of oil in a number of other countries, such as Saudi Arabia in the Middle East, and Brunei in Southeast Asia, has made them very wealthy.

*Brunei's vast oil wealth has enabled the sultan (ruler) to build a magnificent new palace. It is called Istana Nurul Iman, and is only open to the public at the end of the Islamic fasting month of Ramadan.*

*"Floating markets" are a common sight on the busy waterways of the Far East.*

*Vanilla vines grow well in the warm climate of Indonesia, and women harvest the pods by hand.*

### FAR EAST

East Asia is often called the Far East. In the 19th century, European traders and travellers used this name to distinguish east Asia from the Middle East. The Far East includes China, Japan, and Korea.

## KOREA

The Korean peninsula juts out from northern China towards Japan. The two Korean nations were at war between 1950 and 1953. They have lived in constant mistrust of each other since the war ended, but are now trying to mend the divisions between them. South Korea has a booming economy and is heavily supported by the United States. North Korea is Communist and poorer. The climate favours rice growing, with warm summers and icy winters.

*Construction work is a common sight in South Korea, as new offices and factories are built for the country's expanding industries.*

### SOUTHEAST ASIA

Many different people live in the warm, tropical southeastern corner of Asia. There are ten independent countries in the region. Some of them – Burma (Myanmar), Laos, Thailand, Cambodia (or Kampuchea), and Vietnam – are on the mainland attached to the rest of Asia. Further south lie Brunei, Malaysia, and the tiny island nation of Singapore. Indonesia stretches across the foot of the region. It is a scattered nation of more than 13,500 islands. The islands of the Philippines are to the east. Although some of these countries are very poor, Southeast Asia as a whole has one of the most rapidly developing economies in the world.

*Hundreds of different languages are spoken in the Indian sub-continent, but Indian schools teach pupils to read and write Hindi, which is the country's official language.*

### INDIAN SUBCONTINENT

The triangular landmass of south Asia extends south from the Himalaya Mountains to the warm waters of the Indian Ocean. This region is also known as the Indian subcontinent. It includes not only India but also Pakistan, Nepal, Bangladesh, and Bhutan. At the very southern tip of India lies the island nation of Sri Lanka.

*The port of Shanghai lies at the mouth of the River Yangtze.*

## RIVER YANGTZE

The Yangtze (or Chang Jiang), the world's third-longest river, flows 6,380 km (3,964 miles) through the middle of China, from its source in Tibet to the sea at Shanghai. In 1997, the first stage was completed on the Three Gorges Dam, China's largest construction project since the building of the Great Wall.

---

*Find out more*

CHINA
INDIA
JAPAN
RELIGIONS
RUSSIAN FEDERATION
SOUTHEAST ASIA

ASIA

Asia is the world's largest continent. It is a region of contrasts: both in its landscape, and peoples. The break up of the Soviet Union produced five new central Asian republics. The countries in the south are mainly Muslim, but are divided by religious differences and conflicts.

AFGHANISTAN
**Area:** 652,090 sq km (251,770 sq miles)
**Population:** 23,900,000
**Capital:** Kābul

ARMENIA
**Area:** 29,800 sq km (11,506 sq miles)
**Population:** 3,100,000
**Capital:** Yerevan

AZERBAIJAN
**Area:** 86,600 sq km (33,436 sq miles)
**Population:** 8,400,000
**Capital:** Baku

BAHRAIN
**Area:** 680 sq km (263 sq miles)
**Population:** 724,000
**Capital:** Manama

BANGLADESH
**Area:** 143,998 sq km (55,598 sq miles)
**Population:** 147,000,000
**Capital:** Dhaka

BHUTAN
**Area:** 47,000 sq km (18,147 sq miles)
**Population:** 2,300,000
**Capital:** Thimphu

BRUNEI
**Area:** 5,770 sq km (2,228 sq miles)
**Population:** 358,000
**Capital:** Bandar Seri Begawan

BURMA
**Area:** 676,550 sq km (261,200 sq miles)
**Population:** 49,500,000
**Capital:** Rangoon

CAMBODIA
**Area:** 181,040 sq km (69,000 sq miles)
**Population:** 14,100,000
**Capital:** Phnom Penh

CHINA
**Area:** 9,396,960 sq km (3,628,166 sq miles)
**Population:** 1,300,000,000
**Capital:** Beijing

CYPRUS
**Area:** 9,251 sq km (3,572 sq miles)
**Population:** 802,000
**Capital:** Nicosia

EAST TIMOR
**Area:** 15,007 sq km (5,794 sq miles)
**Population:** 778,000
**Capital:** Dili

GEORGIA
**Area:** 69,700 sq km (26,911 sq miles)
**Population:** 5,100,000
**Capital:** Tbilisi

INDIA
**Area:** 3,287,590 sq km (1,269,338 sq miles)
**Population:** 1,070,000,000
**Capital:** New Delhi

INDONESIA
**Area:** 1,904,570 sq km (735,555 sq miles)
**Population:** 220,000,000
**Capital:** Jakarta

IRAN
**Area:** 1,648,000 sq km (636,293 sq miles)
**Population:** 68,900,000
**Capital:** Tehran

IRAQ
**Area:** 438,320 sq km (169,235 sq miles)
**Population:** 25,200,000
**Capital:** Baghdad

ISRAEL
**Area:** 20,700 sq km(7,992 sq miles)
**Population:** 6,400,000
**Capital:** Jerusalem

JAPAN
**Area:** 377,800 sq km (145,869 sq miles)
**Population:** 128,000,000
**Capital:** Tokyo

JORDAN
**Area:** 89,210 sq km (34,440 sq miles)
**Population:** 5,500,000
**Capital:** Amman

KAZAKHSTAN
**Area:** 2,717,300 sq km (1,049,150 sq miles)
**Population:** 15,400,000
**Capital:** Astana

NORTH KOREA
**Area:** 120,540 sq km (46,540 sq miles)
**Population:** 22,700,000
**Capital:** Pyongyang

SOUTH KOREA
**Area:** 99,020 sq km (38,232 sq miles)
**Population:** 47,700,000
**Capital:** Seoul

KUWAIT
**Area:** 17,820 sq km (6,880 sq miles)
**Population:** 2,500,000
**Capital:** Kuwait City

KYRGYZSTAN
**Area:** 198,500 sq km (76,640 sq miles)
**Population:** 5,100,000
**Capital:** Bishkek

LAOS
**Area:** 236,800 sq km (91,428 sq miles)
**Population:** 5,700,000
**Capital:** Vientiane

LEBANON
**Area:** 10,400 sq km (4,015 sq miles)
**Population:** 3,700,000
**Capital:** Beirut

MALAYSIA
**Area:** 329,750 sq km (127,317 sq miles)
**Population:** 24,400,000
**Capital:** Kuala Lumpur

MALDIVES
**Area:** 300 sq km (116 sq miles)
**Population:** 318,000
**Capital:** Male'

MONGOLIA
**Area:** 1,565,000 sq km (604,247 sq miles)
**Population:** 2,600,000
**Capital:** Ulan Bator

NEPAL
**Area:** 140,800 sq km (54,363 sq miles)
**Population:** 25,200,000
**Capital:** Kathmandu

OMAN
**Area:** 212,460 sq km (82,030 sq miles)
**Population:** 2,900,000
**Capital:** Muscat

PAKISTAN
**Area:** 796,100 sq km (307,374 sq miles)
**Population:** 154,000,000
**Capital:** Islamabad

PHILIPPINES
**Area:** 300,000 sq km (115,831 sq miles)
**Population:** 80,000,000
**Capital:** Manila

QATAR
**Area:** 11,000 sq km (4,247 sq miles)
**Population:** 610,000
**Capital:** Doha

RUSSIAN FED.
**Area:** 17,075,400 sq km (6,592,800 sq miles)
**Population:** 143,000,000
**Capital:** Moscow

SINGAPORE
**Area:** 620 sq km (239 sq miles)
**Population:** 4,300,000
**Capital:** Singapore City

SRI LANKA
**Area:** 65,610 sq km (25,332 sq miles)
**Population:** 19,100,000
**Capital:** Colombo

SYRIA
**Area:** 185,180 sq km (71,500 sq miles)
**Population:** 17,800,000
**Capital:** Damascus

TAIWAN
**Area:** 36,179 sq km (13,969 sq miles)
**Population:** 22,600,000
**Capital:** Taipei

TAJIKSTAN
**Area:** 143,100 sq km (55,251 sq miles)
**Population:** 6,200,000
**Capital:** Dushanbe

THAILAND
**Area:** 513,120 sq km (198,116 sq miles)
**Population:** 62,800,000
**Capital:** Bangkok

TURKEY
**Area:** 779,450 sq km (300,950 sq miles)
**Population:** 71,300,000
**Capital:** Ankara

TURKMENISTAN
**Area:** 488,100 sq km (188,455 sq miles)
**Population:** 4,900,000
**Capital:** Ashgabat

U. A. E.
**Area:** 83,600 sq km (32,278 sq miles)
**Population:** 3,000,000
**Capital:** Abu Dhabi

UZBEKISTAN
**Area:** 447,400 sq km (172,741 sq miles)
**Population:** 26,100,000
**Capital:** Tashkent

VIETNAM
**Area:** 329,560 sq km (127,243 sq miles)
**Population:** 81,400,000
**Capital:** Hanoi

YEMEN
**Area:** 527,970 sq km (203,849 sq miles)
**Population:** 20,000,000
**Capital:** Sana

## STATISTICS
**Area:** 46,366,908 sq km
(17,940,146 sq miles)
**Population:**
3,954,612,000
**Highest point:** Mount
Everest (Nepal)
8,848 m (29,029 ft)
**Longest river:** Yangtze
(China) 6,380 km
(3,964 miles)
**Largest lake:** Caspian
Sea 371,000 sq km
(143,205 sq miles)

| | | | | | |
|---|---|---|---|---|---|
| Volcano | Mountain | Ancient¤ monument | Capital¤ city | Large¤ city/¤ town | Small¤ city/¤ town |

**SCALE BAR**

0    500    1000    km

0    500    1000    miles

### MOUNT EVEREST
The Himalayan mountain range runs along the
China-Nepal border southeast from the Pamir
mountains. It is a group of rugged peaks and
valleys, sometimes described as the "roof of the
world". The highest point in the Himalayas is
Mount Everest (right) – the world's highest
mountain.

### URAL MOUNTAINS
*The Ural Mountains
form a natural border
between Asia
and Europe.*

### KURILE ISLANDS
*The Kurile Islands are
part of the Russian
Federation, but Japan
claims the southernmost
islands in this chain as
part of its own territory.*

### SEOUL
Modern office blocks crowd together in
Seoul, the capital city of South Korea, but a
few ancient buildings still survive. The South
Gate (below) was built at the end of the
14th century as part of a wall that once
surrounded the city. Today, Seoul is
spreading far beyond its original boundaries
as rapid industrial growth creates a need for
more offices, factories, and homes.

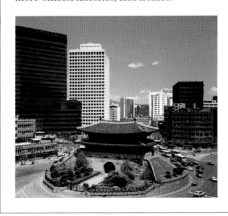

### EAST TIMOR
*In 1975 Indonesia invaded the
Portuguese colony of East Timor,
the eastern part of the island of
Timor. The following year the region
was made a province of Indonesia. In
a UN-monitored referendum in 1999,
voters rejected Indonesian rule and in
2002 East Timor became an
independent state.*

### JAVA
Rice terraces (right)
provide the staple food for
Indonesia. These fields are
on the island of Java, which
has only seven per cent of
Indonesia's land area but is
the home of some 60 per cent
of the country's people.

# HISTORY OF
# ASIA

THE VAST CONTINENT OF ASIA is home to the oldest civilizations and religions in the world. Because Asia contains many virtually impassable deserts and mountain ranges, individual countries developed separately from each other. However, links between these countries sprang up as merchants travelled along the Silk Road, Indian kings invaded neighbouring countries, Buddhist monks crossed the Himalayas, and Arab traders sailed across the Indian Ocean. As a result, the great Hindu, Buddhist, and Islamic religions spread across the continent. For much of the last 500 years, Europe controlled large parts of Asia, but since 1945 Asian countries have gained their independence. Many of them are now world-class economies.

## EARLY CIVILIZATIONS
Asia's extreme land forms, such as the towering peaks of the Himalayas, which separate India from China, meant that early Asian cultures had little contact with each other, or the rest of the world. As a result, the first great Asian civilizations, such as the Indus Valley civilization in the Indian subcontinent, and the Shang Dynasty in China, developed very different and distinct cultures.

*Bactrian (two-humped) camel pottery made in China.*

## HINDUISM
Hinduism began in the ancient civilizations of the Indus Valley, in India, around 2500 B.C. Over the centuries, the religion spread across India to Sri Lanka and the islands of Southeast Asia. Hinduism is the oldest religion in the world still practised today, and provides a thread linking together all of India's history.

## ARAB TRADERS
Arab merchants were great travellers and adventurers, crossing deserts and oceans in search of new markets in which to buy and sell their goods. On their journeys, they converted local people to their Islamic religion, founded by Muhammad in Arabia in the early 600s. As a result, Islam spread across Asia as far as the southeastern islands.

## SILK ROAD
The Silk Road was an important trading route that stretched across Asia from Loyang, China's capital, in the east to the Mediterranean Sea in the west. It was called the Silk Road because of the Chinese silk that was traded along its length. The road was not continuous, but was made up of a series of well-marked routes connecting major towns. Here merchants bought and sold their goods, creating a link between Asia and Europe.

*Buddhist monks shave their heads and wear saffron-coloured robes.*

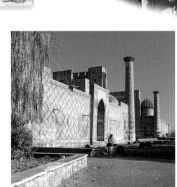

## BUDDHIST MONKS
Siddhartha Gautama, the founder of Buddhism, was born in India c. 563 B.C. By his death c. 483 B.C., his teaching had spread throughout India. From about A.D. 100, Buddhist monks took Buddhism across the Himalayas to China, and along the Silk Road into central Asia. Today, most of the world's Buddhists live in Asia.

## MONGOLS
The Mongols were fierce warriors who lived as nomads on the steppes, or grasslands, of central Asia. In the 1200s they created an empire that stretched from China into eastern Europe. Their power declined in the 1300s, but in 1369 one of their leaders, Tamerlane the Great, became ruler of central Asia. He built many fine mosques in his capital, Samarkand.

## EUROPEAN DOMINATION

In 1498, Portuguese explorer Vasco da Gama sailed to India around the southern tip of Africa. He was the first European to reach Asia by sea. Other Europeans followed, and over the next 400 years, Europeans dominated much of Asia, first as traders and merchants, then as conquerors and colonizers. Only Persia (present-day Iran), Afghanistan, Thailand, and Japan remained free from European control.

Portuguese colonial house in Macau

## WORLD WAR II

During World War II (1939-45), the Japanese invaded China and much of Southeast Asia in order to create an empire. Some welcomed the Japanese invaders, because they threw out the European colonial masters and gave the people a greater degree of independence. After Japan's defeat in 1945, Britain, France, the Netherlands, and the USA returned to take control of their former colonies.

# COMMUNIST ASIA

In 1949, the Communist Party finally gained power in China after years of civil war. Communists also took control in North Korea, Mongolia, North Vietnam, Cambodia, and Laos. The Communist governments of these countries improved people's living standards, but failed to match the economic success of Japan and other Asian countries.

The Red Guard, followers of Chinese Communist leader Mao Zedong

Chinese students bearing a portrait of Mao Zedong (1893-1976)

Chinese demonstrate their revolutionary fervour in 1967

## ASIA

**c. 2,500 B.C.** Hinduism is founded in India.

**c. 563-c. 483 B.C.** Life of Buddha.

**500s B.C.** The Silk Road is established.

**250 B.C.** Buddhism spreads to Sri Lanka and Southeast Asia.

**A.D. 100** Monks take Buddhism to China and into central Asia.

**850-1200** Chola kings of India take Hinduism to Sri Lanka and into Southeast Asia.

**1279** Mongol Empire under Kublai Khan reaches greatest extent.

**1369** Tamerlane the Great creates a new Mongol Empire in the city of Samarkand.

**1498** Vasco da Gama sails to India.

**1600** British merchants establish an East India Company in order to trade with India.

**1619** Dutch begin to control the East Indies.

**1757** British take over Bengal and expand their rule in India.

**1850s** French begin to control Southeast Asia.

**1937** Japanese troops invade China.

**1941-45** World War II rages in eastern Asia and the Pacific.

**1947-48** British rule in India comes to an end.

**1949** Indonesia becomes independent.

**1999** Portuguese hand Macau back to China.

## INDEPENDENCE

Following World War II, the European countries began to grant their Asian colonies independence. India became independent from Britain in 1947-48, and Indonesia gained its independence from the Netherlands in 1949. The last colony – the Portuguese territory of Macau – was handed back to China in 1999.

# TIGER ECONOMIES

Japan and other countries began rebuilding their economies after World War II. They concentrated on heavy industries such as car manufacturing and shipbuilding, and on hi-tech industries such as computing and electronics. Today Japan is the world's second biggest economy, while Taiwan, South Korea, Singapore, and others have become industrial powerhouses.

***Find out more***

CHINA, HISTORY OF
INDIA, HISTORY OF
JAPAN, HISTORY OF
SOUTHEAST ASIA, history of
WORLD WAR II

# ASSYRIANS

ABOUT 3,000 YEARS AGO, a mighty empire rose to power in the Middle East where Iraq is today. This was the Assyrian Empire. It lasted for more than 300 years and spread all over the surrounding area from the River Nile to Mesopotamia. Under King Shalmaneser I (1273-1244 B.C.) the Assyrians conquered Babylon and many other independent states, and eventually united the region into one empire. With an enormous army, armoured horses, fast two-wheeled chariots, and huge battering rams, the Assyrians were highly skilled, successful fighters, ruthless in battle. The Assyrian Empire grew quickly with a series of warlike kings, including Ashurbanipal II and Sennacherib. Great wealth and excellent trading links enabled the Assyrians to rebuild the cities of Nimrud and Nineveh (which became the capital), and to create a new city at Khorsabad. Assyria was a rich, well-organized society, but by the 7th century B.C. the empire had grown too large to protect itself well. In about 612 B.C., the Babylonian and Mede peoples destroyed Nineveh, and the Assyrian Empire collapsed.

**WARRIORS**
The Assyrians were famed and feared for their strength in battle and for torturing their victims. They developed the chariot and fought with swords, shields, slings, and bows.

*Men armed with spears and swords accompanied the king on lion hunts.*

**ASSYRIAN EMPIRE**
In the 7th century B.C. the Assyrian Empire reached its greatest extent. It stretched down to the Persian Gulf in the south and the Mediterranean coast in the west, and included Babylon.

**LION HUNT**
Hunting and killing lions was a favourite pastime of the Assyrian kings. Lions represented the wild strength of nature. It was considered a noble challenge to seek them out and kill them, although captive lions were also hunted. Only the king was allowed to kill a lion.

**ROYAL LIFE**
Stone reliefs tell us much about the lives of the Assyrian royalty. This relief sculpture shows King Ashurbanipal II (668-633 B.C.) drinking wine in his garden with his queen. It looks like a quiet, domestic scene, but on another section of this sculpture there is a head hanging from a tree. It is the head of Teumann, the king of the Elamites, whose defeat the king and queen are celebrating.

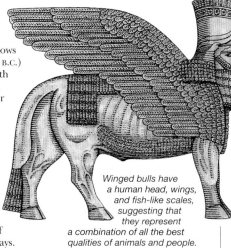

*Winged bulls have a human head, wings, and fish-like scales, suggesting that they represent a combination of all the best qualities of animals and people.*

**WINGED BULLS**
Massive stone sculptures (right) of winged bulls were placed on each side of important doors and gateways.

*Assyrian slaves had to drag the massive sculptures to the palace.*

*Find out more*
BABYLONIANS
MIDDLE EAST

# ASTRONAUTS
## AND SPACE TRAVEL

The astronaut wears a special undergarment with tubes that water flows through, keeping the astronaut's body cool.

The different parts of the suit, such as the gloves and helmet, are locked in position.

On 12 APRIL 1961, the world watched in wonder as Yuri Gagarin of Russia blasted off from Earth aboard a huge rocket and entered space. He was the first cosmonaut, the Russian word for astronaut, a person trained to work in space. Eight years later, Neil Armstrong walked on the Moon and became the first human being to step onto another world away from our planet. Since then, a few hundred other astronauts, both men and women, have voyaged into space. Astronauts have jobs to do during their missions. They help with the construction of the International Space Station and perform scientific experiments under the weightless conditions of space. Today, astronauts are preparing for the next major landmarks in space exploration – to go back to the Moon and then perhaps to Mars.

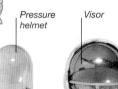

Pressure helmet

Visor

Cap

Communications headset

Water inlet and outlet

There is no air in space to carry sound waves, so astronauts communicate by radio.

Main tanks provide oxygen for the astronaut to breathe.

Communications input socket

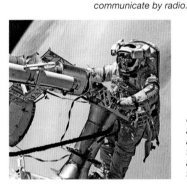

Wrist clamp

Reserve oxygen tanks provide emergency oxygen supply.

Oxygen inlets and outlets

Extra vehicular glove

Control panel allows the astronaut to adjust the temperature and oxygen flow in the suit.

Battery provides power for spacesuit systems.

Urine transfer collection

Integrated thermal micrometeoroid garment

Strap-on fastener

Cosmonaut Salizhan S. Shapirov installing navigation and communication equipment outside the International Space Station.

Urine-collection device worn by the astronaut is like a big nappy.

Layers of different plastics make the suit strong yet flexible.

Lunar overshoe

## SPACESUIT

Space is a perilous place for a human being. There is no air to breathe, and without a spacesuit for protection, an astronaut would explode. This is because the human body is built to function under the constant pressure of the Earth's atmosphere, which is not present in space.

### WEIGHTLESSNESS

We have weight because of the pull of the Earth's gravity. In space, gravity holds the astronauts and their spacecraft in orbit around the Earth. But there is no force holding the astronauts to their spaceship, so they float around inside it. This is called weightlessness.

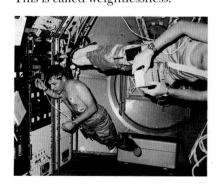

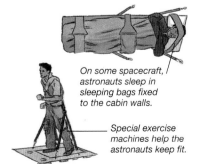

On some spacecraft, astronauts sleep in sleeping bags fixed to the cabin walls.

Food and drinks come in special packs that do not spill. There is an oven to heat food.

Special exercise machines help the astronauts keep fit.

### TRAINING

People have to undergo long training programmes to become astronauts. They also must be very fit. These cosmonauts are practising working under weightless conditions using a life-size model of a *Salyut* spacecraft inside a huge water tank.

### LIVING IN SPACE

While on board a spacecraft, astronauts consume the same kind of food and drink as they do on Earth. There is usually no bath or shower; astronauts wash with damp pieces of cloth instead. Regular exercise is essential, because living in weightless conditions can weaken bones and muscles.

*Find out more*

GRAVITY
ROCKETS AND MISSILES
SOVIET UNION, HISTORY OF
SPACE FLIGHT

# ASTRONOMY

THERE ARE AMAZING SIGHTS to be seen in the heavens – other worlds different from our own, great glowing clouds of gas where stars are born and immense explosions in which stars end their lives. Astronomers are scientists who study all the objects in the universe, such as planets, moons, comets, stars, and galaxies. Astronomy is an ancient science. The early Arabs and Greeks looked up to the sky and tried to understand the moons, stars, and planets. However, most of these objects were too distant for early astronomers to see in any detail. It was only after the invention of the telescope in the 17th century that people really began to learn about the universe. Today, astronomy makes use of a vast array of equipment to explore space. Astronomers use ground-based telescopes of many kinds, launch spacecraft that visit the other planets in the solar system, and send up satellites to study the universe from high above the Earth's surface.

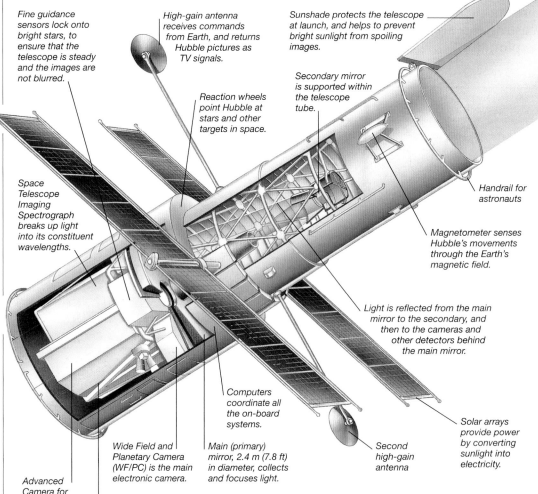

Fine guidance sensors lock onto bright stars, to ensure that the telescope is steady and the images are not blurred.

High-gain antenna receives commands from Earth, and returns Hubble pictures as TV signals.

Sunshade protects the telescope at launch, and helps to prevent bright sunlight from spoiling images.

Reaction wheels point Hubble at stars and other targets in space.

Secondary mirror is supported within the telescope tube.

Space Telescope Imaging Spectrograph breaks up light into its constituent wavelengths.

Handrail for astronauts

Magnetometer senses Hubble's movements through the Earth's magnetic field.

Light is reflected from the main mirror to the secondary, and then to the cameras and other detectors behind the main mirror.

Computers coordinate all the on-board systems.

Wide Field and Planetary Camera (WF/PC) is the main electronic camera.

Main (primary) mirror, 2.4 m (7.8 ft) in diameter, collects and focuses light.

Second high-gain antenna

Solar arrays provide power by converting sunlight into electricity.

Advanced Camera for Surveys is very sensitive, but has a more restricted view than the WF/PC.

Near-Infrared Camera and Multi-Object Spectrometer contains three infrared detectors.

## OBSERVATORY
Astronomers study space from observatories (above) that are often at the top of a mountain where there is a clear view of the sky. This photograph took several hours to make. The stars trace circles because the rotation of the Earth makes them appear to move across the sky.

## SPACE TELESCOPE
The optical telescope is one of the main tools of an astronomer. Most astronomical optical telescopes focus light from distant stars using a large curved mirror instead of lenses. This is because it is not possible to construct a lens big enough, and even if it were, a lens would produce distorted images. Launched in 1990, the Hubble Space Telescope is an optical telescope that orbits high above the Earth in order to avoid the blurring effect produced by the Earth's atmosphere.

## RECEIVING DATA ON EARTH
All signals to and from the Hubble Space Telescope pass through NASA's Goddard Space Flight Center, Maryland, USA. Here, engineers constantly monitor the spacecraft's health. Hubble astronomers work at the Space Telescope Science Institute, and control the telescope's observing schedule. Astronomers from far-off countries use Hubble through remote control. An astronomer (right) receives a Hubble image of the Tarantula nebula (a group of stars).

# EXPLORING THE UNIVERSE

Stars and other objects in the universe produce streams of tiny particles and many kinds of waves, such as radio waves. Except for light, these waves and particles are all invisible, but astronomers can study them to provide information about the universe. The atmosphere blocks many of the rays, so detectors are mounted on satellites that orbit above the Earth's atmosphere.

## INFRA-RED RAYS

Objects in space can also send out infra-red (heat) rays. Satellites and ground-based telescopes pick up these rays. They can reveal the centres of galaxies, and gas clouds called nebulae (right), where stars are forming.

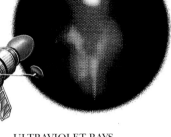

## X-RAYS

Special satellites carry detectors that pick up x-rays. These satellites have discovered black holes, which give out x-rays as they suck in gases from nearby stars. This is an x-ray image of a supernova, which is an exploding star.

## GAMMA RAYS

Some satellites detect gamma rays, which are waves of very high energy. Gamma rays come from many objects, including pulsars, which are the remains of exploded stars. This is a gamma ray map of our own galaxy.

## ULTRAVIOLET RAYS

Astronomers can learn about the substances in stars by analyzing ultraviolet (short wavelength) rays that come from them. A computer-generated picture produced by detecting ultraviolet rays (left) gives the composition and speed of gases that circle around in the outer atmosphere of a star.

## VISIBLE LIGHT

Telescopes on the ground and on satellites detect the light rays that come from planets, comets, stars, and galaxies. The Earth's atmosphere distorts light rays, making pictures slightly fuzzy. However, new computer- controlled telescopes are able to reduce this distortion.

*A supernova remnant as seen through an optical telescope.*

*Radio image of a quasar. A quasar is a kind of powerful galaxy with a very bright centre.*

## RADAR SIGNALS

Astronomers produce radar maps of planets and moons by bouncing radio waves off their surfaces. The radar map of Venus (left) was recorded by the *Pioneer Venus* spacecraft of the United States. The map is colour-coded to represent plains and mountains on the planet's surface.

## RADIO WAVES

Many bodies produce their own radio waves, which are picked up by the large dishes of radio telescopes. Objects called pulsars, quasars, and radio galaxies were discovered in this way.

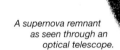

## NEUTRINOS

Tiny particles called neutrinos come from stars. Most neutrinos pass right through the Earth, but special detectors lying deep underground can detect a few of them. By studying neutrinos, astronomers can find out about the Sun and exploding stars.

*An array of sensitive light detectors pick up flashes of light produced when neutrinos enter the tank.*

## SKYWATCHERS OF THE PAST

In the third century B.C., the Greek scientist Aristarchus suggested that the Earth and planets move around the Sun. The telescope, first used to observe the heavens by Italian scientist Galileo, proved this to be true and led to many other discoveries. In the 1920s, the astronomer Edwin Hubble found that stars exist in huge groups called galaxies and that the universe is expanding in size.

*The ancient observatory at Jaipur, India, contains stone structures that astronomers built to measure the positions of the Sun, Moon, planets, and stars.*

*Neutrino detectors consist of large tanks of water, in which flashes of light occur as the neutrinos pass through.*

### Find out more
BLACK HOLES
MOON
PLANETS
SATELLITES
SPACE FLIGHT
STARS
SUN
TELESCOPES
UNIVERSE

# ATHLETICS

MOST SPORTS FANS like athletics, which has produced some of the greatest achievements in sports over the years. These are the feats of strength and activity, and are performed on specialized tracks or fields. Track sports include sprinting, middle-distance running, walking, and hurdles, which involves leaping over low gates while running. They may take place on a track, a road, or a cross-country route. Field events are held in special arenas and include the high jump, the long jump, and several throwing events. All athletic events require stamina, speed, power, and determination. In the shortest sprinting events, competitors may reach speeds of 36 km/h (22 mph). Many people do not compete but pursue athletics purely for their fitness and health benefits.

MARATHON
Men and women of very mixed abilities take part in marathon races, run over a distance of 42.2 km (26 miles, 1,155 feet). Marathons usually follow a route around the closed streets of a city, such as New York.

RUNNING EVENTS
Races take place around the track in a counter-clockwise direction. Runners in races up to 400 m (1,312 feet) must stay in lanes.

JUMPING EVENTS
These include triple jumps and the pole vault, for men only, and the long and high jumps, for both men and women. Competitors in the long and triple jumps land in sandpits; in the high jump and pole vault, they land on soft foam beds.

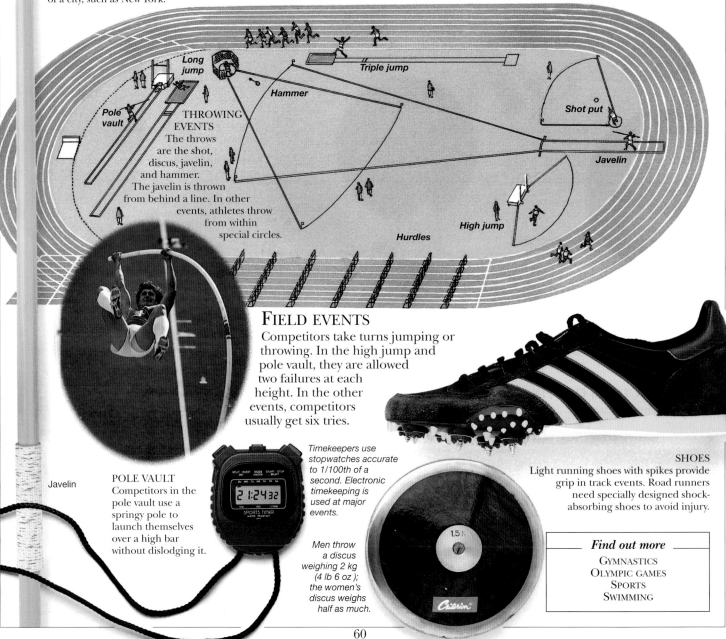

Long jump

Triple jump

Pole vault

Hammer

THROWING EVENTS
The throws are the shot, discus, javelin, and hammer. The javelin is thrown from behind a line. In other events, athletes throw from within special circles.

Shot put

Javelin

High jump

Hurdles

## FIELD EVENTS
Competitors take turns jumping or throwing. In the high jump and pole vault, they are allowed two failures at each height. In the other events, competitors usually get six tries.

Javelin

POLE VAULT
Competitors in the pole vault use a springy pole to launch themselves over a high bar without dislodging it.

Timekeepers use stopwatches accurate to 1/100th of a second. Electronic timekeeping is used at major events.

Men throw a discus weighing 2 kg (4 lb 6 oz ); the women's discus weighs half as much.

SHOES
Light running shoes with spikes provide grip in track events. Road runners need specially designed shock-absorbing shoes to avoid injury.

*Find out more*
GYMNASTICS
OLYMPIC GAMES
SPORTS
SWIMMING

# ATLANTIC OCEAN

THE UNDERWATER LANDSCAPE of the Atlantic is dominated by the mid-Atlantic ridge, the world's longest mountain chain. Some of the ridge's peaks rise above sea level as volcanic islands, such as Iceland and the Azores. The deepest part of the Atlantic, the Puerto Rico Trench, plunges to 9,200 m (30,185 ft) below sea level. The Atlantic Ocean is rich in oil and natural gas. In recent years, offshore oil reserves have been exploited in the Gulf of Mexico, the Niger Delta and the North Sea. Sand, gravel and shell deposits are also mined by the USA and UK for use in the construction industry. The Atlantic is the most productive and heavily utilized fishing ground in the world, providing millions of tonnes a year. The Atlantic Ocean has been crossed by shipping routes for many centuries. It is still heavily used for sea-borne trade, especially the bulk transport of raw materials, such as oil, grain, and iron, to industrial centres.

**SUBTROPICAL SCILLIES**
The Gulf Stream is a warm ocean current that flows up the east coast of North America, and then across to western Europe, driven by north-easterly trade winds. These winds carry moisture and warmth from the ocean to the land. In England's Scilly Islands, subtropical plants flourish in winter because of the impact of the current.

The Atlantic Ocean is bounded by the Americas in the west, and by Europe and Africa in the east. Along the mid-Atlantic ridge, a long submarine mountain chain, high volcanic peaks pierce the water's surface as islands.

## ATLANTIC TOURISM
The volcanic islands which have emerged along the ocean's mid-Atlantic ridge, especially the Canaries, Azores and Madeira, are major tourist attractions. The fertile black soil of the Canaries is ideal for the cultivation of bananas, tomatoes, sugar cane and tobacco. The mild sub-tropical climate attracts winter visitors from Europe.

**SUBMARINE ACTIVITY**
During the Cold War, from the 1950s to the 1980s, the Atlantic Ocean was patrolled by both the US and Russian navies. Since the 1990s, US and Russian scientists are sharing advances in submarine technology – developed for defence purposes – to survey, map, and analyze the unexplored world beneath the Atlantic.

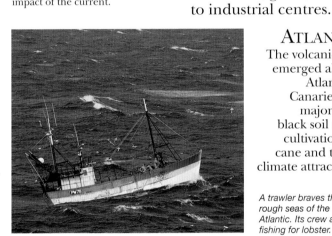

*A trawler braves the rough seas of the Atlantic. Its crew are fishing for lobster.*

## ATLANTIC FISHING
The Atlantic Ocean, a productive fishing ground for centuries, contains over half the world's total stock of fish. In the North, cod, haddock, mackerel, and lobster are the main catch, while the South Atlantic catch is dominated by hake, tuna, and pilchard. Freezer trawlers, that can catch and process a tonne or more of fish in just an hour, are in danger of over-fishing the Atlantic. Countries claim exclusive rights to zones extending 370 km (200 nautical miles) from their coastlines to conserve fish stocks.

**NAVIGATION**
Compasses are vital in cross-ocean navigation. The compass needle points to magnetic north, in the Canadian Arctic.

**ICELANDIC HEATING**
Iceland was formed by volcanic action along a fault line in the Earth's crust, the ridge, 65 million years ago. Iceland still has over 100 volcanoes, many still active. The vast natural heat reserves beneath Iceland's icy surface, are being harnessed to provide hot water and heating for much of the population.

*Plumes of steam rise from a geothermal power station (left). Iceland has the most silfataras (volcanic vents) and hot springs in the world. The intense heat deep underground creates bubbling hot springs and mud pools.*

---

***Find out more***

OCEANS AND SEAS
SHIPS AND BOATS
SUBMARINES
VOLCANOES
WIND

# OVERSEAS TERRITORIES AND DEPENDENCIES

 **ASCENSION**
**Area:** 88 sq km (34 sq miles)
**Status:** British dependent territory of St Helena
**Claimed:** 1673
**Population:** 1,200
**Capital:** Jamestown (St Helena)

 **BERMUDA**
**Area:** 53 sq km (20.5 sq miles)
**Status:** British Crown colony
**Claimed:** 1612
**Population:** 64,400
**Capital:** Hamilton

 **BOUVET ISLAND**
**Area:** 58 sq km (22 sq miles)
**Status:** Norwegian dependency
**Claimed:** 1928
**Population:** None
**Capital:** None

 **FAEROE ISLANDS**
**Area:** 1,399 sq km (540 sq miles)
**Status:** Self-governing territory of Denmark
**Claimed:** 1380
**Population:** 46,300
**Capital:** Tórshavn

 **FALKLAND ISLANDS**
**Area:** 12,173 sq km (4,699 sq miles)
**Status:** British dependent colony
**Claimed:** 1832
**Population:** 3,000
**Capital:** Stanley

 **SAINT HELENA**
**Area:** 122 sq km (47 sq miles)
**Status:** British dependent territory
**Claimed:** 1673
**Population:** 7,400
**Capital:** Jamestown

 **TRISTAN DA CUNHA**
**Area:** 98 sq km (38 sq miles)
**Status:** British dependent territory of St Helena
**Claimed:** 1612
**Population:** 300
**Capital:** Jamestown (St Helena)

**SOUTH GEORGIA & THE SOUTH SANDWICH ISLANDS**
**Area:** 3,592 sq km (1,387 sq miles)
**Status:** British dependent territory
**Claimed:** 1775
**Population:** No permanent residents
**Capital:** None

## ATLANTIC YACHT RACING
Cross-ocean racing began in 1866, with a race from Connecticut, USA, to Cowes in the Isle of Wight, which took 13 days. Single-handed ocean races became popular in the 1960s.

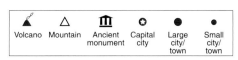

## BERMUDA TRIANGLE
The Bermuda Triangle lies between Bermuda, Florida, and Puerto Rico. Many ships, submarines, and aeroplanes have disappeared in its waters. In 1872 a deserted sailing ship, the *Mary Celeste*, was found drifting across the Atlantic – its ten crew members were never located.

**SCALE BAR**
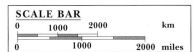

# INDEPENDENT STATES

 **CAPE VERDE**
**Area:** 4,030 sq km (1,556 sq miles)
**Population:** 463,000
**Capital:** Praia

 **ICELAND**
**Area:** 103,000 sq km (39,770 sq miles)
**Population:** 290,000
**Capital:** Reykjavík

# ATMOSPHERE

There is no definite upper limit to the atmosphere. The final layer before outer space is called the exosphere; it contains hardly any air at all.

A layer of very thin air called the thermosphere extends from about 80 to 480 km (50 to 300 miles) above the ground. It contains the ionosphere – layers of electrically charged particles, from which radio waves can be bounced around the world.

The mesosphere extends from 50 to 80 km (30 to 50 miles) above the Earth. If meteors fall into this layer, they burn up, causing shooting stars.

Under the mesosphere lies the stratosphere. It extends from 11 to 50 km (7 to 30 miles) up. The stratosphere is a calm region. Airliners fly here to avoid the winds and weather lower down.

Although it is the narrowest layer, the troposphere contains most of the gas in the atmosphere. It reaches about 11 km (7 miles) above the ground, but this varies around the globe and from season to season. Most weather occurs in the troposphere.

WITHOUT THE ATMOSPHERE, it would be impossible to live on Earth. The atmosphere forms a layer, like a blanket around the Earth, protecting us from dangerous rays from the sun and from the cold of outer space. It contains the air that we breathe, together with water vapour and tiny pieces of dust. Air contains the gases oxygen, carbon dioxide, and nitrogen, which are necessary for life; water vapour forms the clouds that bring rain. The atmosphere is held by the pull of the Earth's gravity and spreads out to about 2,000 km (1,250 miles) above the Earth. Three quarters of the air in the atmosphere lies beneath 10,700 m (35,000 ft) because the air gets thinner higher up. The air at the top of Mount Everest is only one third as thick as it is at sea level. That is why mountain climbers carry an air supply and why high-flying aircraft are sealed and have air pumped into them.

## LAYERS OF THE ATMOSPHERE

The Earth's atmosphere is divided into several layers. The main layers, from the bottom upwards, are called the troposphere, the stratosphere, the mesosphere, the thermosphere, and the exosphere.

### OZONE LAYER

Within the stratosphere, there is a thin layer of the gas ozone. Ozone is a form of oxygen that absorbs ultraviolet rays from the sun. Without the ozone layer, these rays would reach the ground and kill all living creatures. Pollution and the use of certain chemicals are destroying the ozone layer.

Compared to the size of the Earth, the atmosphere forms a very narrow band – approximately equivalent to the skin around an orange.

## SKY AND SUNSET

When rays of light travel through the atmosphere, they hit pollen, dust, and other tiny particles. This causes the rays to scatter, or bounce off in all directions. Some colours of light are scattered more than others.

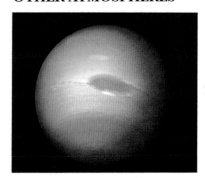

## OTHER ATMOSPHERES

Other planets' atmospheres are very different from Earth's. On Neptune (above), the atmosphere is mainly methane gas. Jupiter and Saturn have thick, cloudy atmospheres of hydrogen. None of these planets can support life.

**BLUE SKY**
The atmosphere scatters mainly blue light; this is why the sky looks blue. The other colours of light are scattered much less than blue so that they come to Earth directly. This causes the area of sky around the sun to look yellow.

**SUNSET AND SUNRISE**
At sunset and sunrise, when the sun is below the horizon, the light travels through much more of the atmosphere before we see it. The blue light is scattered so much that it is absorbed, or soaked up, by the atmosphere. Only red light reaches us, so the sky looks red.

*Find out more*
AIR
CLIMATES
OXYGEN
PLANETS
WEATHER

# ATOMS AND MOLECULES

*A drop of water contains about 3,000 million billion molecules.*

LOOK AROUND YOU. There are countless millions of different substances, from metals and plastics to people and plants. All of these are made from about 100 different kinds of "building blocks" joined together in different ways. These building blocks are tiny particles called atoms. Atoms are so small that even the tiniest speck of dust contains more than one million million atoms. Some substances, such as iron, are made of just one kind of atom; other substances, such as water, contain molecules – atoms joined together in groups. Such molecules may be very simple or very complex. Each water molecule contains two hydrogen atoms and one oxygen atom; plastics are made of molecules which often contain millions of atoms. An atom itelf is made up of a dense centre called a nucleus. Particles that carry electricity, called electrons, move around the nucleus. Scientists have discovered how to split the nucleus, releasing enormous energy which is used in nuclear power stations and nuclear bombs.

*A molecule of water contains three atoms – two hydrogen atoms and one oxygen atom.*

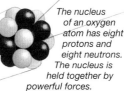

*Protons and neutrons are made up of quarks.*

*Electrons whiz around the nucleus. An atom of oxygen has eight electrons.*

*There is a lot of empty space in an atom. If the nucleus were the size of a tennis ball, the nearest electron would be 1 km (about half a mile) away.*

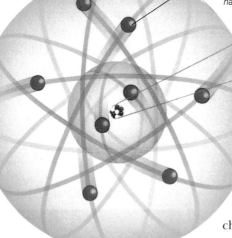

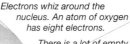

*The nucleus of an oxygen atom has eight protons and eight neutrons. The nucleus is held together by powerful forces.*

## PROTONS AND NEUTRONS

The nucleus of an atom contains particles called protons and neutrons. These contain even smaller particles called quarks. Protons carry electricity. However, they carry a different kind of electricity from electrons. They have a "positive charge", whereas electrons have a "negative charge". Neutrons have no electric charge.

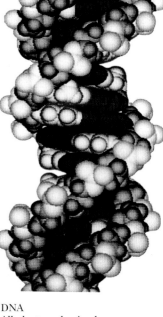

DNA
All plants and animals contain molecules of DNA (deoxyribonucleic acid). DNA carries the blueprint for life: coded information in DNA molecules determines the characteristics of each living thing and its offspring. A DNA molecule consists of millions of atoms arranged in a twisted spiral shape.

## DISCOVERING THE ATOM

About 2,400 years ago, the Greek philosopher Democritus believed that everything was made up of tiny particles. It was not until 1808 that English scientist John Dalton proved that atoms exist. Around 1909, New Zealand scientist Ernest Rutherford (below) discovered the nucleus.

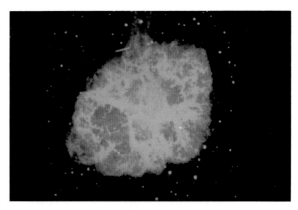

## IMMORTAL ATOMS

The particles that make up atoms never disappear but are constantly journeying through the universe as part of different substances. All these particles originated with the formation of the universe around 15,000 million years ago. The atoms that make everything on Earth were formed from these particles in stars, which then exploded like the crab nebula (above).

*Find out more*
CHEMISTRY
OXYGEN
PHYSICS
PLASTICS
REPRODUCTION

# AUSTRALIA

LOCATED BETWEEN THE INDIAN AND PACIFIC OCEANS, Australia is an island continent, and the sixth largest country in the world. It is a land of varied landscapes, including tropical rainforests, vast deserts, snow-capped mountains, rolling tracts of pastoral land, and magnificent beaches. The country boasts a great number of natural features, the most famous of which are the Great Barrier Reef and Uluru (Ayers Rock). Australians have an outdoor lifestyle and enjoy a high standard of living. Almost 90 per cent of the country's 19.7 million people live in the fertile strip of land on the east and southeast coast. Many of them live in Melbourne and Sydney, Australia's two largest cities, and in the nation's capital, Canberra. Today few people live in the dry Australian interior known as the Outback. The original inhabitants of Australia, the Aborigines, learned to survive in the harsh conditions there. However, only a small number of the 410,000 Aboriginal population live a traditional life in the Outback today. Other Australians are descendants of settlers from Britain, continental Europe and Southeast Asia.

Australia lies southeast of Asia, with the Pacific Ocean to the east and the Indian Ocean to the west. It is the only country that is also a continent. Together with several nearby islands, Australia covers a total area of 7.61 million sq km (2.94 million sq miles).

## SURFING
Surfing is a favourite Australian sport. Surfing carnivals are held regularly in many towns. Polynesian people invented the sport hundreds of years ago; recently it has expanded to include windsurfing, trick surfing, and long-distance surfing. Surfers often travel vast distances to reach a beach with the best waves of the day.

*At a surfing carnival lifeguards give demonstrations of lifesaving. Surfing competitions are hotly contested and often draw many spectators.*

*During the celebrations of Australia's 200th anniversary, ocean-going sailing ships gathered in Sydney's famous harbour.*

## SYDNEY
Sydney is the oldest and largest city in Australia. Sydney was founded in 1788 as a British prison colony with about 1,000 prisoners and their guards; today it is home to more than 4 million people. The city stands around Port Jackson, a huge natural bay spanned by Sydney Harbour Bridge. Sydney is a busy industrial centre and tourist resort.

### BEACH CULTURE
The majority of Australians live in towns and cities along the coast. Therefore the beach is the most popular venue for leisure pursuits. Australia's climate is ideal for beach activities such as surfing, swimming, sailing and beach volleyball. Mild winter temperatures mean that these sports can be enjoyed all year round.

### FILMMAKING
The Australian film industry produces a number of important films each year. Some, such as *Picnic at Hanging Rock* (1975), which tells of the mysterious disappearance of a group of Australian schoolgirls, have received international acclaim.

*Australia's currency is the Australian dollar. On one side the coins feature a portrait of the Queen of England, who is the head of state.*

## TASMANIA

The island of Tasmania lies off the southeast coast of Australia and is a state in itself, with a population of nearly half a million. The island has a cooler, damper climate than the rest of the country and is famous for its fruit, vegetables, and sheep. Tin, silver, and other products are mined. Much of western Tasmania is unpopulated and covered in dense forest where native wildlife, such as the Tasmanian devil, below, survives in large numbers.

### GREAT DIVIDING RANGE
Running along the eastern coast of the continent from Cape York to Ballarat is a 3,700 km (2,300 mile) mountain chain called the Great Dividing Range. The tallest mountain is Kosciuszko, at 2,228 m (7,310 ft). Other peaks are much lower. The mountains divide the fertile coastal plains from the dry interior. The steep hills were once a major barrier to travel; even today only a few roads and railways cross from east to west.

*The Three Sisters formation in New South Wales belongs to the Great Dividing Range.*

*Outback ranchers ride motorbikes or horses to round up cattle and sheep.*

*Ancient rock and bark paintings show that Aboriginal culture flourished nearly 40,000 years before European settlers arrived.*

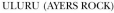

## OUTBACK

Very few people live in Australia's interior, called the Outback. However, sheep and cattle are farmed on the dry land. Some ranches, called stations, cover hundreds of square kilometres. Because of the great distances, Outback Australians live isolated lives and communicate by radio.

### STRIP MINING
Australia has huge mineral wealth, and mining is an important industry. The country produces one third of the world's uranium, which is essential for nuclear power. In recent years iron ore has been excavated in large strip mines where giant digging machines remove entire hills.

### ULURU (AYERS ROCK)
One of the most impressive natural sights in Australia is Uluru (formerly known as Ayers Rock). This huge mass of sandstone stands in the middle of a wide, flat desert and is 335 m (1,142 ft) high. Although it lies hundreds of kilometres from the nearest town, Uluru is a major tourist attraction with its own hotel. The rock is particularly beautiful at sunset, when it seems to change colour.

# PERTH

Founded in 1829, Perth (below) is the state capital of Western Australia and its financial and commercial heart. Most Australian people live in cities, and the population of Perth reflects the European ancestry of a large percentage of today's Australians.

## CANBERRA

Canberra, the capital city of Australia, is situated in the Australian Capital Territory (A.C.T.), an area of 2,360 sq km (911 sq miles) completely surrounded by the state of New South Wales. The capital was designed as a city of parks and gardens by American landscape architect, Walter Burley Griffin. Construction of the city began in 1913. Canberra is a political and educational centre rather than a commercial or industrial town.

*Hay Street mall (left) is a pedestrian shopping precinct located in Perth's central business district.*

# ADELAIDE

Adelaide (right) is the capital and chief port of South Australia. A well-planned city, it was designed in a grid pattern by Colonel William Light, the first surveyor-general of South Australia. The city is bordered by 6.9 sq km (2.7 sq miles) of parkland, and was named for Queen Adelaide, wife of King William IV of England.

# MELBOURNE

The capital city of Victoria and the second largest city in Australia, Melbourne (below) displays a dramatic mixture of old and new. Melbourne was founded in 1835 by an Australian farmer, John Batman. Nearly 20 years later, gold was discovered in Victoria and Melbourne's population climbed sharply. Today, Melbourne is a leading seaport, and the commercial and industrial centre of Victoria.

# BRISBANE

The state capital of Queensland and its largest city, Brisbane (right) is a bustling seaport lying above the mouth of the Brisbane river at Moreton Bay. In this way, it is similar to Australia's other state capitals, all of which were founded near rivers close to ocean harbours. Like other state capitals, Brisbane too is the commercial centre of its state, with its main business district situated near the waterfront.

*St Paul's Cathedral stands proudly amid modern architecture in Melbourne. The building was designed by William Butterfield in the 1880s in a Gothic style.*

---

### *Find out more*

ABORIGINAL AUSTRALIANS
AUSTRALIA, HISTORY OF
AUSTRALIAN WILDLIFE
ARCHITECTURE
CITIES

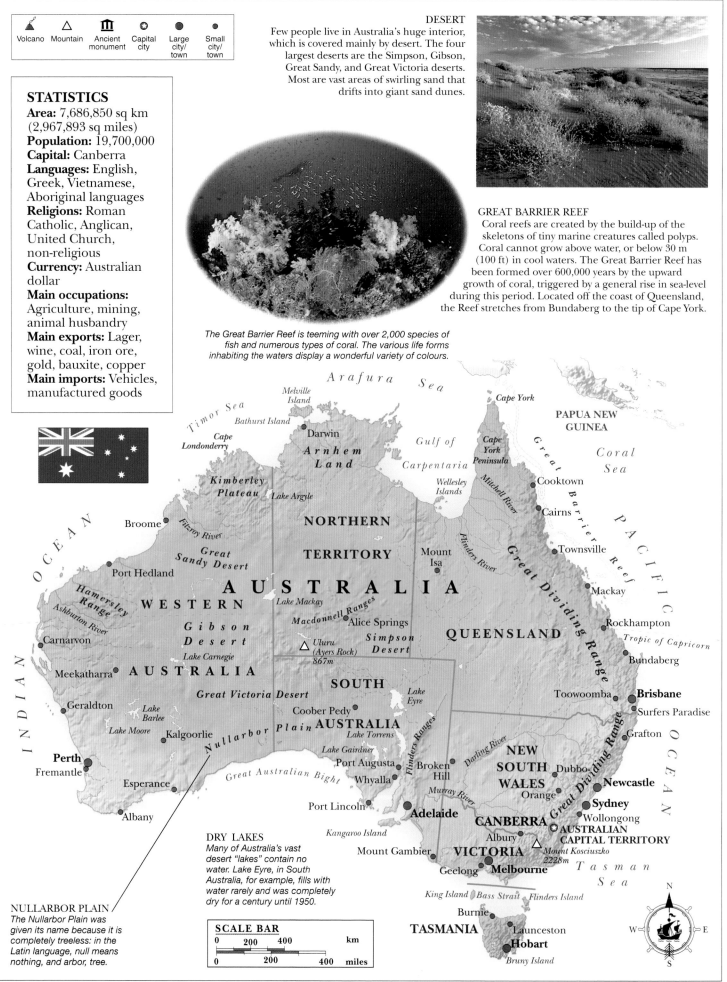

## STATISTICS

**Area:** 7,686,850 sq km
(2,967,893 sq miles)
**Population:** 19,700,000
**Capital:** Canberra
**Languages:** English,
Greek, Vietnamese,
Aboriginal languages
**Religions:** Roman
Catholic, Anglican,
United Church,
non-religious
**Currency:** Australian
dollar
**Main occupations:**
Agriculture, mining,
animal husbandry
**Main exports:** Lager,
wine, coal, iron ore,
gold, bauxite, copper
**Main imports:** Vehicles,
manufactured goods

### Map Legend
- Volcano
- Mountain
- Ancient monument
- Capital city
- Large city/town
- Small city/town

### DESERT
Few people live in Australia's huge interior,
which is covered mainly by desert. The four
largest deserts are the Simpson, Gibson,
Great Sandy, and Great Victoria deserts.
Most are vast areas of swirling sand that
drifts into giant sand dunes.

### GREAT BARRIER REEF
Coral reefs are created by the build-up of the
skeletons of tiny marine creatures called polyps.
Coral cannot grow above water, or below 30 m
(100 ft) in cool waters. The Great Barrier Reef has
been formed over 600,000 years by the upward
growth of coral, triggered by a general rise in sea-level
during this period. Located off the coast of Queensland,
the Reef stretches from Bundaberg to the tip of Cape York.

*The Great Barrier Reef is teeming with over 2,000 species of
fish and numerous types of coral. The various life forms
inhabiting the waters display a wonderful variety of colours.*

### DRY LAKES
*Many of Australia's vast
desert "lakes" contain no
water. Lake Eyre, in South
Australia, for example, fills with
water rarely and was completely
dry for a century until 1950.*

### NULLARBOR PLAIN
*The Nullarbor Plain was
given its name because it is
completely treeless: in the
Latin language, null means
nothing, and arbor, tree.*

### SCALE BAR
0  200  400  km
0  200  400  miles

# HISTORY OF
# AUSTRALIA

AS RECENTLY AS 1600, the only people who knew about Australia were the aboriginal peoples who had lived there for more than 40,000 years. The rest of the world had no idea that the continent existed. In 1606, the Dutch explorer William Jansz landed in northern Australia. Although he did not know it, he was the first European to see the country. Further exploration of the coastline by Dutch and British explorers revealed that Australia was an island. In 1770, the British captain James Cook claimed the east coast of Australia for Britain and named it New South Wales. The British sent convicts to their new colony, forming the basis of Sydney, today the country's largest city. Throughout the 19th century, the population of Australia grew as more convicts arrived, followed by immigrants. For many of them life was tough, but the British colony grew richer when gold was discovered in 1851. Farming also became established. In 1901, Australia became an independent commonwealth, although it remained close to Britain for many years and Australian troops fought in both world wars on the side of Britain. More recently, Australia has branched away from Britain and set up links with other countries.

ABORIGINES
The first aboriginal peoples probably arrived in Australia from the islands of Southeast Asia about 40,000 years ago. In 1770, there were about 300,000 Aborigines in Australia.

Convict ships in the bay

Chopping wood to make timber huts

The convicts carried supplies onto the shore.

At first, the convicts (prisoners) were miserable and hungry.

The first British settlement in Australia was at Port Jackson in Sydney Harbour, next to the location of the present-day Sydney Opera House.

## BOTANY BAY
In 1770, the English explorer James Cook dropped anchor in Botany Bay, south of what is now the city of Sydney. In 1788, the first 750 British settlers arrived in Australia. These people were convicts – guarded by 250 soldiers – who had been transported abroad to relieve the overcrowded British prisons. They lived in a prison camp set up on the shores of Sydney Harbour. The colonists came close to starvation, but gradually their lives improved. The tents they lived in were replaced by brick and timber huts, and eventually the colony began to prosper. In 1868, the transportation of convicts ended, leaving more than 160,000 convicts living in Australia.

## EXPLORATION

The first explorers of Australia mapped out the coastline but left the interior largely untouched. In 1606, the Dutch navigator William Jansz briefly visited northeastern Australia. Between 1829 and 1830, the English explorer Charles Sturt explored the rivers in the south but failed to find the inland sea that many people assumed existed in the centre of Australia. In 1840, Edward Eyre, from England, discovered the vast, dry salt lakes in South Australia before walking along its southern coast. In 1860 and 1861, the Irishman Robert O'Hara Burke and Englishman William Wills became the first people to cross Australia from south to north. It was not until the 1930s that Australia was completely surveyed.

Burke and Wills
Sturt
Eyre
Cook
Jansz

Alice Springs
Perth
Brisbane
Sydney
Adelaide
Melbourne

*Map showing the routes of the different explorers of Australia*

## BURKE AND WILLS

In 1860 and 1861, Burke and Wills succeeded in crossing Australia from south to north. However, they both died of starvation on the return journey south.

## GOLD RUSH

Gold was discovered in 1851 in New South Wales and Victoria. Thousands of prospectors rushed from all over the world, including China, to make their fortunes in Australia. The national population rose from 400,000 in 1850 to 1,100,000 by 1860. Conditions were tough for the gold miners, and in 1854 a group of miners at Eureka Stockade at Ballarat, near Melbourne, refused to pay the licence fee required to mine for gold. The government sent in troops; 24 miners and six soldiers were killed in the battle that followed.

*The Aborigines were amazed to see the crowds of white people landing in their territory.*

## OVERCOMING ABORIGINES

During the 19th century, the European settlers disrupted the aboriginal way of life. Many aboriginal languages and customs died out as their land was taken. Children were taken away from their parents to be educated in the European way. As a result, the Aborigine population fell from 300,000 in 1770 to about 60,000 by 1900.

## IMMIGRATION

In 1880, there were only two million people on the vast Australian continent. A century later, almost 15 million people lived there. Most had come to Australia from Britain, Italy, and Greece. In a deliberate attempt to boost the population after 1945, the Australian government offered to pay part of the passage for poor Europeans. About two million people took advantage of the scheme, which ended in 1965, with one million coming from Britain alone. Asians and other non-white peoples were denied entry until the 1960s. Many children travelled on their own. The group of immigrants (left) are on their way to a farm school in Western Australia from Waterloo Station, London, England.

## URANIUM MINING

Australia is rich in minerals, like uranium, the raw material used to fuel nuclear power stations and produce nuclear bombs. Although uranium mining increased dramatically during the 1970s, many Australians opposed it because of the dangers of radiation from uranium. In addition, many of the uranium deposits lie within aboriginal tribal lands. Protests have therefore regularly occurred to prevent the exploitation of this dangerous mineral.

_____ *Find out more* _____
ABORIGINAL AUSTRALIANS
AUSTRALIA
COOK, JAMES
EMIGRATION AND IMMIGRATION
NUCLEAR AGE

# AUSTRALIAN WILDLIFE

This map shows the main kinds of habitat in Australia.

- ☐ Tropical forest
- ☐ Tropical Grassland
- ☐ Temperate forest
- ☐ Desert
- ☐ Mountain

*Tasmania*

OF ALL THE CONTINENTS, Australia has the most unusual assortment of animals and plants. Almost half of the world's 314 kinds of marsupials (pouched mammals) are found only in Australia. Marsupials include kangaroos, koalas, possums, gliders, and bandicoots. The platypus and echidna – the only mammals that lay eggs – also live in Australia. The Australian landscape is very varied. In the northeast are steamy tropical rain forests and swamps which are home to crocodiles and wading birds. In the central part of Australia there are vast hot deserts made up of sand and rocks. Australia has more desert than any other continent, and there is sometimes no rainfall in these areas for several years. In the south, where the climate is milder, eucalyptus trees grow on rolling grasslands and shrubby bushland.

## FUNNEL-WEB SPIDER
The large, hairy funnel-web spider is so named because it builds a funnel-shaped web to catch its prey. These spiders are feared by humans because their bite is extremely poisonous.

## EUCALYPTUS
There are about 500 different kinds of eucalyptus trees in the world. Almost all of them came originally from Australia. The koala depends mainly on the leaves of a few species of eucalyptus tree for food.

## KOALA
The koala is found only in the eucalyptus forests of Australia. It spends most of its life in the trees, feeding at night and sleeping for up to 18 hours each day.

*Kangaroos are herbivores (plant eaters); they feed mostly on grasses and leaves.*

*Strong back legs are well adapted for jumping. A kangaroo can bound along at about 70 km/h (43 mph).*

## GRASSLAND
Kangaroos live in grassland areas. These areas consist mainly of kangaroo grass, which grows in clumps about 50 cm (20 in) high. Tough, spiky, spinifex plants grow in the drier areas. Many of the grasslands are now used to grow crops and graze farm animals.

## KANGAROO
There are about 50 different kinds of kangaroo in Australia, including the red kangaroo shown here. Kangaroos have huge back legs and strong tails. The red kangaroo is one of the largest – a male can grow to more than 2 m (6 ft) in height.

## RED-NECKED WALLABY
Wallabies are smaller members of the kangaroo family. The red-necked wallaby shown here is nicknamed "the brusher" because it prefers brush and scrubland areas rather than open countryside. It is also called the red wallaby, Eastern brush wallaby, and Bennett's wallaby.

## WOMBAT
Wombats live in grassland areas, dry woodlands, and shrublands. They dig a complicated tunnel system with their strong legs and large claws, and come out of their burrow at night to eat plants such as spear grass.

*A young kangaroo is called a joey. A new-born joey crawls into its mother's pouch, where it stays for more than 30 weeks, sucking milk. Once the joey has left its mother, it returns only to feed.*

## WEDGE-TAILED EAGLE
With a wingspan of 2.5 m (8 ft), the wedge-tailed eagle is one of the world's largest eagles. It soars over bush and desert areas of Australia searching for rabbits and similar prey.

*Shield bugs are so named because they have a shield-shaped plate on the body. They feed on the sap inside plants and are also known as sap suckers.*

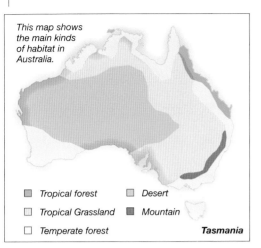

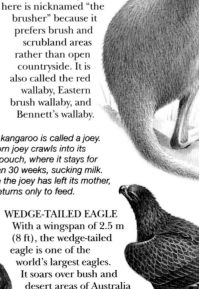
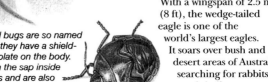
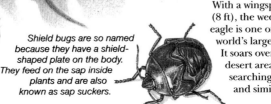
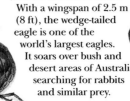

## RAIN FOREST

Tropical rain forests grow along a strip of Australia's northeast and north coast, together with luxurious palms, bunya-bunya pines, tree ferns, and colourful orchids. There are many other forests, including subtropical rain forests of kauri pine and scrub box near the mid-eastern coast of Australia, and cooler temperate rain forests of Antarctic beech in parts of the southeast and on the island of Tasmania.

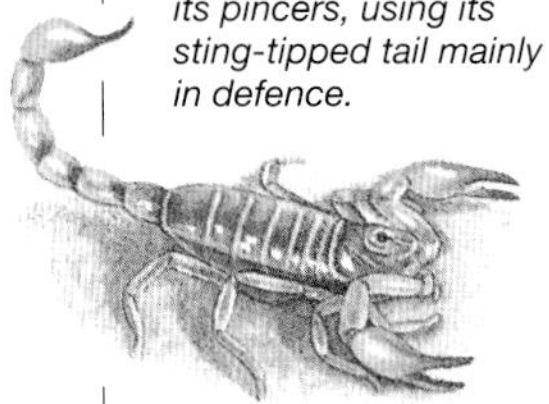

*The desert scorpion catches its food of insects and worms with its pincers, using its sting-tipped tail mainly in defence.*

## BOWERBIRD

In the warmer forests, male bowerbirds build small structures called bowers to attract a female. They use twigs, leaves, stems, and petals to make the bower. Each kind of bowerbird makes its own kind of bower, sometimes using bottle caps and other shiny pieces of rubbish.

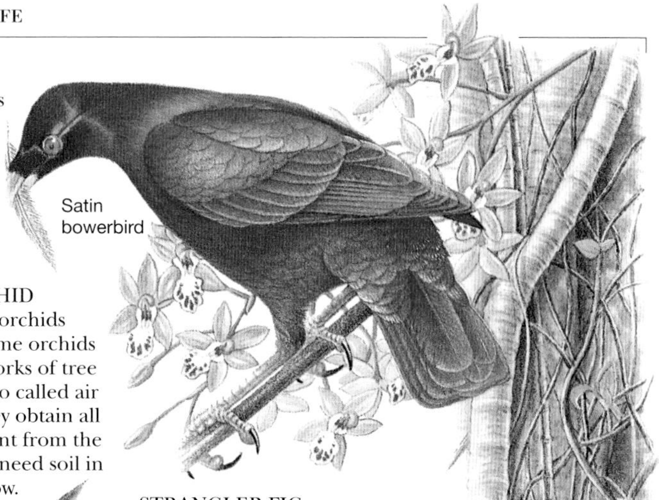

Satin bowerbird

## ORCHID

More than 600 kinds of orchids grow in Australia. Some orchids grow high in the forks of tree branches and are also called air plants because they obtain all their nourishment from the air and do not need soil in order to grow.

## STRANGLER FIG

Many tangled vines grow among the rain forest branches. The strangler fig twines around a tree trunk for support as it grows. Its thick stems may choke the tree to death.

## LORIKEET

There are seven different kinds of lorikeet in Australia; the one shown here is the rainbow lorikeet. Lorikeets are colourful, noisy relatives of parrots, and gather together in large flocks. They have brush-like tongues for sipping nectar from orchids and other flowers.

# DESERT

Australia has many poisonous animals, including snakes, spiders, and scorpions. Many poisonous animals live in the vast deserts in the centre of the country. Dry scrubland and desert cover more than half of Australia. One of the most common trees is the mulga, a shrub-like acacia that provides some food and shelter in the burning heat.

## POSSUM

Possums, gliders, and ringtails are active at night. They live in wooded areas and eat mainly food from plants, particularly nectar from the flowers of the evergreen banksia shrubs.

*The honey possum's brush-like tongue laps up nectar from the banksia flower. The possum helps the banksia reproduce by carrying its pollen to the next plant.*

## NATIONAL PARKS

Australia has more than 2,000 national parks and wildlife reserves, which cover 80 million hectares (197 million acres). These parks include Seal Rock in New South Wales and Lamington National Park, shown here.

*Australia is home to many kinds of snakes, including the Diamond Python.*

## DESERT PEA

The Sturt's desert pea is named after the British explorer Charles Sturt (1795-1869). It grows in sandy deserts and blooms only after rainfall. Its seeds may lie in the soil for many years, waiting until the next rainstorm before they can develop.

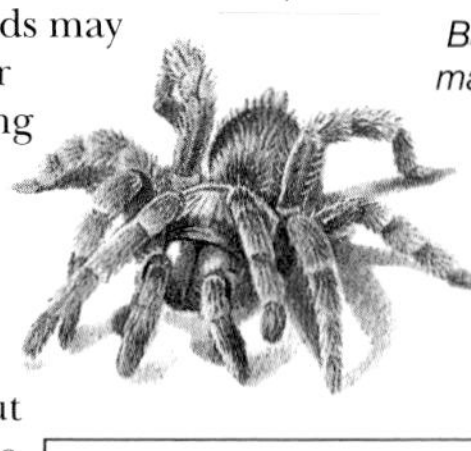

*Barking spiders make a noise by rubbing their mouthparts together. They catch frogs, insects, and small reptiles.*

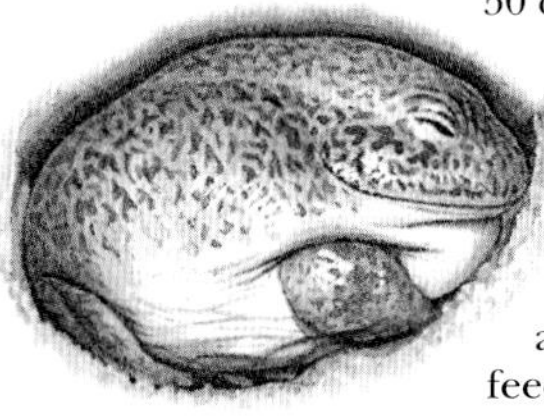

## DINGO

Australia's wild dog – the dingo – probably first came to Australia about 40,000 years ago with the aboriginal settlers. Dingoes eat a variety of food, including rabbits, birds, reptiles, and wallabies. They also kill sheep, which makes them unpopular with farmers.

## WATER-HOLDING FROG

During the dry season this Australian frog burrows about 50 cm (20 in) below the surface of the soil and forms a bubble-like layer of skin around its body. Only its nostrils are uncovered. After it rains the frog wakes, rubs off the cocoon, and digs its way out. It lays its eggs in the puddles, absorbs water through its skin, feeds, then burrows again.

*Find out more*

AUSTRALIA
AUSTRALIA, HISTORY OF
FOREST WILDLIFE
MAMMALS
NATIONAL PARKS
SPIDERS AND SCORPIONS

# AUSTRIA

| Volcano | Mountain | Ancient monument | Capital city | Large city/ town | Small city/ town |
|---|---|---|---|---|---|

AUSTRIA OCCUPIES a strategic position at the heart of Europe. Both the River Danube and the Alpine passes in the west, have been vital trade routes for many centuries, linking south and east Europe with the north and west. Until 1918, Austria was part of the Habsburg Empire, which dominated much of Central Europe. Today, it is a wealthy, industrialized economy. In the northeast, the fertile plains that surround the Danube provide rich farming country, and potatoes, beet and cereals are grown there. In the west, the magnificent mountain scenery of the Alps attracts millions of visitors. Austria is rich in mineral resources, especially iron. It uses hydroelectric power, generated by fast mountain streams, to provide power for its steel and manufacturing industries.

Austria is a landlocked country, located at the heart of Europe. To the west it is Alpine. The northeast is the fertile valley of the Danube.

## STATISTICS
**Area:** 83,850 sq km (32,375 sq miles)
**Population:** 8,100,000
**Capital:** Vienna
**Languages:** German, Croat, Slovene
**Religions:** Roman Catholic, Protestant, Muslim, Jewish
**Currency:** Euro

### AUSTRIAN COFFEE
Coffee was introduced to Vienna by the Turks in the 17th century. Coffee, accompanied by pastries or chocolate cakes, is a famous Viennese speciality.

### MOZART
The composer Wolfgang Amadeus Mozart (1756-91) was born in Salzburg and spent his childhood there. His remarkable early talent and the continuing popularity of his music draw many visitors to the city. This miniature comes from the Mozart Museum in Salzburg.

*This miniature features Mozart and his sister Maria-Anna (1751-1829).*

*The Schönbrunn Palace, the summer residence of the Habsburgs*

## VIENNA
The Habsburg family ruled Austria for several centuries, and Vienna was the capital of their empire. Vienna stands on the River Danube, and is a gateway between East and West Europe. The city is most famous for its magnificent 17th-century architecture. Today, it is a major centre of trade and industry.

### THE TIROL
The Alpine district of western Austria is known as the Tirol. The region has a very strong identity and folk culture, and historically it was an important link between Germany and Italy. Salt, copper mining, and dairy farming are important to the economy of the Tirol. Tourists are drawn by its spectacular beauty, especially in winter when skiing is a major attraction.

SCALE BAR
0   50   100   km
0   50   100   miles

| Find out more |
|---|
| COMPOSERS |
| EUROPE |
| EUROPE, HISTORY OF |

# AZTECS

MORE THAN SEVEN HUNDRED YEARS AGO a civilization was born in what is now Mexico. The Aztecs, founders of this civilization, were the last native American rulers of Mexico. They were a wandering tribe who arrived in the Mexican valley during the 13th century. The Toltec and Olmec Indians had already established civilizations in this area, and influenced the Aztecs. Over the next 200 years the Aztecs set up a mighty empire of some 12 million people. The Aztecs believed that the world would come to an end unless they sacrificed people to their sun god, Huitzilopochtli. They built pyramids and temples where they sacrificed prisoners from the cities they had conquered. In 1519 Spanish conquistadors (adventurers) arrived in Mexico and defeated the Aztecs. Montezuma II, last of the Aztec emperors, was killed by his own people, and the Aztec empire collapsed.

*Victim being sacrificed on top of the temple.*

*Preaching priest*

*Aztec pyramid with temple at top*

*The bodies of sacrificed victims were thrown to the ground.*

*Causeway*

*Temple precinct at Tenochtitlán*

## TENOCHTITLÁN
The Aztec capital, called Tenochtitlán, was a "floating city", built in Lake Texcoco, on one natural and many artificial islands. To reach the mainland, the Aztecs built causeways (raised roads) and canals between the islands. Today Mexico City stands on the site.

## AZTEC ARTISTS
The Aztecs made beautiful jewellery using gold, turquoise, pearls, shells, and feathers. They also used other valuable stones, such as obsidian and jade.

## HUMAN SACRIFICES
Aztec priests used knives with stone blades to kill up to 1,000 people each week, offering the hearts to their sun god, Huitzilopochtli.

## TRIBUTES
The Aztecs became very rich by collecting tributes (payments) from conquered tribes. Cloth, maize (a type of corn), pottery, and luxury goods were brought to Tenochtitlán from the conquered cities by porters, and exchanged in four huge markets. Officials made lists of all the tributes in picture writing. The Aztecs declared war on any tribe that refused to pay tribute.

*Ceremonial jade mask*

### Find out more
CONQUISTADORS
SOUTH AMERICA, history of

# BABYLONIANS

ONE OF THE FIRST CIVILIZATIONS developed about 6,000 years ago in the Middle East, between the Tigris and Euphrates rivers. This region was known as Mesopotamia, meaning "land between rivers". The land was fertile, and farming methods were highly refined. The people were among the first to develop a system of writing, use the wheel, and build cities. One of these cities was Babylon, founded in about 2000 B.C. It became the capital city of Babylonia (now part of Iraq). Babylon was an important trading centre. It was also a religious centre and the site of many splendid temples. Its people were strong and prosperous under the great king Hammurabi, who united the different areas into one empire. Babylon became even more magnificent later, under King Nebuchadnezzar II. In 538 B.C., the Persian king Cyrus the Great conquered Babylon; Alexander the Great conquered it again in 331 B.C. When the Romans eventually captured Babylon, the capital city lost its importance, fell into ruins, and became part of the Roman Empire.

### CYLINDER SEAL
The Babylonians wrote using cylinder seals. These seals were often made of semiprecious stone and were very delicately carved. To sign or stamp a document, a person rolled a cylinder seal over damp clay. This seal shows clearly the god Shamash, the goddess Ishtar (with wings), and the god, Ea.

*Ziggurat*

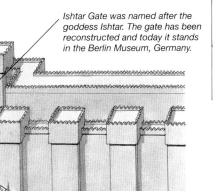

Ishtar Gate was named after the goddess Ishtar. The gate has been reconstructed and today it stands in the Berlin Museum, Germany.

### BABYLONIAN EMPIRE
Babylon was one of several important cities in Mesopotamia. For about 2,000 years, its fortunes rose and fell. At its height, under King Hammurabi, and later King Nebuchadnezzar II, the Babylonian empire controlled the entire southern area of Mesopotamia.

## BABYLON
The city of Babylon was rebuilt many times before its final destruction. It reached the height of its glory in about 600 B.C. It was an impressive city, with massive walls and elaborate religious buildings, including a pyramid-like ziggurat. Babylon also had a fabulous Hanging Garden – one of the Seven Wonders of the Ancient World.

### RUINS OF BABYLON
About 90 km (55 miles) south of Baghdad, Iraq, lie the ruins of ancient Babylon. Although the ruins are sparse, it is still possible to see where the palaces and ziggurat once stood. During the 19th century, archeologists excavated the site. Today, various parts of the ancient city wall have been rebuilt, as shown above.

### HAMMURABI
Under King Hammurabi (1792-1750 B.C.), Babylon gained control of a large part of Mesopotamia. Hammurabi is famous for the laws he introduced, which are carved on a stela, or pillar, of stone. The stone shows a portrait of Hammurabi standing before Shamash, the god of justice. Beneath this are the laws of Babylon, carved in cuneiform (wedge-shaped) writing. They deal with all aspects of life and show that Babylon was a sophisticated civilization.

### NEBUCHADNEZZAR
Nebuchadnezzar II (605-562 B.C.) was one of the most famous kings of Babylonia. Among other conquests, he captured Jerusalem and forced thousands of its people into exile in Babylonian territory. This story is told in the Bible, in the Book of Daniel. Nebuchadnezzar is said to have gone mad at the end of his reign, as shown in this picture of Nebuchadnezzar by the English artist William Blake (1757-1827).

### Find out more
ALPHABETS
ASSYRIANS
PHOENICIANS
WONDERS
of the ancient world

# BADGERS AND SKUNKS

Muscular body · Tough, wiry fur · Small ears · Small eyes and poor eyesight · Short, thick legs · Keen sense of smell · Long, strong claws

DAWN AND DUSK are the favourite hunting times for badgers and skunks, which prowl at night in search of food. Badgers and skunks are members of the weasel family, found in Europe, North America, Asia, and Africa. Badgers are heavy, sturdy animals, with broad, muscular bodies. They use their strong claws for digging underground homes called burrows, where they rest by day. Their thick fur is black, white, and brown. Like badgers, skunks have black and white markings, but their tails are large and bushy. Skunks live in open woodland areas of North and South America. There are three kinds – striped, spotted, and hog-nosed. Striped and hog-nosed skunks live in underground burrows; the spotted skunk lives underground but can climb trees. Badgers and skunks have an effective way of fending off enemies. They have scent glands on their bodies that produce a very unpleasant smell when the animal is threatened.

## SETTS
Eurasian badgers live in family groups in a system of tunnels called a sett, which they often build on a bank, or among tree roots. Over the years the badgers extend the sett. A large sett may be 100 years old and have more than 20 entrances; it may house up to 15 badgers. The badgers regularly bring fresh bedding of grass, leaves, and moss to their rest chambers, dragging out the old lining and leaving it near the entrance.

Boar (male badger) · Sow (female badger) · Cubs (young)

Chinese ferret badger

American badger

### HONEY BADGER
The African ratel feeds on honey and is also called the honey badger. The badger relies on a bird called the honey guide bird to lead it to bee and wasp nests, which the badger then breaks into with its strong claws. The thick fur and loose skin of the honey badger seem to shrug off any stings from the bees and wasps.

*Badgers are easily recognized by the vivid black and white markings or "badges" on their faces.*

## SKUNK
The striking black and white pattern on the striped or common skunk warns other animals to keep away. The skunk is famous for spraying enemies with a stinking substance from glands near its anus. If the spray touches the eyes of another animal, it can cause temporary blindness. There are 10 different kinds of skunk. They eat small animals, insects, birds' eggs, and fruit.

*Skunk stamps its front feet to warn others it is about to spray.*

## BADGER CUBS
Two or three cubs are born in late winter or early spring. They play outside the sett entrances during the summer months.

## STRIPES
Many badgers and skunks have stripes on their faces or along the sides of their bodies. These stripes provide camouflage by helping to break up the animal's outline in twilight. No two faces are exactly the same, so the stripes may also enable the animals to recognize one another.

**Find out more**

ANIMALS
MAMMALS
NESTS AND BURROWS

# BALLET

The tips of female dancers' toe shoes are stiffened to allow them to dance on tiptoe without hurting their feet.

MUSIC, DANCE, and mime combine in ballet to tell a story. Ballet began as entertainment for the royal families of Europe more than 300 years ago, and classical ballet style has developed gradually since then. The original French names for steps and jumps are still used. In the 19th century, "romantic" ballet became popular. Dancers in floating white dresses performed *La Sylphide* and *Giselle*. In the early 20th century, the Russian Sergei Diaghilev founded the Ballets Russes, one of the greatest of all ballet companies which performed all over the world. In ballet, each step and movement is planned in advance. This is called choreography. Great choreographers such as the Russian Fokine (1880-1942) arranged dances for the Ballets Russes. Most ballet dancers begin training at an early age. Ballet dancing is hard work and requires hours of practice.

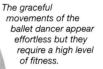

The graceful movements of the ballet dancer appear effortless but they require a high level of fitness.

## MODERN BALLET
In the early 20th century some dancers broke away from classical ballet and moved towards a freer sort of dance. Dancer Isadora Duncan was a pioneer of this more natural style in which performers express ideas in strong movements. Later, choreographer Martha Graham established a modern dance technique. Today, dancers often study the discipline of classical ballet before adopting modern styles.

## FONTEYN AND NUREYEV
Towards the end of her career, British ballerina Margot Fonteyn began dancing with a young Russian, Rudolf Nureyev. This famous partnership, shown here in *Romeo and Juliet,* inspired them both and delighted their audiences.

## ANNA PAVLOVA
The Russian ballerina Anna Pavlova (1881-1931) was one of the greatest dancers of all time. She worked from the age of 10 to perfect her dancing. Her most famous solo was *Dying Swan,* which was created for her by Fokine.

First    Second    Third    Fourth    Fifth

### THE FIVE POSITIONS
All ballet movements begin and end with one of the five positions; they were created in the 18th century to provide balance and to make the feet look elegant.

___ *Find out more* ___
COMPOSERS
DANCE
MUSIC
ROCK AND POP
THEATRE

# BALL GAMES

IN MANY SPORTS AND GAMES, players kick, bowl, or throw a ball around a playing area. They sometimes use bats, rackets, cues, and clubs – as well as their hands, feet, and heads – to roll or drive the ball. The balls vary in shape and size. Most are round, either solid and hard as in billiards and baseball, or hollow as in tennis. Football players use a round ball made of pigskin. In badminton the "ball", called a shuttlecock or bird, has feathers.

Ball games began in prehistoric times. At first they were part of religious ceremonies. People believed ball games would prolong the summer or direct the winds. The Ancient Greeks were among the first to play a ball game for pleasure. Ball games were a vital part of life for the Mayas and Aztecs of Central America. Today, popular ball games range from racket sports such as tennis and squash, to team games such as soccer and baseball.

**JAI ALAI**
Jai alai, a Spanish game, is also called pelota. Players use a curved scoop called a cesta to hurl a ball (the pelota) at the front wall of the court.

*Pool balls are numbered from 1 to 15.*

*The leather cover of an English football protects an inflated rubber inner lining.*

*Three fingerholes enable players to grip a bowling ball.*

*In table tennis, the "racket" is a solid paddle.*

## TEAM GAMES
Most of the world's major team sports are ball games, including baseball, basketball, and football. Team games move very fast. Team members need individual skills, such as the ability to run fast, but team skills such as passing the ball are equally important. Team games encourage friendship, discipline, and the ability to work with others.

**RACKET GAMES**
In racket games such as squash, players use a racket to propel the ball over a net or against a wall. The racket is usually a mesh of strings stretched on a frame. Players compete individually (singles) or in pairs (doubles). Some racket sports do not need a racket: handball players use a glove or the hand as their racket.

**GOLF**
Golfers use clubs to aim the small ball at a hole in the ground. Other ball games require careful aim too. In bowling, the object is to knock down ten or five pins with one ball. Bowlers aim their balls close to a target ball, or jack. In pool and billiards, players aim balls at pockets around a table.

**TENNIS**
Tennis evolved from a curious game called real, or royal, tennis, which is still played today in a few countries. Real tennis began in France nearly a thousand years ago; its court has open windows, doors, and sloping roofs. Modern tennis is called lawn tennis. It is sometimes played on a grass lawn but usually on a hard surface, such as clay. The top international tennis competitions are held in Wimbledon in England, the United States, Australia, and France. Leading tennis players earn huge sums from prize money and equipment sponsorship.

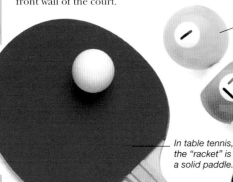

**BASEBALL AND CRICKET**
Baseball is the national sport of the United States. Winners of the National and American league pennants (championships) compete in the World Series each year. A gentler version, softball, is a popular amateur sport. Cricket players use a wooden bat and a hard ball. Cricket is popular in England, Australia, the West Indies, Pakistan, and India.

---

***Find out more***

AZTECS
CRICKET
FOOTBALL AND RUGBY
SPORTS

---

# BALLOONS AND AIRSHIPS

HAVE YOU EVER WATCHED BUBBLES RISE as water boils? That is how balloons and airships fly. They do not need wings to lift them into the air; instead they use a huge, bubble-like bag that floats up because it contains a gas that is lighter than the air around it. In the early days the gas was usually hydrogen, which was explosive and dangerous. Today, most balloons use hot air, and airships use helium gas. The main difference between balloons and airships is that balloons go where the wind takes them; airships have engines and can fly wherever the pilot chooses. People flew in balloons and airships long before aeroplanes were invented. But in the 1930s, aeroplane design improved, and airships and balloons were gradually forgotten. In recent years, however, ballooning has become popular again, and new airships are being built.

### MONTGOLFIER BROTHERS
The French brothers Joseph and Jacques Montgolfier built the first balloon that carried people into the air. It made its first free flight in Paris, France, on 21 November 1783, 120 years before the Wright brothers built the first aeroplane.

### *HINDENBURG* DISASTER
The airships of the 1930s were huge, and the German *Hindenburg* was the largest, with a length of more than 244 m (800 ft). The *Hindenburg* was filled with flammable hydrogen; in 1937 it burst into flame and was destroyed.

Envelope is not rigidly constructed, but is held in shape by the pressure of the gas inside it.

In order to save helium, some airships have special air bags, called ballonets, inside the envelope (the large gasbag). Air is let out instead of helium as the ship goes up, then sucked back in as the airship goes down.

Air let out from ballonet

Propeller fans allow the airship to take off and land vertically and manoeuvre in the air with great precision.

The gondola carries water ballast (weight to stabilize the craft) which can be let out to help gain height quickly.

Gondola made of Kevlar, a light, extremely strong plastic

Air let out from ballonet

## AIRSHIP
Airship engines can propel the craft in any direction. This airship has swivelling propeller fans that drive it up, down, or forward. It can fly at a speed of more than 90 km/h (55 mph).

## HOT-AIR BALLOONS
Hot-air balloons consist of a wicker basket and a bright, colourful envelope made of nylon. The envelope can be made in almost any shape, from a camel to a castle. Filling the envelope takes a lot of hot air. The heat from burning propane gas produces the hot air. The propane gas is stored as a liquid in metal cylinders carried in the basket.

### GONDOLA
Crew and passengers ride in a cabin called a gondola. This makes an ideal observation platform, because an airship flies slowly and steadily and can stay in the air for hours. The pilot controls the airship with a joystick similar to that in an aeroplane.

Balloons sometimes carry sand as ballast which can be thrown out of the basket in order to gain height rapidly.

Before each balloon flight, the envelope is laid on the ground and held open, and the propane burner is lit to inflate the envelope with hot air.

As the balloon fills up with hot air, it gradually rises. When there is enough hot air to lift the basket, the flight can begin.

Once in flight, an occasional blast of hot air from the propane burner is enough to keep the balloon at a steady height.

*Find out more*
AIR
AIRCRAFT
GAS
PLASTICS
TRANSPORT, HISTORY OF

# BALTIC STATES
## AND BELARUS

THE THREE BALTIC STATES – Lithuania, Latvia, and Estonia – were once Soviet republics. They were the first republics to declare their independence from the Soviet Union in 1991. Traditionally all three countries, with their fertile land and high rainfall, depended on agriculture and rearing dairy cattle. The Soviets, however, encouraged the growth of heavy industry and manufacturing, turning these small republics into industrial nations. When the republics became independent, they had to deal with price rises, food shortages, and pollution. Despite these problems they are beginning to forge links with east and west Europe, and new industries are being developed. Tourists are beginning to come to the historic cities of Tallinn and Riga, and the peoples of these countries are rediscovering their history and culture, long suppressed by the Russians.

The Baltic Republics occupy a small stretch of Baltic coast, flanked to the east by Russia, and to the west by Poland and the Russian enclave of Kaliningrad. Belarus lies along the southern border. The Baltic Sea provides an outlet to the North Sea.

ESTONIAN NATIONALITY
During the Soviet era, many Russians were settled in the Baltic States. This led to tensions with the Baltic peoples, who tried hard to maintain their own national identity. In Estonia, two-thirds of the population is Estonian. Their language is Finno-Ugric, related to both Finnish and Hungarian.

### RIGA
The capital of Latvia lies on the west of the Dvina River, 15 km (9 miles) upstream from the Baltic Sea. The city was founded in 1201, and became an important Baltic trading centre. Surviving medieval buildings, such as the castle and cathedral, reflect its prosperity. However, much of this historic legacy was destroyed during the German occupation in World War II (1941-44). It is now a major industrial centre and port, although it is ice-bound between December and April.

### THE BALTIC COAST
All the Baltic states face the Baltic Sea. In winter, the Baltic Sea is frozen, but in summer Baltic resorts attract tourists. Industrial pollution is damaging this coastline.

BELARUS
**Area:** 207,600 sq km (80,154 sq miles)
**Population:** 9,900,000
**Capital:** Minsk
**Languages:** Belorussian, Russian

ESTONIA
**Area:** 45,125 sq km (17,423 sq miles)
**Population:** 1,300,000
**Capital:** Tallinn
**Languages:** Estonian, Russian

LATVIA
**Area:** 64,589 sq km (24,938 sq miles)
**Population:** 2,300,000
**Capital:** Riga
**Languages:** Latvian, Russian

LITHUANIA
**Area:** 65,200 sq km (25,174 sq miles)
**Population:** 3,400,000
**Capital:** Vilnius
**Languages:** Lithuanian, Russian

SCALE BAR
0   50   100   km
0   50   100   miles

Volcano   Mountain   Ancient monument   Capital city   Large city/town   Small city/town

*Find out more*
EUROPE, HISTORY OF
OCEANS AND SEAS
SOVIET UNION, HISTORY OF

# BARBARIANS

BY THE FOURTH CENTURY A.D., the once great Roman Empire was in decline. A great threat came from tribal groups living outside the boundaries of the empire. The Romans despised these tribes. They thought they were uncivilized because they did not live in cities. Today we often call these tribes barbarians. But in fact they were superb metalworkers, farmers, and great warriors, with well-organized laws and customs. Around A.D. 370 hordes of one particular tribe, the Huns, moved from central Asia and pushed other tribes further westwards and through the frontiers of the Roman Empire. Some of the tribes nearest the empire asked the Romans for shelter. But in 406 hordes of Alans and Vandals swept into Gaul (modern France); in 410 the Visigoths, under Alaric, attacked and captured Rome, and barbarians flooded the Roman Empire. In 1452 the Huns, led by Attila, attacked northern Italy. The Empire was constantly under attack by many Barbarian tribes. Each tribe ruled the area it conquered in its own way.

**ATTILA THE HUN**
The nomadic Huns were jointly ruled by Attila (434-453) and his brother Bleda. In 452, after killing Bleda, Attila invaded Italy.

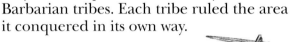

**SACK OF ROME**
In 410 Alaric, king of the Visigoths, captured and looted the great city of Rome which had been unconquered for 800 years. The sacking of Rome shocked the civilized world, but the empire itself did not collapse until 476.

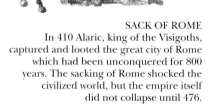

## CRAFTWORK

Each barbarian tribe had its own culture, laws, and customs. Even before the year 500 many barbarians had lived inside the Roman Empire, and many eventually became Christians. The barbarians were not just warriors. Their metalwork and jewellery were particularly beautiful.

*Gold buckle set with garnet*

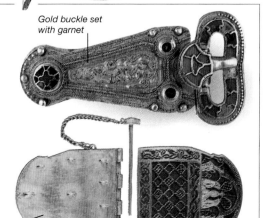

*This gold and enamelled fibula was used to fasten a barbarian man's cloak.*

BARBARIAN INVASIONS
By A.D. 500, barbarian tribes had overrun the Western Roman Empire. They divided their territory into separate kingdoms. With time, the invaders adopted some Roman ways, laws, and some Latin words. This map shows the routes of the barbarian invasions in the fifth century.

---

***Find out more***
CHARLEMAGNE
EUROPE, HISTORY OF
ROMAN EMPIRE
VIKINGS

# BATS

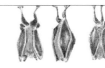

WHEN MOST OTHER CREATURES return to their homes for the night, bats take to the air. Bats are the only mammals capable of flight. They are night-time creatures with leather-like wings that enable them to swoop and glide through the darkness catching moths and other airborne insects. Although most bats are insectivores (insect eaters), some feed on fruit, nectar, pollen, fish, small mammals, and reptiles. Bats usually give birth to one or two young each year. The young are left in a nursery roost, clustered together for warmth, while the mothers fly off to feed. There are about 1,000 different kinds of bats, including red bats, brown bats, and dog-faced bats. They make up one quarter of all mammal species, yet few people have ever seen one. Today, many kinds of bats are becoming rare as their roosts are destroyed and their feeding areas are taken over for farming and building. In Britain, all bats and their roosts are protected by law.

**VAMPIRE BAT**
The vampire bat of South America bites mammals and birds to feed on their blood, but it does not usually attack humans.

*Bats sleep upside down in a nesting place called a roost.*

*Bat's wings are supported during flight by long, thin arm and finger bones. When resting, the bat hangs in its roost by its clawed back feet.*

**FISHING BAT**
The South American fishing bat has long legs and sharp claws for catching fish. It uses echolocation to detect ripples on the water's surface, then flies low with its feet dangling in the water. When the bat hooks a fish, its legs pull the slippery prey up to its mouth, where sharp teeth hold the fish securely.

*At the top of each wing is a claw which the bat uses to cling onto rocks as it clambers about in the caves where it lives.*

**HORSESHOE BAT**
There are 145 different kinds of horseshoe bats. Their name comes from the fleshy, curved flaps on their noses, which help with echolocation. The greater European horseshoe bat has a wingspan of more than 30 cm (12 in).

## FRUIT BAT
The fruit bat is the largest bat; some measure almost 2 m (7 ft) from one wing tip to the other. It is also called the flying fox because it has a fox-like face. Fruit bats roost in trees or caves and fly out at dawn and dusk to feed on fruit, flowers, and leaves. Fruit bats are found in Africa, southern Asia, and Australia. In areas where they live in large numbers, fruit bats cause great damage by eating farm crops.

## ECHOLOCATION
Bats find their way in the dark by making squeaks and clicks, which are so high-pitched that most humans cannot hear them. This is called echolocation. The sounds made by the bat bounce off a nearby object such as a tree or a moth. The bat can detect the returning echoes with its large, forward-pointing ears, and in a split second it has worked out the size, distance, and direction of the object.

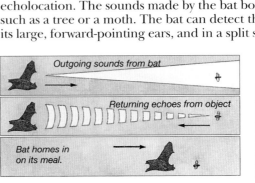

*Outgoing sounds from bat*

*Returning echoes from object*

*Bat homes in on its meal.*

| *Find out more* |
| --- |
| ANIMALS |
| ANIMAL SENSES |
| FLIGHT, ANIMAL |
| MAMMALS |
| WHALES AND DOLPHINS |

# BEARS AND PANDAS

Small ears

Large head

Small eyes with poor eyesight

Short muzzle

Keen sense of smell

Huge, powerful paws

ALTHOUGH BEARS are often portrayed as cuddly, they are among the most dangerous of all creatures. There are seven kinds of bears. The largest is the polar bear. It stands nearly 3 m (10 ft) tall and weighs more than half a tonne. The smallest bear is the sun bear from Southeast Asia, which measures about 1.2 m (4 ft) from head to tail. Other bears include the grizzly and the sloth bear. Bears are heavily built mammals, which eat both flesh and plants. Giant pandas, which eat mostly bamboo shoots, are related to bears. The giant panda is a large black and white creature that weighs about 135 kg (300 lb). Today they are very rare. The red panda, which is much smaller, is more closely related to the raccoon. All bears and the giant panda have poor eyesight, so they find their food mainly by smell.

DANCING BEAR
Bears have sometimes been taken from their natural habitats and trained to entertain people, but this cruel practice is now banned in most countries.

## BLACK BEAR

There are two kinds of black bear – one from North America and the other from Southeast Asia. Not all American black bears are completely black. Some are dark brown or reddish brown. Black bears are skilful tree climbers and run fast – up to 40 km/h (25 mph). American black bears inhabit the forests of North America, and many live in national parks.

PAWS
A bear's paws are large, broad, and powerful, with tough, thick claws. Pandas have unusual paws. A modified wristbone acts like a thumb, allowing the panda to grasp bamboo shoots (above).

## GIANT PANDA

The giant panda is also called the panda bear. Giant pandas live in central and western China and eat mostly bamboo shoots. There are only a few hundred giant pandas left in the wild, and they have become a worldwide symbol of conservation.

## GRIZZLY BEAR

The huge grizzly bear has no enemies apart from humans. Grizzly bears live in North America, Europe, and Asia. The grizzly is also called the brown bear. A female grizzly bear gives birth to two or three cubs in a winter den. Grizzly bears eat almost anything, including spring shoots, autumn fruits, animal flesh, and honey taken from bees' nests.

RACCOON
There are 18 kinds of raccoon; all are found in the Americas. They are fast, agile creatures related to bears. Raccoons are active mainly at night, when they feed on fish, nuts, rubbish dumps, farm crops, and livestock.

In autumn, grizzly bears scoop up salmon that have swum upriver to spawn (lay their eggs).

*Find out more*
ANIMALS
CONSERVATION
and endangered species
MAMMALS
NORTH AMERICAN WILDLIFE
POLAR WILDLIFE

# BEAVERS

THERE ARE TWO KINDS of beavers – the European and the North American. Both are rodents – a group of animals that includes rats, mice, and squirrels. Beavers have long, sharp front teeth for gnawing at plants and trees. These teeth are open-rooted and continue to grow throughout life. Beavers are excellent builders. They use their teeth like chisels to bite through branches, which they drag away to build dams and lodges in rivers and streams. Although beavers go on land to find food, they are aquatic animals and spend most of their time in or near water. They are good swimmers, using their webbed back feet for speed. A beaver can dive and hold its breath underwater for several minutes. The beaver has a flat, scaly tail which it uses for steering and also for extra speed, thrusting the tail up and down in the water like a powerful paddle. Beavers also use their tails to warn others of danger by slapping the tail on the surface of the water. During the 18th and 19th centuries, beavers were hunted for their thick fur, which was used to make coats and hats. In some parts of North America beavers almost died out completely. Today, however, trapping beavers for their fur is controlled and these animals are no longer in danger of extinction.

**TEETH**
The beaver's huge front incisor teeth can cut through bark and wood to fell small trees for food and for dam building.

**DAMS**
Using sticks, stones, and mud, beavers build a dam at a suitable place across a stream. The water around the dam spreads out to form a lake, which is where the beavers build their lodge.

*Beaver can hold and manipulate small items, such as twigs and stones for the dam, with its front paws.*

*Beaver uses its flat tail as a rudder when it is swimming underwater.*

**WOOD FOR DAMS**
As wood becomes scarce, beavers may have to travel greater distances to find more. They float tree branches along canals and add them to the dam.

*Some lodges are more than 3 m (10 ft) high.*

*Adult beaver brings leafy twigs home to food store.*

## FEEDING
Beavers are herbivores (plant eaters). Their food varies according to the season. In autumn and winter, beavers feed on bark and soft wood, particularly aspen and willow. They store twigs and branches underwater in the lake or river where they live. Even when the surface of the water is frozen hard in winter, beavers can swim from the underwater entrance of their home to bring back stored food. In spring and summer, beavers feed on grass, leaves, and water plants.

**BREEDING**
Young beavers are called kits. They are born in spring and can swim a day or two after birth.

*Underwater entrances help keep kits safe from predators.*

**UNDERWATER ENTRANCE**
The lodge has several underwater entrances. Inside the lodge the beavers are safe from predators such as wolves, which cannot dig through the strong walls or swim down through the entrances.

## LODGE
A beaver family lives in a structure called a lodge, built from tree branches and mud. Inside the lodge, the beavers hollow out a dry chamber above the water level. This is where they rest and sleep. In autumn the adults coat the outside of the lodge with a layer of mud. The mud freezes in winter and gives protection against predators.

*Find out more*
ANIMALS
CONSERVATION
and endangered species
MAMMALS
MICE, RATS, AND SQUIRRELS

# BEES AND WASPS

HONEYBEES, BUMBLEBEES, and common wasps are a familiar sight to many of us, but there are thousands more, such as carpenter bees, stingless bees, mud wasps, and potter wasps. Bees and wasps first existed millions of years ago and live in almost every part of the world. These insects fly well, and the movement of their powerful wings makes the buzzing sound. Many bees and wasps are solitary, living in a nest in the ground or in a hollow plant stem. Some, such as bumblebees and honeybees, live in large groups, or colonies, in trees, roofs, and rock crevices. In a bumblebee colony the queen resembles her workers and shares many of their jobs. In a honeybee colony, however, the queen does not share these jobs and spends most of her life laying eggs. A honeybee colony may contain 50,000 bees.

*Beekeepers used to destroy the hive and the bees to harvest honey from straw hives, or skeps.*

*Honey is a food that bees produce and store inside the hive. The bees feed on honey through winter.*

*Queen honeybee lays 1,500 eggs every day during summer.*

*Eggs hatch into larvae after a few days. The larvae become pupae, then adult bees.*

*Workers gather food, care for young, and clean and protect the hive.*

*Drone (male) mates with queen bee, then dies.*

## BEEHIVE
Beekeepers provide hives where the honeybees raise their young and store their food of honey. Inside the hive are rows of wax combs full of eggs, growing larvae (grubs) and pupae, the queen with her drones (males) and workers, and cells of stored pollen and honey. In a hive there may be about 40,000 worker bees, a few hundred drones, and one queen.

## PARASITIC WASPS
These wasps paralyze spiders and insects, then lay eggs on their victim. These eggs hatch into larvae that eat the animal alive.

*Wasp eggs develop into larvae inside the nest.*

## WASP'S NEST
After the winter hibernation, the queen wasp builds a papery nest. The queen scrapes up and chews wood, mixes it with saliva to make a pulp, then builds the nest with the pulp. The queen wasp lays eggs in hexagonal (six-sided) cells inside the papery nest, then catches and chews up insects to feed to the growing larvae. The larvae develop into worker adults who continue to enlarge and reinforce the nest. The males and the new queen are produced later in the season. A big nest may house 5,000 workers. They fly out to feed on plant sap, fruit, and nectar.

*Shaft of wasp's sting*

## COMMON WASP
Yellow and black markings warn other animals of the wasp's venomous sting. Some wasps use the sting as a defence against predators and to kill or subdue prey. Bees sting only if they are provoked.

*Only female wasps (the queen and workers) sting.*

## BEE DANCE
When a honeybee finds a good source of food, it informs other bees in the hive by "dancing" in a figure of eight pattern. The bee dance shows the other bees where the source of nectar or pollen is in relation to the position of the sun.

---

***Find out more***
ANIMALS
FLOWERS AND HERBS
INSECTS

# BEETLES

WHIRLIGIG BEETLES, CLICK BEETLES, and deathwatch beetles belong to the largest group of animals in the world. Of all the animals known to science, one in three belongs to the group of insects called beetles. Many beetles can fly, and have hard, often colourful wing cases. These wing cases are modified forewings. They fold over the insect's back when the beetle is not in flight, and protect the wings beneath. During flight, the front wing cases are usually raised to allow the main wings to beat. Some beetles are active predators; the long-legged tiger beetle, for example, hunts down and eats smaller insects. Others, such as the Colorado beetle, eat only plant material. A few beetles are a nuisance to humans; Colorado beetles destroy potato crops, and elm bark beetles spread Dutch elm disease, destroying thousands of elm trees. But many kinds of beetles help to recycle dead leaves, dead animals, and other plant and animal material. Beetles are among only a few creatures that can break down dead wood.

**GLOW-WORM**
The glow-worm is a beetle. It has organs on the underside of its tail, which produce a pale green glowing or flashing light. The light is used by the female to attract a mate or, in some species, a meal.

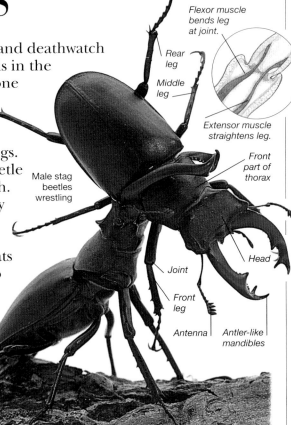

*Flexor muscle bends leg at joint.*

*Rear leg*

*Middle leg*

*Extensor muscle straightens leg.*

*Front part of thorax*

*Male stag beetles wrestling*

*Head*

*Joint*

*Front leg*

*Antenna*

*Antler-like mandibles*

*Tiger beetle*   *Wasp beetle*   *Two-lined collops beetle*   *Weevil*

**DUNG BEETLE**
Dung beetles are so named because they feed on, and lay eggs in, animal droppings. The larvae (grubs) hatch and feed on the droppings before developing into pupae (chrysalises). Some dung beetles shape a lump of dung into a ball and roll it into their burrow before laying eggs in it.

*Some dung beetles are also called scarab beetles. The Ancient Egyptians believed they were sacred.*

## STAG BEETLE

Stag beetles take their name from their antler-like mandibles (jaws). Enlarged mandibles are found only on the male, and are so heavy that the beetle cannot give a strong bite. The huge mandibles are mainly for show, as when males threaten and wrestle with each other in order to mate with a female.

**LADYBIRD**
The bright colours of ladybirds warn predators not to attack them because they taste bad. Many ladybirds feed on greenfly and other aphids that damage garden plants. This makes ladybirds popular insects with humans.

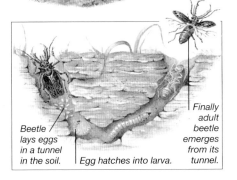

*Beetle lays eggs in a tunnel in the soil.*

*Egg hatches into larva.*

*Finally adult beetle emerges from its tunnel.*

## COCKCHAFER BEETLE

The cockchafer beetle is a slow, awkward flier. It is attracted to light and often crashes into windows. The larvae, called white grubs, live in soil where they eat the roots of grasses and other plants. Adult cockchafer beetles are sometimes called May bugs or June bugs.

**LIFE CYCLE OF A WOOD-BORING BEETLE**
A beetle starts life as an egg, then hatches into a larva (grub). The larvae of some beetles, such as the longhorn, eat wood and make tunnels in wooden furniture. During its life inside the wood, a larva changes into a pupa, then into an adult. As it leaves the wood, the adult woodborer beetle makes an exit hole. Old furniture sometimes contains hundreds of these tiny holes, which are nicknamed woodworm.

*Find out more*
ANIMALS
FLIGHT, ANIMAL
INSECTS
MOUNTAIN WILDLIFE

# BENIN KINGDOM

THE KINGDOM OF BENIN lay in the Niger River delta area of what is now southern Nigeria. Benin began as a city-state in the 11th century, and by about 1450, was a wealthy kingdom that continued to flourish for another 300 years. Two peoples, the Binis and Yoruba, made up the kingdom, which was ruled by powerful kings called obas. The wealth of the kingdom came from trade, either across the Sahara with other African peoples or on the coast with Europeans. The centre of the kingdom was Benin City. It contained a huge royal palace, where the obas lived. The people of Benin were skilled craftworkers, who produced wonderful carvings and brasses. The Portuguese arrived in the region in the 15th century, and in 1897, the British conquered the kingdom, and made it part of colonial Nigeria.

**BENIN**
Benin Kingdom was situated in West Africa on the site of present-day Benin City, which is named after the kingdom.

Ceremonial sword

This wide-bladed sword was designed for ornamentation rather than use in combat.

An oba, or great king, flanked by two of his courtiers

A brass plaque that decorated the wooden pillars supporting the oba's palace.

## OBAS
The obas were immensely wealthy and controlled trade. One of the most important obas was Ewuare the Great (r. 1440-80), who made Benin City powerful. Obas ruled through ministers, to whom they delegated some authority. The people of Benin revered the obas as gods, and made sacrifices to them.

Benin anklet

### BENIN CITY
Dutch traveller Olfert Dapper described Benin City in 1688 as large and prosperous, surrounded by a high earth wall. It contained many fine buildings including the obas' palace. There were also special areas for craftspeople.

### TRADE AND SLAVERY
For hundreds of years, Benin traded with African kingdoms to the north. From about 1480, the Portuguese began buying slaves, cloth, pepper, and ivory from Benin. The obas stopped trading slaves in 1550, but in the 1600s they again began selling slaves to the Europeans.

## BENIN KINGDOM
**1000s** Benin City is founded.

**1450** Benin at its most powerful.

**1486** First Portuguese explorer visits Benin.

**1500s** English, Dutch, and French merchants start trading.

**1680s** Benin resumes slave trade.

**1688** Olfert Dapper writes a history of Benin.

**1897** British capture Benin City and burn it.

## BENIN BRONZES
The kingdom of Benin was famous for its "bronzes", most of which were actually brass castings. The "bronzes", some of which were large and striking heads, represented obas and other dignitaries. Craftworkers also made likenesses of European traders who came to the region. Other Benin art included ivory carvings and plaques. These and other artefacts were made by guilds of craftspeople, who lived in special areas in Benin City called wards.

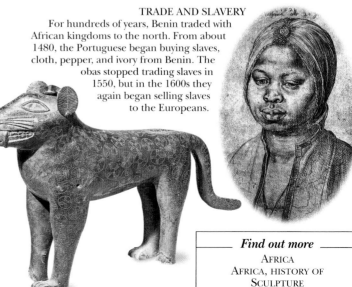

_Find out more_
AFRICA
AFRICA, HISTORY OF
SCULPTURE

# BICYCLES AND MOTORCYCLES

A motorcyclist wears tough leather clothing and a crash helmet made of impact-resistant plastic. These give protection if the motorcyclist falls off.

The rider controls the bike's speed by twisting the right-hand grip.

Motorcycles stop with disc brakes. Holes in the discs help get rid of water quickly and keep them working well in the rain.

Most motorcycles have a chain connected to the gearbox that drives the back wheel. A few have a rotating shaft instead.

The rider changes gear by clicking a foot lever up or down.

APART FROM WALKING, there is no simpler and cheaper way to travel than on a bicycle. Bicycles were invented in Europe little more than 200 years ago; today, they are popular the world over, not only because they are less expensive than cars but also because they do not produce pollution. Motorcycles are not as simple or cheap. Like bicycles, though, they are small and manoeuvrable, which makes them ideal for nipping in and out of city traffic. Specially built off-road motorcycles can be ridden in places no car can reach. When you first ride a bicycle, it is hard to believe you will stay up. At slow speeds, staying up depends on your sense of balance. But once a bicycle is going fast enough, it stays up by itself. This is because the frame is a special shape that makes a bicycle very stable.

PENNY-FARTHING BICYCLE
In the days before bicycle chains were invented, riders had to perch high on a bicycle which had a huge front wheel in order to travel at speed.

## MOTORCYCLES
In 1885, the German carmaker Gottlieb Daimler built the first motorcycle by fixing an engine to a bicycle frame. Today's smallest motorcycles, called mopeds, are also closely related to the bicycle. A moped engine is so small that the rider may have to pedal to help the machine up hills. By contrast, the biggest motorcycles are powerful enough to reach speeds of 260 km/h (160 mph), faster than all but the fastest sports cars.

CORNERING
Motorcyclists lean over to go around bends. If they did not, the front wheel might turn, but bike and rider would go straight on under their own momentum. Leaning over balances out this effect. The faster the bike corners, the more it has to lean.

## BICYCLES
In about 1790, the Comte de Sivrac of France invented the first wooden bicycle. In 1885, Englishman J. K. Starley produced the safety bicycle which is the design most modern bicycles are based on.

Mountain bikes have thick tyres and sturdy frames, enabling them to travel over rough tracks.

GEARS
Many bicycles have gears. Gears allow the bicycle to travel fast or slow while the rider pedals at a comfortable rate. Moving the gear lever lifts the chain from one cog to another.

RACERS
Racing bikes are light and fast. The rider crouches low over the handlebars to minimize air resistance.

A large cog turns the wheel slowly. This produces extra force for climbing uphill.

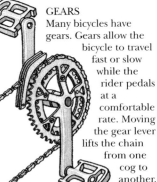

TANDEMS
Bicycles for two people are called tandems. The two riders sit in line and pedal together; their combined effort makes the tandem speed along.

UNICYCLES
Unicycles have only one wheel. They are so tricky to ride that they make good circus acts.

TRICYCLES
Bicycles with three wheels, called tricycles, cannot fall over, but it takes more effort to pedal them.

A small cog turns the wheel quickly. This allows the bike to travel fast downhill or along flat ground.

*Find out more*
SPORTS
TRANSPORT, HISTORY OF
WHEELS

The Big Bang, 13.7 billion years ago

# BIG BANG

NEARLY FOURTEEN BILLION YEARS AGO, the universe exploded out of virtually nothing. The first scientist to propose this astonishing theory, now known as the Big Bang, was George Lemaître (1894-1966). His idea was supported by the work of Edwin Hubble (1889-1953), which showed that the universe is expanding. If this is so, the entire cosmos must have originated from a single point of explosion. But what was that single point? Scientists call it a "singularity" – a tiny, infinitely dense dot that once contained all the matter of the universe. Such a thing is impossible to imagine, and even astronomers do not really understand it. Yet within a few minutes of the Big Bang, the single point would have been converted into an immense, expanding cloud of gas. Over millions of years this became the galaxies, stars, and planets of the universe.

**FRED HOYLE**
It was astronomer Fred Hoyle (1915-2001) who suggested the term "Big Bang", as a joke. He believed the universe had no beginning and no end.

Galaxies started to form a billion years after the Big Bang.

Stars begin to form in a spinning cloud of dust and gas.

The solar system formed, 4.6 billion years ago.

First life forms appeared on Earth, 3.8 billion years ago.

## RED SHIFT
The light from some stars looks redder than it should. This is due to the Doppler Effect, and shows that these stars are moving away from us. Distant galaxies also look redder but because the whole of space is expanding their lightwaves are stretched when they reach us. This is called red shift.

Longwave

Shortwave

The Earth

Shortwave

Star

Star

Star

If a star is moving away, its light waves are stretched out and shift towards the red end of the spectrum.

If a star is staying in the same position relative to Earth, then the wavelengths of light emitted remain unchanged.

If a star is moving towards the Earth, light waves are compressed and shift to the blue end of the spectrum.

As the ambulance moves away, the siren's sound waves stretch, increasing their wavelength and lowering their pitch.

## CHAIN OF EVENTS
Scientists believe that the universe was created in an explosive event called the Big Bang. At the instant of creation, matter was concentrated in an infinitely small, dense dot called a singularity. This then began to expand and cool, allowing the conversion of energy into particles. After thousands of years, these particles joined to make atoms of hydrogen and helium that would eventually form galaxies and stars.

## DOPPLER EFFECT
Christian Doppler (1803-53) showed that sound waves are compressed if the source is moving towards your ear, and stretched if it is moving away. This alters the pitch of the sound you hear. The same principle applies to light waves arriving from distant stars.

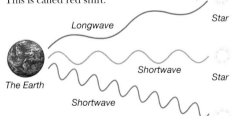

The sound waves of an ambulance siren are compressed as it comes nearer, reducing their wavelength and raising their pitch.

_Find out more_
ASTRONOMY
PHYSICS
STARS
UNIVERSE

# BIOLOGY

THE NATURAL WORLD is full of marvels and mysteries: the beautiful colours of a flower, the magnificent display of a peacock, the magic of new life when a child is born. Biology is the science of all living things, from the tiniest microscopic organisms (living things) to the largest whales in the sea; it is the study of all plants and animals and their environments, or surroundings. Biologists study how living things grow, feed, and move, how they reproduce, and how they evolve (change) over long periods of time. Biology covers an enormous range of topics and deals with millions of species (kinds) of organisms. Because of this, biology is divided into different specialized branches such as anatomy, which deals with the structure of living things, and physiology, which is concerned with the way animals and plants function. Biology is important in other sciences and professions that deal with living things, such as agriculture, forestry, and medicine.

**LABORATORY**
A biologist works in a specially equipped room called a laboratory. Biologists use a variety of techniques to study animals and plants. They may dissect (cut up) specimens, or use powerful microscopes to probe into the structure of tiny microscopic organisms, such as cells and bacteria.

## BOTANY
The study of plants and flowers is called botany. It is one of the two main branches of biology.

*Stamen of flower*

*Cross-section of stamen*

*Botanists study the structure of plants and how they reproduce.*

## ZOOLOGY
Zoology, the other main branch of biology, is the scientific study of animals.

*Clump of a frog's newly laid eggs, called frogspawn*

*Zoologists study the life and growth of animals.*

*Tiger pierid butterfly of Central and South America*

*Hairstreak butterfly of South America*

## TAXONOMY
Biologists classify living organisms into different groups so they can understand the relationships between them. This is called taxonomy. For instance, butterflies and moths belong to the same taxonomic group, called Lepidoptera.

## EVERYDAY BIOLOGY
There are biological processes going on all around us. For example, bread dough rises when it is left in a warm place. This is because live yeast in the dough gives off gas that make the dough expand, a process called fermentation.

*Yeast is made up of single-celled living organisms. Yeast cells obtain their energy from the dough mixture and give off carbon dioxide gas in the process.*

*Once the bread is cooked, it is full of little holes made by the gas bubbles.*

*Carbon dioxide gas makes the dough rise.*

## HISTORY OF BIOLOGY
The Greek philosopher Aristotle was one of the first biologists. He studied birds and animals in about 350 B.C. During the 17th century, the English scientist Robert Hooke discovered living cells through the newly invented microscope. In 1953, English scientist Francis Crick and American scientist James Watson discovered the structure of deoxyribonucleic acid (DNA), the chemical that controls all cells and life patterns.

Francis Crick (left) and James Watson

## HUMAN BIOLOGY
Human biology is concerned with all the different systems of the human body. These include the digestive system, the circulatory system, the respiratory (breathing) system, the reproductive system, the nervous system, and the muscular and skeletal systems.

---

### Find out more
CHEMISTRY
DARWIN, CHARLES
EVOLUTION
GENETICS
HUMAN BODY
PLANTS
REPRODUCTION

# BIRDS

Outer feathers produce lift for flight.

Short, strong beak for cracking open seeds.

Brightly coloured plumage attracts a female in the breeding season.

IN THE ENTIRE ANIMAL WORLD, birds are the only living creatures with feathers. They are also warm-blooded, like mammals. There are about 9,000 different kinds of birds, living in all parts of the world. They include exotic, colourful birds such as parrots, garden birds such as robins and thrushes, water birds such as ducks, sea birds such as puffins and penguins, and many more. Most birds are well adapted for flying and have large, powerful chest muscles to allow them to flap their wings. Their bones are light, with tiny honeycombed holes to keep them lightweight, which assists them during flight. Feathers are light too. They protect the bird's body and keep it warm. Wing feathers fit together to form a smooth, airtight surface for gliding. Tail feathers provide balance and help the bird steer in midair. A few birds, however, cannot fly. Flightless or nearly flightless birds include ostriches, penguins, and the rare kakapo, a kind of parrot from New Zealand. Birds do not have teeth, which would be too heavy; instead they have a strong, light bill, or beak. Most birds, particularly eagles and other birds of prey, have good eyesight and hearing. Their sense of smell, however, is poor.

Male chaffinch in flight

Long tail feathers act as a rudder, to help with steering during flight.

## PLUMAGE
A bird's feathers are called its plumage. Some birds, such as the wren and the sparrow, have brown plumage for camouflage. Other birds have plumage with dazzling colours and patterns. It is usually the males that have bright plumage, to help them attract a mate during the breeding season. The distinctive colouring also helps the members of a flock keep together.

Skeleton of a pigeon

Humerus (upper arm bone)

Skull

Radius and ulna (forearm bones)

Mandibles (jaws)

Spine (backbone)

Keel on breast bone

Internal system of a starling

Beak (bill)

Lungs

Gullet

Kidney

Crop

Ribs

Sternum (breast bone)

Femur (thigh bone)

Heart

Pelvis (hip bone)

Liver

Pygostyle (tail bone)

Tibia (shin bone)

Tarsus (ankle bone)

Gizzard

Cloaca

Intestine

THE BIGGEST AND SMALLEST BIRDS
The tiny bee hummingbird is one of the world's smallest birds. It measures about 5 cm (2 in) from beak to tail, and is so light that 17 bee hummingbirds would weigh only 28 gm (1 oz). The ostrich, which is more than 2.5 m (8 ft) tall, is the world's largest bird, but it cannot fly at all.

## BIRD BONES
Most of the bones in a bird's skeleton are hollow, to save body weight. Wings are controlled by powerful muscles attached to the keel, which is a ridge along the edge of the breastbone.

## INSIDE A BIRD
Most of a bird's body is taken up by the muscles, heart, lungs, and digestive system. Birds have two stomachs, as in the starling shown here. The first stomach, the crop, stores food; the second, the gizzard, grinds the food to a pulp.

This ostrich head looks huge in comparison to a tiny bee hummingbird.

A bee hummingbird is so small that it can fit in the palm of your hand.

Curlew feeding

# BEAKS AND BILLS

The beak is also called the bill. It is the bird's tool for all kinds of jobs. Bills are made of a hard substance called keratin, and are used for feeding, preening (trimming the edges of feathers), making a nest, and fighting off predators. The shape of the bill shows what sort of food the bird eats. Hooked bills are good for tearing flesh.

Wing feather of a macaw

## CURLEW BILL
A long, thin bill for probing into seashore mud to find worms and shellfish.

Rachis (stiff shaft)

## GULL BILL
An all-around shape for probing, cutting and tearing food, and holding slippery fish.

Barbs

## PARROT BILL
The hooked tip is for grasping and tearing up soft fruit. The strong base cracks open seeds and pips.

## MACAW BILL
The huge, heavy macaw's bill breaks up nuts and seeds. Many macaws and other parrots are becoming rare because the tropical rain forests in which they live are being destroyed.

Flat part of feather, called the vane

Quill or base of feather, embedded in skin.

Blue tit egg

Hard, chalky eggshell

Baby bird

Food store of yolk

# FEATHERS

Tiny hummingbirds have less than 1,000 feathers; swans have more than 25,000. Feathers are made mainly of keratin, which is also found in human hair and nails.
Feathers have a central shaft, or rachis. On each side of the shaft, hooks called barbs lock together like a zip to make a flat part called the vane. Flight feathers make a smooth wing surface; down feathers keep the bird warm.

Soft, downy parrot feather

Peacock feathers

Colourful patches on feathers, known as "eyes", are used for the breeding display.

# NESTS AND EGGS

Birds do not give birth to babies the way that mammals do. Instead, they lay eggs with hard shells, then sit on them to keep them warm. The baby bird develops inside the shell, nourished by the yolk. After a few weeks the bird pecks its way out of the shell. Some birds, such as flamingos, build big nests for their eggs. Others, such as guillemots, do not make nests, but lay eggs on a cliff edge. Some cuckoos lay eggs in another bird's nest and abandon them, leaving the owner of the nest to raise the young.

Day-old blue tit nestlings

# BIRD BEHAVIOUR

During the day, birds are busy looking after their young, communicating with other birds, eating, and preening. Bird behaviour such as migrating in winter or pecking at food is instinctive, so it does not have to be learned. Some birds, such as the tawny frogmouth of Australia, feed at night, but during the day the frogmouth sits very still, looking like a tree stump.

BREEDING DISPLAY
During the breeding season, the male blue bird of paradise hangs upside down in a tree, showing off his feathers to attract a female. The males of some kinds of birds, such as the grouse, fight over a patch of ground called a lek. Without a territory, no females will come to mate.

Blue bird of paradise

NESTLINGS
Most newly hatched birds are helpless, for they have no feathers and cannot see. They stay in the nest to be fed and protected by one or both parents until their feathers grow. A parent bird may make dozens of trips back to the nest each day, bringing food for the chicks.

Eyelids still joined together

### Find out more
CROWS, JAYS, AND RAVENS
DUCKS, GEESE, AND SWANS
EAGLES
and other birds of prey
OSTRICHES AND EMUS
OWLS
SEA BIRDS
SONGBIRDS

# BLACK DEATH

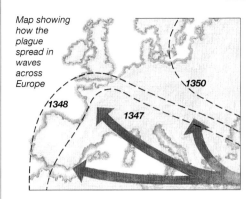

Map showing how the plague spread in waves across Europe

1350

1348

1347

THE MEDITERRANEAN ISLAND OF SICILY was a terrifying place in 1347. Everywhere people were dying of a mysterious disease. Those who caught it usually had violent stomach cramps and boils under their arms. Dark patches covered their bodies, and death followed within three days. The disease became known as the Black Death because of the dark patches; today we know it was bubonic plague. It spread into Italy and France. By the end of 1348 millions had died – about one third of the population of Europe. There was panic as the Black Death advanced. People avoided each other, fearful that they might catch the plague. Many townspeople fled into the countryside carrying the disease with them. There was a shortage of food because there were fewer people to farm the land. Fields were filled with rotting animal bodies.

## SPREAD OF PLAGUE
The Black Death began in Asia. It spread through Turkey, then arrived on ships at Sicily in October 1347, and reached Britain near the end of 1348. The plague reappeared every few years until the early 18th century; outbreaks were even reported in the early 19th century.

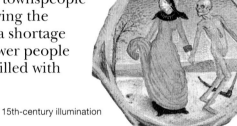

15th-century illumination

## THE BLACK DEATH
Death came to rich and poor alike. Some, thinking the plague was a punishment from God, whipped themselves and prayed to be saved.

*Large plague grave where victims were buried*

## CROSS OF DEATH
Crosses were painted on the doors of plague-ridden houses. Criminals and volunteers put the dead bodies on carts and buried them in large graves.

## BUBONIC PLAGUE

Fleas living on black rats carried the bubonic plague. The fleas passed on the disease when they bit people. A more infectious form of the plague – pneumonic plague – was spread by coughing.

## TREATMENT OF PLAGUE

Doctors used herbs or cut open people's veins to let out "bad" blood. But these methods failed. Many people refused to go near sufferers, even sick members of their own family.

## PEASANTS REVOLT
The Black Death killed so many people that there was a shortage of workers. The survivors demanded higher wages and organized revolts in France and England against high taxes and strict, out-of-date laws.

---

### Find out more
DISEASE
MEDIEVAL EUROPE
PEASANTS REVOLT

# BLACK HOLES

WHEN A GIANT STAR EXPLODES and collapses, it can create an object of incredibly high density. This object has such massive gravitational pull that nothing can escape, not even light. It is called a stellar black hole. Anything coming into the gravitational field of the black hole is invisible. Its presence is betrayed by spirals of matter swirling into it, rather like water draining into a plughole. Black holes may also develop at the centre of galaxies from clouds of gas, rather than from the remains of giant stars. These are called supermassive black holes and can have up to hundreds of thousands of times the mass of our Sun. The gravitational force is so immense that thousands of stars may be dragged into the vortex. As they become squeezed together on the edge of the funnel, they form a whirlpool concentration of gas, dust, and smashed stars that flares with brilliant light.

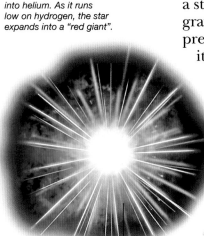

Inside a large star, nuclear fusion converts hydrogen into helium. As it runs low on hydrogen, the star expands into a "red giant".

The star finally dies in an explosion that is called a supernova.

**ALBERT EINSTEIN**
Physicist Albert Einstein (1879-1955) proposed a general relativity theory which showed that light is bent by gravity, so it can be trapped inside a black hole.

**SUPERNOVA REMNANT**
The cloud of debris and gas created by a supernova is called a supernova remnant. At the centre sits the black hole. When the mass of the original star is not enough to create a black hole, the result may be a pulsar neutron star. This spins rapidly, emitting beams of light.

## STAR CYCLE
Astronomers believe that many massive stars end as black holes. As it uses up the last of its fuel, a large star expands to become an even bigger "supergiant" star. Eventually it explodes as a supernova. The centre then collapses to become a neutron star, or a black hole.

If enough debris falls back on to the stellar core it can become a black hole.

## GRAVITATIONAL WELL
If space is shown as a flat plane, then a black hole is like a dent or funnel in the surface. Any object that strays within the area of the dent will probably spiral towards the middle. Eventually, it swirls down the "gravitational well", into a region from which even light cannot escape.

An object is drawn by gravity towards the black hole.

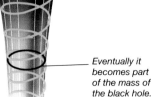

Once the object has plunged into the vortex there is no escape.

Eventually it becomes part of the mass of the black hole.

Gas drawn from nearby blue supergiant star

The accretion disc swirling into the black hole

**ACCRETION DISC**
Matter spiralling into a black hole is known as an accretion disc. It may contain stars and planets as well as debris and gases. You can't see black holes but the material falling into them causes them to give out enormous amounts of radiation.

---

*Find out more*
ASTRONOMY
EINSTEIN, ALBERT
GRAVITY
STARS

# BOOKS

NEARLY ALL THE IDEAS and discoveries that have been made through the ages can be found in books. The book is one of humankind's great inventions, and it is very adaptable. There are many kinds of books, from fiction or storybooks to nonfiction (information) books, such as how-to books, dictionaries, and encyclopedias like the book you are reading. Egyptians made the first books 5,000 years ago. They wrote them on scrolls of papyrus – paper made from reeds. The Romans invented the book as we know it today, using treated animal skin called parchment for pages. For hundreds of years all books were handwritten. They were rare and precious. The Chinese invented printing in the 9th century; it arrived in Europe during the 15th century. Printing made it possible to produce more than one book at a time, so as books became cheaper, more people began to read them and knowledge was spread more widely.

**AUTHORS AND EDITORS**
The author writes the book and submits it to the editor, who checks for errors and prepares the manuscript for the printer.

**LINDISFARNE GOSPELS**
Monasteries were centres of learning throughout the Middle Ages in Europe (5th-15th centuries). They preserved the skills of writing and bookmaking. Monks in England wrote the Lindisfarne Gospels 1,300 years ago. It is a copy of part of the Bible, handwritten and beautifully decorated with pictures.

Cardboard stiffens the cover.

Gluing cloth onto cardboard makes a "case".

Fitting the pages into the spine is called casing-in.

Spine cloth is glued on to reinforce the sewn ends.

Pages are folded into sections of 16 and sewn together.

Glued endpapers hold the pages on the case.

## MAKING A BOOK
To make modern books, printers use computers to set the type (arrange the words on the page) and cameras to make the printing plates. Machines print, fold, stitch, and bind the books in a single operation.

## PAPERBACKS
Books with soft paper covers became widespread in the early 20th century. They were cheaper to produce than hardcover books, so more people could afford to buy and read them.

PENGUIN BOOKS
Huntingtower
JOHN BUCHAN
WILLIAM FAULKNER
3/6

## THE PUBLISHER
Thousands of new books are published every year by companies such as DK. They decide which books to print and pay the cost of book production. Publishers also advertise books and distribute them through bookshops.

## LIBRARIES
A library is a collection of books. There are private libraries and public lending libraries. Many schools and universities have libraries where pupils and students can use books and other resources for their course work. The librarian arranges books by authors' names, and in subject order. Fiction and nonfiction books are kept on different shelves.

## SHAPES AND SIZES

Books are published in many different shapes and sizes, on an enormous range of subjects from general knowledge to Bible stories, and information on the world around us. They range from pocket-sized books, which can be carried around easily, to larger books, and even novelty-shaped or pop-up books. Books for younger children may have large type for easier reading; smaller pocket-sized books are useful for quick at-a-glance reference. The size of a book often relates to the use to which it will be put. Encyclopedias, for instance, tend to be large because they contain a lot of information.

*Some books contain activities such as models to make.*

### AUDIO BOOKS
Books that you listen to are called audio books. The author or an actor records the words onto a tape or compact disc (CD), which can be played in the same way as a music tape or CD. Many people use audio books for learning a language, by listening to the tape again and again. Newspapers, specialist magazines, novels, and reference works are also recorded for use by blind people.

*Shaped books are fun.*

### THE JACKET
Many books have a wrapping around them called a jacket. It often has flaps, which tuck behind the cover to hold the jacket in place. A jacket protects a book, as well as showing the author's name and the title of the book. Jacket flaps may also contain information about the author and the contents of the book. The publisher's logo, or identifying mark, and name appear on the jacket, as well as the book's barcode.

*The jacket carries details about the author.*

*The title of the book must be clear.*

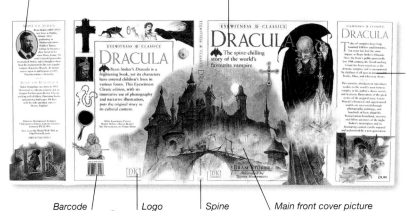

*The front flap has lots of information about the book.*

Barcode    Logo    Spine    Main front cover picture

### TABLE OF CONTENTS
Many books, particularly information books, have a table of contents. This tells the reader what is inside the book, and gives page references for the chapters or sections. There may be a list at the beginning of the book of everyone who worked on it, and an index at the end, directing the reader to information.

*Cardboard scenes leap from pop-up books.*

### ILLUSTRATIONS
Pictures and photographs are an important part of many books, particularly children's books. They may be decorative, or may be used to explain difficult concepts, or ideas, within the text. Illustrated children's books have a long history: the first picture books for children appeared in the mid-1600s. Today, many well-known artists, or illustrators, work to produce books for children.

**Find out more**

INFORMATION TECHNOLOGY
MUSEUMS AND LIBRARIES
PAPER
PRINTING
REFERENCE BOOKS

# BRAIN AND NERVES

EVERY THOUGHT AND MOVEMENT that we make is controlled by the brain. The brain is more complex than any computer ever invented. It enables us to think, speak, hear, see, feel, and move. It works non-stop, day and night. The brain consists of billions of living units called neurons or nerve cells. Neurons carry millions of messages to the brain along the spinal cord, which runs down the back and links the brain to the rest of the body. When these messages, or nerve signals, reach the brain, it sorts them out and sends instructions to the rest of the body along the nerves. Nerves are like wires, made of bundles of nerve cells. Sensory nerves take signals from the eyes, ears, and skin to the brain; motor nerves take signals from the brain to the muscles, telling them when to move the body. The average adult human brain weighs about 1.4 kg (3 lb) and has a texture like jelly. It is protected inside the head by the skull.

**SLEEP**
When we sleep, the body rests but the brain is still working, controlling our breathing and heartbeat. We remember some of our night thoughts as dreams.

**CEREBRAL HEMISPHERES**
The largest parts of the brain are the two folded cerebral hemispheres. Our thoughts are based in these hemispheres. The outer layer of the brain is called the grey matter. It is rich in nerve cells. The inner layer is called the white matter. It consists mainly of nerve fibres. If the two hemispheres were spread out, they would cover an area the size of a pillowcase.

Skull

White matter

Meninges are membranes which surround and cushion the brain within the skull.

Hypothalamus has overall control of the internal organs and is linked to the pituitary gland and hormonal system.

Pituitary gland

Cerebellum processes and coordinates signals going out to muscles from hemispheres.

Spinal cord

Brain stem

Area associated with touch

Area involved with consciousness, creativity, and personality

Area that controls the muscles which make body movements

Area that controls vision

Area that controls hearing, smell, and taste

Area associated with coordination and balance

Area that controls breathing and blood pressure

Nerve

Nerve cell

Grey matter

White matter

**NERVE REFLEX**
When you prick your finger, sensory nerves carry signals to the spinal cord. Here they pass through intermediate nerve cells and then straight back out to the muscles, making them pull the finger away. This is called a reflex – an automatic reaction that we make without thinking.

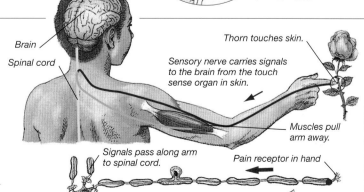

Brain

Spinal cord

Thorn touches skin.

Sensory nerve carries signals to the brain from the touch sense organ in skin.

Muscles pull arm away.

Pain receptor in hand

Signals pass along arm to spinal cord.

Nerve cell

Motor nerve carries signals to muscles in arm.

**NERVE CELLS**
Each nerve cell has a main cell body with fine spidery connections called dendrites, and a long, wirelike fibre called the axon. The axon connects with thousands of other nerve cells, creating millions of pathways for nerve signals.

*Find out more*
HEART AND BLOOD
HUMAN BODY
MUSCLES AND MOVEMENT

# BRAZIL

Brazil borders every country in South America, except Chile and Ecuador. Its Atlantic border is 7,400 km (4,600 miles) long.

**BRAZIL, THE LARGEST COUNTRY** in South America, is a land of contrasts. To the south, it is dominated by the rolling grasslands of the Brazilian highlands, while arid deserts lie to the northeast. Three-fifths of Brazil's total land area is covered by the world's largest rain forest, which forms the drainage basin of the Amazon, the world's second-longest river. Increasingly, the rain forest is being cleared for agriculture, cattle ranching, mining, and the timber industry as Brazil's rapidly growing population places more pressure on the land. Rural poverty drives many people to overcrowded cities. São Paulo, the fastest growing city on the continent, is a major industrial centre. Brazil was colonized in the 16th century by the Portuguese, who imported African slaves to work on sugar plantations. Today, Brazil is the largest Roman Catholic nation in the world, and has a vibrant mix of Indian, Portuguese, and African cultures.

## RIO DE JANEIRO

Rio de Janeiro is located on the Atlantic coast, and sprawls across bays, islands, and the foothills of the coastal mountains. It is dominated by the distinctive shape of Sugarloaf Mountain and the monumental statue of Christ the Redeemer. Founded by the Portuguese in 1565, it was capital of Brazil from 1763 to 1960. Today, this rapidly growing city is a major international port, and a commercial, manufacturing and cultural centre. It is also famous for its beaches, annual carnival, and exciting nightlife.

## SHANTY TOWNS

For many people living in rural poverty, cities seem to offer a chance of employment and a better life. Yet a severe lack of housing in Brazil's major cities has led to the growth of *favelas*. These shanty towns, built of wood and corrugated iron, sprawl over land which is unfit for other development.

*About 22 per cent of the world's coffee comes from Brazil. It is grown in the warm fertile soils of central and southern Brazil.*

### RIO CARNIVAL

Every year, just before Lent, Rio de Janeiro is transformed by a five-day carnival. Huge parades snake their way through the city. Brightly dressed singers, musicians, and dancers fill the streets with colour, spectacle, and the sound of *samba* music.

### GOLD RUSH

Brazil's mineral wealth ranges from iron and tin to gold and precious stones, such as diamonds and topaz. Since the 1980s, thousands of miners have flooded to the Serra Pelada region, burrowing into the hillside with their bare hands in search of gold.

*Carnival party-goers compete with each other for the prize for the most outrageous costume and best-decorated float.*

*Swarms of gold prospectors, known as garimpeiros, cover this Brazilian hillside. They chip away rock with pick axes, hoping they might find their fortune in gold.*

# AMAZONIAN RAIN FOREST

The largest surviving area of rain forest in the world is in the Amazon river basin. It is the most biologically diverse habitat in the world and supports millions of species of plants and animals. Scientists estimate that more than 2,000 species can live in just one rain forest tree. The annual average temperature is 26°C (79°F), while annual rainfall can be as high as 2,000 mm (80 in). Rain forest soils are easily washed away when trees and plants are removed. As more and more land is cleared for farming and timber, the rain forest is lost forever.

*When rain forests are cleared in equatorial regions, heavy rainfall erodes the soil, leaving a green desert. Crops cannot grow in these conditions and many animals lose their natural habitat.*

*Tropical hardwoods are a valued resource and large logging companies are responsible for much of the loss of rain forest habitat. When landless peasants settle in the Amazonian rainforest, they clear the forest and farm the land until it degenerates to scrub, or is sold to cattle ranchers.*

Brazil nuts

## FOREST RESOURCES

The Amazonian rain forest is rich in many resources, from plants with medicinal properties and rubber trees which produce latex, to brazil nuts. Brazil nuts (left) can be eaten or crushed to make oil. They are exported worldwide.

## AMAZONIAN INDIANS

It is estimated that some 220,000 native Brazilians still live in the rain forest. These peoples, also known as the Amazonian Indians, live a traditional way of life. They survive by hunting, fishing, and clearing small patches of forest for farming corn and manioc. Many Indian groups have been wiped out by disease or by land-hungry miners, settlers, and loggers. Today, most live in protected areas.

*In Manaus (right) during the dry season, trucks reverse down to the edge of the Amazon to receive cargo.*

## WATER HIGHWAY

The mighty Amazon river has the greatest volume of water of any river in the world. It is navigable along its entire 6,400-km (4,000-mile) length. It is a major transport artery, carrying 10 per cent of all Brazilian cargo. The river teems with barges, passenger ships, and patrol boats. River ports, such as Manaus and Belém, are important commercial centres.

*This boy is a Yanomami Indian. His people's traditional way of life was destroyed when gold prospectors ejected them from their lands.*

## MANAUS

Manaus was a rich city in the 19th century, its wealth based on the rubber industry. Today, it is a centre for the cattle-ranching, mining, and timber industries of Amazonia. It is also an important cultural centre in this remote region, and is famous for its domed opera house. With a population of one million, Manaus is a magnet for the rural poor who continue to settle there.

*Find out more*

FESTIVALS
FOOTBALL AND RUGBY
FOREST WILDLIFE
RIVERS
SOUTH AMERICA

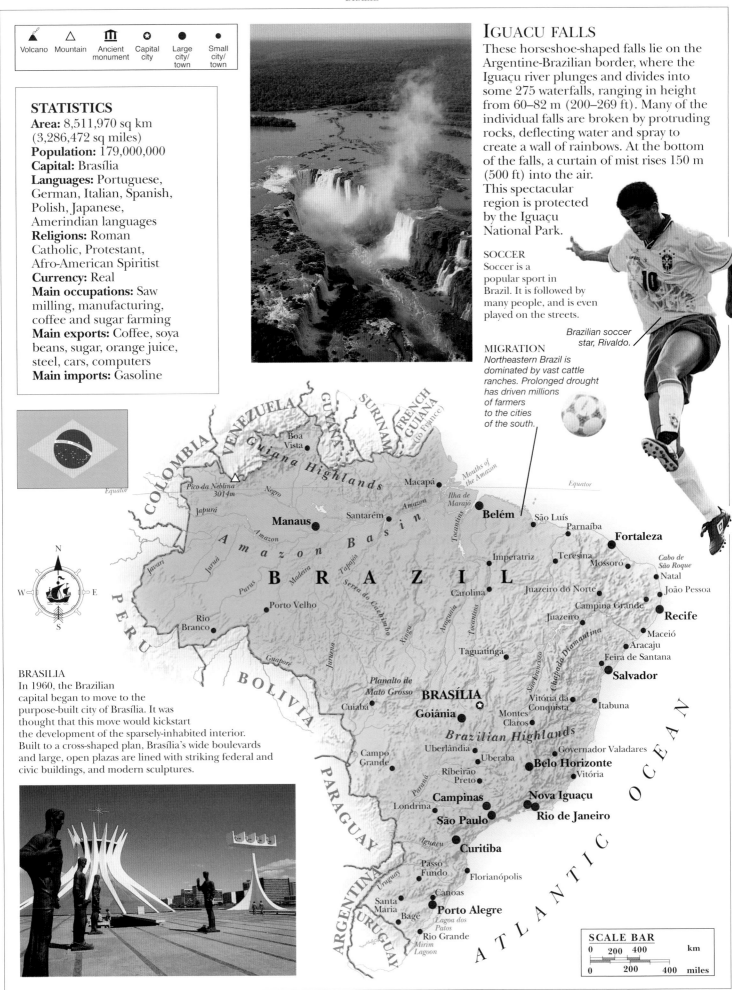

## STATISTICS
**Area:** 8,511,970 sq km (3,286,472 sq miles)
**Population:** 179,000,000
**Capital:** Brasília
**Languages:** Portuguese, German, Italian, Spanish, Polish, Japanese, Amerindian languages
**Religions:** Roman Catholic, Protestant, Afro-American Spiritist
**Currency:** Real
**Main occupations:** Saw milling, manufacturing, coffee and sugar farming
**Main exports:** Coffee, soya beans, sugar, orange juice, steel, cars, computers
**Main imports:** Gasoline

# IGUACU FALLS
These horseshoe-shaped falls lie on the Argentine-Brazilian border, where the Iguaçu river plunges and divides into some 275 waterfalls, ranging in height from 60–82 m (200–269 ft). Many of the individual falls are broken by protruding rocks, deflecting water and spray to create a wall of rainbows. At the bottom of the falls, a curtain of mist rises 150 m (500 ft) into the air. This spectacular region is protected by the Iguaçu National Park.

## SOCCER
Soccer is a popular sport in Brazil. It is followed by many people, and is even played on the streets.

*Brazilian soccer star, Rivaldo.*

## MIGRATION
*Northeastern Brazil is dominated by vast cattle ranches. Prolonged drought has driven millions of farmers to the cities of the south.*

## BRASILIA
In 1960, the Brazilian capital began to move to the purpose-built city of Brasília. It was thought that this move would kickstart the development of the sparsely-inhabited interior. Built to a cross-shaped plan, Brasília's wide boulevards and large, open plazas are lined with striking federal and civic buildings, and modern sculptures.

### Map labels
Volcano  Mountain  Ancient monument  Capital city  Large city/town  Small city/town

COLOMBIA — VENEZUELA — GUYANA — SURINAM — FRENCH GUIANA (to France)
Boa Vista
Guiana Highlands
Pico da Neblina 3014m
Equator
Negro
Japurá
Amazon
Macapá
Mouths of the Amazon
Ilha de Marajó
Belém
São Luís
Parnaíba
Fortaleza
Manaus
Santarém
Amazon Basin
Javari
Jurua
Amazon
Madeira
Purus
Tapajós
Serra do Cachimbo
B R A Z I L
Imperatriz
Teresina
Mossoró
Cabo de São Roque
Natal
PERU
Porto Velho
Tocantins
Carolina
Juazeiro do Norte
João Pessoa
Campina Grande
Recife
Rio Branco
Guaporé
Jurueña
Xingu
Araguaia
Tocantins
Juazeiro
Maceió
Aracaju
Feira de Santana
Taguatinga
São Francisco
Chapada Diamantina
Salvador
BOLIVIA
Planalto de Mato Grosso
Cuiabá
BRASÍLIA
Goiânia
Vitória da Conquista
Montes Claros
Itabuna
Brazilian Highlands
Campo Grande
Uberlândia
Uberaba
Governador Valadares
Belo Horizonte
Vitória
PARAGUAY
Ribeirão Preto
Paraná
Campinas
Nova Iguaçu
Londrina
São Paulo
Rio de Janeiro
Iguaçu
Curitiba
ATLANTIC OCEAN
Passo Fundo
Florianópolis
Uruguay
Canoas
Santa Maria
Bagé
Porto Alegre
Lagoa dos Patos
Rio Grande
Mirim Lagoon
ARGENTINA — URUGUAY

### SCALE BAR
0   200   400   km
0   200   400   miles

# BRIDGES

TRAVEL ON LAND is easier, safer, and more direct with bridges. Motor vehicles and trains can speed over lakes, rivers, and deep valleys. Bridges raise busy roads over others so that the roads do not meet. Major roads and railways enter cities on long bridges sometimes called viaducts. Footbridges allow people to cross roads, rivers, and railways safely.

The first bridges were made by placing tree trunks across rivers, and laying flat stones on rocks in shallow streams. Later, people made rope bridges by weaving plants together, and built stone bridges with strong arches. Similar kinds of bridges are built today with concrete and other strong, modern materials instead of natural materials. Steel beams and cables are used as supports. The world's longest bridge crosses Lake Pontchartrain in the United States. It is almost 39 km (24 miles) long. Land cannot be seen from its centre.

### SUSPENSION BRIDGE
A pair of long steel cables fixed to high towers suspends the roadway. Suspension bridges can span the longest distances because they are lightweight.

### ARCH BRIDGE
A curved arch firmly fixed to the banks supports the bridge. Arches are very strong structures.

### CANTILEVER BRIDGE
Each half of the bridge is balanced on a support in the river. Where the two halves meet, there may be a short central span.

### CABLE-STAYED BRIDGE
Sets of straight steel cables attached to towers hold up the bridge from above.

### BASCULE BRIDGE
Sections of the bridge tilt like a drawbridge, allowing ships into port.

### BEAM BRIDGE
Several columns in the river-bed or the ground support the bridge from beneath. Sometimes the bridge is made of a hollow girder through which cars and trains can run.

## BUILDING A BRIDGE
The supports and ends of the bridge are built first, firmly fixed in the ground or the riverbed and banks. The deck of the bridge carrying the road or railway is then built out from the ends and supports, or lifted onto them.

### SUSPENDING THE CABLES
The towers of a suspension bridge are built first. Steel ropes are then placed over the towers. A machine moves along the ropes, spinning long lengths of wire into strong steel cables.

### RAISING THE DECK
Long lengths of cable, called hangers, are fixed to the suspending cables. The deck of the bridge is made in sections elsewhere. The sections are taken to the bridge, lifted into position, and attached to the hangers.

## KINDS OF BRIDGES
There are various ways of building bridges to span rivers and other barriers. Most bridges rest on solid supports. Pontoon bridges, which are found on some lakes, float on the surface of the water.

## AQUEDUCTS
Bridges that carry water are called aqueducts. The aqueduct may be part of a canal, or it may bring a water supply to a town or city. The Romans built many aqueducts with high stone arches, several of which survive today.

### THE LONGEST SPANS
The Akashi-Kaikyo Bridge in Japan, has the longest single span of any bridge. The central span is 1,990 m (6,530 ft) long. The bridge was completed in 1997. The Humber Bridge, England, (left) has the fourth longest single span, at 1,410 m (4,626 ft).

### TACOMA BRIDGE DISASTER
The Tacoma Narrows Bridge in Washington, United States, failed in 1940. The wind made the bridge twist back and forth until the deck gave way. Nobody was hurt.

> **Find out more**
> ARCHITECTURE
> BUILDING

# ANCIENT
# BRITAIN

THE TERM ANCIENT BRITAIN describes the period of British history from about 3500 B.C. until the Romans invaded in A.D. 43. Prehistoric people had lived in Britain for many thousands of years before this, but evidence shows that real changes began during the Neolithic, or New Stone Age, when early people in Britain, like those elsewhere, learned to make pottery, and to grow their own food by farming. They were also the first people in Britain to leave behind large-scale monuments, which they built with simple stone tools. They, and the people of the Bronze and Iron Ages, who included the Celts, are known as Ancient Britons. They lived in a harsh environment, but developed stunning art, and became skilled warriors.

### SKARA BRAE
Britain's best-preserved prehistoric village is Skara Brae, Orkney. Skara Brae dates back to the Stone Age, around 5,000 years ago. There were very few trees on Orkney, so the people built their houses out of stone. They even used stone to make the furniture – including beds and cupboards – which still survives.

## STONEHENGE
Europe's greatest prehistoric monument is Stonehenge, a massive stone circle used for religious ceremonies, which stands on Salisbury Plain, England. Stonehenge was built in stages between 2950 and 2500 B.C. Its gigantic stones are called sarsens. These came from about 30 km (18.6 miles) away. No one knows how the Ancient Britons moved them to Stonehenge.

Each sarsen was about 9 m (29.5 ft) tall (6 m/19.7 ft above ground), and weighed some 40 tonnes.

Tops of sarsen stones had dimples, which fitted into holes on lintels.

Ancient Britons may have dragged stones on sleds or rollers.

Builders may have used poles as levers to raise the huge lintel stones.

This sarsen formed part of an inner arrangement of stones.

Builders used levers and ropes to haul a stone into position.

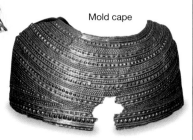

Mold cape

### METALWORKING
Britain's metalworkers became highly skilled. In about 2500 B.C., they found out how to use copper and gold. Soon after, they were working in bronze, and discovered iron c. 800 B.C. They continued to use gold, making beautiful objects such this finely worked cape which was buried in a warrior's grave at Mold, North Wales.

### MAIDEN CASTLE
This hill fort in Dorset, England is big enough to contain a sizeable village. It was built in the 6th century B.C., and enlarged some 200 years later. Its Iron Age inhabitants protected themselves with huge ditches, throwing up the earth to make ridges.

### WOAD
Ancient Britons decorated their bodies with a blue dye made from the woad plant. They made the dye by mixing up a paste of woad leaves and water, and rolling this into a ball. When the ball dried, the paste on the inside turned blue. The Ancient Britons probably wore the dye to make themselves look fearsome in battle.

Woad leaves provide a rich blue dye.

Woad plant

---

*Find out more*

BRONZE AGE
CELTS
ROMAN EMPIRE
STONE AGE
UNITED KINGDOM, HISTORY OF

---

# BRITISH EMPIRE

Surrounding fence kept out enemies and any dangerous wildlife.

THE LARGEST EMPIRE THE WORLD has ever seen – the British Empire – began in the 1600s as merchants set up trading colonies on the east coast of America. More colonies were established in the Caribbean, India, and, after 1770, Australia, Oceania, and Africa. By 1920, the British Empire had reached its greatest extent. It grew through military conquest and the need for British industry to acquire raw materials. A vast civil service, and Christianity, held it together. But such a large empire was too big to last, and by the end of the 20th century almost every colony had received its independence.

## JAMESTOWN

In 1607, Britain set up its first permanent overseas colony at Jamestown, Virginia, on the east coast of North America. The settlement was named after King James I, and consisted of log cabins surrounded by a protective wooden fence.

Settlers built cabins of wood from local forest.

Women looked after the animals and helped to harvest the crops.

## CAPTURING CANADA

In the early 1600s, the French established colonies along the St Lawrence River in Canada. The British set up the Hudson's Bay Company in 1670 to trade furs and other goods with Inuits from the north of Canada. This caused tension between the British and French in the region. In 1759, the British army, under General Wolfe, captured Quebec, the capital of French Canada. The British defeated the French army, and took control of the whole of Canada.

## THE RAJ

In 1600 Queen Elizabeth I set up the East India Company. It soon controlled large parts of India. Following the Indian Mutiny of 1857, the British government took over. By 1886, Britain controlled the whole Indian subcontinent. For the Victorians, India was the "jewel in the crown", and British rule was known as the "Raj" after the Hindu word meaning "reign".

## THE INDIAN MUTINY

In 1857, a mutiny broke out among Indian troops, who feared they might be converted to Christianity, and suspected their gun cartridges were greased with pig fat (offensive to Muslims), or cow fat (offensive to Hindus). The British put down the mutiny, and took steps to reform the Indian government and army.

## IMPERIAL TRADE

During the 18th and 19th centuries, the Empire helped Britain become the world's major industrial power. The Empire supplied Britain with raw materials, notably cotton, tea, rubber, and minerals. In return, Britain exported manufactured goods to all parts of the Empire. To support this trade, Britain acquired ports, including Malta and the Falkland Islands.

## AUSTRALIA

The first colonists in Australia were British convicts sent out from 1788 to serve their sentences. Later arrivals included Irish people fleeing famine, and others seeking a new life in the wide open spaces of Australia. The discovery of gold in 1851 caused a rush of prospectors, leading to great social and economic change. In 1901, the six separate colonies in Australia were joined together as a single country.

## IMPERIAL DREAM

Thousands of British men and a few women went to serve abroad. Some, such as Cecil Rhodes (1853-1902), made their fortunes in the empire, and believed British rule was the most advanced form of government the world had seen. Rhodes did much to enlarge the empire in Africa. He dreamed of a railway from Cairo to Cape Town passing entirely through British territory.

## MISSIONARIES

As the empire expanded, British Christian missionaries set out to convert the local people. They set up schools and hospitals, and did much to bind the different parts of the empire together through Christianity and the British way of life. One of the most famous missionaries was Scotsman David Livingstone. In 1841 he arrived in Cape Town; by the time of his death in 1873, he had explored most of Africa.

## WORLD WAR I

In 1914, war broke out between Britain and Germany. World War I involved 2.8 million troops from all over the empire. Indian troops fought on the Western Front. Australian and New Zealand (ANZAC) troops fought at Gallipoli, and African forces overran German colonies in Africa.

Britain and its overseas possessions

## EXTENT OF EMPIRE

The British Empire reached its greatest extent in the years after the end of World War I in 1918, when former German and Turkish possessions were added to it. King George V (1865-1936) of Britain ruled over an empire that contained 410 million people – one in five of the world's population. It spread over 29,500,000 sq km (11,400,000 sq miles), and touched every continent.

## DECOLONIZATION

The first countries to gain independence were the white dominions of Canada (1867), Australia (1901), and New Zealand (1907). Non-white countries followed. The Indian subcontinent became independent in 1947-48; Ghana and Malaya left the empire in 1957. Decolonization (withdrawal from the empire) continued through the 20th century, sometimes violently. By 1997, Britain governed only 13 tiny colonies, some uninhabited.

## COMMONWEALTH

In 1931, more than 50 newly independent British colonies joined what is known as the British Commonwealth. The British queen, Elizabeth II, is its head, even though most members are republics or have their own monarchs. Commonwealth leaders meet once every two years to discuss matters such as trade.

## THE BRITISH EMPIRE

**1497** John Cabot claims Newfoundland for England.

**1600** East India Company established.

**1607** Jamestown founded.

**1620s** Caribbean island colonies established.

**1763** Britain gains Canada under Treaty of Paris.

**1783** Britain loses US colonies.

**1788-1867** British convicts are transported to Australia to serve their sentences there.

**1814** Britain acquires its first African colony in the Cape.

**1867** Canada becomes the first dominion in the British Empire.

**1876** Queen Victoria is created Empress of India.

**1886** Britain takes control of India.

**1901-10** Australia, New Zealand, and South Africa become British dominions.

**1920s** Empire at its greatest extent.

**1931** Statute of Westminster recognizes full independence of the dominions.

**1947** India and Pakistan become independent.

**1997** Britain returns Hong Kong to China.

_Find out more_

EMIGRATION AND IMMIGRATION
UNITED KINGDOM
UNITED KINGDOM,
history of
VICTORIA, QUEEN

# BROADCASTING

TO MEDIEVAL FARMERS, THE WORD broadcast meant to scatter seeds across a wide area of ploughed earth, to make sure that as many of them as possible take root. When the radio was invented at the beginning of the 20th century, the same word was used to describe how sound programmes could be sent out far and wide across the world. When television appeared 40 years later, it became possible to broadcast pictures as well as sound. Broadcasting companies, such as the British Broadcasting Corporation (BBC), were first set up in the 1920s to transmit (send out) radio programmes that included news, weather reports, information from the government, music, and drama. Today there are thousands of radio and TV companies. Radio and TV also let us enjoy sport, concerts, plays, and films in our own homes, and learn new skills from educational programmes.

**TOWN CRIER**
Before radio, TV, and newspapers, news was read out loud on the streets by special "newsreaders" called town criers.

## NEWS STUDIO
One of the main functions of broadcasting is to give regular news reports, usually from a studio. Technicians make sure the sound system works and signals are sent out correctly. Journalists research and write the news stories. Newsreaders present the news. Reports, or bulletins, may include live information from outside broadcasts, and interviews with people who are in the news.

*The studio manager organizes the running order of news stories and brings in outside broadcasts and interviews.*

*Schoolchildren try their skills as newsreaders in a mock-up news studio.*

### BROADCASTING COMPANIES
Nearly every country has its own national broadcasting company, such as the BBC in Britain or the National Broadcasting Company (NBC) in the US. These may be paid for by public funds or a licence fee. There are also large commercial broadcasters, paid for by advertising or sponsorship. Smaller stations serve local communities.

Broadcasting House, London, home of the BBC

### FREE ACCESS
The clockwork radio was invented and developed in the 1990s. Now, most people on the planet can access radio, even without a power supply, and keep up with local and international news.

### NEWS GATHERING
Journalists work round the clock to collect the most up-to-date news information. Teams of reporters, photographers and sound engineers are sent to the scenes of major events. Some reporters, such as those reporting on the traffic or covering dramatic events, use helicopters.

Live 8 concert in London, 2005

### REACHING THE PEOPLE
Major news items are broadcast almost instantly even to the remotest communities. Huge numbers of people all over the world can join in events such as the first moon landing or the Live 8 concerts, as these events actually happen.

**Find out more**
INFORMATION TECHNOLOGY
NEWSPAPERS
RADIO
TELEVISION AND VIDEO

# BRONZE AGE

THE BRONZE AGE refers to a period of time during which the predominant metal employed by a culture was bronze. It usually succeeds the Stone Age and the Copper Age and is followed by the Iron Age. The Bronze Age spans c. 3500 to 1000 B.C. but its onset occurred at different times in different parts of the world. During this period, civilizations sprang up in Egypt, Mesopotamia, the Hwang Ho Valley in China, on the Aegean Islands of the Mediterranean, and in the Indus Valley. People learnt to grow crops and domesticate animals, so they no longer needed to move to find food. This allowed communities more time to learn how to use metals. Bronze was formed by melting copper and tin together and was found to be harder and longer lasting than other metals. It was used to make weapons and ornaments, sometimes by pouring hot molten bronze into moulds, for example to make metal pins, or by being heated and beaten into shape. Metalworkers also used gold and copper for luxury items such as jewellery.

MESOPOTAMIA
One of the earliest Bronze Age civilisations began in Mesopotamia, a plain lying between the Tigris and Euphrates rivers. Its fertile land was farmed by the Sumerians, Assyrians, and Akkadians.

## AEGEAN CIVILIZATIONS

The rise of the Aegean civilizations coincided with the start of bronzeworking in the region. Several important cultures arose during the Aegean Bronze Age (c. 3000 to 1100 B.C.): chiefly the Cycladic, Minoan, Mycenaean, and Trojan cultures. People became highly skilled in architecture, painting, and other crafts. Metalworkers used bronze to make weapons, such as this Mycenaean dagger blade (right) and tools for everyday use such as axes, adzes, and tweezers. People were often buried with a variety of valuable bronze weapons, household utensils, or ornaments. The Aegean people produced bronze objects in great quantity.

THE MYCENAEANS
The city of Mycenae was ruled by the legendary king Agamemnon, whose remains were found wearing the gold funeral mask shown right. Mycenae was famous for its grand palace, walled fortress, and the beehive-shaped tombs where kings were buried. The Mycenaeans were wealthy and powerful, and dominated the Aegean region from 1450 B.C. onwards.

### BRONZE AGE

3500 B.C. Beginning of the Bronze Age in the Middle East. First cities built in Mesopotamia, and people begin to use bronze.

3250 B.C. First picture writing develops in Mesopotamia.

3000 B.C. The wheel appears in Mesopotamia, and the plough is first used in China.

2800 B.C. Rise of Bronze Age culture of the Indus Valley, an agriculturally based civilization in India.

2650 B.C. Start of great pyramid building era in parts of Egypt.

2500 B.C. Use of bronze spreads across Europe. First stage of Stonehenge built in England.

2100 B.C. Sumerian city of Ur reaches the height of its power.

c. 1600 B.C. Bronze Age begins in China. Manufacture of magnificent bronze ceremonial vessels.

c. 1200 B.C. Rise of the Assyrian empire.

1000 B.C. Iron begins to replace bronze as the main metal used.

SHANG DYNASTY
The Bronze Age coincided with the rise of the Shang dynasty (c. 1650 to 1027 B.C.), which was located in the Hwang Ho Valley in China. Its Bronze Age lasted from 1500 to 1000 B.C.. Shang techniques for metalworking and writing spread throughout the area. Most bronze vessels (such as the ritual water vessel shown below) were made for use in religious ceremonies. Bronze was also used to make weapons and chariot fittings for soldiers of the great Shang armies.

## WRITING
## AND THE WHEEL

The earliest form of writing, called cuneiform, emerged during the Bronze Age. It was invented by the Sumerians, who also made the first wheels. Wheels were used on wagons and war chariots, and to make pottery. The chariot shown left is from the city of Ur and is being pulled into battle by wild asses.

### Find out more

ASSYRIANS
BABYLONIANS
CELTS
GREECE, ANCIENT
PREHISTORIC PEOPLES
SUMERIANS

# BUDDHISM

ONE OF THE WORLD'S great religions, Buddhism, began in India about 2,500 years ago. It grew and spread, and today there are more than 350 million Buddhists, mainly in Asia. All Buddhists follow the teachings of Buddha, a name which means "Enlightened One". Buddha himself was born in about 563 B.C. He was originally called Siddhartha, and was a wealthy prince who became horrified at the suffering in the world. He left his wealth and family, assumed the name Gautama and began to meditate (think deeply). After three years he achieved enlightenment, or complete understanding, became a monk, and travelled extensively to pass his ideas on to others.

### GOLDEN PAGODA
Buddhist temples usually contain relics of Buddha such as robes or a sandal. Some, such as the Golden Pavilion in Kyoto, Japan, are magnificent buildings inlaid with gold and decorated with diamonds.

Buddhists believe that everyone is reborn after their old body has died. The quality of their new life depends on their karma. Karma is the total of all the good and bad deeds they did in the life they have just left. Buddhists aim to achieve absolute peace – a state they call nirvana. Buddha taught that nirvana could be achieved by following the Eightfold Path: rightness of views, intention, speech, action, livelihood, concentration, mindfulness, and effort.

### BUDDHAS
Although they vary greatly in size, images of the Buddha all look similar. They represent Buddha sitting on a lotus flower. In the home a small Buddha forms part of a shrine. The image reminds followers of the goodness of Buddha and helps them meditate and pray.

*Buddhists burn incense at the shrine and leave offerings of flowers.*

### FESTIVALS
**Bodhi Day** – the day Gautama became the Buddha.

**Parinirvana** – passing of the Buddha into nirvana.

**Wesak or Vesakha Puja** – a three-day festival to celebrate the main events of Buddha's life.

**Dharmachakra Day** – when Buddha gave his first sermon.

### MONKS
Buddhist monks give up most possessions. They keep only their saffron yellow robes, a needle, a razor, a water strainer, and a large piece of cloth to receive alms (gifts). Monks spend their time praying, teaching, and meditating. Each day they go out to collect food. In some Buddhist countries, boys spend a short time at a monastery as part of their schooling.

### WHEEL OF LIFE
Buddhists share with Hindus a belief in the Wheel of Life, also called the Wheel of the Law. This is the continuous cycle of birth and rebirth that traps people who have not yet achieved nirvana. The spokes of the wheel remind the Buddhist of the Eightfold Path.

*Find out more*
ASIA
CHINA
HINDUISM
JAPAN
RELIGIONS

# BUILDING

## CRANE
The crane extends as the building rises. It may also be fixed on top of the building.

*The frame is constructed of beams made of steel or concrete.*

*A hoist fixed to the side of the building carries workers to the top.*

SKYSCRAPERS TOWER above the streets in many cities. The tallest free-standing building, the CN Tower in Toronto, Canada, reaches 553 m (1,815 ft) into the sky. The highest office building is Taipei 101 in Taiwan, at 508 m (1,666 ft). How are such enormous buildings constructed so that they stay up?

A house has walls built of wood, stone, or brick. They hold up the house, supporting themselves as well as the floors and roof. A skyscraper built like this would fall down. The walls could not support the heavy weight of such a high building. So hidden inside a skyscraper is a frame made of steel or concrete. The frame supports the floors and walls, which are often made of glass. Also hidden are the foundations beneath the skyscraper, which support the weight of the building.

### REINFORCED CONCRETE
Liquid concrete is pumped into moulds crossed with steel rods. It sets hard, producing a very strong material called reinforced concrete.

### MOBILE MIXER
A truck with a revolving drum brings concrete to the site. As the drum turns, it keeps mixing the concrete so that it does not set.

*A powerful pump pushes the liquid concrete through the pipe from the ground to the upper floors of the building.*

### PILES
Beams of steel or concrete, called piles, support the building's base. A huge mechanical hammer, called a pile driver, forces the piles into the ground.

## BUILDING SITE
Workers on a building site always wear hard hats to protect their heads. They use many machines to construct a tall building such as a skyscraper. Parts of the building, such as steel beams and concrete slabs, are made elsewhere and brought to the site. Cranes lift the parts into position, and workers fit them together.

*Excavators dig out a huge pit to make the foundation of the building.*

### BULLDOZER
The site is levelled with powerful bulldozers. The curved blade clears vegetation and piles up the soil.

### EXCAVATOR
Trenches and holes are dug with excavators. The bucket digs out soil and dumps it into waiting trucks.

### FOUNDATIONS
Every building is supported by a foundation. This usually consists of a huge pit which contains a base made of reinforced concrete. The frame is built on top of the base, which supports the huge weight of the building.

### SCAFFOLDING
Builders erect scaffolding made of steel tubes so that they can get to any part of a building. In the Far East, strong scaffolding is often made from lengths of bamboo tied together.

## BUILDING MATERIALS
Since early times, people have built with wood and stone. Bricks are made from clay. Stone blocks and bricks are laid in rows and joined together with sand and cement. Wood is cut into parts and assembled into structures. Concrete, made by mixing sand, stones, cement, and water, can be moulded to form any structure.

### Find out more
ARCHITECTURE
ESCALATORS AND LIFTS
HOUSES

108

# BUSES

THE WORD BUS comes from the Latin word omnibus, which means "for all". This is an apt description, for buses were the first kind of public transport, and are still usually the cheapest. The first buses date from the early 19th century when cities grew tremendously during the Industrial Revolution, and working people had to travel further to get to work. Before this time, only people who owned horses and carriages were able to travel long distances. Today, there are buses in cities and villages throughout the world. In most big cities, buses usually run regularly on an organized network of routes, and pick up people at special bus stops. In more remote places, the bus may be just a truck that passes through once in a while and stops wherever there are passengers.

**CITY BUS**
In busy English cities, where the streets are crowded and there are plenty of passengers, some buses, such as this London bus, have two decks.

**ROAD BUS**
Away from cities, buses can be longer to provide space for both passengers and luggage. Some road buses, such as this one from Iraq, may be articulated (hinged) to manoeuvre around hairpin bends on mountain roads.

**SCHOOL BUS**
Many children's first bus ride is on a school bus which takes them to school in the morning and brings them home safely in the afternoon. In comparison to other road vehicles, buses have a very good safety record.

**INTERCITY BUS**
Long-distance buses and coaches, such as those that travel across the United States, have comfortable reclining seats, toilets, coffee machines, and videos.

**COUNTRY BUS**
In less industrialized parts of the world, there are often no railways and most people cannot afford a car, so the bus is the only way to travel. Buses bounce along dusty roads, packed inside and out with people and all their luggage, including chickens, dogs, and other animals.

**TRAMS AND TROLLEY BUSES**
In some cities, such as Amsterdam in the Netherlands, you can catch a tram or a trolley bus instead of a bus. Trams glide along rails laid in the road and run on electric power picked up from overhead cables through rods on the roof. Trolley buses are powered in the same way, but they run on ordinary wheels rather than a track.

## BUSES
In the richer countries of the world, buses are becoming increasingly sophisticated. Many city buses have electronic ticket machines and doors that open and shut automatically, and some buses have computers to guide them along the route. In poorer countries, people frequently crowd into battered vans and pickup trucks, all of which serve the same function as buses.

*Find out more*
CARS
TRANSPORT, HISTORY OF
TRUCKS AND LORRIES

# BUTTERFLIES AND MOTHS

AS BRILLIANT IN COLOUR as many exotic flowers, butterflies are among the most beautiful of all creatures. Butterflies are more familiar to us than moths because they are active by day, whereas moths are active mainly by night. However, there are more than 147,500 different kinds of moths compared to about 17,500 kinds of butterflies. Together these creatures make up the insect group called Lepidoptera. Moths and butterflies have a life cycle in four stages – egg, caterpillar (larva), pupa (chrysalis), and imago (adult). The change in form from caterpillar to butterfly is called metamorphosis. All butterflies and moths are plant eaters and live wherever plants grow, except in extremely cold regions. Some, such as red admiral butterflies, hibernate (sleep) during winter. Others, such as bogong moths, migrate long distances to find food. A few butterflies and moths are pests to humans. Cabbage white caterpillars devour garden vegetables, and clothes moth caterpillars eat the natural fibres in clothing.

Wings and body are covered with scales.

Butterflies often have slim, non-furry bodies.

Most butterflies have thin antennae with clubbed ends.

Forewing

Hind wing

## MORPHO BUTTERFLY

Butterflies, particularly those living in tropical regions, are often more brightly coloured than moths. The blue morpho shown above is found in South America.

SILKWORM
The silkworm is the caterpillar of a moth. It spins a cocoon of silky thread around its body, then changes into a pupa inside the cocoon. People produce silk thread from silkworm cocoons.

Swallowtail butterfly

The owl butterfly lays its eggs in batches. The eggs become darker as the time for hatching approaches. Their actual size is only about 1 mm (1/20th inch).

## MOTH

Moths usually fly at night. Their wings are often but not always dull in colour. When the moth is at rest, it holds its wings to the side of its body. A moth's body is usually plump and hairy, and the antennae are feathery or fernlike. This *brahmaeid* moth from Southeast Asia has fernlike antennae.

EGG TO CATERPILLAR
After mating, a female moth lays eggs on or near a suitable source of food for the caterpillars to eat when they hatch. The eggs of some kinds of moths hatch only when the weather becomes warmer after a cold spell. This usually means that spring has arrived; the plants are beginning to grow again, and they provide food for the hungry caterpillars.

Egg

Caterpillar cuts open egg with its strong jaws and emerges from egg head first.

Hairy head waves around as the pink-striped body struggles to escape from the shell.

Legs

Caterpillar eats the eggshell, which contains important nutrients.

## FEEDING

Each type of caterpillar feeds on a certain kind of vegetation. It spends almost all its time eating; as a result caterpillars can cause great damage to plants and farm crops. Caterpillars stop eating only to moult, or discard their skin when it has become too tight. The caterpillar expands in size before the new skin hardens.

Oak silkmoth caterpillar eats a leaf.

Caterpillar works along leaf blade between veins.

In a few minutes the leaf is almost gone.

Large, powerful jaws rapidly snip off and chew small pieces of food.

Not all moths are dull in colour – many are beautiful, including the moths shown here.

Jaws are hardened with a substance called chitin.

Caterpillar is attached to twig by silken thread.

Caterpillar spins silk girdle around its body, then skin of caterpillar begins to split.

Silk girdle is finished. The pupa is starting to form inside.

New skin of pupa

Caterpillar of the citrus swallowtail butterfly attaches its body to a twig and prepares to change into a pupa (chrysalis).

Spinnerets produce silken thread.

Empty skin and legs of caterpillar

## CATERPILLAR TO CHRYSALIS
Before its final moult, a caterpillar stops feeding and may change colour. It finds a safe place to pupate (change into a pupa, or chrysalis). It anchors itself to a stem with silk thread from spinnerets at its rear end. Many moth caterpillars spin a silken cocoon around themselves for protection. Leafroller caterpillars curl leaves around their bodies and, using their mandibles (mouthparts), stitch them together with silk.

## PUPA TO BUTTERFLY
The pupa stage is often called the resting stage. But inside its hard skin the creature is undergoing an amazing transformation, controlled by its chemical hormones. After several weeks, the skin of the pupa splits and the adult butterfly or moth emerges. Its damp, crumpled wings soon spread and dry.

### SCALES
Tiny overlapping scales cover the wings of moths and butterflies. The colours and arrangement of the scales create the beautiful pattern of the whole wing.

With folded wings, the Indian leaf butterfly looks just like a dead leaf.

Adult blue morpho butterfly with wings closed

### CAMOUFLAGE
Seen alone, a butterfly or moth may look so colourful that it would easily be noticed. But in many species the wing colours and patterns are designed to blend in with the natural surroundings. The shape of the wing may also closely resemble a natural object such as a leaf or a fruit.

Resting pupa of blue morpho butterfly disguised as a leaf

Butterfly begins to emerge.

Blood pumps into wing veins to expand them. Wings gradually dry and harden.

Indian leaf butterfly with wings open

## CONSERVATION
Hundreds of species of moths and butterflies are in danger of extinction. They are threatened because the areas where they live are cleared for farms and homes. Butterflies and moths are also killed and sold to collectors because of their great beauty.

Spanish moon moth is now a protected species.

Queen Alexandra's birdwing butterfly is in danger because the forests where it lives are being cut down.

Large blue butterflies were extinct in Britain, but have now been reintroduced.

The Taenaris macrops butterfly from New Guinea feeds on ripe bananas.

When the wings are open, the eyespots flash like the eyes of a predator.

### EYESPOTS
The eyespots on a butterfly's wings look like the eyes of a predator such as the owl above.

### Find out more
ANIMALS
CAMOUFLAGE, ANIMAL
FLIGHT, ANIMAL
INSECTS

# LORD
# BYRON

Childe Harold and Ianthe

IN MARCH 1812 a young English poet said, "I woke one morning and found myself famous". His name was George Gordon, Lord Byron, and the first two parts of his long poem *Childe Harold's Pilgrimage* had just been published. The poem describes the life of a young man who was adventurous, but rather an outsider from society. Characters like this became known as "Byronic heroes", and readers were fascinated by their exciting stories. Like his heroes, Lord Byron was an adventurer, too. He travelled widely, and published a number of long poems, such as *Don Juan, The Corsair,* and *The Vision of Judgement.* These were full of action, but also poked fun at the society of the time. Byron's works made him one of the best-known writers in Europe. He was part of the Romantic movement in literature, which regarded imagination and feelings as important.

**1788** Born in London.

**1798** Inherits title, Sixth Baron Byron.

**1807** Publishes first book, *Hours of Idleness;* it is attacked by the *Edinburgh Review.*

**1809** Byron responds with the satire *English Bards and Scotch Reviewers.*

**1812** *Childe Harold's Pilgrimage* (cantos 1 and 2).

**1816** Leaves England for Europe; travels widely.

**1819** Publishes the first two cantos (parts) of *Don Juan.*

**1821** Writes several plays and the satire *The Vision of Judgement.*

**1824** Dies at Missolonghi in Greece.

**CHILDE HAROLD**
Like Byron himself, the character of Childe Harold travelled all over Europe, commenting on everything he saw – scenery, people he met, and his own feelings. Readers liked the fact that the poem was a mixture of adventure story and travel guide.

Lord Byron

## SCANDAL

The British public liked Byron's poems, but was scandalized by his lavish lifestyle, his love affairs, and his satires on politicians and the nobility. In 1816 Byron and his wife separated, and British society turned against him. He was forced to leave the country, and never returned.

**NEWSTEAD ABBEY**
Byron inherited the Gordon family home, Newstead Abbey, in Nottinghamshire. The house had once been a monastery and was in a poor state of repair. Byron spent little time there. The poet built up huge debts as a result of his lifestyle, and sold Newstead to raise money.

Newstead Abbey

## TRAVELS

Byron travelled throughout Europe, going to far-flung places such as Spain, Albania, and the eastern Mediterranean. Few British people visited those countries at that time. He lived for several years in Italy, but loved Greece most of all. Byron used his knowledge of continental Europe in his poems, and his work has always been as popular in Europe as in his native Britain.

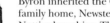

Greek soldiers under siege.

**WAR IN GREECE**
During Byron's lifetime, Greece was ruled by Turkey, but the Greeks wanted independence. In 1821 the Greeks revolted. Three years later, Byron went to join the freedom fighters. He gave a lot of money to the rebels and set up his own brigade of fighters. But in 1824, Byron was struck down by a fever at the town of Missolonghi, and died before he had a chance to join the fighting.

---

***Find out more***
LITERATURE
POETRY
WRITERS AND POETS

---

# BYZANTINE EMPIRE

As THE ROMAN EMPIRE began to decline in the 3rd century A.D., the Byzantine Empire began to emerge. In 330, the Roman Emperor Constantine moved the capital of the Roman Empire from Rome to Byzantium in Turkey. He renamed the capital Constantinople (now Istanbul), and it became the centre of the new Byzantine Empire. At first the empire, named after Byzantium, consisted only of the eastern part of the Roman Empire. But after the Western Roman Empire collapsed, the Byzantine Empire began to expand. Christianity became the state religion, and Constantinople became a Christian centre. Artists and scholars from all over Europe and the Middle East came there to study. Under Emperor Justinian I, the Byzantine Empire regained much of the territory of the old Roman Empire. Trade, art, and architecture thrived. But the empire suffered many attacks. By 642 Muslim Arabs had overrun Byzantine territories in North Africa and the Middle East. Gradually the empire lost its lands in Asia Minor (Turkey) and southeast Europe. In 1453 the Ottomans captured Constantinople, and the Byzantine Empire ended.

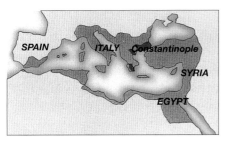

**BYZANTINE EMPIRE**
In A.D. 565, the Byzantine Empire stretched from Spain in the west to Syria in the east. By 1350, the empire had shrunk to a fragment of its former area.

Central dome measures 31 m (100 ft) across.

Marble floors

**HAGIA SOPHIA**
Justinian I (483-565) built the Hagia Sophia (Church of Holy Wisdom) in the centre of Constantinople. It was the largest Christian church in the Eastern world and was intended to provide a spiritual centre for the Byzantine Empire. After 1453, the church became a mosque (Muslim house of worship). Today the Hagia Sophia is a museum.

**CONSTANTINE THE GREAT**
In 314, Constantine the Great (288-337) became Roman emperor. At that time Christianity was forbidden, but in about 312, Constantine himself had been converted, some say by the sight of a cross in the sky. Christianity became the official religion of the Byzantine Empire and is now known as the Eastern Orthodox Church.

**SIEGE OF CONSTANTINOPLE**
By the year 1453, the Ottoman Turks had overrun the entire Byzantine Empire and reached the gates of Constantinople. Under the leadership of Sultan Muhammad II, the Ottomans besieged the city and captured it after two months. The Christian inhabitants of Constantinople were allowed to remain in the city, which became the capital of the Muslim empire.

## BYZANTINE EMPIRE

**395** Roman Empire splits into East and West, with Constantinople as the capital of the Eastern Empire.

**476** The Western Roman Empire collapses; the Byzantine or Eastern Empire takes over the whole Roman Empire.

**527-65** During the reign of Justinian I, the Byzantine Empire reconquers much of the old Roman Empire.

**635-42** Byzantine Empire loses control of the Middle East and North Africa to the Arabs.

**1071** Byzantine Empire loses Asia Minor to the Turks. Calls in help from Europe.

**1333** Ottoman Turks gain a foothold in Europe and begin to encircle Constantinople.

**1453** Constantinople falls to the Ottoman Turks; the Byzantine Empire comes to an end.

*Find out more*
CHRISTIANITY
OTTOMAN EMPIRE
ROMAN EMPIRE

# JULIUS CAESAR

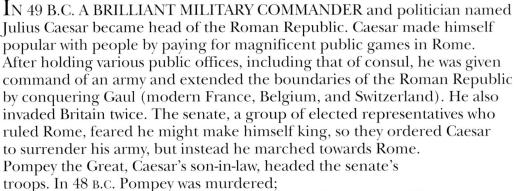

IN 49 B.C. A BRILLIANT MILITARY COMMANDER and politician named Julius Caesar became head of the Roman Republic. Caesar made himself popular with people by paying for magnificent public games in Rome. After holding various public offices, including that of consul, he was given command of an army and extended the boundaries of the Roman Republic by conquering Gaul (modern France, Belgium, and Switzerland). He also invaded Britain twice. The senate, a group of elected representatives who ruled Rome, feared he might make himself king, so they ordered Caesar to surrender his army, but instead he marched towards Rome. Pompey the Great, Caesar's son-in-law, headed the senate's troops. In 48 B.C. Pompey was murdered; and in 45 B.C. Caesar was elected dictator. But a year later he was violently assassinated.

100 B.C. Born in Rome.
65 B.C. Elected public games organizer.
62 B.C. Elected praetor, a law official.
60 B.C. Forms First Triumvirate.
59 B.C. Elected consul.
58 B.C. Begins Gaul campaign.
55 B.C. Invades Britain.
49 B.C. Fights civil war. Becomes dictator.
48 B.C. Defeats Pompey.
46 B.C. Defeats Pompey's supporters.
45 B.C. Made dictator for life.
44 B.C. Assassinated.

As Caesar wondered whether or not to cross the River Rubicon, legend has it that a vision of a larger-than-life man appeared, playing a trumpet, luring him across the river. Caesar took it to be a sign from the gods, and gave the order for his troops to proceed.

## TRIUMVIRATE
In 60 B.C. Caesar, wanting to be elected consul, allied his fortunes with Pompey (above) and Crassus, another leading politician, to form a three-man group (a triumvirate), which was the most powerful political group in Rome.

## CROSSING THE RUBICON
Caesar's victories in Gaul made him very popular with many Romans. However, others feared and distrusted him. In 49 B.C. the senate ordered him to give up his army. Caesar refused and crossed the River Rubicon to invade Italy and begin the civil war.

Each army unit, or legion, carried its own standard, shaped like an eagle.

CAESAR'S DEATH
Many politicians in Rome thought that Caesar had too much power. Led by Marcus Brutus and Gaius Cassius, a number of Pompey's supporters plotted against Caesar and decided to kill him. On 15 March (the Ides of March), 44 B.C., the plotters attacked Caesar in the senate and stabbed him to death. Civil war raged after his death; finally, his adopted son Octavian emerged as victor, and the Roman Empire was born.

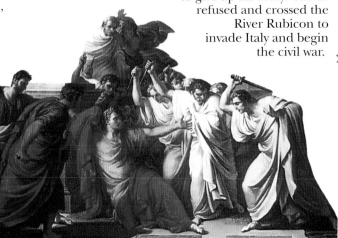

LAUREL CROWN
Victorious Roman military commanders often wore laurel wreaths to symbolize their power. Later, emperors would wear a crown of gold olive leaves after a great victory.

*Find out more*
ITALY, HISTORY OF
ROMAN EMPIRE

# CAMELS AND LLAMAS

A CAMEL IS MORE SUITED TO life in the desert than almost any other beast. With a hump full of fat on its back as a permanent store of fluids, the camel is able to travel great distances without eating or drinking. Then, when food is plentiful, the camel's enormous stomach can hold huge amounts of grass and water. There are two kinds of camels – the dromedary and the Bactrian. The guanaco of South America is closely related to the camel, but it has no hump; other members of the camel family include the alpaca, llama, and vicuna, also from South America. Both camels and llamas have long, sturdy legs and are good runners. They have long necks, and their eyes, ears, and nostrils are set high on the head so they can detect danger from a distance. Camels, llamas, and alpacas have been used as beasts of burden for thousands of years. Most dromedary camels are domesticated and kept for meat and other products; Bactrian camels still live wild in the Gobi Desert, in northern Asia.

Thick fur keeps Bactrian camel warm at night and cool in the day.

Long, curved neck allows camel to reach for food plants.

Wide, padded feet splay out to keep camel from sinking into soft sand.

Long, thick eyelashes protect eyes from scorching sun, freezing frost, and sandstorms.

### SURVIVING A SANDSTORM
In a sandstorm the camel kneels down on its thick kneepads, presses its ears flat, shuts its long-lashed eyes, seals its mouth, and closes its nostrils almost completely. In this way the camel avoids breathing in too much of the sand and dust whipped up by the storm.

## LLAMA
Weighing about 140 kg (300 lb), an average llama is almost 1.2 m (4 ft) tall at the shoulder. Llamas were first domesticated by people more than 4,000 years ago. Cars, lorries, and trains have largely replaced them, but llamas are still used in South America for transport. Both llamas and alpacas are killed for meat and for their hides. These llamas are carrying goods in Peru.

## SHIP OF THE DESERT
Famous for carrying people across the hot lands of North Africa and the Middle East, the camel is often called "the ship of the desert". Camels provide people with milk and meat, and their hair and hides are used to make tents, rugs, and clothes. Camels have tough lips that can grip thorny plant food. They seldom need to drink, but when water is plentiful they can drink 100 litres (about 25 gallons) at one time.

GUANACO
The graceful guanaco shown here lives wild in the foothills of the Andes Mountains, in South America. Vicunas live wild too, higher up on the Andean mountain pastures. The vicuna is an officially protected species, but both vicunas and guanacos are still hunted for their meat, hides, and wool.

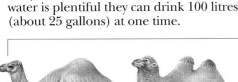

Almost all the 14 million camels in the world are dromedaries.

The Bactrian, or Asian camel, has long, shaggy fur and two humps.

### CAMEL HUMPS
The dromedary or Arabian camel has one hump; the Bactrian or Asian camel has two. An average adult camel is about 2.1 m (7 ft) tall at the hump and weighs approximately 500 kg (1,100 lb).

___
***Find out more***
AFRICA
ANIMALS
DESERT WILDLIFE

# CAMERAS

ALTHOUGH THE FIRST PHOTOGRAPH was taken only about 180 years ago, cameras are much, much older. Hundreds of years ago, the Chinese found that light entering a dark room through a pinhole would project a fuzzy image of the world outside onto the opposite wall. Many years later, in 1500 in Europe, a room like this was called a camera obscura, which is Latin for "darkened room". In the 17th century some artists drew sketches with the aid of a camera obscura which had a lens instead of a pinhole to make the image sharper and brighter. The discovery of chemicals that darkened when exposed to light finally made it possible to fix the image permanently – on paper, on glass plates, or on film. Today, digital cameras use light-sensitive electronic sensors instead of film. Sophisticated electronic technology in most cameras ensures that each picture gets the right amount of light (autoexposure) and is perfectly sharp (autofocus). But all cameras still work on the same basic principle as the camera obscura of old.

Grip sensors shut down LCD displays to conserve power when camera is not being held

Pop-up flash unit

Sensors read metal strips on the film cassette to detect which type of film is being used

Motordrives advance film and reset shutter after each shot

Autofocus zoom lens

Light enters camera

### SINGLE-LENS REFLEX CAMERA
The single-lens reflex (SLR) camera (above) may use either film or a digital sensor. It is popular with photographers for its versatility, and because the viewfinder shows exactly the same view that the camera will record. The lens can be interchanged with others to give a wide view or to magnify the subject.

## KINDS OF CAMERAS
There are many different types of cameras, including film, digital, compact, single-lens reflex, disposable, instant-picture, and large-format cameras. Most film cameras use 35 mm (1.4 in) film. Large-format cameras take huge sheets of film up to 255 mm (10 in) wide. Today, tiny digital cameras are also built into most mobile phone handsets.

### DIGITAL CAMERA
A digital camera captures images electronically rather than on standard film and stores them on removable memory cards. Images can then be transferred to a computer and printed out or sent over the Internet.

Photos stored on the camera's memory card can be viewed on the LCD (liquid crystal display).

### DIGITAL PHOTO PRINTERS
Some digital cameras can be connected directly to printers in order to print out photos, and many printers have slots for memory cards to be inserted. This makes transferring images to a computer unnecessary.

### POLAROID CAMERA
The Polaroid "instant-picture" camera uses slim envelopes of plastic instead of a roll of film. Inside is a sheet of film and a pod of chemicals that bursts to process the picture in just 90 seconds.

### MOVIE CAMERAS
The movement we see in the cinema is an illusion. A movie (cinema) film is really a series of still pictures projected on to the screen in such quick succession that they seem to merge into one another. If the subject is in a slightly different place in each picture it looks as if it is moving. Most movie cameras take 24 pictures, or frames, every second, on a very long strip of film wound steadily through the camera. The film stops while each picture is taken, then advances quickly, ready for the next picture.

### LARGE-FORMAT CAMERA
In early cameras, the lens was focused by moving a bellows – a concertina-like cloth tunnel – in and out. Many photographers still use large-format bellows cameras for high-quality studio work.

---

***Find out more***

FILMS
LIGHT
PHOTOGRAPHY
TELESCOPE
TELEVISION AND VIDEO

---

# ANIMAL
# CAMOUFLAGE

A BUTTERFLY that looks like a flower, a bird that resembles a log, a fish that seems as lifeless as a stone – many animals and plants survive by blending in with their surroundings. This is called camouflage. Camouflage includes colour, shape, and patterning. For example, it is difficult to spy a newborn deer among the trees because of its pale brown colour and speckled coat. A dead-leaf mantis is also difficult to see because of its leaf shape, and a chameleon can change its colour to match the colour of its surroundings. Camouflage helps animals hide from predators. It also helps predators such as tigers and leopards ambush their prey without being seen. Some animals such as rabbits camouflage themselves by staying absolutely still when in danger so their movements do not give them away.

Chameleon quickly changes colour to brown when it moves onto a leafless branch.

Chameleon matches the green colouring of its leafy branch.

## ARCTIC HARE
The Arctic hare is brown in summer to match its surroundings of soil and shrubs. In autumn it sheds its fur and grows a new white coat, for camouflage in the winter snow. The Arctic fox preys on the Arctic hare. In winter the Arctic fox also has a white coat for camouflage.

## CHAMELEON
The chameleon is famous for changing its colour and pattern to match its surroundings. Its colour alters when cells in the skin change size, moving their grains of colour nearer the surface or deeper into the skin. When the Jackson's chameleon shown here was taken off its branch, its colour changed from green and yellow to mottled brown. But it took the chameleon about five minutes to do so.

### STICK INSECT
The spindly stick insect is very difficult to recognize among twigs and branches because of its shape and colour. It can fold its thin legs alongside its body and look even more like a twig. When danger threatens, it stays absolutely still – like a stick.

### TIGER STRIPES
The tiger is camouflaged by its stripes, which match the light and dark patterns of sunlit grasses. The tiger hunts mainly by ambush, creeping stealthily towards its prey in the undergrowth, then charging over the last few metres.

> ### Find out more
> ANIMALS
> BIRDS
> FISH
> INSECTS
> LIONS, TIGERS, and other big cats
> RABBITS AND HARES

# CANADA

THE SECOND LARGEST COUNTRY in the world is also one of the emptiest. Much of Canada is virtually uninhabited. The northern part of the country is a hostile wasteland of snow and ice for much of the year. Few people live among the high Rocky Mountains in the west. Even in the huge wheat-growing plains in the centre there are few people. The majority of Canada's 31.5 million inhabitants live in the southeast, close to the border with the United States. Most Canadians speak English, but for some, particularly those in the province of Québec, French is the first language. This is because they are descendants of the French who settled in Canada in the 16th century. The languages of the native North American and Inuit inhabitants are rarely heard today. Much of Canada's trade is with its neighbour, the United States. However, Canada has close links with many European, Asian, and African nations.

Canada occupies the northern half of North America, stretching from the Pacific to the Atlantic oceans. Part of the country lies within the Arctic Circle. At 6,416 km (3,987 miles) the Canadian-US border is the world's longest continuous frontier between two nations.

## TORONTO

More than four million people live in the city of Toronto. It is Canada's business centre and capital of the province of Ontario. Toronto has many skyscrapers, including the 553 m (1,815 ft) high Canadian National Tower.

*Maple syrup is obtained by cutting into the maple tree and directing the flow of its sap into a collecting vessel.*

## SPORTS AND LEISURE

Winter sports such as skiing, skating, and ice hockey are popular in Canada because winters are long and there is plenty of snow and ice. Modern ice hockey was invented in Canada in the 1870s and is now played nearly everywhere in the world. During the summer, sailing, canoeing, and field hockey are also popular.

*Ice hockey is the Canadian national sport. The country produces some of the best players in the world.*

## ROCKY MOUNTAINS

Western Canada is dominated by the Rocky Mountains, which stretch from the United States border in the south to Alaska in the north. The mountains are covered in trees and are a haven for bears and other wildlife.

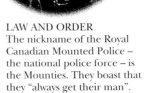

### LAW AND ORDER

The nickname of the Royal Canadian Mounted Police – the national police force – is the Mounties. They boast that they "always get their man".

## NATURAL RESOURCES

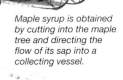

Canada is rich in minerals such as zinc and iron ore and has huge reserves of oil, coal, and natural gas. Just off Canada's east coast lies the Grand Banks, one of the world's richest fishing areas. Waters within 320 km (200 miles) of Canada's coastline are reserved for Canadian fishermen only. The vast forests that grow across the country are a major source of timber. The country's exports are mainly sent south to the United States; the two countries have formed a free-trade zone, which means that exports or imports between them are not taxed.

**PROVINCES** showing date of joining the Confederation of Canada

**ALBERTA** 1905
**Area:** 661,190 sq km (255,286 sq miles)
**Population:** 3,223,400
**Capital:** Edmonton

**BRITISH COLUMBIA** 1871
**Area:** 947,800 sq km (365,946 sq miles)
**Population:** 4,220,000
**Capital:** Victoria

**MANITOBA** 1870
**Area:** 649,950 sq km (250,946 sq miles)
**Population:** 1,174,600
**Capital:** Winnipeg

**NEW BRUNSWICK** 1867
**Area:** 73,440 sq km (28,355 sq miles)
**Population:** 751,300
**Capital:** Fredericton

**NEWFOUNDLAND AND LABRADOR** 1949
**Area:** 404,720 sq km (156,649 sq miles)
**Population:** 517,000
**Capital:** St. John's

**NOVA SCOTIA** 1867
**Area:** 55,490 sq km (21,425 sq miles)
**Population:** 937,500
**Capital:** Halifax

**ONTARIO** 1867
**Area:** 1,068,630 sq km (412,298 sq miles)
**Population:** 12,449,500
**Capital:** Toronto

**PRINCE EDWARD ISLAND** 1873
**Area:** 5,660 sq km (2,185 sq miles)
**Population:** 137,700
**Capital:** Charlottetown

**QUÉBEC** 1867
**Area:** 1,540,680 sq km (594,857 sq miles)
**Population:** 7,568,600
**Capital:** Quebec

**SASKATCHEWAN** 1905
**Area:** 652,330 sq km (251,865 sq miles)
**Population:** 995,300
**Capital:** Regina

**TERRITORIES** showing date of joining the Confederation of Canada

**NORTHWEST TERRITORIES** 1870
**Area:** 1,346,106 sq km (519,734 sq miles)
**Population:** 42,900
**Capital:** Yellowknife

**NUNAVUT** 1999
**Area:** 2,093,190 sq km (808,185 sq miles)
**Population:** 29,700
**Capital:** Iqaluit

**YUKON TERRITORY** 1898
**Area:** 483,450 sq km (186,660 sq miles)
**Population:** 31,200
**Capital:** Whitehorse

*In Québec, winding streets connect the Lower Town sector on the waterfront and Upper Town on Cape Diamond, a bluff rising 91 m (300 ft) above the St. Lawrence.*

## QUÉBEC

The city of Québec (above) is the oldest city in Canada and the capital of the province of Québec. The French style of its buildings reminds the visitor that many of the city's first colonists came from France. Québec city was founded in 1608 by the French explorer Samuel de Champlain, and Québec itself remained a French colony until the British took it over in 1759. Today Québec is the centre of French Canadian culture. French is still the official language, and most of the population is Roman Catholic. The Québecois, the people of Québec, see themselves as different from other Canadians, and over the years many of them have campaigned for independence.

*This observation deck has a 360-degree view of Vancouver. It is perched on top of Harbour Centre Tower.*

**VANCOUVER**
Vancouver is Canada's leading Pacific port. Situated in southwestern British Columbia, Vancouver overlooks the Strait of Georgia and is surrounded by mountains. The city's many landmarks date from the 1880s and span architectural styles from Renaissance and Art Deco to Modern and Post Modern.

## YUKON TERRITORY

Few people live in the Yukon Territory in northwestern Canada but the region is rich in silver, zinc, lead, and gold. During the 1890s it was the site of the Klondike gold rush. Prospectors and adventurers who came to the Yukon hoping to strike gold founded Whitehorse, which became the territorial capital in 1952. Winters in the Yukon are long and cold, but in summer the weather becomes warm, with temperatures reaching 16°C (60°F). This allows the growth of many kinds of vegetation, which take on a rich variety of colours in the autumn. Moose, caribou, beavers, and bears are common in the Yukon.

---

*Find out more*

CANADA, HISTORY OF
INUIT
MOUNTAINS
NATIVE AMERICANS
SPORT

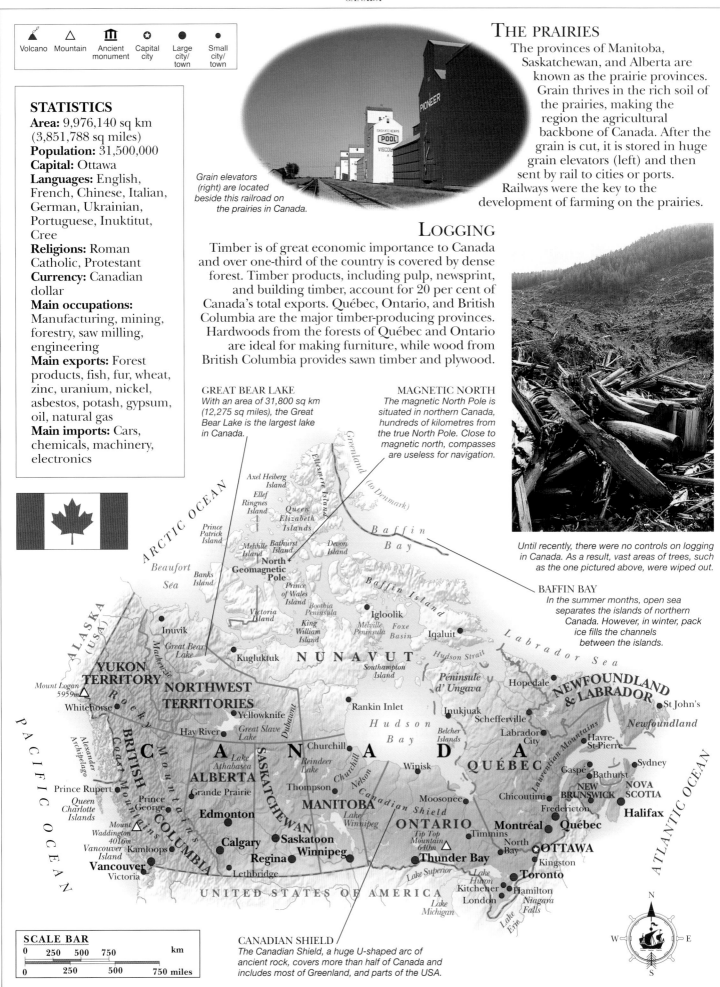

## STATISTICS
**Area:** 9,976,140 sq km (3,851,788 sq miles)
**Population:** 31,500,000
**Capital:** Ottawa
**Languages:** English, French, Chinese, Italian, German, Ukrainian, Portuguese, Inuktitut, Cree
**Religions:** Roman Catholic, Protestant
**Currency:** Canadian dollar
**Main occupations:** Manufacturing, mining, forestry, saw milling, engineering
**Main exports:** Forest products, fish, fur, wheat, zinc, uranium, nickel, asbestos, potash, gypsum, oil, natural gas
**Main imports:** Cars, chemicals, machinery, electronics

## THE PRAIRIES
The provinces of Manitoba, Saskatchewan, and Alberta are known as the prairie provinces. Grain thrives in the rich soil of the prairies, making the region the agricultural backbone of Canada. After the grain is cut, it is stored in huge grain elevators (left) and then sent by rail to cities or ports. Railways were the key to the development of farming on the prairies.

*Grain elevators (right) are located beside this railroad on the prairies in Canada.*

## LOGGING
Timber is of great economic importance to Canada and over one-third of the country is covered by dense forest. Timber products, including pulp, newsprint, and building timber, account for 20 per cent of Canada's total exports. Québec, Ontario, and British Columbia are the major timber-producing provinces. Hardwoods from the forests of Québec and Ontario are ideal for making furniture, while wood from British Columbia provides sawn timber and plywood.

*Until recently, there were no controls on logging in Canada. As a result, vast areas of trees, such as the one pictured above, were wiped out.*

**GREAT BEAR LAKE**
*With an area of 31,800 sq km (12,275 sq miles), the Great Bear Lake is the largest lake in Canada.*

**MAGNETIC NORTH**
*The magnetic North Pole is situated in northern Canada, hundreds of kilometres from the true North Pole. Close to magnetic north, compasses are useless for navigation.*

**BAFFIN BAY**
*In the summer months, open sea separates the islands of northern Canada. However, in winter, pack ice fills the channels between the islands.*

**CANADIAN SHIELD**
*The Canadian Shield, a huge U-shaped arc of ancient rock, covers more than half of Canada and includes most of Greenland, and parts of the USA.*

**SCALE BAR**

# HISTORY OF
# CANADA

*Canada's most popular emblem is the leaf of the local tree, the red maple.*

ABOUT TWENTY-FIVE THOUSAND YEARS AGO Canada's first people walked across the land that then existed between Siberia and Alaska. Fishing people from Europe began to explore the rich coast of Canada about 1,000 years ago, and the original Native American inhabitants of the country lost control when British and French settlers began to establish trading posts for fur during the 17th century. Britain and France fought each other for the land, and in 1759 Britain won control of the whole country. A century later, Canada became independent of British rule but remained a British dominion (territory). After World War II, Canada became very prosperous and developed a close business relationship with the United States. During the 1970s French Canadians demanded more power and threatened to make the province of Quebec independent. However, Canada is still united.

*Native Americans were the first inhabitants of Canada.*

*Snowshoes*

*Wood cabin*

*European traders exchanged goods with Native Americans who trapped wild animals for their furs.*

*Traders travelled by canoe to trading posts. Transport by canoe also opened the way to missionaries and explorers in Canada.*

## HUDSON'S BAY COMPANY

Both the British and French set up companies in the 17th century to trade in valuable Canadian furs. These companies grew wealthy and powerful and acted like independent governments. The British Hudson's Bay Company ruled much of northern Canada until 1869 when its lands were made part of the Dominion of Canada.

### PIERRE TRUDEAU

Since the 1960s Canada has become increasingly independent of Britain. A new flag was adopted in 1965 and two years later a world fair – Expo '67 – was held to show off Canadian skills in the centenary year of independence. In 1968 Pierre Trudeau (right) was elected as prime minister. A great intellectual, he was a strong supporter of a unified Canada.

## CABOT AND CARTIER

The Italian explorer John Cabot, sailing for England, was the first European, after the Vikings, to visit Canada when he sailed along the coast of Newfoundland in 1497. The French explorer Jacques Cartier sailed up the mouth of the St. Lawrence River in 1534. Following these two voyages, both Britain and France laid claim to Canada.

*John Cabot*

**Yukon Territory**

**Northwest Territories**   **Nunavut**

**British Columbia**

**Alberta**   **Manitoba**

**Saskatchewan**

**Ontario (formerly Upper Canada)**

**Newfoundland and Labrador**

**CANADA IN 1867**

*Prince Edward I.*

*Nova Scotia*

*New Brunswick*

**Quebec (formerly Lower Canada)**

### DOMINION

In 1867, the four British colonies of Nova Scotia, New Brunswick, and Upper and Lower Canada formed the self-governing Dominion of Canada. Six more colonies joined after 1867. Newfoundland joined in 1949 and Nunavut was created in 1999.

---

*Find out more*

CANADA
COOK, JAMES
INUITS
NATIVE AMERICANS
VIKINGS

# CARIBBEAN

The Caribbean Sea is about 1,943,000 sq km (750,193 sq miles) in area. It is enclosed on three sides by Central America, South America, and the Caribbean Islands.

STRUNG OUT LIKE a rope of pearls, there is a long row of tropical islands curving for more than 3,200 km (2,000 miles) between Mexico and Venezuela. Together they are usually called the Caribbean islands, sometimes the West Indies. Some are tiny, uninhabited rocks or coral reefs; others are much larger islands with thriving populations. On Martinique for instance, 432,900 people live around the wooded slopes of several volcanoes which tower hundreds of metres above the sea. There are 13 countries and 12 other territories in the Caribbean. Cuba, with a population of 11.3 million people, is the biggest nation. Although each country has its own distinctive culture, many have connections with other countries. These links are left over from the 18th and 19th centuries, when the whole region was colonized by European kingdoms. The ruling nations brought African slaves to the Caribbean to harvest sugar cane. Today, descendants of these slaves make up a large proportion of the population.

### TOURISM
The Caribbean islands are very beautiful, with lush trees, colourful birds, long sandy beaches, and months of sunshine. The region attracts tourists from all over the world. This has created many new jobs, particularly in the towns. Tourism is now the main source of income for several islands.

### CRICKET
Cricket is a reminder of the Caribbean's colonial past. It is played, and passionately supported, in many of the former British colonies. For international test matches, the Caribbean islands join forces and compete as the West Indies. The West Indies were victorious in the cricket World Cup in 1975 and 1979.

*Brian Lara (right) plays cricket for the West Indies. With 400 runs, he holds the world record for the highest test match score.*

### AGRICULTURE
More than half the people of the Caribbean earn a living from agriculture. Many work for a landowner, producing crops such as sugar and coffee. They may also rent or own a small plot of land. On this land they grow food to feed their families or to sell in local markets.

### BASTILLE DAY
The islands of Guadeloupe and Martinique are part of France and the people have strong links with this country. They speak the French language, use the French franc for money, fly the French flag, and celebrate French holidays such as Bastille Day. Other Caribbean islands have close political and financial links with Britain, the Netherlands, or the United States.

### ARCHITECTURE
Brilliant colours enhance the traditional shapes of Caribbean architecture. Similarly, Caribbean music, literature, art, and food are a unique mixture of European and African culture.

### Find out more
CENTRAL AMERICA
COLUMBUS, CHRISTOPHER
CRICKET
SLAVERY

| Volcano | Mountain | Ancient monument | Capital city | Large city/town | Small city/town |
|---------|----------|------------------|--------------|-----------------|------------------|

 **ANGUILLA**
**Area:** 91 sq km
(35 sq miles)
**Status:** British dependent territory
**Claimed:** 1650
**Population:** 12,700
**Capital:** The Valley

 **ANTIGUA AND BARBUDA**
**Area:** 440 sq km (170 sq miles)
**Population:** 67,900
**Capital:** St. John's

 **ARUBA**
**Area:** 193 sq km
(75 sq miles)
**Status:** Dutch autonomous region
**Claimed:** 1643
**Population:** 70,800
**Capital:** Oranjestad

**BAHAMAS**
**Area:** 13,935 sq km
(5,380 sq miles)
**Population:** 314,000
**Capital:** Nassau

 **BARBADOS**
**Area:** 431 sq km
(166 sq miles)
**Population:** 270,000
**Capital:** Bridgetown

 **CAYMAN ISLANDS**
**Area:** 259 sq km (100 sq miles)
**Status:** British dependent territory
**Claimed:** 1670
**Population:** 41,900
**Capital:** George Town

 **CUBA**
**Area:** 114,524 sq km
(44,218 sq miles)
**Population:** 11,300,000
**Capital:** Havana

 **DOMINICA**
**Area:** 751 sq km
(290 sq miles)
**Population:** 69,700
**Capital:** Roseau

 **DOMINICAN REPUBLIC**
**Area:** 48,442 sq km
(18,704 sq miles)
**Population:** 8,700,000
**Capital:** Santo Domingo

**GRENADA**
**Area:** 344 sq km
(133 sq miles)
**Population:** 89,300
**Capital:** Saint George's

 **GUADELOUPE**
**Area:** 1,779 sq km
(687 sq miles)
**Status:** French overseas department
**Claimed:** 1635
**Population:** 440,000
**Capital:** Basse-Terre

 **HAITI**
**Area:** 27,750 sq km
(10,714 sq miles)
**Population:** 8,300,000
**Capital:** Port-au-Prince

 **JAMAICA**
**Area:** 10,991 sq km
(4,244 sq miles)
**Population:** 2,700,000
**Capital:** Kingston

 **MARTINIQUE**
**Area:** 1,101 sq km
(425 sq miles)
**Status:** French overseas department
**Claimed:** 1635
**Population:** 393,000
**Capital:** Fort-de-France

 **MONTSERRAT**
**Area:** 101 sq km
(38 sq miles)
**Status:** British dependent territory
**Claimed:** 1632
**Population:** 9,000
**Capital:** Plymouth

**NETHERLANDS ANTILLES**
**Area:** 992 sq km (385 sq miles)
**Status:** Dutch autonomous region
**Claimed:** 1816
**Population:** 221,000
**Capital:** Willemstad

 **PUERTO RICO**
**Area:** 8,897 sq km
(3,435 sq miles)
**Status:** US commonwealth territory
**Claimed:** 1898
**Population:** 3,890,000
**Capital:** San Juan

 **ST. KITTS AND NEVIS**
**Area:** 269 sq km
(104 sq miles)
**Population:** 38,800
**Capital:** Basseterre

 **ST. LUCIA**
**Area:** 616 sq km
(238 sq miles)
**Population:** 162,100
**Capital:** Castries

 **ST. VINCENT AND THE GRENADINES**
**Area:** 388 sq km (150 sq miles)
**Population:** 116,800
**Capital:** Kingstown

 **TRINIDAD AND TOBAGO**
**Area:** 5,128 sq km (1,980 sq miles)
**Population:** 1,300,000
**Capital:** Port-of-Spain

 **TURKS AND CAICOS ISLANDS**
**Area:** 500 sq km (193 sq miles)
**Status:** British dependent territory
**Claimed:** 1766
**Population:** 19,400
**Capital:** Cockburn Town

**VIRGIN ISLANDS**
**Area:** 352 sq km
(136 sq miles)
**Status:** US unincorporated territory
**Claimed:** 1917
**Population:** 124,800
**Capital:** Charlotte Amalie

 **VIRGIN ISLANDS, BRITISH**
**Area:** 153 sq km (59 sq miles)
**Status:** British dependent territory
**Claimed:** 1672
**Population:** 21,700
**Capital:** Road Town

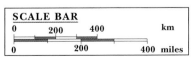

**SCALE BAR**

| 0 | 200 | 400 | km |
|---|-----|-----|-----|

| 0 | 200 | 400 | miles |
|---|-----|-----|-----|

## ISLAND GROUPS

The larger islands of the Caribbean between Cuba and Puerto Rico are often called the Greater Antilles, to distinguish them from the Lesser Antilles to the east. The small islands from the Virgin Islands to Dominica are sometimes called the Leeward Islands; and the islands to the south (Martinique to Grenada), the Windward Islands.

# HISTORY OF THE
# CARIBBEAN

FOR CENTURIES THE BEAUTIFUL Caribbean islands were home to Arawak and Carib peoples, who may have originated in South America. Skillful navigators, they established settlements and lived by farming and fishing. In 1492, the European explorer Christopher Columbus arrived in the Caribbean. Others followed, leading to 500 years of European domination, as first the Spanish, and then the British, French, and Dutch fought for control of the islands. The Europeans enslaved, or killed the native populations, and brought Africans in slave ships to work on sugar plantations. During the 20th century, many islands won their independence from Europe. Today, many of the Caribbean islands depend on a single crop, such as sugar or bananas.

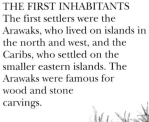

**THE FIRST INHABITANTS**
The first settlers were the Arawaks, who lived on islands in the north and west, and the Caribs, who settled on the smaller eastern islands. The Arawaks were famous for wood and stone carvings.

Sugar cane

Thousands of Africans were imported into the Caribbean as slaves.

## SLAVERY
When the Spanish conquered the Caribbean in the early 1500s, they enslaved the local people, and forced them to work on sugar, fruit, spice, and coffee plantations. As these slaves died, more were shipped over from Africa. Britain was the main slave-trading nation. British ships took slaves across the Atlantic, and carried sugar and other crops back to Europe.

RASTAFARIANISM
Many people on Jamaica and other Caribbean islands are Rastafarians. They believe black people will eventually return to Africa to achieve their freedom. Rastafarians take their name from Prince Ras Tafari, better known as Haile Selassie. The emperor of Ethiopia from 1930-74, he was the only African ruler to keep his country independent of European control.

**THE CARIBBEAN**

**1492** Christopher Columbus lands in the Bahamas.

**1500s** Spain takes control of the Caribbean.

**1700s** British, French, Dutch, and Danes take over many of the islands.

**1804** Haiti becomes the first independent black nation in the Caribbean.

**1834** Slaves freed as slavery abolished in British Empire.

**1898** Cuba wins independence from Spain.

**1962** Jamaica and Trinidad and Tobago gain independence from Britain.

**1983** USA overthrows left-wing regime in Grenada.

**1994** US-led invasion overthrows dictatorship in Haiti.

## INDEPENDENCE
In 1962, both Jamaica and Trinidad and Tobago gained independence from Britain. Over the next 20 years, eight more British colonies became independent. However, some of the Caribbean still remains under American, Dutch, or French rule.

There was much cause for celebration when Jamaica finally won independence.

CUBA
In 1959, Fidel Castro (b. 1927) overthrew Cuba's corrupt government, and set up a Communist regime. He reformed the country, providing free education and health care for all, but nearly caused a nuclear war in 1962 when the USA objected to the placing of Russian missiles on the island.

*Find out more*
BRITISH EMPIRE
CARIBBEAN
COLUMBUS, CHRISTOPHER
EMIGRATION AND IMMIGRATION
SLAVERY

# CARS

IF YOU COULD line up all the world's cars end to end, they would form a traffic jam stretching all the way to the moon; and the line is getting longer, because a new car is made every second. Most cars are family cars, used for trips to school, work, and shops, to see friends and take holidays. But there are also a number of special-purpose cars, including taxis, sports cars, police patrol cars, and ambulances.

Petrol or diesel engines power modern cars, just as they did the first cars of the 19th century. But the cars of today are very different from cars even 30 years ago. The latest cars have low, sleek shapes that are attractive and also reduce drag, or air resistance. Other features include powerful brakes for stopping quickly and electronic engine control systems that allow cars to travel faster and use less fuel.

## HOW A CAR WORKS
In most cars, the engine is at the front and drives the back or front wheels (or all four wheels) through a series of shafts and gears. There are usually four or five different gears; they alter the speed at which the engine turns the wheels. In low gear, the wheels turn slowly and produce extra force for starting and climbing hills. In high gear, the wheels turn fast for travelling at speed.

A car radiator is full of water. A pump keeps water flowing around the engine to keep it cool. As the car moves forward, cold air rushes through the radiator, cooling the water before its next circuit around the engine.

The steering wheel turns the steering gear via a long shaft.

Tread, or grooves on the tyres, improve traction (grip) in the rain.

This car has a manual gearbox, which means the driver uses the gear lever to change gear. In some cars, gear changes are automatic.

Turning the steering wheel inside the car turns a system of gears that point the front wheels towards the left or right.

Suspension springs and shock absorbers soften a bumpy ride for the passengers and keep the wheels firmly on the ground as the car travels over uneven surfaces.

Pressing on the brake pedal pushes a special liquid down tubes, which in turn push on pistons at each wheel. These pistons squeeze the brake pads against steel discs or drums attached to the wheels, slowing down the wheels and stopping the car.

## ANTI-POLLUTION DEVICE
Waste gases from the engine of a car are highly toxic (poisonous). To keep them under control some cars have special filters, called catalytic converters, fitted to the exhaust system. These filters remove poisonous gases.

## TYPES OF CARS
Cars have numerous uses, and there are many different kinds of cars available to suit almost any task. Most family cars combine a large interior with speed and fuel economy. However, for other, more specialized vehicles, speed, luxury, or power may be the most important design feature.

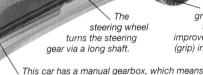

### SPORTS CAR
With its large engine, sleek design, and usually seating for only two people, a sports car is designed purely for speed. Some can travel at about 300 km/h (200 mph).

## CRASH PROTECTION
Driver and passengers are cocooned in a strong steel cage to protect them in a crash. But the rest of the car is designed to crumple easily and absorb some of the impact. Wearing seat belts can protect car passengers from injury in a crash.

### LUXURY CAR
Large, carefully crafted cars such as the world-famous Rolls-Royce are among the most beautiful and expensive automobiles in the world.

### OFF-ROAD VEHICLE
Rugged vehicles built specially for driving across country have powerful engines, four-wheel drive, and heavy ridged tyres for extra grip.

# HISTORY OF THE CAR

People laughed at the first rickety "horseless carriages" of the 1880s. But rapid technical progress soon made it clear that cars were here to stay. In 1903, cars could already reach speeds of more than 110 km/h (70 mph). But they were expensive and often broke down. Since then cars have become steadily cheaper and more reliable. Now they are everyday transport for millions of people throughout the world.

## NICOLAS CUGNOT

The first road vehicles were powered by steam. In 1769, Nicolas Cugnot, a French soldier, built a steam carriage for dragging cannon. It travelled about 5 km/h (3 mph) and had to stop about every 10 minutes to build up steam.

## DAIMLER AND BENZ

In the 1880s, German engineers Karl Benz and Gottlieb Daimler worked independently to produce the first petrol engine. In 1885, Karl Benz built his flimsy motorized tricycle (left), the first petrol-powered car.

## PANHARD AND LEVASSOR

In the 1890s, two Frenchmen, René Panhard and Emile Levassor, built the first car with the engine in the front, the arrangement found in most cars to this day.

*The production line for the Ford Model T*

## FORD MODEL T

Early cars were handmade and cost so much money that only the rich could afford them. In 1908, Henry Ford opened a factory to produce large numbers of the Model T (above). This was the first car cheap enough to be purchased by more people.

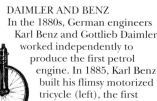

*Rear airfoil*

*Wide tyres, called slicks, are smooth to minimize rolling resistance, but wide to give a good grip on the track.*

*Powerful disc brakes can slow the car from 300 km/h to 65 km/h (200 mph to 40 mph) in less than three seconds.*

*The light aluminium body is carefully shaped to keep drag to a minimum.*

*The frame is made from ultra-light carbon-fibre composites.*

## NEW DESIGNS

Prototypes (test models) of new cars are packed with electronics and computers that can do anything from parking the car automatically to finding the best route through town. Many parts of these cars are made from plastics and other new materials; some new engine designs contain ceramic components instead of metal ones.

*Enormously powerful engine with 8 or 10 cylinders drives the car along at speeds up to about 400 km/h (250 mph).*

*A computer continually adjusts the suspension to make sure the wheels do not bounce up from the track.*

*Aerofoils at the front and back work like upside-down aeroplane wings. Air rushing over them pushes the car firmly onto the track, which improves traction.*

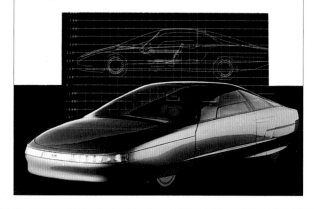

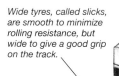

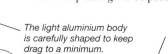

## RACING CAR

Grand Prix racing cars are designed for speed alone, so they are built very differently from road cars. They have big, powerful engines and are made of special light materials. Their ultra-low shape allows them to slice through the air easily so they can travel as fast as possible. Indeed, the driver has to lie almost flat to fit in.

*Find out more*
BUSES
ENGINES
POLLUTION
ROADS AND MOTORWAYS
TRANSPORT, HISTORY OF
TRUCKS AND LORRIES
WHEELS

# CARTOONS

T UMBLING AND SPINNING on the TV screen, cartoon characters make impossible feats look easy. But the process of creating a cartoon is slow and requires great patience. An artist must make 12 drawings of the figure to produce just one second of movement. This kind of film, called an animated cartoon, first appeared on the cinema screen about 100 years ago. But it was the American Walt Disney who made cartoons famous. In 1937 he produced his first feature-length film, *Snow White and the Seven Dwarfs*. Today, animated films can be created using computers as well as by traditional methods. An animated film is just one example of a cartoon. Originally, the word meant the paper pattern an artist made for a painting; today a cartoon usually means a funny drawing. Political cartoons criticize politicians and other public figures, and the imaginary characters in comic strip cartoons help us laugh at ourselves when life gets us down.

The background picture stays the same throughout the movement.

The cels are put in order onto a peg bar.

Each picture is coloured in on the back of the cel.

Registration holes at the bottom of each cel keep the image straight.

## CARTOON FILM
Nine separate drawings follow each other rapidly to create a smooth-flowing sequence of a boy pulling his sweater over his head.

## ANIMATION
To make an animated film, artists draw each stage of every movement on clear plastic pages called cels. The background is painted on a separate cel, and shows through the clear cels. Photographing the cels in the correct sequence makes the figures move. Artists may produce a million drawings for one feature-length film.

### COMPUTER ANIMATION
Animators can now create whole films entirely on computer. Computer-generated cartoons work on the same principle as traditional animation, except the images are created in 3D using computer software instead of being drawn on cels. Advances in technology mean that computer animation can be very lifelike. The Incredibles (2004) won an Oscar for its animation.

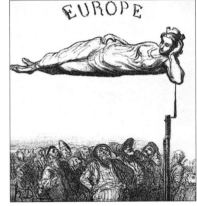

## HISTORICAL CARTOONS
Cartoons can help politicians attack their opponents. Daumier, a 19th-century French artist, was a harsh critic of the French government. In this cartoon Daumier balanced a figure representing Europe on the tip of a bayonet, to show how unstable European politics had become.

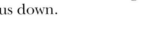

## COMIC STRIP
The comic strip tells a story in a series of pictures. Sometimes the meaning is clear from the pictures alone; sometimes speech balloons put words in the characters' mouths. Characters such as Snoopy (above) and Superman have amused generations of children, and many adults follow their adventures.

*Find out more*
DRAWING
FILMS
MAGAZINES
NEWSPAPERS

# CASTLES

THE MASSIVE WALLS AND TOWERS of a castle were designed to make it impossible for enemy soldiers to destroy it. Inside was a whole world in miniature – lords and ladies, government officials, soldiers, servants, animals, gardens, treasure stores, and dungeons where prisoners could be tortured. The best site for a castle was on a hill surrounded by water. If there were no natural features, the builders made an artificial hill or dug a deep ditch and filled it with water to make a moat. A well-built castle with a good military commander in charge could withstand an enemy siege for many months. Most castles were built between the 9th century and the 16th century, when many countries were almost constantly at war. Early castles were small and made of wood; the later stone buildings housed town-sized populations; many are still standing today. The invention of gunpowder at the end of the 13th century made castles hard to defend. As times grew more peaceful, kings and lords moved into comfortable country houses.

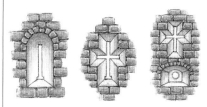

**LOOPHOLES**
Archers fired through loopholes – narrow slits in the walls which were wider on the inside to make aiming easier. The inner walls were often higher than the outer walls, so archers could fire at the attackers over the heads of their own soldiers.

Siege engines had to be tall enough for attackers to fire down on castle soldiers.

Sandbags protected the attacking archers.

Towers which stuck out from the walls gave archers a clear view of the attackers trying to climb the walls.

Even if the attackers built a bridge across a moat, they could be stopped by boiling water or hot sand dropped on them from above.

## DEFENDING A CASTLE

During a siege, attackers tried to climb over the walls, smash them down with siege engines, or starve out the inhabitants. The defenders used archers with bows and arrows to keep attackers away from the walls. If the archers failed, soldiers pushed the attackers' scaling ladders away with poles and poured tubs full of boiling water or hot sand onto the enemy below. Deep moats or solid rock foundations stopped the attackers from digging under the walls. In peacetime, the knights and soldiers of the castle trained for war by jousting and playing war games in elaborate tournaments.

Attackers used a battering ram to break down drawbridge.

Deep moats surrounded castle walls.

# HOW CASTLES DEVELOPED

International wars, especially the Crusades in the Middle East, led to bigger armies, more powerful weapons, and stronger, more sophisticated defences. These wars speeded up castle building.

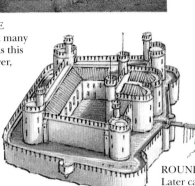

### NORMAN CASTLE
The Normans built many stone castles such as this one (above) at Dover, England, between the 11th and 13th centuries.

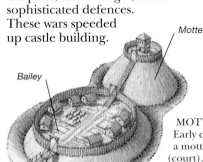

Motte

Bailey

### MOTTE AND BAILEY
Early castles were built as a motte (hill) and bailey (court). They were made of wood and burned easily.

"Fairy tale" turret

### SPANISH CASTLE
Some castles, such as the Alcázar in Segovia, Spain, became magnificent royal palaces.

### ROUND TOWERS
Later castles had round towers. Rocks bounced off the curved surface and did less damage.

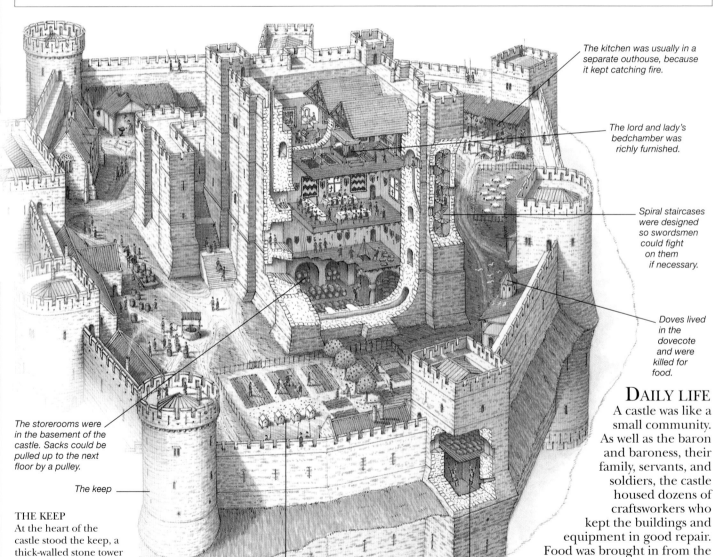

The kitchen was usually in a separate outhouse, because it kept catching fire.

The lord and lady's bedchamber was richly furnished.

Spiral staircases were designed so swordsmen could fight on them if necessary.

Doves lived in the dovecote and were killed for food.

The storerooms were in the basement of the castle. Sacks could be pulled up to the next floor by a pulley.

The keep

### THE KEEP
At the heart of the castle stood the keep, a thick-walled stone tower several storeys high. This was the last refuge in a siege, but in peacetime it was also home to the lord's family and followers.
The entrance to the keep was always on the first floor, through the guardroom. Above this was a great hall for feasting, and sometimes sleeping. The lord's own rooms were on the top floor.

Bees were kept to provide honey, and herbs were grown for medicinal purposes.

Prisoners were kept in chains in the dungeons.

## DAILY LIFE
A castle was like a small community. As well as the baron and baroness, their family, servants, and soldiers, the castle housed dozens of craftsworkers who kept the buildings and equipment in good repair. Food was brought in from the surrounding countryside or grown in the castle garden.

*Find out more*

CRUSADES
KNIGHTS AND HERALDRY
MEDIEVAL EUROPE
NORMANS

# CATS

WHEN YOU WATCH a cat stalking a bird, it is easy to see how cats are related to lions and tigers. All cats are excellent hunters. They have acute senses and sharp teeth and claws, and they are strong and agile. Cats do most of their hunting at night, and have evolved excellent eyesight in dim conditions. Even a domestic cat, or house cat, could survive in the wild by catching mice, small birds, insects, and other creatures. Many exotic pedigree (purebred) cats, however, might not be able to live for long in the wild, since most are used to a pampered lifestyle indoors.

    The ancestor of our domestic cats is a wild tabby-coloured cat – the African wild cat – that has existed for about one million years. This small wild cat spread through Africa, Asia, and Europe, until it was gradually tamed by people in Africa, where it helped protect food stores from rats and mice. Since then, domestic cats have been bred by people into many different types, from striped tabbies and Persian longhairs to the tailless Manx cat. Three thousand years ago, domestic cats were a common sight in Egypt, where they were held in great esteem. Today there are more than 500 million domestic cats around the world.

**WILD CATS**
The wild cat looks similar to the domestic tabby cat, but it has a heavier build and a larger head. Wild cats have black stripes on their legs and tail.

**AGILITY**
Cats have exceptional balance and often climb trees, walls, and fences when they are hunting or exploring. Cats also have extremely quick reflexes in case of a fall. As a cat drops, the balance organs inside its ears tell it at once which way is up. The cat rights its head, followed by its body, then lands safely on all four paws.

*Cat suddenly falls.*

*Head twists around first.*

*Body follows head around.*

*Legs stretch out for landing.*

**BLACK CATS**
For thousands of years, black cats have been associated with magic and witchcraft. They are still believed by some people to bring both good and bad luck.

*Long flexible tail helps cat balance on narrow ledges.*

*Large ears can pick up faint sounds.*

*Touch-sensitive whiskers for feeling in the dark*

*Claws retracted in sheaths to keep them sharp*

*Pupils open wide in dim light to let in more light.*

*Pupils are narrow in bright light to let in less light.*

**EYES**
In dim conditions, a cat's pupils open wide to let the maximum amount of light into the eye. The tapetum lucidum, a mirror-like layer inside the eye, reflects the light at the back of the eye. This is why a cat's eyes shine in the dark.

## DOMESTIC CAT
There are more than 100 official breeds of domestic cat, and many more unofficial breeds. Cat experts are continually creating new varieties by selective breeding. The Bombay cat (left) is a new breed which was developed in the United States in the 1970s. It was bred by mating a Burmese with an American Black Shorthair. Although the Bombay has very short, dense hair, it still shows all the main features of a typical cat.

# KITTENS

Young cats are called kittens. They spend hours chasing their tails, springing on each other, and having mock fights. Their play has a serious purpose. It helps them develop hunting skills, quick reactions, and strength and suppleness for those times when they have to fend for themselves.

## GROOMING
Cats are famous for their cleanliness. Every day they spend at least an hour washing their fur with saliva and licking it with their rough-surfaced tongues. This makes the fur smooth and glossy. It also helps keep body heat in, removes pests, and stimulates the skin's blood flow.

## SLEEPING
The average cat sleeps 16 hours each day, usually in short intervals called cat naps. A cat's body is designed for quick bursts of action, with much rest between.

# BEHAVIOUR

Domestic cats resemble their wild ancestors in several ways. Although most domestic cats do not have to catch their own food, they show many signs of hunting behaviour such as being particularly active at dawn and dusk, and stalking and pouncing on pretend prey. Much of this behaviour is instinctive, or inborn, and does not have to be learned. A cat that is brought up away from all other cats still behaves in this way.

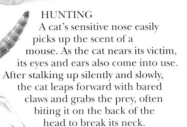

## HUNTING
A cat's sensitive nose easily picks up the scent of a mouse. As the cat nears its victim, its eyes and ears also come into use. After stalking up silently and slowly, the cat leaps forward with bared claws and grabs the prey, often biting it on the back of the head to break its neck.

## LEAPING
Long, supple legs, with strong muscles and flexible joints, give cats great jumping ability. A cat usually looks before it leaps, moving its head from side to side so that it can judge the distance accurately. If the jump is too big, the cat may try to find another route.

*During lactation (milk-feeding), the kittens suck milk from teats on their mother's abdomen.*

*The mother cat guards her young until they are able to fend for themselves.*

## HAIRLESS CAT
The sphynx breed of cat was developed in the 1960s from a kitten that was born without fur. The sphynx has bare skin except for a few fine, dark, downy hairs on its face, paws, and tail tip. It is unlikely that a hairless cat such as this one could survive in the wild for long.

# BREEDING

Female cats, or queens, are pregnant for about nine weeks. They give birth to between one and 10 kittens, but two to five kittens is average. A family of young kittens is called a litter. Newborn kittens are helpless. Their eyes are closed for the first week or more, and they do not begin to crawl for about two weeks. They feed on their mother's milk at first. After about eight weeks they gradually stop taking milk and begin to eat solid foods. This process is called weaning. About four weeks later, the mother cat is ready to mate again.

*Ancient Egyptians kept domestic cats to guard grain stores. Cats became so celebrated that some were worshipped as gods, and statues such as the one shown here were made.*

*Find out more*
ANIMAL SENSES
ANIMALS
EGYPT, ANCIENT
LIONS, TIGERS, and other big cats
MAMMALS

# CAUCASUS REPUBLICS

THESE RUGGED AND MOUNTAINOUS republics lie between the flat steppelands of the Russian Federation and the high plateaux of Southwest Asia. All three countries were once part of the Soviet Union, and gained their independence in 1991. The region is rich in natural resources, with many contrasting climates and landscapes. Georgia's western borders on the Black Sea coast are lush and green with a warm, humid climate, while much of Armenia is semi-desert and high plateau. Farming is important for all three countries; crops include apricots, peaches, cereals, citrus fruits, grapes and tea. The mountains are rich in mineral resources, such as iron, copper and lead, while the Caspian Sea has plentiful oil. There are over 50 ethnic groups living in the Caucasus, each retaining their own language and culture. Since independence, there have been growing ethnic and religious tensions.

Georgia, Azerbaijan, and Armenia are sandwiched between the high mountains of the Greater and Lesser Caucasus. The Black Sea borders the west of the region, while the landlocked Caspian lies to the east. Beyond the Caucasus Mountains to the north lies the Russian Federation.

## CAUCASUS
*The Caucasus in the north of the region form a high mountain barrier isolating it from the Russian Federation. Many peaks in the Caucasus rise to more than 4,600 m (15,000 ft).*

## OIL RIGS
In 1900, Azerbaijan was one of the world's main oil producers, supplying the entire Soviet Union. Caspian Sea oil resources are still being exploited, although lack of investment in rigs has reduced the potential output. Oil is piped from Baku, the centre of the industry, to Iran, Russia, Kazakhstan, and Turkmenistan.

## BLACK SEA
*The Black Sea is an inland sea between Asia and Europe. It is connected to the Mediterranean Sea by the Bosporus, the Sea of Marmara and the Dardanelles.*

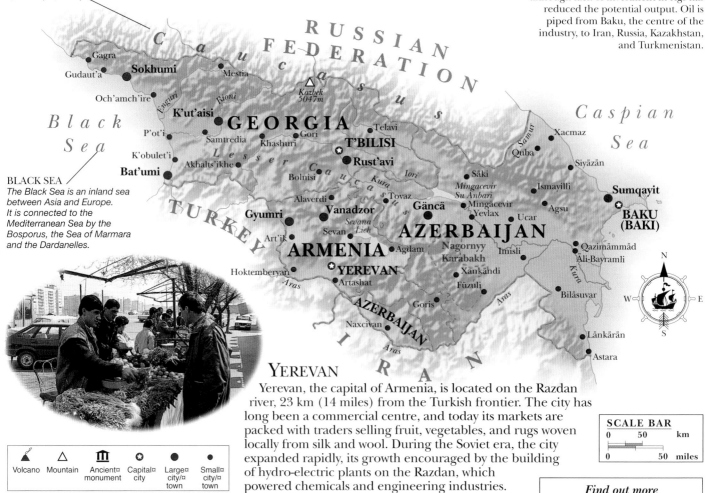

## YEREVAN
Yerevan, the capital of Armenia, is located on the Razdan river, 23 km (14 miles) from the Turkish frontier. The city has long been a commercial centre, and today its markets are packed with traders selling fruit, vegetables, and rugs woven locally from silk and wool. During the Soviet era, the city expanded rapidly, its growth encouraged by the building of hydro-electric plants on the Razdan, which powered chemicals and engineering industries.

| Volcano | Mountain | Ancient¤ monument | Capital¤ city | Large¤ city/¤ town | Small¤ city/¤ town |

**ARMENIA**
**Area:** 29,000 sq km (11,505 sq miles)
**Population:** 3,100,000
**Capital:** Yerevan

**AZERBAIJAN**
**Area:** 86,600 sq km (33,436 sq miles)
**Population:** 8,400,000
**Capital:** Baku

**GEORGIA**
**Area:** 69,700 sq km (26,911 sq miles)
**Population:** 5,100,000
**Capital:** Tblisi

### SCALE BAR
0    50    km
0    50    miles

### Find out more
ASIA
ASIA, HISTORY OF
MOUNTAINS
OIL
SOVIET UNION, HISTORY OF

# CAVES

BENEATH THE SURFACE of the Earth lies a secret world. Caves run through the rock, opening out into huge chambers decorated with slender stone columns. Underground rivers wind through deep passages, and waterfalls crash down on hidden lakes. Caves such as these are many thousands of years old; they were formed as water slowly dissolved limestone rocks. But not all caves are underground. Sea cliffs contain caves that have been eroded by the waves. Caves also develop inside glaciers and within the solidified lava around volcanoes.

Caves are damp, dark places. Some are only large enough to contain one person; others, such as the network of caves in Mammoth Cave National Park, United States, stretch for hundreds of kilometres. One of the world's deepest caves, in France, lies almost 1.5 km (1 mile) below the ground. Prehistoric peoples used caves for shelter. Caves at Lascaux, France, contain wall paintings and ancient tools that are perhaps 20,000 years old. A few cave dwellers still live today in parts of Africa and Asia.

## STALACTITES
Slender stalactites often hang from a cave roof. Drops of water seeping down from above dissolve a white mineral called calcite from the rock. As the water dries, small amounts of calcite are left behind. These build up to form stalactites. This process is usually very slow; stalactites grow only about 2.5 cm (1 in) in 500 years.

*Water drop falls from tip of stalactite.*

## STALAGMITES
Water dripping from the roof or from a stalactite falls to the cave floor, leaving layers of calcite on the floor. In this way a pillar called a stalagmite slowly builds upwards.

## HOW CAVES FORM
Large cave systems lie beneath the ground in regions made of limestone rock. For thousands of years, rainwater, which is naturally acidic, dissolved away the limestone. Small cracks formed, slowly widening to create deep holes, which became underground caves and rivers as water continued to erode the rock.

*Ridges and grooves in the limestone surface*

*Water seeps through rock joints; rock develops cracks which widen into potholes.*

*Step-like rock formations*

*Stalactites and stalagmites take thousands of years to grow.*

*Stream emerges over waterfall.*

*Craggy limestone cliffs*

*Sinkhole – point at which a stream plunges underground*

*Sparse vegetation*

*A stalactite and stalagmite may grow and meet to form a column from floor to roof.*

*Steep channel carved by stream.*

*Ground water fills a previously dry cavern to the level of the water table, which can rise and fall over time.*

*Underground lake*

*Later passage eroded by stream.*

*Stream emerges via cave mouth and flows along the valley bottom.*

*Potholers marvel at the fascinating rock formations around an underground lake at the mouth of a cave in France.*

## POTHOLING
The sport of exploring caves is called potholing. Clambering about in caves is a dirty and often wet pastime, so potholers wear tough clothing. Other important equipment includes nylon ropes, a helmet with a light, and ladders made of steel cables. Potholers work in teams and may stay in a cave for several days. Potholing can be dangerous; rain can cause flooding, and potholers can be trapped by sudden rockfalls.

### Find out more
BATS
GEOLOGY
PREHISTORIC PEOPLES
ROCKS AND MINERALS
VOLCANOES

# CELTS

TWO THOUSAND YEARS AGO, much of western Europe was inhabited by a fierce, proud, artistic people known as the Celts. They were skilled warriors, farmers, and metalworkers. For several hundred years their art and culture dominated northwest Europe. All Celts shared a similar way of life, but they were not a single group of people. They included many different tribes such as the Atrebates of southern Britain and the Parisii of northern France. Most Celts lived in villages or hill forts, some of which developed into small towns. But the Celts never formed a unified nation. Between 3000 B.C. and A.D. 100 they were absorbed into the Roman Empire. Today Celtic-speaking people can still be found in parts of Britain, Ireland, and France.

**BOUDICEA**
In A.D. 61, Boudicea (or Boadicea), queen of the Iceni, a Celtic tribe in Britain, led a massive revolt against Roman oppression. The Britons, however, were no match for the well-organized Romans, and the revolt was suppressed.

*Livestock were kept for food and dairy produce.*

*Huts were covered in clay and thatch to protect them from bad weather.*

*Woven wooden frame of hut*

*The Celts wove their own cloth on looms.*

## THE HOME
Celtic families lived together in one large hut. Some huts were made of stone; others of wattle and daub – wood-framed huts covered in clay to make a hard wall. Thatch was often used to keep the rain out. An iron caldron hung over a fire for cooking meat or boiling water. Bread was cooked in a domed clay oven. Members of the family wove cloth, worked as farmers, or made pots.

### DRUIDS
Druids, a very important group in Celtic society, were priests who led religious ceremonies, acted as judges and advisers, and were responsible for teaching the sons of chiefs. Druidism involved the worship of many gods. Oak trees and mistletoe were also sacred to Druids.

## METALWORKING
The Celts worked with many different metals including iron, bronze, copper, gold, and silver. Farm tools, weapons, shields, chariots, and helmets were made from metal, and many were beautifully decorated with distinctive plants and animals, as shown on the border around this page.

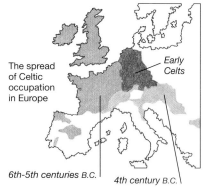

*The spread of Celtic occupation in Europe*

*Early Celts*

*6th-5th centuries B.C.*    *4th century B.C.*

**CELTIC LANDS**
The earliest Celts lived in central Europe, in what is now southern Germany. By about 500 B.C. Celts had spread out to cover much of Europe, from Ireland to the Black Sea.

---
### Find out more
BRITAIN, ANCIENT
IRON AGE
---

# CENTIPEDES
## AND MILLIPEDES

WITH MORE LEGS than most other creatures, the centipede is a speedy predator. This active hunter runs swiftly after insects and other small prey, and sometimes chases millipedes, too. Centipedes and their slower-moving relatives, the millipedes, belong to the larger animal group called arthropods, which means "jointed feet". They may have as many as 180 pairs of legs – centipedes have one pair on each body segment; millipedes have two pairs on each segment. There are about 3,000 kinds of centipedes and 10,000 kinds of millipedes. Both kinds of creatures are found in dark, moist woodland areas, in soil, in leaf litter, and in rotten wood. Most centipedes lay their eggs in the soil, leaving the young to hatch and fend for themselves. Millipedes lay eggs in batches of between 30 and 100. Some millipedes leave the eggs in the soil; others make a nest from hardened excrement or spin a silk cocoon for protection. Millipedes are mainly plant eaters. They are important recyclers of dead leaves and wood, chewing them up and returning the nutrients to the soil in their droppings.

**VELVET WORM**
The wormlike peripatus, or velvet worm, has many legs and is similar in shape to centipedes and millipedes. This picture shows a peripatus attacking a forest millipede by covering it with sticky threads.

*Flat body allows centipede to creep easily into cracks.*

*Antennae (feelers) sense the movement and scent of prey.*

## GIANT BANDED CENTIPEDE
The giant banded centipede is a fearsome predator of worms, slugs, and insects. A centipede finds its prey by using the two long antennae (feelers) on its head. Then it sinks its long clawlike fangs into the victim. These fangs are not true teeth. They are legs adapted to inject poison. The jaws cut up the prey and pass the pieces into the centipede's mouth.

*Rear legs are longer than front legs.*

*Orange-red spots along the millipede's body are glands that produce foul-smelling fluid.*

*Spotted snake millipede*

## MILLIPEDE
As the millipede pushes its way slowly through the soil, its legs move in waves, 10 to 20 legs at a time. The millipede's mouthparts are specialized for scraping and chewing plant material. Most millipedes feed on decomposing plant matter; others eat plant roots and are pests on farm crops. A few millipedes live in rocky habitats and caves and prey on animals. Most millipedes, including this spotted snake millipede, produce a foul-smelling substance to deter predators.

*Garden centipede*

**GARDEN CENTIPEDE**
The common garden centipede attacks any animal of its own size, including other centipedes. Garden centipedes have 15 pairs of legs and are found mainly in damp places under logs, stones, bark, and leaves.

**POISONOUS CENTIPEDE**
Some centipedes are huge, such as the long scolopendra centipedes of Africa, Asia, and the Americas. They grow to about 30 cm (12 in) long. These giant centipedes sometimes wander into houses, where they feed on household pests. Their poisonous bite can be dangerous, so these centipedes are best avoided.

*Millipede's legs move together in waves when it is walking.*

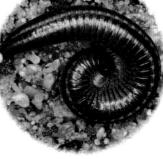

*The hard exoskeleton, or outer casing, on a millipede's body is divided into many segments. These segments overlap and allow the millipede to curl its body up in self-defence when threatened.*

*These creatures are well named – centipede means "a hundred legs", and millipede means "a thousand legs".*

> ### Find out more
> ANIMALS
> INSECTS

135

# CENTRAL AFRICA

The Equator runs through the countries of Central Africa, exercising a strong influence on both climate and vegetation. The extreme north of the region borders the arid Sahara Desert. The south is dominated by the Congo River basin and equatorial rain forest.

MUCH OF CENTRAL AFRICA is covered by dense rain forest, drained by the Congo River which flows in a sweeping arc for 4,666 km (2,900 miles). Most of the countries in this region were once French colonies. Their fortunes have varied since independence in the 1960s. The Democratic Republic of Congo has rich mineral deposits and fertile land, but civil wars and conflict with Rwanda (1996-97) have kept it poor. Chad has also suffered from civil wars while the Central African Republic is one of the world's poorest countries, the victim of an unstable government. To the west, Gabon, Cameroon, and Congo have profited from oil and timber, and are comparatively stable. Everywhere, most people support themselves by farming. In the humid tropical lowlands, diseases such as malaria are widespread, and infant mortality is high.

FULANI
The Fulani are nomads who spread across West Africa and into Chad, Guinea, and Cameroon during the 11th century. From the 14th century, they converted to Islam, spreading the faith through persuasion and conquest. Some Fulani are still cattle-herding pastoralists, while others have adopted settled agriculture, or live in towns.

TIMBER INDUSTRY
The equatorial rain forests of Central Africa are a major source of hardwoods, such as mahogany, ebony, and teak. Timber is an important export for several countries, especially Gabon and Cameroon. However, the timber industry poses a severe threat to the rain forests, which take many years to recover. In addition, most timber companies are foreign-owned, and take profits out of the countries.

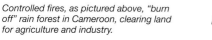
Controlled fires, as pictured above, "burn off" rain forest in Cameroon, clearing land for agriculture and industry.

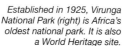
Established in 1925, Virunga National Park (right) is Africa's oldest national park. It is also a World Heritage site.

## OIL WEALTH
The Congo, Gabon, and Cameroon have all discovered extensive offshore oil reserves in the Atlantic Ocean. Exports of oil are vital economically, as they can earn these countries foreign currency. In the Congo, oil accounts for 85 per cent of the country's exports. This over-dependence on oil can be disastrous when world oil prices fluctuate. Oil is also Gabon's main export, and profits from oil have been ploughed back into its health service, one of the best in Africa.

VIRUNGA NATIONAL PARK
Virunga National Park is located in the northeast corner of the Democratic Republic of Congo, and was created in 1925. It is dominated by the Virunga Mountains, a range of both dormant and active volcanoes which extend into Rwanda and Uganda. The mountains are cloaked with cloud forests, and are a famous refuge for gorillas, an endangered species. Lake Edward occupies much of the centre of the park, and the open countryside surrounding it is populated by herds of elephants and okapi.

LIBREVILLE
Gabon's capital, Libreville ("free town"), was founded by freed slaves in 1849. It lies on a string of hills which enclose a port. The modern European-style centre is ringed by traditional African villages.

*Find out more*
AFRICA
AFRICA, HISTORY OF
AFRICAN WILDLIFE
SLAVERY

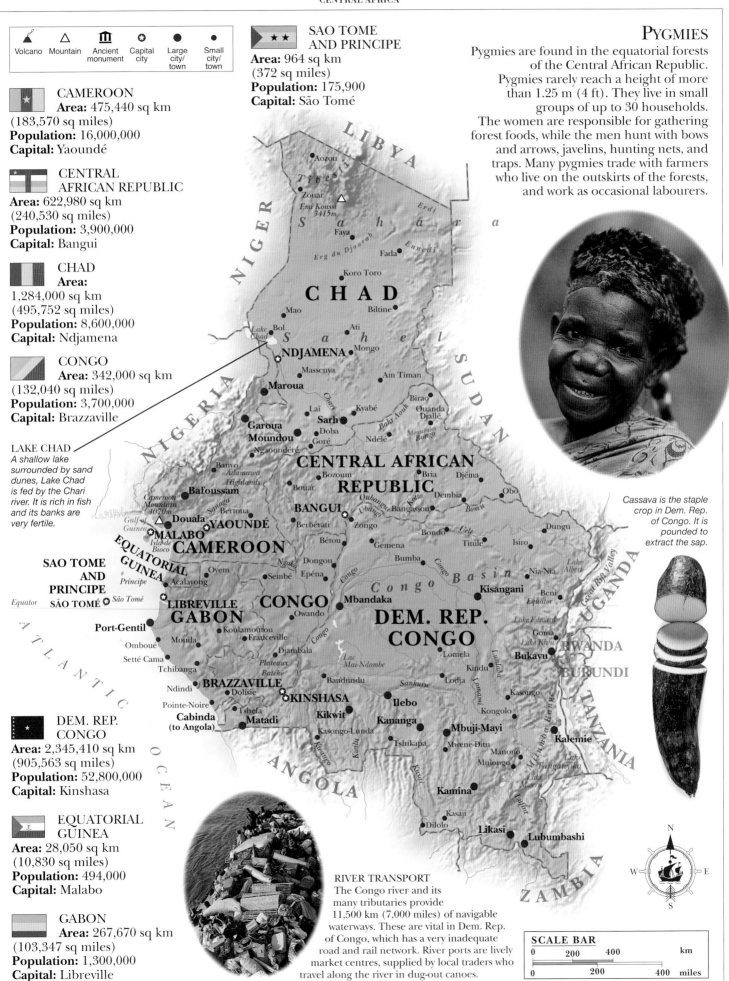

**Volcano** ⚑   **Mountain** △   **Ancient monument** 🏛   **Capital city** ✪   **Large city/town** ●   **Small city/town** ∙

## CAMEROON
**Area:** 475,440 sq km
(183,570 sq miles)
**Population:** 16,000,000
**Capital:** Yaoundé

## CENTRAL AFRICAN REPUBLIC
**Area:** 622,980 sq km
(240,530 sq miles)
**Population:** 3,900,000
**Capital:** Bangui

## CHAD
**Area:** 1,284,000 sq km
(495,752 sq miles)
**Population:** 8,600,000
**Capital:** Ndjamena

## CONGO
**Area:** 342,000 sq km
(132,040 sq miles)
**Population:** 3,700,000
**Capital:** Brazzaville

**LAKE CHAD**
*A shallow lake surrounded by sand dunes, Lake Chad is fed by the Chari river. It is rich in fish and its banks are very fertile.*

## SAO TOME AND PRINCIPE
**Area:** 964 sq km
(372 sq miles)
**Population:** 175,900
**Capital:** São Tomé

## PYGMIES
Pygmies are found in the equatorial forests of the Central African Republic. Pygmies rarely reach a height of more than 1.25 m (4 ft). They live in small groups of up to 30 households. The women are responsible for gathering forest foods, while the men hunt with bows and arrows, javelins, hunting nets, and traps. Many pygmies trade with farmers who live on the outskirts of the forests, and work as occasional labourers.

*Cassava is the staple crop in Dem. Rep. of Congo. It is pounded to extract the sap.*

## DEM. REP. CONGO
**Area:** 2,345,410 sq km
(905,563 sq miles)
**Population:** 52,800,000
**Capital:** Kinshasa

## EQUATORIAL GUINEA
**Area:** 28,050 sq km
(10,830 sq miles)
**Population:** 494,000
**Capital:** Malabo

## GABON
**Area:** 267,670 sq km
(103,347 sq miles)
**Population:** 1,300,000
**Capital:** Libreville

**RIVER TRANSPORT**
The Congo river and its many tributaries provide 11,500 km (7,000 miles) of navigable waterways. These are vital in Dem. Rep. of Congo, which has a very inadequate road and rail network. River ports are lively market centres, supplied by local traders who travel along the river in dug-out canoes.

**SCALE BAR**

| 0 | 200 | 400 | km |

| 0 | 200 | 400 | miles |

# CENTRAL AMERICA

LIKE LINKS IN A CHAIN, the seven Central American countries seem to tie together the continents of North and South America. The climate is hot and steamy; trees, plants, and jungle animals thrive around the marshy coasts and on the high mountains. More than 2,500 years ago Native Americans made Central America their home. Some of the people who live there today are direct descendants of these early inhabitants. Many are *mestizos*: people with both Native American and European ancestors. European people first came to Central America in about 1500, and the Spanish empire ruled the area for more than three centuries. By 1823, many of the countries had gained independence, but this did not bring peace and prosperity to their people. Most Central Americans are still very poor and have no land. There are too few jobs and not enough food. Governments in the region have been unable to solve these problems, and wars and revolutions are common.

Central America forms an isthmus, or narrow land bridge, from Mexico in the north to Colombia in the south.

There are many active volcanoes in Central America. The largest is Tajumulco in Guatemala.

The soil in the valleys is very fertile.

Jungle covers the eastern coastal plain and many mountains.

## MAYAS

Between A.D. 250 and 900 Native American people called Mayas lived in Central America, where they created a vast empire. They built great cities at Palenque and Tikal (in present-day Mexico and Guatemala) and constructed huge stone temples and palaces in the shape of pyramids. To feed the people in the cities, the Mayas became skilled at cultivating food. They used ingenious farming methods to grow plentiful crops on the small areas of suitable land.

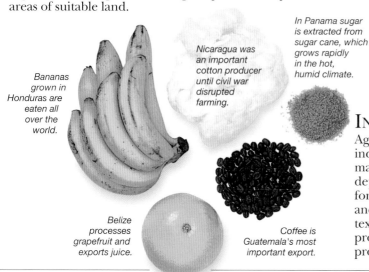

Bananas grown in Honduras are eaten all over the world.

Nicaragua was an important cotton producer until civil war disrupted farming.

In Panama sugar is extracted from sugar cane, which grows rapidly in the hot, humid climate.

Belize processes grapefruit and exports juice.

Coffee is Guatemala's most important export.

### PEOPLE
More than 38 million people live in Central America, mostly in the countryside and in small towns. The biggest city is Guatemala City, which has a population of over 2 million. Most people speak either Spanish or one of the local Native American languages. In Belize, many people speak English. Many Central Americans are Christians, and the Roman Catholic Church is an important influence in everyday life and culture.

### EDUCATION
Civil wars and other armed conflicts have disrupted normal life in Central America. One result is that many people are illiterate. However, in Nicaragua there is a major campaign to teach people to read.

## INDUSTRY
Agriculture is the major industry in Central America; many of the countries depend on one main crop for their income. Both Belize and El Salvador also make textiles and light industrial products. Guatemala produces oil for export.

*Find out more*

AZTECS
CARIBBEAN
CONQUISTADORS
MEXICO

| Volcano | Mountain | Ancient monument | Capital city | Large city/town | Small city/town |
|---|---|---|---|---|---|

## STATISTICS
**Area:** 523,160 sq km (201,993 sq miles)
**Population:** 38,756,000
**Number of independent countries:** 7

# PANAMA CANAL
The Panama Canal is a great international waterway connecting the Atlantic and Pacific Oceans. It is more than 80 km (50 miles) long and up to 150 m (500 ft) wide, with a minimum depth of 12 m (39 ft). Over 13,000 ships from all over the world pass through the canal's locks each year. Most of their cargo travels to and from the United States.

PACIFIC COASTAL STRIP
Half the population of Central America lives on the western slopes, which are higher and drier than the lowlands that border the Caribbean coast. Most people in the west work as farmers, producing coffee, bananas, sugar cane, and cotton.

### SCALE BAR
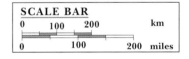

BELIZE
**Area:** 22,960 sq km (8,865 sq miles)
**Population:** 256,000
**Capital:** Belmopan
**Currency:** Belizean dollar

COSTA RICA
**Area:** 51,100 sq km (19,730 sq miles)
**Population:** 4,200,000
**Capital:** San José
**Currency:** Colón

HONDURAS
**Area:** 112,090 sq km (43,278 sq miles)
**Population:** 6,900,000
**Capital:** Tegucigalpa
**Currency:** Lempira

EL SALVADOR
**Area:** 21,040 sq km (8,124 sq miles)
**Population:** 6,500,000
**Capital:** San Salvador
**Currency:** Colón

NICARAGUA
**Area:** 130,000 sq km (50,193 sq miles)
**Population:** 5,500,000
**Capital:** Managua
**Currency:** Córdoba

GUATEMALA
**Area:** 108,890 sq km (42,043 sq miles)
**Population:** 12,300,000
**Capital:** Guatemala City
**Currency:** Quetzal

PANAMA
**Area:** 77,080 sq km (29,761 sq miles)
**Population:** 3,100,000
**Capital:** Panama City
**Currency:** Balboa

COSTA RICA
More than half of Costa Rica's people live on a broad, fertile plateau surrounded by volcanic ranges (above). Small farms dot the area; coffee, corn, rice, and sugar are grown on the hillsides. Unlike other Central American countries, Costa Rica enjoys political stability.

# CENTRAL ASIA

A LANDSCAPE OF HIGH MOUNTAINS, fertile valleys, and extensive deserts, Central Asia was once peopled by nomads, who roamed the land with their animal herds, searching for new pastures. The Silk Road, a trade route from China to Europe, once passed through the region, and a number of towns were founded along it. From 1922 to 1991 most of the region was part of the Soviet Union. During this period traditional ways of life began to disappear, and new technology made the land more productive. Today, the independent states of the region use mountain streams to generate electricity, and divert water to irrigate the arid land. A large range of crops – vegetables, wheat, fruit, and tobacco – are grown. Cotton is a major crop, and is exported by Uzbekistan. Afghanistan, to the south, has been plagued by warfare. Its economy is in a state of collapse due to the conflict.

In the east and south, the Central Asian mountains form a barrier between Central Asia, and China and Pakistan. To the west lies Iran and the eastern shores of the Caspian Sea. To the north lie the flat steppelands of Kazakhstan.

SAMARQAND
One of the oldest cities in Central Asia, Samarqand was situated on the ancient Silk Road from China to Europe. Some of its finest buildings date to the 13th and 14th centuries, when Samarqand was the centre of an Islamic empire. The monuments of the Registan Square (below) are decorated with mosaics, marble, and gold.

*Samarqand is still a major trading centre, exporting silk and cotton, fruit, vegetables, and tobacco.*

*Animal breeding is important to the Kyrgyz because they have so little land to farm. The Kyrgyz are known for their skilled horsemanship.*

## KYRGYZ NOMADS
Mainly from Kyrgyzstan, the Kyrgyz are a nomadic people, who traditionally live on the high plateaux by herding sheep, goats, yak, horses, and camels. They lived in *yurts*, felt-covered frame tents. During the Soviet era many Kyrgyz were forced to settle on large collective farms.

CARPETS
Woollen carpets from Turkmenistan and Uzbekistan have distinctive geometrical designs. They are made by hand-knotting the wool. They are used as saddle-cloths, wall-hangings, and prayer mats.

## ARAL SEA
In Uzbekistan, cotton-farmers are diverting the flow of the Amu Darya to water their fields. The inland Aral Sea, also fed by the river, is drying up. More than half the sea's water has been lost since 1960 and its salinity has increased fourfold. The sea is too salty for fish, and fishing ports are now surrounded by grounded ships and barren land. Fertilizers have poisoned drinking water, leading to health problems.

COTTON HARVEST
Uzbekistan is one of the world's largest cotton-cultivators. Cotton is also grown elsewhere in Central Asia, which is the most northerly of the great cotton regions of the world. Uzbekistan makes and exports machinery used to harvest and process the cotton. The gathering of the white, fluffy cotton is highly mechanized.

*Find out more*

ASIA
DAMS
ISLAM
OCEANS AND SEAS
SOVIET UNION, HISTORY OF

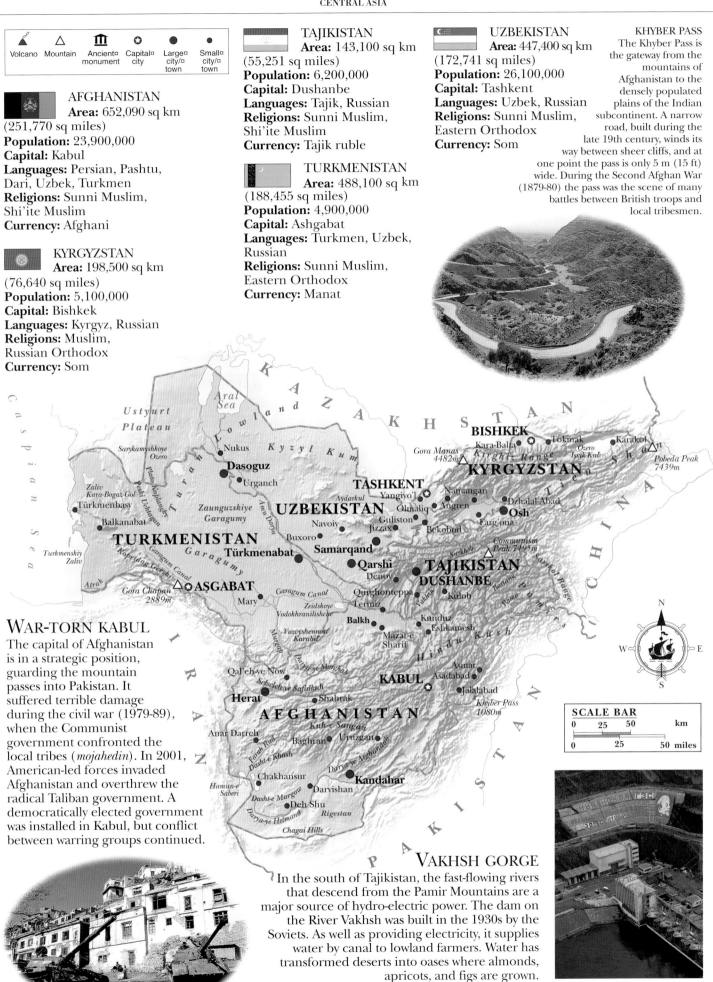

Volcano  Mountain  Ancient monument  Capital city  Large city/town  Small city/town

## AFGHANISTAN
**Area:** 652,090 sq km (251,770 sq miles)
**Population:** 23,900,000
**Capital:** Kabul
**Languages:** Persian, Pashtu, Dari, Uzbek, Turkmen
**Religions:** Sunni Muslim, Shi'ite Muslim
**Currency:** Afghani

## KYRGYZSTAN
**Area:** 198,500 sq km (76,640 sq miles)
**Population:** 5,100,000
**Capital:** Bishkek
**Languages:** Kyrgyz, Russian
**Religions:** Muslim, Russian Orthodox
**Currency:** Som

## TAJIKISTAN
**Area:** 143,100 sq km (55,251 sq miles)
**Population:** 6,200,000
**Capital:** Dushanbe
**Languages:** Tajik, Russian
**Religions:** Sunni Muslim, Shi'ite Muslim
**Currency:** Tajik ruble

## TURKMENISTAN
**Area:** 488,100 sq km (188,455 sq miles)
**Population:** 4,900,000
**Capital:** Ashgabat
**Languages:** Turkmen, Uzbek, Russian
**Religions:** Sunni Muslim, Eastern Orthodox
**Currency:** Manat

## UZBEKISTAN
**Area:** 447,400 sq km (172,741 sq miles)
**Population:** 26,100,000
**Capital:** Tashkent
**Languages:** Uzbek, Russian
**Religions:** Sunni Muslim, Eastern Orthodox
**Currency:** Som

## KHYBER PASS
The Khyber Pass is the gateway from the mountains of Afghanistan to the densely populated plains of the Indian subcontinent. A narrow road, built during the late 19th century, winds its way between sheer cliffs, and at one point the pass is only 5 m (15 ft) wide. During the Second Afghan War (1879-80) the pass was the scene of many battles between British troops and local tribesmen.

## WAR-TORN KABUL
The capital of Afghanistan is in a strategic position, guarding the mountain passes into Pakistan. It suffered terrible damage during the civil war (1979-89), when the Communist government confronted the local tribes (*mojahedin*). In 2001, American-led forces invaded Afghanistan and overthrew the radical Taliban government. A democratically elected government was installed in Kabul, but conflict between warring groups continued.

## VAKHSH GORGE
In the south of Tajikistan, the fast-flowing rivers that descend from the Pamir Mountains are a major source of hydro-electric power. The dam on the River Vakhsh was built in the 1930s by the Soviets. As well as providing electricity, it supplies water by canal to lowland farmers. Water has transformed deserts into oases where almonds, apricots, and figs are grown.

# CHARLEMAGNE

TWELVE CENTURIES AGO one man ruled most of western Europe. Charlemagne could hardly read or write, yet he built up a vast empire. Charlemagne was a Frank, one of the peoples who had invaded the Roman Empire when it collapsed in the 5th century, and who then settled in northern France. When he became king in A.D. 768, his territory was small, and threatened by its French neighbours. Charlemagne soon overcame them all and then invaded northern Italy. He was a great warrior. He fought the people of Hungary, and the Saxons in Germany. He also invaded Spain and stopped the Muslims living there from threatening the rest of Europe. Charlemagne's aim was not just to rule more countries; he wanted to convert the inhabitants to Christianity. To achieve this goal he became ruthless with those who opposed him. However, he was not an especially cruel ruler. He reformed the countries he conquered, and, perhaps because he was not an educated man, he encouraged learning and set up many schools. The Pope, who was head of the Christian Church, rewarded Charlemagne by crowning him Emperor of the Romans in 800, for Charlemagne's European empire was the first to be formed since the fall of Rome. When he died 14 years later, Charlemagne was the most powerful ruler in Europe.

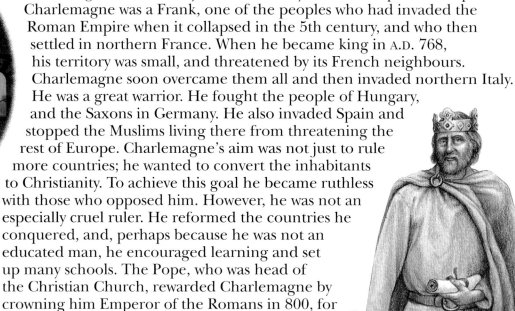

## THRONE
Charlemagne was a very powerful ruler, but his marble throne was plain and undecorated. The throne was a copy of the one described in the Bible from which King Solomon ruled his kingdom of Israel. Charlemagne built a chapel in his palace to house his throne. The chapel survives today as part of Aachen Cathedral, in Germany.

## CORONATION
Pope Leo III crowned Charlemagne Emperor of the Romans on Christmas Day in 800, at St. Peter's Basilica in Rome. Charlemagne became the first Roman emperor for more than three centuries. Although he accepted the title, he believed that it had little value.

## WHAT HE LOOKED LIKE
There are few known portraits of Charlemagne, but those that remain show a tall, bearded, blond-haired man.

*This coin dates from Charlemagne's period of rule.*

## HOLY ROMAN EMPIRE
Charlemagne's domain (coloured pink here) covered most of Europe. Though his empire was split up after his death, what remained later became known as the Holy Roman Empire (coloured green). The last emperor, Francis II, resigned the title in 1806. Some say he abolished the empire to stop Napoleon Bonaparte, emperor of France, from taking the title. Others say Napoleon ended it because he didn't want a rival emperor in Europe.

Holy Roman Empire

Charlemagne's empire

Part of both empires

## ROYAL TOMB
Scenes from Charlemagne's life cover his tomb in Aachen Cathedral. One panel shows his armies besieging the town of Pamplona in Spain. The tomb is richly decorated with gold, and set with precious stones.

### Find out more
BARBARIANS
MEDIEVAL EUROPE
NAPOLEON BONAPARTE

# CHEMISTRY

HAVE YOU EVER WONDERED why cooking changes raw, tough food into a tasty meal? Cooking is just one example of a chemical reaction that converts raw materials into new substances. Chemists use chemical reactions to make plastics, medicines, dyes, and many other materials that are important in everyday life. They also study what substances are made of and how they can be combined to make new materials. Chemicals are the raw materials used by a chemist. More than 4 million different chemicals have been made by chemists; there are about 35,000 chemicals in common use. These chemicals can be made by combining simple substances, called elements, into more complicated substances called compounds. Early chemists considered four elements – fire, water, air, and earth. Today, we know there are 92 that occur in nature, and a few others that can be made in laboratories. The most common element in the universe is hydrogen, which is the main component of stars.

APPARATUS
Chemists use special flasks and jars to mix chemicals, together with equipment that is electronic and automated.

## CHEMICAL REACTIONS

When different substances combine together to form new materials, a chemical reaction occurs. Some reactions need heat to start them off; others produce heat as the reaction proceeds.

Sodium is a soft, silvery metal.

Chlorine is a poisonous yellow-green gas.

Sodium chloride is a non-poisonous white powder.

### ELEMENTS AND COMPOUNDS
Elements are substances which are made of a single kind of atom. When different elements combine, their atoms join to produce molecules of a new substance, which is called a compound. For example, common salt is a compound called sodium chloride. It is made by combining the element sodium and the element chlorine. When the two elements combine, they form a compound which is entirely different from either of the elements used to produce it.

Chemists use a shorthand to describe chemicals. $H_2O$ is the symbol for water and shows that each water molecule contains two hydrogen atoms (H) and one oxygen atom (O).

## HISTORY OF CHEMISTRY
The Egyptians were the first chemists. The word chemistry comes from *Chem*, the name for Ancient Egypt. Modern chemistry began around 1790 when a Frenchman, Antoine Lavoisier, explained how chemical reactions work. In 1808, an English scientist, John Dalton, showed that substances were made from atoms. By 1871, a Russian teacher, Dimitri Mendeleyev, had produced the periodic table, which classifies elements according to their properties and is the cornerstone of chemistry.

### ALCHEMY
Early chemistry, called alchemy, was a mixture of magic and guesswork. From about A.D. 300, alchemists tried to make gold from lead, mercury, and other cheap metals. They also tried to find an elixir, or preparation, to prolong life. Although the alchemists did not succeed in these aims, they found ways of separating substances and making them pure. They also discovered many new substances.

___ *Find out more* ___
ATOMS AND MOLECULES
EGYPT, ANCIENT
HEAT
PHYSICS
SCIENCE, HISTORY OF

# CHINA

TO DESCRIBE CHINA you need to use enormous numbers. The country is vast, covering more than 9.3 million sq km (3.6 million sq miles). China's written history stretches back 3,500 years – longer than any other nation's. 1,300 million people live there, and one-fifth of the world's population is Chinese. In such a large country, there are many variations, including four major language families. The land, too, is tremendously varied. The east and southeast, where most people live, is green and fertile. Other parts of the country are barren deserts of sand and rock. Organizing and feeding the huge and varied Chinese population is a mammoth task. Since 1949 China has been ruled by a Communist government that has tried to provide adequate food, education, and health care to every part of the nation. During the late 1970s, Communist party moderates embraced economic reforms that lifted government controls and encouraged private enterprise. Consequently, China became the world's third-largest economy in the mid 1990s. China's human rights record, however, is still criticized because of political oppression at home and in Tibet.

China is the fourth-largest country in the world. It is situated in eastern Asia. The Russian Federation and Mongolia lie to its north, and Southeast Asia and the Indian subcontinent to its south and west. The East China Sea is to its east.

TRANSPORTATION
Private cars are almost unknown in China. The bicycle is the main method of transport for people and luggage.

*Chinese farmers make use of every suitable piece of land, carving steps or terraces in the hillsides to grow rice and other crops.*

*Rice is grown in flooded fields called paddies.*

Tiananmen Square, Beijing

BEIJING
The capital city of China is Beijing, formerly Peking. Modern Beijing spreads out around the older central area. To the north and west are houses and Beijing University. The industrial area is to the east of the centre. At the heart lies Tiananmen (Gate of Heavenly Peace) Square. Here parades and celebrations take place on national holidays. In 1989, the government forcibly disbanded a pro-democracy student demonstration here, killing thousands.

## AGRICULTURE AND LAND USE
Most Chinese people are crowded together in just 15 per cent of the total land area, mainly in river valleys in the east. Three in ten live in huge cities; the rest live in the countryside. There they grow rice and wheat and raise pigs and other livestock. Much of the rest of the country is mountainous and wild. The Takla Makan Desert in the west is dry and cold, and few people live there.

NEW YEAR
China's most important festival is the celebration of New Year. Each year is named after an animal and people celebrate with colourful processions. Tangerines with leaves are the lucky fruits of the New Year. Odd numbers are unlucky so people always give presents of tangerines in pairs.

## FAMILY LIFE
The family is the most important institution in Chinese life. Children respect their parents and look after them in their old age. China's population is growing, and the government now rewards parents who limit their families to just one child. This policy works well in the cities, but in farming communities, people need large families to labour in the fields.

## HAN CHINESE

China has a large number of ethnic groups. The Han Chinese people make up about 90 per cent of the total population. Their ancestors may have come east from Turkestan, which is now partly in western China and partly in Central Asia and Afghanistan. However, it is possible that Han Chinese people descended from Mongolian tribes who moved south.

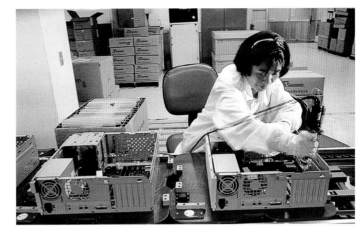

## INDUSTRIAL TAIWAN

Boasting a highly educated and ambitious workforce, Taiwan is one of Asia's wealthiest economies. The country produces about 10 per cent of the world's computers, and is the world's leading television producer. It also specializes in shoe-manufacturing. Taiwan's mineral industry is not a significant earner as mineral resources are relatively modest.

### PANDAS

The giant panda lives only in the mountainous forests of southwestern China. It feeds almost exclusively off bamboo. The woody grass is low in nutrients, so pandas must eat about 38kg (84 lb) of it every day to survive. The panda is classified as an endangered species, and fewer than 1,600 remain in the wild today. They live in areas of forest set aside as nature preserves by the Chinese government.

### LHASA

Monasteries in Lhasa, capital of Tibet, are reminders that the city was once the centre of Lamaism (Tibetan Buddhism). The religion is an important part of Tibetan life, and at one time one-sixth of all Tibetan men were monks. The head of the religion, the Dalai Lama, was also the ruler of the country. However, in 1950 Communist China invaded Tibet, and has ruled the region ever since.

### SHANGHAI

The largest city in China, Shanghai (right), is one of the world's biggest seaports. For centuries China was closed to the west, but in 1842 the Treaty of Nanking, between China and Britain, opened the port to western trade. Since then Shanghai has been the leading commercial and industrial centre in China. Today, about half of China's foreign business passes through the city.

*The spectacular Potala Palace (left), in Lhasa, was built in the 17th century.*

*To Western eyes in the Middle Ages, the Chinese junk (left) seemed an ungainly figure. However, the junk is still widely used today, thus proving its seaworthiness.*

## JUNK

The junk is an ocean-going sailing vessel of ancient unknown origin. By the Middle Ages, Chinese junks had sailed to the waters of Indonesia and India. The junk carries up to five sails consisting of panels of linen or matting flattened by bamboo strips. Each sail can be spread or closed at a pull, like a venetian blind. A massive rudder, which steers the boat, takes the place of a keel or a centreboard, and keeps the boat from tipping over or drifting with the wind. The hull is partitioned by solid bulkheads, which add greatly to the boat's strength.

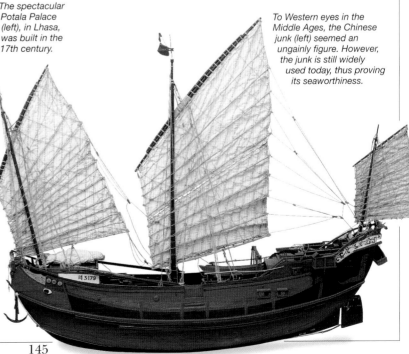

Most Chinese people work in agriculture. However, over 25 per cent of China's 750 million-strong workforce is employed in industries such as textiles (left) and electronics.

# MEDICINE

Medicine in China is a mixture of East and West. Modern surgical and drug techniques are borrowed from Europe and the United States. However, doctors still use traditional cures that have been popular for thousands of years, including herbs and other natural remedies. To relieve pain, Chinese doctors sometimes use acupuncture, a technique in which fine needles are inserted into specially-chosen parts of the body. "Barefoot doctors", or locally-trained healers, keep people healthy in the countryside with natural remedies.

Acupuncture charts show the positions of meridians, or lines of energy, where the acupuncturist inserts needles.

A Chinese apothecary, or chemist, makes use of a wide range of natural plant and animal cures.

## INDUSTRY

Chinese factories have been modernized since 1949, but in comparison with the factories of Japan or the United States, some are still old-fashioned. However, China is the world's leading manufacturer of television sets and produces other electrical goods, farm machinery, machine tools, toys, and textiles. With such a huge population, there is no shortage of workers.

The Chinese eat with chopsticks. They hold both sticks in one hand, and pinch the tips together to pick up food.

Buddhist monks in Tibet, southwest China, spend much time studying and writing.

## FOOD

Rice is one of the main ingredients of Chinese food, as are noodles and many vegetables. Dried foods, soya beans, fish, and meat are also used in Chinese cooking, which varies considerably in the different regions of China.

# CHINESE LANGUAGE

Mandarin, the main language of China, is spoken in all but the southeast coastal areas. Within each language there are many dialects, or regional variations. Although each vocabulary is different, all the variations are written in the same script.

The Beijing Opera performs traditional and new works, mainly with political themes.

Chinese writing consists of thousands of symbols, each one representing a different word or idea.

兒童百科全書

## HONG KONG AND MACAO

At midnight on 29-30 July, 1997, Hong Kong (above) returned to Chinese sovereignty after it had been a British colony for 157 years. Two years later, Hong Kong's neighbour, Macao, ceased to be a Portuguese colony. It officially came under Chinese rule at midnight on 19-20 December, 1999.

## CULTURE

China has a rich and ancient culture: paintings found in some Chinese tombs are more than 6,000 years old. Today, artistic traditions continue in the form of folk dancing and music; films, opera, and theatre are all very popular. Artists are encouraged to produce works that depict the achievements of the Chinese people.

---

### Find out more

ASIA
CHINA, HISTORY OF
COMMUNISM
MAO ZEDONG
MONGOL EMPIRE

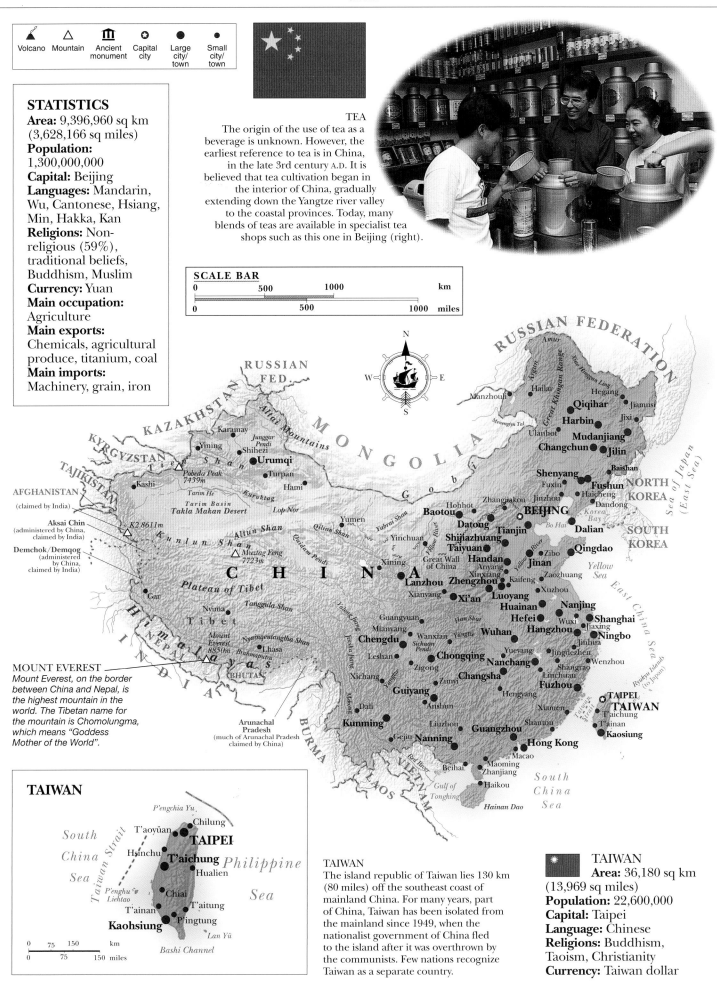

Volcano | Mountain | Ancient monument | Capital city | Large city/town | Small city/town

## STATISTICS
**Area:** 9,396,960 sq km (3,628,166 sq miles)
**Population:** 1,300,000,000
**Capital:** Beijing
**Languages:** Mandarin, Wu, Cantonese, Hsiang, Min, Hakka, Kan
**Religions:** Non-religious (59%), traditional beliefs, Buddhism, Muslim
**Currency:** Yuan
**Main occupation:** Agriculture
**Main exports:** Chemicals, agricultural produce, titanium, coal
**Main imports:** Machinery, grain, iron

### TEA
The origin of the use of tea as a beverage is unknown. However, the earliest reference to tea is in China, in the late 3rd century A.D. It is believed that tea cultivation began in the interior of China, gradually extending down the Yangtze river valley to the coastal provinces. Today, many blends of teas are available in specialist tea shops such as this one in Beijing (right).

**SCALE BAR**
0    500    1000    km
0    500    1000    miles

AFGHANISTAN
(claimed by India)

**Aksai Chin**
(administered by China, claimed by India)

**Demchok/Demqog**
(administered by China, claimed by India)

MOUNT EVEREST
*Mount Everest, on the border between China and Nepal, is the highest mountain in the world. The Tibetan name for the mountain is Chomolungma, which means "Goddess Mother of the World".*

**Arunachal Pradesh**
(much of Arunachal Pradesh claimed by China)

## TAIWAN

*South China Sea*

*Taiwan Strait*

P'engchia Yu
Chilung
T'aoyüan
**TAIPEI**
Hsinchu
**T'aichung**
Hualien
*Philippine Sea*
P'enghu Liehtao
Chiai
T'aitung
T'ainan
P'ingtung
**Kaohsiung**
Lan Yü
*Bashi Channel*

0   75   150   km
0   75   150   miles

### TAIWAN
The island republic of Taiwan lies 130 km (80 miles) off the southeast coast of mainland China. For many years, part of China, Taiwan has been isolated from the mainland since 1949, when the nationalist government of China fled to the island after it was overthrown by the communists. Few nations recognize Taiwan as a separate country.

### TAIWAN
**Area:** 36,180 sq km (13,969 sq miles)
**Population:** 22,600,000
**Capital:** Taipei
**Language:** Chinese
**Religions:** Buddhism, Taoism, Christianity
**Currency:** Taiwan dollar

# HISTORY OF
# CHINA

CHINA HAS A LONGER continuous civilization than any other country in the world, and its civilization has often been far more advanced. People have lived in China for around 500,000 years. They built cities about 5,500 years ago, long before cities existed in Africa, the Americas, or Europe. The Chinese invented paper, ink, writing, silk fabric, printing, and gunpowder. Until this century, China's vast empire was ruled by emperors who came from different dynasties, or royal families. They kept China practically isolated from the rest of the world until the 19th century. But, in 1911 the Chinese people forced the last emperor to abdicate (resign). A republic was established, but it was weakened by civil war and Japanese invasion. In 1949, the Communist party took power and began to transform China into a major industrial nation. Since the late 1970s, the Party has encouraged free enterprise.

*The bodies of the figures were hollow for lightness.*

### TERRACOTTA ARMY
In 221 B.C., Shih Huang Ti became the first emperor of all China. His vast army helped him unite rival Chinese kingdoms. When Shih Huang Ti died in 210 B.C., a life-size copy of his army was made by 700,000 slaves and craftworkers. More than 8,000 terracotta clay archers, soldiers, chariots, and horses were buried in silent rows to guard his tomb.

*Figures were made in separate pieces.*

### CH'IN DYNASTY
China gets its name from the Ch'in dynasty of Shih Huang Ti, which ruled China between 221 and 206 B.C. The dynasty was ruthless and its army was invincible. Army officers often rode in light wooden chariots and could be recognized by their special headgear and armour.

*The weapons were real. When the tomb was discovered in the early 1970s, some weapons were still sharp enough to cut hair.*

### GREAT WALL
The Great Wall of China is the longest wall in the world. It is 3,460 km (2,150 miles) long, 12 m (39 ft) high, and between 6 m (20 ft) and 15 m (49 ft) wide. The wall was built during the reign of Shih Huang Ti to defend China's northern borders against hostile tribes from Central Asia.

### CONFUCIUS
Confucius (551-479 B.C.) was a wise teacher. His ideas greatly influenced the Chinese. He taught that people should be courteous, loyal, and unselfish.

### HAN DYNASTY
The Han dynasty ruled China from 206 B.C. to A.D. 220. It was a peaceful era, during which China greatly expanded its territory. Schools were built and learning was encouraged. Paper and ink were invented at this time. Artists created many beautiful objects, such as the bronze "horse of heaven" (above), made nearly 2,000 years ago.

### T'ANG DYNASTY
China was powerful and rich during the T'ang dynasty (A.D. 618-906). Craftsworkers made beautiful pottery and sculptures, and artists painted superb watercolours on silk. The T'ang empress Wu Tse-t'ien allowed women to take examinations for government posts. The golden bowl below demonstrates the wealth of the dynasty.

### MING DYNASTY
The Forbidden City in Beijing (above) was built during the Ming dynasty (1368-1644). The Ming emperors and their families lived in a palace in the city. Ordinary people were forbidden to enter.

*The dragon is a sign of good luck in China.*

*Clouds represent the sky.*

*Water, topped by foam and waves, represents the sea.*

## DRAGON ROBE
Only an emperor or a member of the imperial family could wear the yellow silk dragon robe. The robe on the left was woven about 100 years ago. The design of the swirling sea, waves, mountains, clouds, and dragons shows that its wearer was the ruler of the universe.

*Mountain represents the Earth.*

### CHINA

**500,000 years ago** China's best-known fossil human, Peking man, makes tools.

**c. 5000 B.C.** First villages established.

**c. 3500 B.C.** First Chinese city built.

**c. 1523-1027 B.C.** Shang dynasty rules northern China. Writing and the calendar are developed; cities are built.

**551-479 B.C.** Life of Confucius.

**221-206 B.C.** Ch'in dynasty unites China. Great Wall built.

**206 B.C-A.D. 220** Han dynasty. Buddhist religion arrives. Paper and ink invented.

**A.D. 618-906** T'ang dynasty. Gunpowder and printing invented.

**868** Earliest known book printed.

**960-1279** Sung dynasty. Compass invented.

**1279-1368** Mongols invade and rule China.

**1368-1644** Ming dynasty. First European traders and missionaries arrive.

**1644-1911** Manchu (Quing) dynasty. Foreign domination increases.

**1911** Emperor gives up throne.

**1912** China becomes a republic.

**1921** Chinese Communist Party founded.

**1931** Japan invades Manchuria.

**1937-45** Japan invades rest of China.

**1945-49** Communists gain control of the country; set up People's Republic of China, led by Mao Zedong.

**1989** Tiananmen Square massacre of pro-democracy students.

## SUN YAT-SEN
In 1911, a rebellion broke out against the corrupt and inefficient Manchu dynasty, and in 1912 a republic was declared. The first president of China was Sun Yat-sen (1866-1925; right). He founded the Kuomintang (Chinese National Party). He tried to modernize the country but his authority was disputed and he soon resigned. However, Sun continued to dominate Chinese politics until his death.

### COLLAPSE OF THE EMPIRE
During the 19th century, many foreign countries forced China to grant them trading rights and allow their citizens to ignore Chinese law. The cartoon above shows Britain, Germany, Russia, Italy, and Japan sharing the Chinese "cake" among them. But the Chinese resented this interference in their affairs and rebelled against the hated foreigners.

### MAO ZEDONG
Mao Zedong (1893-1976) was the leader of the Chinese Communist party, founded in 1921. He fought a civil war with Chiang Kai-shek, leader of the Kuomintang Party, which took power in 1928. In 1949, the Communists expelled Chiang Kai-shek and took power. Mao was leader of China until his death.

### *Find out more*
CHINA
COMMUNISM
JAPAN, HISTORY OF
MAO ZEDONG
MONGOL EMPIRE

# CHRISTIANITY

*Church windows tell Bible stories in pictures made from stained glass.*

FROM VERY HUMBLE ORIGINS, Christianity has grown to be the largest of all world religions. Christians are the followers of Jesus Christ, a Jew who lived almost 2,000 years ago in the land that is now Israel. Jesus was a teacher and a prophet, but Christians believe that he was also the Son of God and that he came into the world to save people from sin, or doing wrong. Jesus was killed by his enemies, but his disciples (group of followers) taught that he rose from the dead and rejoined his father in heaven, a basic Christian belief called the Resurrection. After Jesus' death, his followers began to spread his teaching. Christianity grew, but it was against the law in most lands, and many early Christians died for their beliefs. Today, more than 1,600 million people throughout the world practise Christianity. There are different divisions within Christianity; the three most prominent are Protestantism, the Roman Catholic Church, and the Eastern Orthodox Church. Each has its own way of worshipping. But despite their differences, all Christian groups share a belief in the teachings of Jesus Christ. Most Christians worship by meeting in groups called congregations. They pray together and sing hymns (sacred songs).

*In New Testament stories Jesus compares God to a good shepherd, caring for his "flock" of believers.*

### BIBLE
The Bible is sacred to both Christians and Jews, who believe it contains the word of God. It consists of two parts – the Old and New Testaments. Both Jews and Christians accept the Old Testament, but only Christians accept the New Testament. The New Testament includes the gospels, or teachings of Christ, as told by his followers – Matthew, Mark, Luke, and John. Christians try to follow the central message of the New Testament, which is to love God and their fellow humans and to forgive their enemies.

## COMMUNION
Before he died, Jesus shared a simple meal of bread and wine with his closest followers. He asked them to remember him in this special way. Today the ceremony of Holy Communion, in which worshippers receive bread and wine, is a reminder of Christ's Last Supper and helps Christians feel closer to God. Roman Catholic and Eastern Orthodox churches celebrate communion daily in the form of Mass.

**FEASTS AND HOLY DAYS**
**Advent** Preparation for Christmas.

**Christmas** December 25; birth of Jesus.

**Palm Sunday** Jesus enters Jerusalem, Sunday before Easter.

**Good Friday** Jesus' death, the Friday before Easter Sunday.

**Easter Sunday** late March or April; celebrates Jesus' Resurrection (coming back to life).

*The birth of Jesus is remembered at Christmas. This feast is popular with many non-Christians as well, who enjoy the atmosphere of festive goodwill.*

*Easter is the most important feast in the Christian calendar. It celebrates the rising of Jesus from the dead three days after his crucifixion.*

# ROMAN CATHOLICISM

Roman Catholics make up the largest Christian group. They believe that the Pope, the head of the Catholic Church, is God's representative on Earth. His authority on religious matters is always obeyed. The Pope lives in a tiny independent state in Rome called Vatican City. The Roman Catholic Church is spread worldwide and is the main religion of many countries, including Spain, Ireland, and France. Catholics try to attend Mass on Sundays and to regularly confess their sins to a priest. They pray to God and have special regard for Mary, the mother of Jesus. They also pray to the Christian saints, deeply religious people, some of whom died for their faith.

ROSARY
Catholics use a rosary – a symbolic string of beads – to help them pray. They say a prayer for each bead in the chain.

## ORTHODOX CHURCH

At first Christianity was only "catholic". In A.D. 1054, however, the Christian Church divided. The Pope in Rome and the Patriarch, head of the church of Constantinople (now Istanbul, Turkey), disagreed about the leadership of the Christian world. As a result, the Church in Rome (Catholic) and the Eastern Church (Orthodox) separated. Roman Catholics and members of Eastern Orthodox churches such as those of Russia and Greece share many beliefs. However, Orthodox Christians do not accept the authority of the Pope. Many Christians in eastern Europe and western Asia belong to Orthodox churches. In their churches religious portraits called icons are considered sacred.

## BAPTISM

Adults and children enter the Christian church through baptism, a ceremony in which they are sprinkled with water or immersed in it. Baptism washes away a person's sins. Children are often named, or christened, at their baptism. Parents promise to raise them as good Christians. In some countries baptism takes place outdoors in lakes or rivers. Jesus was baptized in the Jordan River in the Middle East.

*Most of the Christians who worship in the United States are members of Protestant churches.*

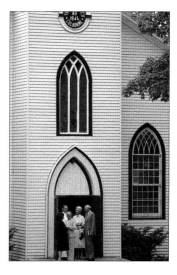

## MOTHER TERESA

Christians believe it is their duty to help relieve the suffering of the poor and sick. Mother Teresa founded the Missionaries of Charity for the homeless and dying in India. She became famous for her work among lepers. In 1979, she was awarded the Nobel Peace Prize. She died in 1997.

*Mother Teresa was born in Albania in 1910, but became an Indian citizen. All the nuns in her missions wear a flowing Indian dress called a sari.*

## PROTESTANTISM

In the early 16th century, some Christians felt that the Roman Catholic Church was no longer correctly following the teachings of Christ. Martin Luther, a German monk, led the protests. Others who agreed with him broke away and formed protest groups in a movement that became known as the Reformation. Today, most Christians who are not members of the Roman Catholic or Orthodox churches are called Protestants. Some Protestant churches, called Evangelical churches, are among the fastest growing Christian groups in the world. They have mainly Afro-Caribbean congregations.

### Find out more

CHURCHES AND CATHEDRALS
JESUS CHRIST
REFORMATION
RELIGIONS

# CHURCHES AND CATHEDRALS

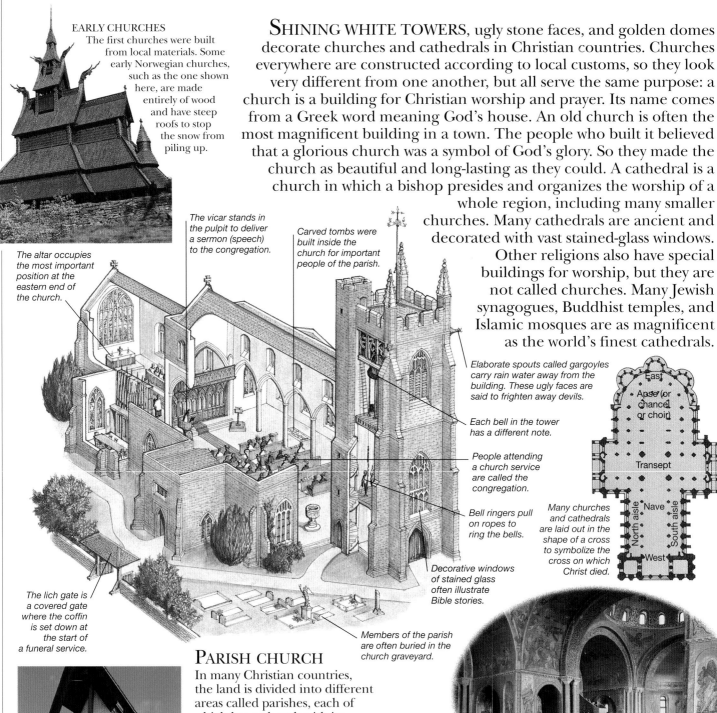

SHINING WHITE TOWERS, ugly stone faces, and golden domes decorate churches and cathedrals in Christian countries. Churches everywhere are constructed according to local customs, so they look very different from one another, but all serve the same purpose: a church is a building for Christian worship and prayer. Its name comes from a Greek word meaning God's house. An old church is often the most magnificent building in a town. The people who built it believed that a glorious church was a symbol of God's glory. So they made the church as beautiful and long-lasting as they could. A cathedral is a church in which a bishop presides and organizes the worship of a whole region, including many smaller churches. Many cathedrals are ancient and decorated with vast stained-glass windows. Other religions also have special buildings for worship, but they are not called churches. Many Jewish synagogues, Buddhist temples, and Islamic mosques are as magnificent as the world's finest cathedrals.

### EARLY CHURCHES
The first churches were built from local materials. Some early Norwegian churches, such as the one shown here, are made entirely of wood and have steep roofs to stop the snow from piling up.

The altar occupies the most important position at the eastern end of the church.

The vicar stands in the pulpit to deliver a sermon (speech) to the congregation.

Carved tombs were built inside the church for important people of the parish.

Elaborate spouts called gargoyles carry rain water away from the building. These ugly faces are said to frighten away devils.

Each bell in the tower has a different note.

People attending a church service are called the congregation.

Bell ringers pull on ropes to ring the bells.

Decorative windows of stained glass often illustrate Bible stories.

The lich gate is a covered gate where the coffin is set down at the start of a funeral service.

Members of the parish are often buried in the church graveyard.

Many churches and cathedrals are laid out in the shape of a cross to symbolize the cross on which Christ died.

East
Apse (or chancel or choir)
Transept
Nave
North aisle
South aisle
West

### PARISH CHURCH
In many Christian countries, the land is divided into different areas called parishes, each of which has a church with its own priest or vicar. In the past, the parish church was the centre of village activities. Here people were baptized as babies, married as adults, and buried when they died.

### CATHEDRAL
From a cathedral, the bishop controls a whole diocese, or group of parishes. Cathedrals get their name from the bishop's cathedra, or throne, which is kept in the cathedral. Many individual cathedrals – and some churches – are named after Christian saints.

St. Mark's Basilica in Venice, Italy, was built between the 11th and 15th centuries.

### MODERN CHURCHES
New churches are still being built today. Some architects follow traditional patterns of church architecture, but many use modern building materials and techniques to produce new and startling effects (left).

___ *Find out more* ___
ARCHITECTURE
CHRISTIANITY
MEDIEVAL EUROPE
RELIGIONS

# SIR WINSTON
# CHURCHILL

IN 1940, BRITAIN badly needed a strong leader. The country was at war with Germany and faced the danger of invasion. Winston Churchill's appointment as prime minister provided the leadership that the British people wanted. He went on to guide the country through the worst war the world had ever experienced. In his underground headquarters he formed the plans which helped to win the war. Churchill's wartime glory came at a surprising time. He was 66 and had held no important government post for many years. He had been almost alone in urging a strong army and navy to oppose the German threat. Working people remembered how he helped crush the general strike of 1926 and cut their wages. But when victory came in World War II, all of this was forgotten, and everyone cheered Churchill as one of the greatest politicians of the age.

**1874** Born at Blenheim Palace, Oxfordshire, England.

**1893** Enters the Royal Military College at Sandhurst.

**1899** Taken prisoner during Boer War in South Africa, but escapes.

**1900** Elected Member of Parliament.

**1906-15** Holds cabinet posts.

**1919** Appointed secretary of state for war.

**1940-45** As prime minister, leads Britain in World War II.

**1951-55** Prime minister.

**1965** Dies.

**YOUNG WINSTON**
As a young soldier and newspaper reporter in India and Africa, Churchill had many adventures. He became world famous when he escaped from a Boer prison in 1899.

**WARTIME PRIME MINISTER**
As wartime leader, Churchill travelled the country visiting bombed cities and raising people's spirits. His simple "V for Victory" sign seemed to sum up British determination to win the war. His most important work took place behind the scenes, where he directed the British war effort. He met the leaders of the then Soviet Union and the United States to draw up plans for fighting the war and for the postwar peace settlement. Above he is seen giving the "V" sign to American sailors.

**HOLDING THE LINE!**

**BRITISH BULLDOG**
Churchill's famous British determination was often portrayed in cartoons and posters. This 1942 American poster shows him as a bulldog.

**PAINTING**
Churchill was an enthusiastic amateur painter. He also wrote many books about history. These hobbies kept him busy after 1945 when he lost his post as prime minister in a disastrous election. He did not return to power until 1951.

**BROADCASTS**
During World War II, Churchill made many radio broadcasts, which inspired the nation. Churchill always explained the situation clearly and listed the dreadful problems which lay ahead, yet he left no doubt that the enemy would eventually be defeated.

*Find out more*

UNITED KINGDOM, HISTORY OF
WORLD WAR I
WORLD WAR II

# CIRCUSES

EARLY CIRCUS ACTS such as tumbling and bull-leaping go back to very ancient times. But the circus that we know today was not developed until 1768, when the Englishman Philip Astley started a trick-riding show in London. He soon added other acts such as tightrope walkers and strong men, and in 1793 John Ricketts set up similar circuses in the United States. These early circuses took place indoors in special buildings; later, travelling tented circuses such as Barnum and Bailey were developed. They moved from town to town, taking the show and its spectacular acts to the audience. Today, the circus combines tightrope acts, juggling, clowns, bareback riders, and animal acts and is one of the most popular forms of family entertainment. Circus work is highly skilled. Venice, Florida, United States, is home to the world's only clown college.

**FLYING TRAPEZE**
Trapeze artistes rely on split-second timing as they perform their midair somersaults. This daring act was invented by the Frenchman Jules Léotard in 1859.

**CIRCUS RING**
Philip Astley discovered that the perfect area for bareback riding was a circle measuring 12.8 m (42 ft) in diameter. This has become the standard circus ring size.

Joseph Grimaldi

Clowns' painted egg heads

## CLOWNS
Every clown is unique. With their funny clothes and makeup, clowns are a special part of every circus. Making people laugh is a serious business, and clowns learn many skills. They may be musicians or acrobats, mimes or comedians. The first real clown, Joseph Grimaldi, was a stage clown in the 19th century, and circus clowns take their nickname, Joey, and their white faces from him. British clowns "register" their makeup by drawing the design on an egg.

**BIG TOP**
Some circuses take place in a huge tent called the big top. The big top must be very strong to resist high winds and to support lighting and rigging for aerial acts. The performers and circus animals live in caravans and trailers.

**RINGMASTER**
At the beginning of each performance the ringmaster strides into the ring, carrying a whip to show that he is in charge. The ringmaster has many responsibilities. Before introducing each act he makes sure that the clothes and equipment are ready. He keeps the mischievous clowns in order and makes sure the show runs smoothly.

Unicyclist

## CIRCUS PARADE
Marching through the street, the parade lets everyone know the circus is in town. Highly-trained horses are part of circus tradition, but many people now think that it is cruel to tame wild animals such as lions and tigers in the ring.

Drummer

Many circus acts rely on balance. The unicyclist's outstretched arms help keep him upright.

Flame eater

Clown

_Find out more_
THEATRE

# CITIES

ONE THIRD OF ALL the world's people live in cities. The world's largest city, Tokyo, Japan, has a population of more than 20 million. But not all cities are vast, because the word city can mean different things. In many places, a city is any large town. In Europe, it is usually a town with a cathedral. And in some places, like the United States, "city" is the name given to an urban area with definite boundaries.

City people need many services: water, power, sanitation, transport, schools, and shops are all essential. Providing these services requires a lot of organization. Badly run cities are unpleasant and unhealthy, with problems such as poor housing, traffic congestion, and pollution. The first cities developed as trading centres in Asia and the Middle East about 7,000 years ago. Rich cities, such as Alexandria in Egypt, became the centres of government and power. Like today's cities, they had markets, banks, hotels, factories, and places of entertainment.

## CAPITAL CITIES
The most important town of any country is called the capital. It is usually the place where the government is based, but it may not be the biggest city in the country. Some capital cities, such as Brasilia, have been specially built in modern times.

*Brasilia was built to replace Rio de Janeiro as the capital of Brazil.*

*Factories require a lot of space, so they are built in the outer parts of cities. They need easy access to roads and railways so they can send their goods to other parts of the country.*

*The city centre usually contains the most stylish shops. Shopping precincts are built close to residential areas on the outskirts of town.*

*Land is expensive in the city centre, so office developments grow upwards rather than outwards.*

*Cities must have a good public transport system, with flyovers or underground railways, to avoid traffic jams.*

*Quiet parks and other recreation areas provide a restful break from the busy city streets.*

## MODERN CITY
The oldest part of the city often forms the centre. Further out are the industrial zones and the areas where people live, all connected by a network of roads.

## PLANNING
Many cities grow up around their historical centres with no overall plan. However, some cities, such as Washington, D.C., have been carefully planned from the start. Streets and squares, transport, sewers, business centres, and sports facilities are all carefully mapped out before any building starts.

*Swiss-French architect Le Corbusier (1887-1965) planned this city for three million people.*

*The city streets follow a grid pattern.*

*Some families live in homes close to the city centre. More live a few kilometres from the centre in less crowded areas called suburbs.*

### Find out more
ARCHITECTURE
INDUSTRIAL REVOLUTION
ROADS AND MOTORWAYS

# CLIMATES

SOME PARTS OF THE WORLD, such as the tropical rain forests of South America, are hot and damp throughout the year. Other regions, such as the Arctic, have long, freezing winters. Conditions such as these are known as the climate of an area. Climate is not the same as weather. Weather can change within minutes; climate describes a region's weather conditions over a long period of time. Every region has its own climate. This depends on how near it is to the equator, which governs how much heat it gets from the sun. Landscape also influences climate; high mountain regions, such as the Himalayas, are cooler than nearby low-lying places. The ocean can prevent a coastal region from getting very hot or very cold, while the weather in the centre of a continent is more extreme. The climate of a region affects landscape and life – clothing, crops, and housing. But climate can change. Today, climatologists, people who study climates, believe that the world's climate is gradually warming up.

THE FREEZING ANTARCTIC
Only hardy creatures, such as penguins, can survive amid the ice and snow of the Antarctic.

The cool forest climate exists only in the northern half of the world.

The treeless landscape of the polar regions is called the tundra.

POLAR CLIMATE
It is cold all year, and ice and snow always cover the ground. No crops grow, and the few people who live there hunt animals for food.

TROPICAL CLIMATE
It is hot all year round in tropical regions, and torrents of rain usually fall every afternoon. Rain forest covers much of the land. In regions where wet and dry seasons occur, tropical grasslands grow.

The Sahara is the largest desert in the world.

In temperate climates, trees shed their leaves in winter.

## WORLD CLIMATES
The different climates of the world run in broad zones around the Earth on either side of the equator. They range from hot and rainy climates at the equator to cold climates at the poles. There are five main climatic zones, each of which is shown on this map by a different colour.

DESERT CLIMATE
In the dry, barren deserts, cold, clear nights usually follow burning-hot days. However, high mountain deserts may have cold, dry winters.

TEMPERATE CLIMATE
Warm summers and cool winters feature in warm temperate climates. Rain may fall all year, or the summer can be dry and sunny, as in Mediterranean regions.

COOL FOREST CLIMATE
Summers are cool and short, and winters are long and cold. Pines and other conifers grow in huge forests which cover much of the land.

Away from the equator, the sun's rays are spread over a wide area.

Sun's rays

Escaping heat

Trapped heat

## CLIMATIC CHANGES
Great climatic changes, such as ice ages, come and go during thousands of years. But severe changes in climate can also occur suddenly or within a few years. Dust from volcanic eruptions can obscure the sun, making a climate cooler. Changes in winds can cause rainfall to shift from a region, bringing drought. Human activities, such as pollution, also affect climate greatly.

GREENHOUSE EFFECT
The atmosphere works like a greenhouse, trapping the sun's heat and warming the Earth. Pollution in the air traps more heat, making the Earth warmer. Unless pollution is reduced, the Earth's climate could be upset.

SAHARA DESERT
The Tuareg nomads are one of the few peoples that live in the punishing climate of the Sahara Desert, coping with the searing heat of the day and the freezing temperatures at night.

SUN AND CLIMATE
The sun's rays warm the equator directly from above, making the tropics hot. Away from the equator, the sun's rays are less direct, making climates cooler.

---

*Find out more*
ATMOSPHERE
DESERTS
EARTH
GLACIERS AND ICECAPS
WEATHER

# CLOCKS AND WATCHES

HAVE YOU EVER COUNTED how many times you look at a clock in one day? Time rules everyday life. To catch a bus, get to school, or meet a friend, you need to be on time. Clocks and watches make this possible. Clocks are timekeeping devices too large to be carried; watches are portable. Some tell the time with hands moving around a dial; others with numbers. All clocks and watches use a controlling device, such as a pendulum, that steadily keeps the time.

Early people relied on the passing of days, nights, and seasons to indicate time. Later, they used other methods, such as sundials, water clocks, and candles with marks on them.

Mechanical timepieces were developed between the 15th and 17th centuries with the invention of clockwork and the pendulum. Springs or falling weights moved gearwheels to drive the clocks. These clocks had hands and a dial, and could be made small enough to allow the invention of the watch. Today, many clocks and watches are electronic and rely on the regular vibrations of a quartz crystal to keep time accurately.

**SUNDIAL**
The sun's shadow moves slowly around a dial marked off in hours. As the shadow moves, it indicates the time. The sundial, which was invented about 5,000 years ago in Egypt, was one of the earliest methods of measuring time.

**WATER CLOCK**
Water flows in and out of bowls so that changing levels of water, or a moving float, indicate the passing time. This Chinese water clock dates back to the 14th century.

**ASTRONOMICAL CLOCK**
This beautiful clock in Prague, Czech Republic, not only shows the hours and minutes but also the signs of the zodiac and the phases of the moon.

Anchor

Ends of anchor engage teeth of escape wheel.

Escape wheel moves with each swing of the pendulum and turns the second hand. Other wheels (not shown) turn hour and minute hands.

Weight pulls cord, driving main wheel that turns other wheels.

Main wheel

Swinging pendulum rocks anchor.

## PENDULUM CLOCK
In the 1580s the Italian scientist Galileo noticed that each swing of a suspended weight, or pendulum, takes a fixed time. He suggested that this regular movement could be used to control a clock. But it was another 70 years before the first pendulum clock was built.

**MECHANICAL WATCHES**
Mechanical watches are controlled by the oscillations of a wheel linked to a spring. The first watch was invented in Germany in about 1500.

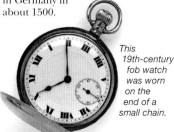

This 19th-century fob watch was worn on the end of a small chain.

**ATOMIC CLOCK**
If it were to run for more than one million years, this atomic clock would be less than one second off! The atomic clock is the most accurate of all clocks. It is controlled by vibrating atoms and is used in science to measure intervals of time with extraordinary accuracy.

Cover and display window

Watch unit and strap

LCD (liquid crystal display)

Microchip

Quartz crystal

Battery

## DIGITAL WATCH
A battery powers a digital watch, and a tiny quartz crystal regulates its speed. Electricity from the battery makes the crystal vibrate thousands of times each second. The microchip uses these regular vibrations to make the numbers on the display change every second, so the watch shows the time very precisely.

*Find out more*
ELECTRONICS
ROCKS AND MINERALS
TIME

# CLOTHES

FROM ELEGANT SILKS to practical working outfits, the clothes people wear reflect how they live. The first clothes were animal skins which kept out the cold and rain. Clothes still give protection against the weather, but society also dictates their shape – a business suit looks out of place on a beach, and nobody goes to the office in a bathing suit. Clothing fashions change from year to year and garments go "out of fashion" quickly. Fashion started as a way to display wealth. When clothes were expensive, only rich people could afford to be fashionable. Through the centuries fashion has evolved as lifestyles changed. For instance, when women had few rights, fashionable dresses restricted movement, just as society limited what women could do. But as women gained more freedom, trousers became popular, and women could move around more easily.

*Hat, scarf, and gloves made from wool help to keep out the winter cold.*

## COLD CLIMATE
Traditionally, clothes for a cold climate are made from animal skins. The fur, worn inside, traps a layer of air which resists the flow of heat from the body. Modern jackets and trousers are made of closely woven nylon and are wind- and waterproof. Down padding traps air between the feathers to keep heat in.

*Veil for modesty*

## THE VEIL
In some cultures women are required to conceal certain parts of the body. This Kunama woman from Eritrea in East Africa is wearing a veil that covers her head and shoulders.

## FUNCTIONAL CLOTHES
Sometimes the function of clothes – the job they have to do – is the most important influence on their design. For example, the function of bad-weather clothes is to keep out cold, wind, and rain; style or colour is not so important. Functional garments are also worn for religious reasons, for different types of work, and for sports. So, religious garments may need to cover the body, factory clothes must be made from durable fabrics, and sports wear should be lightweight.

## BUSINESS SUIT
Dress codes vary at modern workplaces. Some organizations encourage casual wear while others, such as some corporate firms, prefer their staff to come to work in formal suits.

*Multi-layered clothing to keep out heat*

## MAKING CLOTHES
Today most people in Europe and North America buy mass-produced clothes in shops. But homemade clothes are still popular among people who want original clothes in the fabric of their choice, or who cannot afford clothes sold in shops. Paper patterns show how to cut each piece of fabric. Pinning the cut pieces of fabric holds them together to make sewing easier.

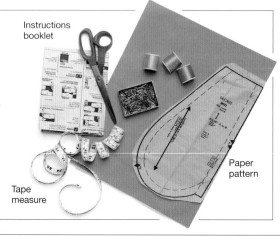

*Instructions booklet*

*Paper pattern*

*Tape measure*

## WARM CLIMATE
People who live in desert climates wear long, loose, cotton robes. The robes have a double function: they protect the skin from the harmful rays of the sun and keep the body cool by trapping layers of air between the folds of cloth. Traditional Arab costume includes a long tunic, cloak, and head cloth.

## BUSTLE

Past fashions can look strange or ridiculous. In the late 19th century the bustle was popular. It made a dress stick out at the back.

*The bustle was a cushion or wire framework tied around the waist under a dress.*

# DRESSES

Clothing has changed through the ages. Ancient Greek dresses were pieces of cloth draped around the body. In 14th-century Europe, dresses were tailored to fit. In the 16th century, women's vests were stiffened with whalebone. Tight boning went on to the end of the 19th century. Fashions changed, and a simple, loose-fitting slip replaced the awkward bustle under women's dresses. The 1920s saw an even greater change: more practical shifts were worn and skirts were short for the first time.

*It took a mass of cloth, lace, whalebone, and steel to complete this elegant-looking 19th-century dress.*

## MINI DRESSES

Clothing gradually grew simpler and less restrictive. In the 1960s, young people had more independence than ever before. Women expressed their freedom by wearing very short skirts.

*Fashionable boots accompanied a variety of outfits in the 1960s.*

## FASHION HOUSES

The most fashionable clothes come from *haute couture* (high fashion) designers. Their companies are called fashion houses. Models show off the designers' new creations at fashion shows called collections. Designer Coco Chanel (1883-1971) revolutionized women's clothing when she created simple and comfortable dresses, suits, and sweaters from jersey, a knitted fabric that stretches as the wearer moves.

*Coco Chanel's clothes were the first fashionable garments that were uncluttered and easy to wear.*

*Early Levi advertisements stressed the strength of the clothes.*

### BLUE JEANS

Inexpensive, easily washed, and hardwearing, blue jeans first appeared in the United States in 1850. A miner digging for gold in the California gold rush asked tailor Levi Strauss to make him a sturdy pair of trousers, because ordinary fabric wore out so quickly. Jeans are made of denim, a tough cotton fabric coloured with the natural blue indigo dye.

# UNIFORMS

People who belong to the same group or organization often wear similar garments so that they can be easily identified. These standard clothes are called uniforms. Uniforms promote a sense of team spirit and companionship that so many people are proud of their uniforms. Some, such as nurses' uniforms, are very functional and protect the wearer while at work.

Schoolgirls     Nurse     Soccer player     Policeman

## PROTECTIVE CLOTHING

Workers such as fire fighters and nuclear power workers need clothes which protect them while they are at work. This fire fighter (above) is wearing a fire-resistant suit that also shields him from high temperatures. An oxygen mask prevents him from suffocating in smoke-filled areas.

*Find out more*

DESIGN
TEXTILES

# COAL

A lump of anthracite, a type of hard black coal

PEOPLE HAVE used coal for cooking and heating for thousands of years. During the 19th century, coal was the world's most important fuel. It powered the steam engines that made the Industrial Revolution possible. Today, coal is still used in vast amounts. Most coal is burned at power stations to produce electricity, and burning coal meets much of the world's energy needs. Coal is also an essential raw material for making many products, the most important of which are iron and steel. Coal is often called a fossil fuel because it is formed from the fossilized remains of plants that are millions of years old. Sometimes a piece of coal bears the imprint of a prehistoric plant or insect. The Earth contains reserves of coal which, with careful use, may last for hundreds of years. But many people are concerned that coal burning adds to global pollution.

## FORMATION OF COAL

**1 PREHISTORIC SWAMP**
Coal began to form in swamps as long ago as 300 million years. Dying trees and other plants fell into the water, and their remains became covered in mud.

**2 PEAT**
The plant remains slowly dried out under the mud, forming layers of peat, a fuel that can be dug from the ground.

**3 LIGNITE**
Layers of peat became buried. Heat and pressure turned the peat into lignite, or brown coal. Lignite is dug from shallow pits called strip mines.

**4 BLACK COAL**
Intense heat and pressure turned deeper layers of peat into a soft black coal called bituminous coal, and anthracite.

## COAL MINERS

For centuries, miners had to cut coal by hand. Now there are drills and computer-controlled cutting machines to help them.

## MINING

Mine shafts are dug down to seams (layers) of coal far below the surface. Miners dig a network of tunnels to remove coal from the seams. In addition to coal, many other useful minerals, such as copper, are mined. The deepest mine is a gold mine in South Africa nearly 4 km (2.5 miles) deep.

Pumps circulate fresh air through the mine.

Skip (shuttle car) lifts coal to surface.

Air shaft

Railway takes miners to the coal faces.

Miners' cage carries miners up and down mine.

Miners use cutting machine to dig out coal at coal face.

Miners have lamps on their helmets which light up everything in front of them in the dark depths of a mine.

Conveyor belts take coal to shaft.

Supports hold roof and sides of tunnels in place.

## USES OF COAL

A few steam-powered trains still burn coal, and some homes have open fires or coal-fired heating systems. The main use for coal is in the production of electricity. Heating coal without air produces coke, which is used to make steel, and coal gas, which may be burned as a fuel. Another product is coal-tar pitch, which is used in making roads. Coal is also treated to make chemicals which are used to produce drugs, plastics, dyes, and many other products.

A large coal-fired power station in Berlin, Germany

---

### Find out more
ELECTRICITY
FIRE
INDUSTRIAL REVOLUTION
IRON AND STEEL
PREHISTORIC LIFE
TRAINS

# COLD WAR

POTSDAM
In 1945, British Prime Minister Winston Churchill, US President Harry Truman, and Premier Joseph Stalin of the Soviet Union (left to right) met at Potsdam, Germany, to decide the future of the Western world. But serious disagreements arose because Stalin was not prepared to release the countries of Eastern Europe from Communist control. This greatly worried the Western leaders.

**W**HEN WORLD WAR II ENDED in 1945, Europe was in ruins. The United States, and what was then the Soviet Union, had emerged as the world's two most powerful countries or "superpowers". By 1949, two new power blocs of countries had formed. The Eastern bloc, led by the Soviet Union, was Communist; the Western bloc, headed by the United States, was Capitalist. Over the next 40 years the two superpowers opposed each other in what became known as the Cold War. Each bloc attempted to become the most powerful by building up stocks of weapons. The Cold War was a time of great tension but during the late 1980s the rivalry eased. Both sides began to disarm, and in 1991 the Soviet Union broke up, bringing the Cold War to an end.

## THE IRON CURTAIN

As soon as World War II ended, Stalin shut the borders of Eastern Europe. Winston Churchill declared that "an iron curtain has descended across the continent" of Europe. The Communists seized control of the countries behind the imaginary Iron Curtain. These countries became Soviet satellites – nations controlled by the Soviet Union. Yugoslavia broke away in 1948; East Germany was added in 1949.

Soviet Union
East Germany
West Germany
Czechoslovakia
Albania

BERLIN AIRLIFT
In 1945, Britain, France, the United States, and the Soviet Union divided Berlin between them. In 1948, Stalin blocked all traffic to West Berlin. But in the Berlin airlift, the Western allies flew in supplies, and Stalin lifted the blockade.

The NATO symbol

NATO
In 1949, the United States and several European countries formed the North Atlantic Treaty Organization (NATO). A military organization, its aim was to prevent a Soviet invasion of Europe. In response to this the Soviet Union formed an alliance of Communist states called the Warsaw Pact.

INF TREATY
From the 1960s onwards, relations between the two superpowers improved. In 1987, US President Ronald Reagan and Soviet General Secretary Mikhail Gorbachev signed the Soviet-American Intermediate-Range Nuclear Forces (INF) Treaty. The INF treaty cut down on the number of nuclear weapons and was a major breakthrough in the Cold War.

KOREAN WAR
In 1950, Communist North Korea, equipped with Soviet weapons, invaded South Korea. The United States led a United Nations force to drive the Communists out. When the United Nations troops invaded North Korea, China sent soldiers to fight them. It was the first time the United States had fought a "hot war" against Communism.

*Find out more*
COMMUNISM
NUCLEAR AGE
SOVIET UNION, HISTORY OF
UNITED NATIONS
VIETNAM WAR
WORLD WAR II

# COLOMBIA

| Volcano | Mountain | Ancient monument | Capital city | Large city/town | Small city/town |

Colombia lies in the far north of the South American continent, and borders both the Caribbean Sea and the Pacific Ocean.

**EMERALDS**
Most of the world's emeralds are found in Colombia, and some of the finest examples are found near the capital, Bogotá.

COLOMBIA IS DOMINATED by the Andes in the west, and the upper reaches of the mighty Amazon in the east. Much of the land is sparsely populated and not suitable for agriculture. The rainforests of the east are rich in wildlife, containing over 1,500 species of birds, numerous monkeys, and endangered felines such as jaguars and ocelots. In the lowlands to the west of the Andes, the subtropical climate provides ideal conditions for growing both coffee, Colombia's main crop, and coca, the basis of Colombia's illegal drugs trade. Originally populated by many native tribes, Colombia was settled by the Spanish in 1525. Colombia became independent in 1819, but has had a history of civil wars and conflict, most recently as a result of the drugs trade.

## STATISTICS
**Area:**
1,138,910 sq km
(439,733 sq miles)
**Population:** 44,200,000
**Capital:** Bogotá
**Languages:** Spanish, Amerindian languages, English Creole
**Religions:**
Roman Catholic
**Currency:**
Colombian peso
**Main occupations:**
Agriculture, mining, drug trafficking
**Main exports:** Coffee, coal, cocaine, gold, platinum, silver, emeralds

Guambiano Indians

## AMERINDIANS

The original American Indian population of Colombia intermarried with Spanish colonists. Today, half of Colombia's population is *mestizo*, which means of mixed European and Indian descent. Yet some 400 Indian tribes survive, speaking more than 180 languages. These Guambiano Indians live on reservations, where they make a living from growing maize, wheat, and potatoes, and selling their craft goods to tourists.

Caribbean Sea

Santa Marta • Ríohacha
**Barranquilla**
**Cartagena**
Gulf of Darien • Sincelejo
Montería • Cúcuta
Barrancabermeja • Bucaramanga
Bello
**Medellín**
Itagüí • Sogamoso
Manizales • Tunja
Armenia **BOGOTÁ**
Tuluá
Buenaventura • Villavicencio
**Cali**
Popayán
Florencia • San José del Guaviare
Pasto • Mitú

PANAMA
PACIFIC OCEAN
ECUADOR
PERU
VENEZUELA
Llanos
Meta
Guaviare
COLOMBIA
BRAZIL
Magdalena
Vaupés
Caquetá
Putumayo
Equator

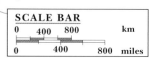

N W E S

## COFFEE
Colombia's main export is coffee, grown on tropical evergreen shrubs which require both high temperatures and high rainfall. Its berry-like fruits are processed to extract the seeds, which are then dried in the sunlight. Further processing frees the seeds from their coverings, and the beans are ready for export. Drying the beans by hand is very hard work, and increasingly machines are being used.

**SCALE BAR**
0   400   800   km
0   400   800   miles

*Find out more*

GEMS AND JEWELLERY
SOUTH AMERICA
SPAIN, HISTORY OF

# COLOUR

A WORLD WITHOUT COLOUR would be a dull place. It would also be difficult to live in. Imagine how hard it would be to tell if traffic lights meant stop or go if there were no red or green. Nature has colour signals too: the bright colours of a tree frog warn other animals that it is poisonous, and the beautiful colours of a flower attract bees to its nectar. Not every creature sees colours in the same way; some animals, such as guinea pigs and squirrels, are colour blind and cannot distinguish between different colours at all. Colour is really the way our eyes interpret different kinds of light. Light is made up of tiny, invisible waves, and each wave has a particular size or wavelength. Each coloured light is composed of different wavelengths, which our eyes are able to detect. White light, such as light from the Sun, is actually a combination of light of all the colours of the rainbow.

## PRISM
A triangular chunk of glass, called a prism, separates all the colours in white light. When light goes through a prism, it is refracted, or bent, because glass slows it down. But every colour goes through at a different speed, and is bent to a different degree. So the colours spread out when they leave the prism.

Indigo

Violet

Blue

Green

Yellow

Orange

Red

## SPECTRUM
When a prism splits white light into colours, they always come out in the same order, with red at one end and violet at the other. This is called the spectrum. When sunlight is refracted by raindrops, a rainbow is produced which contains all the colours of the spectrum.

*Mixing any two primary colours produces secondary colours.*

## MIXING COLOURS
Red, green, and blue are called the primary colours of light. This is because you can mix red, green, and blue light in different proportions to make any colour in the spectrum. In printing there is a different set of primary colours: cyan (green-blue), magenta (blue-red), and yellow. These too can be mixed to give any colour except white.

## PAINT PRIMARIES
Red, yellow and blue are the primary colours of paints. Mixing them together in the correct amounts gives black.

## LIGHT PRIMARIES
When the three primary colours of light are mixed together in the correct proportions they make white. During rock concerts and theatre performances, lighting technicians produce a wide range of colours on the stage by mixing different coloured spotlights.

## COLOURED OBJECTS
Objects look coloured because of the way they reflect the light that hits them. When white light falls on any surface, some colours are absorbed, or taken in, and some bounce off. When we look at the surface, we see only the colours that bounce off. It is this coloured light that produces the colour we perceive the object to be.

## RED SHOES
When daylight hits a pair of red shoes, they look red because they reflect only red light and absorb all the other colours.

## BLACK SHOES?
In blue light, red shoes look black because all the blue light is absorbed, and no light is reflected.

### Find out more
CAMOUFLAGE, ANIMAL
EYES
LIGHT
PRINTING
RAIN AND SNOW

# CHRISTOPHER
# COLUMBUS

IN 1492 THREE SMALL SAILING SHIPS named the *Niña,* the *Pinta,* and the *Santa Maria* left Spain on a daring voyage. Their aim was to find a new sea route to Asia in search of spices and gold. In command was Christopher Columbus, an Italian sailor from Genoa. Unlike other explorers of the time, who were sailing east, Columbus believed that if he sailed west he would reach India and its luxuries within a few months. The Spanish were eager to profit from trade with India and the rest of Asia, and Columbus persuaded Queen Isabella of Spain to pay for his expedition. He set sail on 3 August and two months later sighted land which he believed was Asia. In fact, Columbus had arrived in the Caribbean Islands. He did not realize what he had found, but his journey paved the way for later European settlement in the Americas.

North America

South America

Landed on San Salvador 12 October 1492.

Cuba

Hispaniola

Began homeward voyage 16 January 1493.

THE FIRST VOYAGE
Columbus's voyage to the Caribbean lasted four months. He made three more voyages, reaching Central America on his final voyage.

**PTOLEMY'S WORLD MAP**
The map used by Columbus had been produced by the ancient Greek mapmaker Ptolemy in the 2nd century. The world it showed did not include the continents of North and South America, Australia, or the Pacific.

## EXPLORING THE CARIBBEAN

When Columbus arrived in the Caribbean he was welcomed by the Carib and Arawak people. Native Americans became known as Indians because the early explorers thought they were in India.

Captain's cabin held navigation equipment and a chest to store treasure captured on the voyage.

Food and other supplies were stored here.

Bowsprit was a spar, or horizontal mast, supporting triangular sails.

THE *SANTA MARIA*
Columbus's flagship was a slow, clumsy, wooden cargo ship, no larger than a modern fishing trawler. The ship relied on wind power, and conditions on board were cramped and difficult.

Spare canvas for mending sails.

Off-duty sailors slept wherever there was space.

THE CREW
The *Santa Maria* carried a crew of 40. The main risk of a long voyage was running out of food and fresh water.

*Find out more*

CARIBBEAN
CONQUISTADORS
EXPLORERS

# COMETS AND METEORS

ON A CLEAR NIGHT you may see several shooting stars in the space of an hour. A shooting star, or meteor, looks like a point of light which suddenly darts across the sky and disappears. A meteor occurs when a piece of dust from space, called a meteoroid, burns up as it enters the Earth's atmosphere. As the meteor plummets to Earth at a speed of about 240,000 km/h (150,000 mph), friction with the air produces intense heat which leaves a bright glow in the sky. Meteors usually burn up about 90 km (56 miles) from the Earth's surface.

Many meteoroids are fragments from comets which orbit the Sun. A comet appears as a faint, fuzzy point of light that moves across the night sky for weeks or months. As it nears the Sun, the comet grows a "tail". Then it swings past the Sun and travels away, becoming smaller and fainter. Comets often reappear at regular intervals (every few years) as they travel past Earth on their orbits.

### COMET TAIL
As a comet approaches Earth, the heat of the Sun turns the ice into gas. The gas escapes, along with dust, and forms one or more tails (the gas and dust form separate tails). The tails always point away from the Sun. They get shorter as the comet moves away from the Sun.

Dust tail can be up to about 1 million km (600,000 miles) long. It shines white because the particles of dust reflect sunlight.

Gas tail can be up to 100 million km (62 million miles) long. The gas tail has a bluish glow. This is because the heat of the Sun makes the gas molecules emit blue-coloured light.

The size of a comet's nucleus can range from a few hundred metres across to more than 10 kms (about 6 miles) across.

The solar wind – a blast of charged particles that stream from the Sun – blows the comet's gas tail away from the Sun. When the comet approaches the Sun, its tails follow. The tails lead when the comet moves away from the Sun.

## COMETS
A comet consists of a central core, or nucleus, of dust and ice; a cloud of gas and dust around the nucleus, called the coma; and one or more tails. Astronomers have observed hundreds of comets and believe that about one billion ($10^{12}$) other comets orbit the Sun unseen, far beyond the most distant planet.

In 2004, the Stardust spacecraft flew past comet Wild 2, sending back many pictures including this enhanced, composite image.

Chinese astronomers probably observed Halley's Comet more than 2,200 years ago. The comet also appears in the 11th-century Bayeux tapestry, which shows the Norman Conquest of England.

### HALLEY'S COMET
The English astronomer Edmund Halley (1656-1742) was the first to realize that some comets appear regularly. In 1705 he showed that the comet now called Halley's Comet returns past the Earth every 75 or 76 years.

### METEORITES
Huge lumps of rock called meteorites pass through the Earth's atmosphere without burning up completely. About 25,000 years ago, a meteorite that weighed about 900,000 tonnes (more than 890,000 tons) caused a crater in Arizona, United States (above), 1,200 m (4,000 ft) across. Some scientists believe that the impact of a huge meteorite about 65 million years ago may have destroyed many animal species.

### METEORS
There are two ways in which meteors occur: individually and in showers. This spectacular meteor shower (left) occurred in 1833. Similar impressive displays occur every 33 years during November. At this time the Earth passes through a swarm of meteors, called the Leonids, that spread out along the orbit of a comet.

| *Find out more* |
| --- |
| ASTRONOMY |
| BLACK HOLES |
| EARTH |
| PLANETS |
| ROCKS AND MINERALS |
| STARS |
| SUN |

# COMMUNISM

AFTER 1917, A NEW WORD came into popular use – Communism. For it was then that Russia set up the world's first Communist government. By 1950, nearly one-third of the world's population lived under Communist rule. The word communism comes from the Latin word *communis*, meaning "belonging to all". More than 2,000 years ago, the Greek writer, Plato, put forward the earliest ideas about Communism in his book *The Republic*. Much later, Vladimir Lenin, the Russian revolutionary developed modern Communism from the writings of the German philosopher Karl Marx. Unlike Capitalists, who believe in private ownership, Communists believe that the state should own a country's wealth and industry, and wealth should be shared according to need. In Communist countries, the Communist party controls every aspect of daily life. During the 20th century, Communism was a major political force. But people in Communist countries resented economic hardship and their lack of freedom. From the late 1980s, various countries, including the former Soviet Union, rejected Communist rule.

**CHAINS AROUND THE WORLD**
"The workers have nothing to lose . . . but their chains. They have a world to gain," wrote Marx in his *Communist Manifesto*. On this magazine cover, a worker strikes down "chains" that bind the world.

## KARL MARX
Communism is based on the ideas of Karl Marx (1818-83). His major work, *Das Kapital*, became the Communist "bible". He believed that all history is a struggle between the rich rulers and the poor workers, and that the workers will eventually overthrow their rulers in a revolution. Marx died in exile in London, England.

**SPREAD OF COMMUNISM**
After 1917, Communism spread from Russia to many other countries elsewhere in the world(shown in red above). In Eastern Europe and North Korea, Communist governments were installed by the Soviet army. In China and Southeast Asia, local armed Communist groups took power after fighting long wars.

| CAPITALISM | COMMUNISM |
|---|---|
| Owner    Worker | Worker    Worker |
| Under Capitalism, a few companies own the factories. Workers are paid wages but do not always share the profits. | Under Communism, the factories are owned by the state. The state sets wage levels for workers, and uses profits for other investments. |

### CHINA
In 1949, China became a Communist state under Mao Zedong (1893-1976). China has the largest Communist party in the world, with 63 million members. Since the 1970s China's rulers have gradually abandoned Communist economic policies, encouraging private enterprise to create economic growth. But the party has kept a tight grip on power. It encourages people to take part in group sports, such as tai chi (left).

### FIDEL CASTRO
In 1959, Fidel Castro (left), a Cuban lawyer, led a revolution against Cuba's dictator, President Batista. Castro became head of government, and Cuba became a Communist state. Castro seized all American property and promised freedom to the Cuban people. In the 1960s, Castro encouraged and supported Communist movements throughout Central and South America.

--- *Find out more* ---
CHINA, HISTORY OF
COLD WAR
MAO ZEDONG
RUSSIAN REVOLUTION
SOUTH AMERICA, HISTORY OF
SOVIET UNION, HISTORY OF

# COMPOSERS

AN AUTHOR CREATING A STORY has a choice of more than a hundred thousand words made up from the 26 letters of the alphabet. With only the 12 notes of the chromatic scale – the notes on the piano from any C to the next C above – a composer can make an infinite variety of music of many different styles. These can include jazz, folk, popular, or what is known as classical music.

Composers learn their craft through writing exercises in harmony and counterpoint. Harmony is placing the main tune on the top line with chords (three or more notes sounding together) in support; counterpoint is placing the principal theme in any position with other tunes weaving around it. Composers also discover what instruments can or cannot do, what they sound like, and how to explore their capabilities. The best way to learn all this is to study the music of many composers. Great composers move audiences to tears of joy or sadness with their talent for expressing emotion through music.

*In the 15th century beautiful coloured pictures decorated the margins of composers' works.*

PURCELL
English composer Henry Purcell (1659-95) sang in the king's chapel in London (above) when he was a boy. At the age of 20 he became the organist at Westminster Abbey, London. He composed beautiful chamber music and dramatic operas such as *Dido and Aeneas*.

*Each member of the orchestra uses a line of the score showing only the music for his or her individual instrument.*

## HOW COMPOSERS WORK
Most composers begin by either inventing themes or melodies that are developed for one or more instruments, or by setting words for one or more voices. Sometimes, as with operas and choral works, both voices and instruments are used. Blending them together so that all are heard clearly is a skilled job. The music is written out in a score. As a symphony can last up to an hour, or an opera up to three hours, composing can be seen to be hard work.

*Composers of orchestral music write a complete score, which includes the instrumental parts played by every section of the orchestra.*

*Many composers like to write music sitting at the piano, so that they can play the tunes as they work on them.*

## BAROQUE MUSIC
The music of the 17th and early 18th centuries was called Baroque, after the elaborate architectural styles popular in the same period. It is complex music in which the instruments weave their melodies in and out like threads in a rich, colourful tapestry.

### BACH
The greatest of the Baroque composers was Johann Sebastian Bach (1685-1750) of Germany. The *Brandenburg Concertos*, which he completed in 1721, are among his best-known works.

HANDEL
George Frideric Handel (1685-1759) was born in Germany and moved to England in 1712. He composed music for the English royal family and wrote many famous choral works.

*Handel wrote one of his most famous pieces of music to accompany a royal fireworks display in 1749.*

# CLASSICAL ERA

Serious music is often called classical to distinguish it from popular music. However, for musicians, classical music is the music composed in the late 18th and early 19th centuries. Classical composers extended the harmony and forms of the Baroque era. The symphony developed in this period. Joseph Haydn (1732-1809) composed 104 symphonies.

### MOZART
Wolfgang Amadeus Mozart (1756-91) of Austria was a talented composer and performer by the age of five. He went on to write chamber music, symphonies, and concertos, as well as great operas such as *The Magic Flute*.

*Mozart performed all over Europe when he was only six.*

### BEETHOVEN
The German composer Ludwig van Beethoven (1770-1827; above) was completely deaf for the last 10 years of his life but continued to compose some of the greatest music in the world. His late works moved towards the Romantic movement.

# ROMANTIC MOVEMENT

From about 1820 composers began to experiment with new harmonies and forms, achieving a much wider emotional range. For composers such as Tchaikovsky, formal rules were less important than creating drama, painting pictures in sound, or telling stories.

### TCHAIKOVSKY
The Russian composer Peter Ilyich Tchaikovsky (1840-93) was unhappy in his personal life, which brought great emotional depth to his music. He wrote many well-known ballets and symphonies, including the famous *1812 Overture*.

*Stravinsky's ballet* The Firebird *caused a sensation at its first performance in Paris in 1910.*

*Playing a tune on an electric piano adds the notes to the score on the screen.*

## COMPUTER COMPOSITION
Computers can help composers to write music. The composer can use an electronic instrument to enter the melodies into the computer, where they can be stored, altered, and printed out.

# MODERN MUSIC

In the 20th century there were great changes in serious music. Russian-born composer Igor Stravinsky (1882-1971) experimented with new harmonies, creating sounds that his audiences sometimes found difficult to understand. Composers such as the German Karlheinz Stockhausen (b. 1928) challenged listeners' ideas about music. In *Zyklus*, for example, Stockhausen tells the percussionist to start on any page of the score and play to the end before starting again at the beginning.

## COMPOSERS

**800s** Composers begin to write down their music for the first time. At the same time, monks develop a form of chant, called plainsong, for singing church services.

**1300-1600** Composers of the late Medieval and Renaissance period start to develop harmony by combining different voices together, producing a richer sound called polyphony.

**1597** Jacopo Peri (1561-1633) of Italy composes *Dafne*, the first opera.

**1600s** Baroque music begins, and composers gradually make their music more complicated and elaborate.

**1750-1820** The rise of classical music introduces simpler, popular tunes that more people could enjoy.

**1817-23** Beethoven composes the *Choral symphony*, the first symphony to use a choir.

**1820s** The romantic era begins, and composers start to look for new ways to make their music appeal to the listeners' emotions.

**1850s** Composers in eastern and northern Europe begin to write nationalistic music, based on traditional songs and stories from their countries.

**1865** Richard Wagner's (1813-83) opera *Tristan and Isolde* points the way towards Modern music.

**1888** Russian nationalist composer Nikolai Rimsky-Korsakov composes his *Scheherazade*, based on the *Thousand and One Nights*.

**1900s** The modern era in music begins. Composers of the impressionist movement write music that creates atmosphere, movement, and colour in sound.

**1905** French impressionist composer Claude Debussy (1862-1918) writes *La Mer* (The Sea).

**1924** George Gershwin composes *Rhapsody in Blue* for jazz orchestra and piano.

**1959** German composer Karlheinz Stockhausen (born 1928) writes *Zyklus* for one percussion player.

---

### Find out more
MUSIC
MUSICAL INSTRUMENTS
OPERA AND SINGING
ORCHESTRAS
RENAISSANCE

# COMPUTERS

ACCURATE WEATHER FORECASTING, safe air travel, reliable medical technology – in today's world we take these things for granted, but they would be impossible without computers. Although a computer cannot "think" for itself like a person, it works like an electronic brain, doing tasks and interpreting data (information) very quickly. The computer in an air-traffic control system, for instance, can keep track of hundreds of aircraft at the same time and indicates which routes they should follow to avoid collisions. A personal computer can be used for a variety of tasks from word processing to searching the Internet and sending email. A computer consists of thousands of tiny electronic circuits. Before a computer can work, it must be given a set of instructions, called a program (or software), which tells the mechanical and electronic components inside the computer how to carry out a particular job. Additional components, such as a memory card or an internal modem, can be slotted into the computer as required.

**HIDDEN COMPUTERS**
People usually think of computers as having a screen and a keyboard, but this is not always the case. Many devices, such as washing machines, cars, and cameras, contain tiny computers that are specially programmed to control their function.

**MEMORY**
A computer memory consists of two types of microchips: ROM (Read-Only Memory) contains permanent instructions; RAM (Random Access Memory) holds programs and information as they are needed. The microchips store information in the form of electric charges.

## PERSONAL COMPUTERS

Many homes, schools, and offices use personal computers – small computers designed for use by one person. A personal computer consists of four basic units: a keyboard, to type in information; a memory, to store information and programs; a processing unit, to carry out the instructions contained in the program; and a monitor, for displaying the results of the computer's work.

*Monitor displays data*

*RAM memory chip*

*Power supply*

*The CPU (central processing unit), or microprocessor, is a microchip which does calculations and other similar tasks.*

**TYPES OF DISK**
Information can be stored for long periods on magnetic disks. There are many types of disks, including hard disks, which store vast quantities of data, and floppy disks, which store less information but are removable and can be used to carry data from one computer to another. CD-ROMS (Compact Disc-Read-Only Memory), which hold 650 times as much information as a floppy disk, are the most popular format for multimedia programs.

*A hard disk consists of several magnetic disks. An electromagnet "writes" information onto them and "reads" data from them.*

*Floppy disk*

*CD-ROM*

*ROM memory chip*

*The keyboard has keys similar to those of a typewriter. Pressing the keys feeds information into the computer. Letters or numbers appear on screen, or the computer performs a function.*

**MOUSE**
A device called a mouse moves an arrow on the screen. The mouse ball is connected to two slotted wheels. As each wheel turns, it interrupts a beam of light. From the changes in the light beam, the computer detects where the mouse has moved.

*Mouse*

# HOW COMPUTERS WORK

A computer converts everything it handles, such as letters of the alphabet, into numbers. The numbers are stored in the computer in the form of electronic signals in which "on" stands for 1 and "off" stands for 0. All numbers, letters, and pictures are represented by sequences of 1s and 0s. This is called binary code. The computer does all its different tasks, such as inserting a word into a sentence, by doing rapid calculations with these numbers. Once it has finished its job, the computer changes the numbers into words and pictures that we can understand.

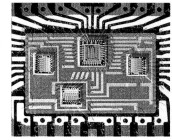

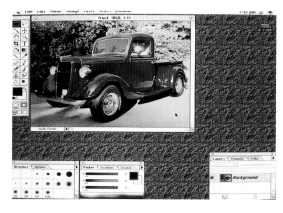

*All computers contain a set of microchips (left). Inside a microchip are millions of tiny electronic parts that store and process electronic signals.*

## SOFTWARE

The programs that make a computer perform different tasks are called software. A computer can perform many different jobs simply by using different software programs, from computer games and word processing packages to painting programs and scientific applications that do complex calculations.

## HARDWARE

Computer machinery is called hardware. There are many different kinds of hardware: personal computers, small portable computers, and large mainframe computers on which many people can work simultaneously. Hardware also includes components such as monitors, printers, and other computer equipment (below).

*Monitor displays information.*

*Hard drive is stored inside tower unit.*

*Speaker*

*CD-ROM drive*

*Zip disk drive*

*Printer produces a paper copy of the material shown on the screen.*

*Keyboard*

*Graphics tablet allows images to be drawn onto the screen with a special pen.*

*Mouse pad*

*Mouse*

*Scanner copies an image from a photograph or book and transfers it into the computer.*

## HISTORY OF COMPUTERS

In 1834, English inventor Charles Babbage designed the first programmable mechanical computer. However, he could not make the machine as it was too complex for the technology of his day. The first electronic computer, ENIAC, was built in the US in 1946. During the 1980s, transistors and microchips enabled computers to become smaller and more powerful. Easy-to-use software programs such as those developed by Microsoft (below) encouraged the spread of computers in people's homes. In the 1990s, web browsers opened the Internet to private individuals.

*In 1975, American Bill Gates (1955-) founded the Microsoft company. By the late 1990s, Microsoft was supplying more than half the world's software.*

*Bluetooth*

*Wi-Fi*

*Router connected to Internet or local network*

*Mobile phone*

## NEW TECHNOLOGY

Computers are becoming increasingly portable and versatile. Wireless or "Wi-Fi" technology means they can connect to the Internet via radio signals, and the similar "Bluetooth" enables them to communicate without cables over short distances with pocket computers, mobile phones, and even printers, keyboards, and mice.

*Using wireless connections, a laptop computer can be used to send e-mails or surf the Internet from almost anywhere.*

*Handheld or "pocket" computers can send and receive e-mails, be used as mobile phones, and let you work on files from your desktop computer.*

> ### Find out more
> ELECTRONICS
> MACHINES
> MATHEMATICS
> ROBOTS
> TECHNOLOGY

# CONQUISTADORS

AT THE BEGINNING OF THE 16TH CENTURY the first Spanish adventurers followed Christopher Columbus to the Caribbean and South and Central America. These conquistadors (the Spanish word for conquerors) were soldiers hungry for gold, silver, and land. They took priests with them, sent by the Catholic Church to convert the Native Americans. The two most famous conquistadors were Hernando Cortés (1485-1547), who conquered the Aztecs of Mexico, and Francisco Pizarro (1470-1541), who conquered the Incas of Peru. Although the conquistadors took only small numbers of soldiers along, they were successful partly because they had brought guns, horses, and steel weapons. But what also came with the conquistadors were European diseases such as smallpox and measles, against which the Native Americans had no resistance. These diseases wiped out more than 70 million Native Americans and destroyed their civilizations. By seizing the land, the conquistadors prepared the way for a huge Spanish empire in the Americas that was to last until the 19th century.

### EL DORADO
The first conquistadors heard legends of a golden kingdom ruled by "El Dorado", the golden man. They kept searching for this amazing place but never found it. Most of the beautiful goldwork they took to Europe was melted down and reused.

### HERNANDO CORTES
In 1519, Cortés set out from Cuba to conquer Mexico, against the governor Velázquez's wishes. Velázquez believed that Cortés was too ambitious. From an early age Cortés had sought adventure and wealth. Eventually his wish was fulfilled and he controlled the whole of Mexico.

Hernando Cortés

Montezuma

## MONTEZUMA MEETS CORTES
When the Aztec emperor Montezuma met Cortés in Tenochtitlán, he believed that Cortés was the pale-skinned, bearded god Quetzalcoatl, who was prophesied to return from the east. He welcomed Cortés with gifts and a ceremony. But Cortés captured him and took over the Aztec empire.

## NEW SPAIN
The Spanish quickly settled in the conquered areas and created the empire of New Spain. The wealth from its silver mines and ranches became the envy of Europe.

■ Aztecs
■ Incas

## NATIVE AMERICANS
After conquest, the Native Americans were treated cruelly and forced to work for the Spanish. Many slaved in the gold mines. It was not long before their old way of life disappeared forever.

### FRANCISCO PIZARRO
In 1532, Pizarro marched into Peru with 200 soldiers. He seized the Inca emperor, Atahualpa, ransomed him for a roomful of gold, then had him killed. The leaderless Inca empire crumbled.

---

### *Find out more*
AZTECS
COLUMBUS, CHRISTOPHER
EXPLORERS
INCAS
MAYA
SOUTH AMERICA, HISTORY OF

---

# CONSERVATION
## AND ENDANGERED SPECIES

ANIMALS AND PLANTS ARE DYING OUT at a greater rate today than ever before. Living things have become extinct throughout the Earth's history – often due to dramatic changes in the climate – but today, humans are posing a greater threat. Thousands of animals and plants are endangered (in danger of extinction) because we cut down forests and drain wetlands to farm or build on the land where they live. We change the environment so much that animals and plants cannot survive. This is called habitat loss. Another great threat is hunting. People hunt animals for their fur, hide, horns, and meat, and sometimes simply because they consider animals a nuisance. Pollution is yet another serious threat, damaging many oceans, rivers, and forests. Conservation is the management and protection of wildlife and its habitats. It includes sheltering and trying to save wild animals and plants from destruction by humans. People are more aware of these threats to wildlife than ever before, and there are conservation organizations in many parts of the world. They work to protect endangered creatures by setting aside areas in the wild where animals and plants can live in safety.

**GREENPEACE**
International organizations such as Greenpeace work in various ways to save endangered polar wildlife, particularly whales and seals. Here, a Greenpeace worker is spraying a seal pup with harmless red dye so that seal hunters will not want to kill the pup for its beautiful fur.

**PYGMY HOG**
There may be only about 100 pygmy hogs left on Earth following the destruction of their grassland home in the Himalayan foothills of Assam, India.

**SIAMESE CROCODILE**
Many crocodiles and alligators have been killed for their skins, to be made into leather bags, shoes, and belts. Today, about 20 members of the crocodile family are in danger of extinction, including the Siamese crocodile and the Orinoco crocodile.

**CACTUS**
The Mexican neogomesia cactus and dozens of other cacti are very rare because plant collectors have taken them from the wild.

Siamese crocodile

**GALAPAGOS TORTOISE**
This huge reptile has suffered from the rats, dogs, and other animals that people have taken to the Galapagos Islands, in the East Pacific Ocean. It is now a protected species.

Neogomesia cactus

**SLIPPER ORCHID**
Many orchids are in danger because collectors bring them away from the wild. Drury's slipper orchid has almost disappeared from its natural region in India, and may soon be extinct.

## CONSERVING NATURE
Conservation involves studying wild places, identifying the animals and plants that live there, and observing what happens to them. The International Union for the Conservation of Nature and Natural Resources (IUCN) collects scientific data and works on conservation in many countries, together with organizations such as the United Nations Environment Programme (UNEP).

**GIANT WETA CRICKET**
There are many kinds of weta crickets in New Zealand. Fossils have been found that are more than 180 million years old. Today, several species of weta cricket are in danger of extinction, including the giant weta cricket shown here.

**RED-KNEED TARANTULA**
The red-kneed tarantula from Mexico (left) is rare because many people keep exotic spiders as pets. This tarantula is not a true tarantula but a member of the bird-eating spider group.

**GREY BAT**
Many kinds of bats are threatened because of the loss of their forest homes to farmland, and because of the increasing use of insecticides on the food they eat. The American grey bat shown right is endangered.

**JAPANESE GIANT SALAMANDER**
The Japanese giant salamander, shown left, is the world's largest amphibian, growing to more than 1.5 m (5 ft) long. Today it is rare. Sometimes people catch it for its meat.

**AFRICAN VIOLET**
The African violet is a well-known houseplant, but it has almost disappeared from its natural habitat – tropical mountain forests in Tanzania, Africa.

**SPADEFOOT TOAD**
There are many kinds of spadefoot toad. The Italian spadefoot toad shown here is particularly endangered.

**DODO**
The dodo was a flightless bird that lived on islands in the Indian Ocean. All dodos were extinct by about 1800.

**GOLDEN LION TAMARIN**
Clearing forests for timber and farmland endangers the lives of many monkeys. Many tamarins and marmosets have been killed in South America, because people mistakenly believed that they spread the diseases malaria and yellow fever.

**MONK SEAL**
Nature reserves have been set up for the Mediterranean monk seal so that it would not be disturbed by tourists on the coasts where it breeds.

**VICTORIA'S BIRDWING BUTTERFLY**
The Victoria's birdwing butterfly was first collected by scientists in 1855, when they shot it with guns. Today this butterfly and many other kinds of butterflies are endangered because collectors kill them.

**JACKASS PENGUIN**
This flightless sea bird is also called the black-footed penguin. Its numbers have decreased in South Africa because of water pollution and because fishing boats catch the fish the penguin eats.

**SUMATRAN RHINOCEROS**
Rhinoceroses are in great danger of extinction, but poachers (illegal hunters) still kill them and sell their horns. The horns are carved into dagger handles or powdered into traditional Chinese medicine. There are only a few hundred Sumatran rhinoceroses left, in Sumatra and mainland Southeast Asia.

**CAPTIVE BREEDING**
One way to help an endangered species recover its numbers is by breeding it in captivity. Experts capture a few animals from the wild, raise them carefully, and encourage them to breed in captivity. Later, they release, or reintroduce, the offspring into a suitable area. The notornis is a flightless bird that scientists believed to be extinct until it was rediscovered in 1948. Eggs from its nests are hatched in an incubator, and the chicks are kept warm with tiny electric blankets. They are fed by someone wearing a puppet-like glove that resembles the parent bird.

## HABITAT LOSS
Tropical rain forests are being destroyed at an alarming rate. Trees are burned or sold for timber, and the land is farmed or used for roads and buildings. Scientists believe that many rain forests contain kinds of animals and plants that we have never seen. For every plant or creature that is threatened or extinct, there may be 100 that we do not know about.

Notornis

**CONTROLLING TRADE**
Some animals and plants are taken from the wild for their skins and other products. Elephants are killed for their ivory tusks. Colourful flowers are made into pulp to make dyes. The Convention on International Trade in Endangered Species (CITES) has lists of hundreds of species, or kinds, of plants and animals. Selling or exporting these animals or their products without a special licence is illegal. All whales, dolphins, and porpoises are on this list; so are all monkeys, apes, and lemurs.

**SNAKE SKIN**
The brightly coloured objects shown above were once the skins of snakes and lizards. The skins are dyed different colours, then made into all sorts of leather goods, including bags and shoes.

**SNOW LEOPARD**
The snow leopard lives high in the mountains of the Himalayas and Central Asia. In winter its fur becomes thicker to keep out the bitter cold. In the past, the snow leopard's winter coat was much prized by fur traders. Today, the snow leopard and many other big cats are protected by the CITES agreement, but they are still hunted illegally in some remote areas.

| *Find out more* |
| --- |
| ANIMALS |
| ECOLOGY AND FOOD WEBS |
| FOREST WILDLIFE |
| NATIONAL PARKS |
| PLANTS |
| POLLUTION |

# CONTINENTS

ALMOST A THIRD OF THE SURFACE of the Earth is land. There are seven vast pieces of land, called continents, which make up most of this area. The rest consists of islands which are much smaller land masses completely surrounded by water. The seven continents are crowded into almost one half of the globe; the huge Pacific Ocean occupies most of the other half. The largest continent is Asia, which has an area of more than 44 million sq km (17 million sq miles).

Most scientists now agree that, about 200 million years ago, the continents were joined together in one huge land mass. Over millions of years they drifted around and changed shape, and they are still moving today. The continents lie on vast pieces of solid rock, called plates, which collide and move against one another. These movements cause volcanoes and earthquakes, push up mountains, and create huge trenches in the Earth's crust.

**3** THE WORLD TODAY
The Americas have moved away from the other continents and joined together, and India has joined Asia. Australia and Antarctica have drifted apart.

Europe
Asia
North America
Africa
South America
Australia
Antarctica

The continents are made of many smaller pieces of land which have been pushed together.

**1** PANGAEA
The continents were joined in one supercontinent, called Pangaea, which began to break apart about 200 million years ago.

Asia
North America
Laurasia
Africa
Europe
India
South America
Gondwanaland
Australia
Antarctica

North America
Asia
Europe
India
Australia
PANGAEA
South America
Antarctica
Africa

**2** BREAK-UP
About 135 million years ago, Pangaea split up into two areas – Gondwanaland and Laurasia.

## CONTINENTAL DRIFT

A glance at the globe shows that the eastern sides of North and South America and the western sides of Europe and Africa follow a similar line. In 1912, Alfred Wegener, a German meteorologist, suggested that the continents once fitted together like pieces of a jigsaw. This huge piece of land then broke up, and the continents drifted apart.

## PLATE TECTONICS

The continents and oceans lie on top of several huge plates of rock about 100 km (60 miles) deep. These plates float on the hot, molten rock in the mantle underneath. Heat from the Earth's interior makes the plates move, carrying the continents with them. Mountains and undersea ridges, deep trenches, and huge valleys form at the edges of the plates as they move and collide.

Pacific Ocean
Trench
South America
Atlantic Ocean
Mountains and volcanoes
American plate
Undersea ridge
Africa
Nazca plate
Molten rock from Nazca plate forces its way up, forming volcanoes along edge of continent.
Nazca plate moves under American plate, forming trench in ocean floor.
Indian Ocean
Hot rock rises from below, pushing the American and African plates apart and forming an undersea ridge.
Mantle
African plate
Indian plate

**MOVING PLATES**

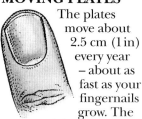

The plates move about 2.5 cm (1 in) every year – about as fast as your fingernails grow. The Atlantic Ocean is widening at this speed as the Americas drift apart from Europe and Africa.

SAN ANDREAS FAULT
The San Andreas fault in the United States is at the border between two plates. They slide against one another, causing severe earthquakes.

# JAMES COOK

IN THE LATE SUMMER OF 1768, a small sailing ship left Plymouth, England, on an expedition to the Pacific Ocean. In charge of the ship was Lieutenant James Cook, who was to become one of the greatest explorers the world has ever known. Cook was an outstanding navigator. He was also a fine captain. He insisted that his sailors eat sauerkraut (pickled cabbage) and fresh fruit, and so became the first captain to save his crew from scurvy, a disease caused by lack of vitamin C. The voyage lasted three years. On his return to England, Cook was sent on two more voyages: one to the Antarctic, the other to the Arctic. On these voyages he became the first European to visit a number of Pacific islands, sailed further south than any other European, and added many lands, including Australia and New Zealand, to the British Empire.

## ENDEAVOUR

Cook's ship, the *Endeavour*, was originally a coal ship. Cook chose this ship because it was sturdy, spacious, and easy to handle. On the *Endeavour* voyage, Cook added many new territories to the British Empire.

*The Endeavour was 30 m (98 ft) long, weighed 360 tonnes and carried 112 sailors and five scientists.*

*Cook stocked up with fresh fruit at every landing.*

*Cook purified the air in the ship once a week by burning vinegar and gunpowder.*

## KEEPING RECORDS
Cook made many maps, took regular measurements, and recorded every event of the voyages in minute detail. The scientists on board collected botanical specimens from the lands they visited. In an age before cameras, artists on board made drawings of all the people, plants, and wildlife they saw to show to people at home. They collected so many specimens in one bay in Australia that they named it Botany Bay. It later became a dreaded prison colony.

*Sydney Parkinson was the ship's artist on board the* Endeavour. *He drew this plant,* Banksia serrata,1, *in around 1760.*

## FIRST VOYAGE
The British Royal Navy sent Cook on his first voyage to observe the planet Venus passing between the Earth and the sun. He also had secret orders from the government to sail into uncharted regions to prove the existence of a southern continent, which they wanted to add to their empire. He did not succeed, but in the attempt he became the first European to visit New Zealand and the east coast of Australia.

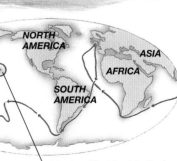

*Sandwich Islands (Hawaii)*

**NORTH AMERICA**

**ASIA**

**AFRICA**

*Pacific Ocean*

**SOUTH AMERICA**

**AUSTRALIA**

*Islanders killed Captain Cook here on 14 February 1779.*

---

### Find out more
AUSTRALIA, HISTORY OF
EXPLORERS
NEW ZEALAND, HISTORY OF

# CORALS
## ANEMONES, AND JELLYFISH

*Tentacles trail more than 15 m (50 ft) from a man-of-war's body.*

Sea wasp

IN THE WARM, TROPICAL SEAS surrounding coral islands are some of the most fascinating sea creatures. Despite being so different in appearance, corals, jellyfish, and anemones belong to the same family. The fabulous corals that make up coral reefs are created by little animals called polyps, which look like miniature sea anemones. Every polyp builds a cup-shaped skeleton around itself, and as the polyps grow and die, their skeletons mass together to create a coral reef. Unlike coral-building polyps, jellyfish can move around freely, trailing their long tentacles below their soft bodies as they swim. Some jellyfish float on the surface and are pushed along with the current. Anemones anchor themselves to rocks, where they wait for fish to swim through their tentacles.

Carijoa coral

### JELLYFISH
The sea wasp jellyfish uses its tentacles to sting fish. Tentacles contain venom which is painful to humans and can cause death.

Clown fish

### CLOWN FISH
These fish live in harmony with sea anemones. The thick, slimy mucus on their bodies keeps them safe from the stinging cells. Clown fish keep anemones clean by feeding on particles of food among their waving tentacles.

### MAN-OF-WAR
The Portuguese man-of-war is not one jellyfish. It is a floating colony of hundreds of jellyfish-like creatures known as polyps. Some polyps form the float, which drifts on the water; others bear stinging tentacles for paralyzing prey; still others digest the prey and pass the nutrients through the body.

*Whip thrown out*

*Stinging tip*

*Stinging cell body*

*Coiled whip*

### STINGING CELLS
Each jellyfish tentacle is armed with deadly weapons. If a fish touches a tentacle, stinging cells containing tiny coiled-up threads are triggered into action. They shoot out a hollow whip like a harpoon, injecting paralyzing poison into the prey.

### CORAL SHAPES
The shape of a coral depends on the arrangement and growing pattern of the tiny polyps that build it. Corals can be dazzling in colour and extraordinary in shape, resembling all sorts of objects. This Carijoa coral looks like a branching tree.

Common sea anemone

*Anemone slowly engulfing a trapped fish.*

## ANEMONE
As a fish stops struggling, the anemone's tentacles shorten and pull it into the mouth, through to the stomach chamber in the "body" of the anemone. Any undigested remains pass out later.

### HOW CORAL REEFS ARE FORMED

*Corals grow in shallow water around an island.*

*Coral reef builds up as island sinks.*

*Island disappears, leaving an atoll.*

Corals live in shallow water around an island where bright sunlight makes them grow. As movements in the Earth's surface make the island sink, corals form a reef. Finally the island disappears, leaving a ring of reefs called an atoll.

### HYDRA
The tiny hydra is a freshwater polyp that lives in ponds. It may be green, brown, or grey in colour. Hydras feed on other tiny water creatures which they catch with their tentacles. Each tentacle has stinging cells that contain poison to paralyze the prey. Hydras reproduce by growing "buds" on their "stalk". The buds break off to form new hydras. This is a form of asexual reproduction.

---
***Find out more***
ANIMALS
DEEP-SEA WILDLIFE
OCEAN WILDLIFE
---

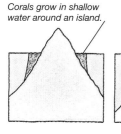

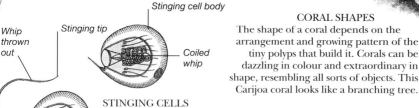

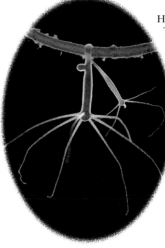

# Cows
## CATTLE, AND BUFFALOES

EVERY TIME WE EAT ice cream or drink milk, we should thank the dairy cow. Each year, cows, or dairy cattle, provide us with millions of litres of milk to make many different dairy products. The dairy cow is just one member of the much larger family of animals called cattle. Humans first domesticated cattle about 5,000 years ago. Today, cattle are bred on every continent for their meat, milk, and hides. There are many different kinds of cattle – all have horns and distinctive split (two-toed) hooves and live in herds. As a group they are often described as ruminants or cud chewers because of the way in which they digest food.

Wild cattle include the water buffalo of Central and Southeast Asia and the rare anoa, found in the rain forest of Celebes, in Indonesia.

**SACRED COW**
Because they provide sustenance, cows are regarded as sacred in parts of Asia. Here the Hindu goddess Parvati is shown seated on a cow.

Horns can be used in defence, but they are sometimes removed by cattle breeders.

Ears can swivel to locate the direction from which a sound comes.

Milk comes from cow's udder.

Tail is used as a fly whisk.

Split (two-toed) hoof

Jersey cow and calf

**CHEWING THE CUD**
Cattle have large, four-chambered stomachs. They eat grass and other plants, which they swallow and partly digest in the rumen (the first chamber of the stomach). Later, the cow regurgitates, or brings up the coarse, fibrous parts of the food as small masses called cud. The cow chews the cud then swallows it again, and it goes into the reticulum (the second chamber). The food then passes into the omasum and finally into the abomasum, where digestion takes place. This complex method means that the cow can extract all the nutrients from the food.

Small intestine

Rumen

Reticulum

Omasum

Abomasum

Large intestine

Food takes more than three days to pass through the entire digestive system.

## CATTLE
There are about 12 billion domestic or farm cattle around the world. Their ancestors were wild cattle called aurochs; the last aurochs died out in 1627. Over many years, breeders have developed various types of domestic cattle. Each is suited to a particular climate and produces mainly meat, milk, or hides for leather. Jersey, Guernsey, Ayrshire, and Holstein are dairy (milk-giving) breeds; Hereford, Angus, Charolais, and Brahman are beef (meat-giving) breeds.

## BISON
Herds of bison, sometimes mistakenly called buffalo, once roamed the North American plains by the millions. A century ago, however, so many had been killed by settlers that only 500 were left alive. Today, there are about 50,000 bison in America, living in protected wildlife parks. The smaller European bison has also been saved from extinction by being bred in captivity, then released into the wild.

North American bison

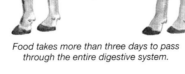

**BUFFALO**
There are about 130 million domestic water buffaloes in Asia, Europe, North Africa, and South America. They pull farm equipment and provide meat and milk. With their wide hooves and thickset legs, water buffalo can walk easily in mud along riverbanks and lakesides. They are often used to farm flooded rice paddies.

---

### Find out more
ANIMALS
FARM ANIMALS
FARMING
MAMMALS
NORTH AMERICAN WILDLIFE

# CRABS
## AND OTHER CRUSTACEANS

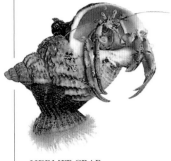

**THOUSANDS OF DIFFERENT** kinds of crabs scuttle over our sandy shores and skulk in rock pools. They range from tiny parasitic crabs living inside mussels to the giant Japanese spider crab, whose legs can be more than 3 m (10 ft) long. Crabs breathe underwater using gills, but some can also survive out of water for a long time. All crabs are protected by strong, hard shells like a suit of armour on the outside of their bodies. Crabs, along with lobsters and crayfish, belong to the animal group called crustaceans. Their bodies are divided into sections, with jointed limbs and two pairs of antennae on the head. A crab begins life as an egg, which develops into a larva, then into an adult crab. Each time the crab reaches another growing stage, it sheds the outer layer of its shell, revealing a new layer beneath.

**HERMIT CRAB**
The hermit crab often makes its home in the empty shell of a whelk, which protects it from predators such as gulls.

**EDIBLE CRAB**
The so-called edible crab is only one of many kinds of crustaceans that are caught, cooked, and eaten by people around the world.

Fiddler crab

Eye on stalk

Antenna

Huge claw for defence

Carapace (shell)

Eight walking legs

## LOBSTER
The lobster scavenges on the seabed for dead fish and other animal remains. One claw has blunt knobs for crushing; the other has sharp "teeth" for cutting. The biggest lobsters are 60 cm (2 ft) long and can live as long as humans – up to 70 years.

Antenna

Crushing claw

Carapace over front part of body

Four pairs of walking limbs

Eye on stalk

Telson (tailpiece)

Six segments on abdomen

## SHRIMPS AND PRAWNS
These little sea creatures are good scavengers. During the day they dig into the sand and hide. At night they emerge to hunt for food using their long feelers. When in danger, prawns and shrimps escape by scooting backwards with a flick of their tail fan.

Long antenna (feeler)

Shrimp

Tail fan

Feeding claw

Tail fan

Prawn

Feeding claw

Long antenna (feeler)

## BARNACLES
These sea crustaceans have no heads. Their long, feathery legs beat the water, collecting tiny food particles. Acorn barnacles live in volcano-shaped shells cemented on to rocks. Goose barnacles attach themselves to driftwood by their stalks.

Goose barnacles

Acorn barnacles

## WHERE CRUSTACEANS LIVE
Some crustaceans such as the yabby (a freshwater shrimp) and the water flea live in rivers and lakes. A few crustaceans live on land. The woodlouse, for example, can be found under dead leaves and in damp woodland areas.

Woodlouse

Water flea

Yabby

*Find out more*
ANIMALS
OCEAN WILDLIFE
SEASHORE WILDLIFE

# CRICKET

PLAYED WITH A BAT AND BALL, cricket is a popular team game. The object is to score the highest number of runs by hitting the ball and running the length of the pitch to the far wicket as many times as possible, before fielders from the other team reach the wicket with the ball. The game is played by two teams of 11 players, each team taking it in turns to bat or field. Batting sessions, called "innings", end when 10 of the 11 players are out. Batters are out if the ball hits the wicket – or would do if the batter's leg was not in the way (leg before wicket)– or if a fielder catches the ball or runs them out. Two umpires on the field judge whether the batter is in or out. Invented by the English, cricket is now played worldwide by men and women. Top competitive nations include India, Pakistan, West Indies, and Australia. "Test" matches between these teams are the highest level of cricket.

*Ball is hit with full face of bat.*

*Good footwork*

**HISTORY OF CRICKET**
Cricket began in England, probably in the 1500s, with club-like bats and a two-stump wicket. From the 1800s it developed into today's game.

## BATTING
The bowler delivers the ball to the striking batter, who can either guard the wicket with defensive strokes, or play attacking strokes to hit the ball and score runs. Batters do not always have to run: four runs are scored automatically if the ball reaches the boundary, and six if it goes over the boundary without bouncing.

*Non-striking batter*
*Wicket*
*Umpire*
*Bowler*
*Mid-off*
*Cover point*
*Pitch is 20 m (22 yd) long.*
*Grass field*
*Silly mid-on*
*Square leg*
*Umpire*
*Backward short-leg*
*Batter*
*Wicketkeeper*
*Gully*
*Slip*
*Silly mid-off*
*Cover*

### EQUIPMENT
To avoid injury, batters and wicketkeepers wear protective gear. Leg pads and gloves must be worn, and many players also wear helmets. Clothing is traditionally white, but in some competitions players wear coloured clothes. Cricket bats are made of willow, which does not split.

*Leg pad*

*Bat*

*Batting glove*

## BOWLING
Each bowler delivers one "over" (six balls) before another bowler takes a turn. Fast bowlers use speed to get batters out. Medium bowlers are not as fast, but they make the ball swerve in the air. Slow bowlers hold the ball in different ways to make it turn when it bounces.

*Cricket ball showing cork and twine core and red leather casing*

### PITCH
The captain of the fielding side places his or her fielders in good positions to prevent runs and to catch the ball when possible. The wicketkeeper and slip are there to catch the batter out if he or she misses the ball. Other fielders stand further away on the boundary. One umpire stands at the bowler's end and another stands at square leg.

*Find out more*
BALL GAMES
HEALTH AND FITNESS
SPORTS

# CROCODILES AND ALLIGATORS

LYING LOW IN THE WATER looking like an old log, but ready to snap up almost any animal, the crocodile seems like a survivor from the pre-historic age, and it is. One hundred million years ago, crocodiles were prowling through the swamps with the dinosaurs. Crocodiles and alligators belong to the reptile group called crocodilians. This group includes 14 kinds of crocodiles, seven kinds of alligators (five of which are commonly called caimans), and one kind of gavial. Crocodilians are carnivorous (meat-eating) reptiles; they lurk in rivers, lakes, and swamps, grabbing whatever prey they can. Crocodiles and alligators eat fish and frogs whole. They drag larger prey such as deer under the water, where they grip the animal in their jaws and spin rapidly, tearing off chunks of flesh. Crocodiles and alligators occasionally eat humans.

Nile crocodiles measure up to 6 m (20 ft) long and weigh more than 1 tonne.

Female carries the young in her mouth.

**CROCODILE**
The fourth tooth on each side of the crocodile's lower jaw is visible when the mouth is closed.

**ALLIGATOR**
Unlike crocodiles, no lower teeth are visible when the alligator's mouth is closed.

**CAIMAN**
The caiman has a broad mouth for eating a variety of prey.

**GAVIAL**
The gavial has a long, slender mouth with sharp teeth for catching fish.

## NILE CROCODILE
The Nile crocodile is found in many watery parts of Africa. Like most reptiles, the female lays eggs, which she looks after until they hatch. The newly hatched young listen for their mother's footsteps and call to her. She gently gathers them into her mouth in batches and carries them to the safety of the water.

**YOUNG**
After about three months, the young crocodiles hatch out of the eggs. The mother guards them closely because they are in danger of becoming food for large lizards and foxes.

**CROCODILE SMILE**
Crocodiles often bask in the sun with their mouths wide open. Blood vessels inside the mouth absorb the sun's warmth. This raises the animal's body temperature and gives the crocodile the energy to hunt for its prey in the evening.

## ALLIGATOR
There are two kinds of true alligators – the Chinese and the American alligators. Today, the Chinese alligator is in great danger of extinction – only a few hundred survive. The American alligator lives in rivers and swamps across the southeastern United States, where it eats fish, water birds, and anything else it can catch. In more populated areas, the American alligator also grabs unwary farm animals.

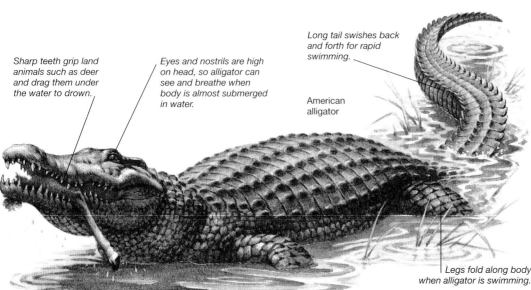

Sharp teeth grip land animals such as deer and drag them under the water to drown.

Eyes and nostrils are high on head, so alligator can see and breathe when body is almost submerged in water.

Long tail swishes back and forth for rapid swimming.

American alligator

Legs fold along body when alligator is swimming.

*Find out more*
ANIMALS
LIZARDS
PREHISTORIC LIFE

# OLIVER
# CROMWELL

ONE OF THE PEOPLE WHO SIGNED King Charles I's death warrant in January 1649 was Oliver Cromwell. A Puritan member of parliament, he had been a prominent parliamentary leader in the English Civil War (1642-49) against the king and his Royalist supporters. Following the king's execution, the monarchy was abolished and a new constitution declared England a republican "Commonwealth". Cromwell headed its Council of State. In 1653 he was made Lord Protector, which gave him the power to decide how to rule the country. However, he faced many difficulties in leading the new Commonwealth, as people held very different political and religious views. Cromwell governed England until his death in 1658, and in 1660, Charles ll was offered the throne, signalling the end of the Commonwealth.

*Though a Puritan, Cromwell loved music, dancing, and hunting.*

**1599** Born in Huntingdon.

**1628** Becomes MP for Huntingdon.

**1629** Becomes a Puritan (strict Protestant).

**1641** Uprising in Ireland.

**1642** Civil War begins.

**1644-45** Cromwell leads the cavalry to defeat Royalists at Marston Moor and Naseby.

**1649** The Commonwealth is declared.

**1649-50** Cromwell's army crushes Irish Royalists.

**1650-51** Scottish Royalists are defeated at the battles of Dunbar and Worcester.

**1653** Made Lord Protector.

**1657** Refuses the Crown.

**1658** Dies – buried in state.

## CROMWELL THE SOLDIER

A brave and level-headed cavalry leader, Cromwell led his men to win many battles. In 1645 he helped to form the New Model Army, which became an awesome fighting force and perhaps the best army in Europe. Their defeat of the Scots at Preston in 1648 finally ended the Civil War.

### THE COMMONWEALTH

The new government tried to create a just and godly "Commonwealth". It banned popular pleasures including Sunday sports, bear-baiting, and cockfighting. Christmas and May Day celebrations were also forbidden. Theatres were closed, but soon reopened.

*Cockfighting was widely popular, especially among Royalists.*

## TROUBLE IN IRELAND

From the 16th century onwards, English Protestants moved into Ireland and dispossessed people of their land. The Irish rebelled against Charles I's rule and he tried to suppress them. In 1649 Cromwell went to Ireland to put down a Royalist uprising. There were terrible massacres at Drogheda and Wexford.

*Cromwell's coat of arms*

### THE LORD PROTECTOR

In 1653 Cromwell was made Lord Protector for Life, to govern with a Council of State and a single-chamber parliament. Later he was asked to take the Crown, but he refused. However, he lived regally and his son Richard succeeded him.

### RELIGIOUS TOLERANCE

Cromwell thought that people should be free to worship God in the way they believed to be right. Religious freedom and tolerance were guaranteed, though not to Catholics and Quakers. In practice, most people enjoyed tolerance.

___ *Find out more* ___

ENGLISH CIVIL WAR
STUARTS
UNITED KINGDOM, HISTORY OF

# CROWS, JAYS, AND RAVENS

THE MEMBERS OF THE CROW FAMILY are among the best known of all birds because of their large size, bold habits, and noisy "crowing" calls. There are 117 kinds of crows. They include carrion crows, jays, magpies, ravens, and rooks. Many crows in Europe, North America, Africa, and Australia live in open countryside and are pests to farmers because they eat seeds and grains. In Asia and South America, however, some jays and magpies live in dense forests and are seldom seen. Crows have varied diets. Apart from seeds, they eat fruit, insects, small mammals, and dead animals, as well as birds' eggs and nestlings. They are good mimics and can imitate the sounds of other birds, animals, and human speech. In bird intelligence tests, members of the crow family, particularly jackdaws and ravens, score higher than any other birds.

### ROOKERIES
Rooks breed in colonies high in the treetops. They build big nests of sticks and twigs early in spring.

### COMMON CROW
Crows can be a nuisance to farmers because they spoil their crops. These clever birds are rarely fooled for long by a scarecrow standing in the field.

*Crows often feed on newly planted seeds.*

### MAGPIE
The magpie is famous as a bird thief. It is attracted by bright objects it spots on the ground. It is known to make off with coins, jewellery, and other shiny objects, which it then hides or buries. Magpies live in Europe, North America, North Africa, and Asia.

## JAY
The brightly coloured European jay lives mainly in woodlands, where it feeds on acorns, beechnuts, fruit, and berries. The blue jay is beautifully patterned in blue and black, and lives among the trees in parks and gardens of central and eastern North America. There are also colourful jays in Asia.

## RAVEN
The raven is the largest of the crow family, with a wingspan of 2 m (6 ft). Ravens were once thought to bring bad luck, probably because they fed on the dead bodies of criminals left hanging on the gallows.

*Leg feathers puffed out*

*Head feathers fluffed out*

### CROW COURTSHIP
Many crows perform elaborate dances and displays in the breeding season, when the male courts the female. Here a male raven puffs out his feathers and bows to his partner while making *kaaa*-ing sounds.

*Male raven performing bowing ceremony*

## JACKDAW
Tree holes and chimney tops provide nesting places for the European jackdaw. It builds a nest of twigs lined with grass, hair, fur, and wool plucked from the backs of sheep. Like magpies, jackdaws are attracted to shiny objects.

---
***Find out more***
BIRDS
FLIGHT, ANIMAL
---

# CRUSADES

NINE CENTURIES AGO the Pope appealed to Christians to recapture the holy city of Jerusalem from the Turkish Muslims who had seized it. Thousands of European Christians – knights, princes, pilgrims, and peasants – responded to the call and set out on a long warring pilgrimage, called a crusade, from western Europe to Palestine (now Israel). Four years later, after battles, starvation, and disease, the surviving crusaders captured the city of Jerusalem. The crusaders set up a Christian kingdom on the shores of Palestine that lasted nearly a century. But in 1187, Saladin recaptured Jerusalem. At least seven more crusades set out. None were successful, but links between Europe and the Middle East were established that still continue today.

### THE CHILDREN'S CRUSADE
In 1212, a tragic crusade occurred when thousands of Christian children set off on foot from Europe to Jerusalem. Most starved to death, or were sold into slavery.

Richard I sailed from London.

Philip of France set off from Vezelay.

● Vezelay

● Regensburg

Verona ●

The Third Crusade made Richard I popular in his own time and earned him the nickname "the Lionheart".

Constantinople

Krak des Chevaliers was the strongest crusader castle.

● Acre

Crusader ship

### ACRE BESIEGED
Huge wooden siege towers helped the crusaders attack the city of Acre. The defenders threw spears, hot sand, and boiling water on them.

### THE THIRD CRUSADE
King Richard I of England (ruled 1189-99) took part in the Third Crusade with the king of France and the Holy Roman Emperor. King Richard I captured the port of Acre, but was caught and held for ransom on his return journey. Ultimately, they failed to take Jerusalem on this crusade, but did make a truce with Saladin allowing Christian pilgrims to enter the city.

### SULTAN SALADIN
Leader of the Muslim forces, Saladin (1137-93) was a great commander. As sultan of Egypt and Syria, he made Egypt one of the most powerful regions in the Middle East.

### JOURNEY TO JERUSALEM
The journey from Europe to the Holy Land was long and dangerous, and many of the crusaders died on the way. Those who went back to Europe from Palestine took silks and spices with them, as well as Islamic learning such as mathematics and astronomy.

### THE CRUSADES
**1096** First Crusade (also known as the People's Crusade) sets off. Many peasants die on the way, though knights survive.

**1097** Crusaders arrive in Constantinople (now Istanbul).

**1098** French and Norman armies capture Antioch.

**1099** Crusaders capture Jerusalem. Divide coastal land into four kingdoms.

**1147-49** Second Crusade attacks Muslims in Spain, Portugal, and Asia Minor.

**1187** Saladin conquers Jerusalem and most of Palestine.

**1189** Third Crusade sets off led by the kings of England and France and Frederick I, the Holy Roman Emperor. Frederick dies on the way.

**1191-92** Crusaders capture Acre but return to Europe.

**1202-04** Fourth Crusade sets off. Crusaders capture Constantinople and steal treasure.

**1217** Fifth Crusade sets off. Crusaders capture Damietta, Egypt, but return it and make a truce.

**1228-29** Sixth Crusade. Emperor Frederick II makes a 10-year truce.

**1248-50** Seventh Crusade. Louis IX of France captures Damietta but is forced to return it.

**1270** Eighth Crusade. Louis IX dies. This final crusade returns to Europe.

---

*Find out more*
CASTLES
WEAPONS

# DAMS

EVERY DAY, FACTORIES and homes use up huge amounts of water. For example, an oil refinery uses 10 times as much water as the petrol it makes. Dams help to provide us with much of the water we need by trapping water from flowing rivers. Building a dam across a river creates a huge lake, called a reservoir, behind the dam. Reservoirs also provide water to irrigate large areas of farmland. A dam can store the water that falls in rainy seasons so that there is water during dry periods. By storing water in this way, dams also prevent floods. Flood barriers can stop the sea from surging up a river and bursting its banks. Some provide electricity as well as water. They contain hydroelectric power stations powered by water from their reservoirs.

Lake Mead

Lift shaft inside dam goes down to hydroelectric power station.

Water from the reservoir enters the intake towers.

Roadway along top of dam

Arched, concrete dam wall

Water flows down pipes to hydroelectric power station.

Pipes carry excess water to the Colorado River so that the dam does not break or overflow.

Hoover dam

Dam shown with water removed from one side.

## CONCRETE DAMS
There are two main types of concrete dam: arch dams and gravity dams. Arch dams (either single-arch or multiple-arch) are tall, curved shells of concrete as little as 3 m (10 ft) thick. Because their arched shape makes them very strong, they do not burst. Large gravity dams are also made of concrete. Their vast weight keeps them from giving way.

Water flows down to Colorado River.

Hydroelectric power station

Overflow water

Tunnel that was excavated to divert river while dam was built.

### HOOVER DAM
The Hoover Dam in the United States, one of the world's highest concrete dams, is 221 m (726 ft) high. It is an arch dam that spans the River Colorado, supplying water for irrigation and electricity to California, Arizona, and Nevada. Lake Mead, the reservoir formed by the dam, is 185 km (115

## EMBANKMENT DAMS
The biggest dams are embankment dams, made by piling up a huge barrier of earth and rock. A core of clay or concrete in the centre keeps water from seeping through the dam. The side is covered with stones to protect it from the water. The world's highest dam is the Rogunsky Dam in Tajikistan, an embankment dam 325 m (1,066 ft) high.

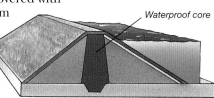
Waterproof core

### THE EFFECTS OF DAMS
The reservoir that forms in the valley behind a dam floods the land, often damaging the environment. For example, the Aswan High Dam in Egypt was built to control the flooding of the River Nile, but changing the river's flow has destroyed the fertility of the surrounding land.

*A dam prevents fish, such as salmon, from swimming up and down a river. Some dams have a fish ladder, a pipe, or pools through which fish can swim past the dam.*

### FLOOD BARRIERS
Movable dams, called flood barriers, are built on rivers to control flooding. Built in 1982, this barrier across the River Thames in England protects London from flooding by North Sea gales. Large, curved gates rise if the river gets too high.

_____ *Find out more* _____
ELECTRICITY
FARMING
LAKES
RIVERS
WATER

# DANCE

WHEN PEOPLE HEAR MUSIC, they often tap their feet and clap their hands. Dancing is a natural activity, and there are many different styles, ranging from the hectic breakdance to the graceful, elegant waltz. However, all forms of dance share the same rhythmic movements that people have enjoyed since time began. Prehistoric cave paintings show people moving in a lively way. They kept time by clapping and stamping. Later, dancers began to move in patterns with more formal steps, and dancing in couples or in groups at balls or dances became a part of social life. In many countries special costumes are part of folk-dancing traditions.

**RITUAL DANCE**
In religious rituals, dance is a way of thanking the gods or asking for their help. These Native Americans are performing a fertility dance. It is important that the steps are always danced in the same order.

*Square dancers often dress up in cowboy or cowgirl style.*

*This modern jazz dancer combines the grace and elegance of traditional ballet with soft, fluid poses that more closely express personal feelings. The swirling movements of her dress complement and enhance her performance.*

**SQUARE DANCING**
Square dancing is very sociable. Four couples form a square and change partners in a sequence of moves. A caller shouts out instructions such as "Swing your partner to the right". This traditional North American dance has many variations.

## MODERN DANCE
Most traditional dances have a prearranged series of steps and movements, but modern dance forms encourage dancers to move more freely. Contemporary dance emerged at the beginning of the 20th century. US dancer Isadora Duncan was one of the first performers to move away from orthodox ballet and develop her own style. Jazz dance emerged in the 1920s and has been central to modern dance.

*Love – putting on a ring*

*Marriage – tying the love knot around the bride's neck*

**MIME**
Mime mixes dance and acting to create a language without words which can be understood by people from many cultures. The dancer shown here is from India, but mime is also part of other Eastern and Western dance styles.

*Modern dancers often devise their own steps and perform barefoot.*

*There are six styles of Indian classical dance. These styles usually involve miming out stories from ancient mythology.*

**ROCK AND ROLL**
The emergence of rock and roll music in the 1950s led to the first mass form of modern dance. The music had a strong beat and lyrics that young people could relate to. Rock and roll steps were wild and daring, and were very different to conservative social dancing.

**DANCE AND WORSHIP**
In India, almost all performing arts are linked to religion. *Bharatanatyam* is a classical dance style from Tamil Nadu, southern India. It is linked to ancient temple dances. Performers paint their hands and feet with red dye. In ancient times, the dancers came from special families and were known as *devadasis*.

***Find out more***
BALLET
FILMS
INDIA

# CHARLES
# DARWIN

1809 Born in Shrewsbury, Shropshire, England.

1825-27 Studies medicine at Edinburgh University.

1827 Studies divinity at Cambridge, but spends more time on biology, zoology, and geology.

1831-36 HMS *Beagle* voyage.

1858 Evolutionary theory first explained to the world.

1859 Publishes *On the Origin of Species* – it is a best-seller.

1882 Dies; buried at Westminster Abbey, London.

ON 27 DECEMBER 1831, HMS *Beagle* sailed from Plymouth, England to survey the east and west coasts of South America. On board was the ship's naturalist, Charles Darwin. The ship sailed beyond the Americas to the Pacific Ocean, where Darwin made many scientific discoveries, especially on the Galapagos and Keeling Islands. As a schoolboy, Darwin had often been in trouble with his headmaster for spending time on chemistry experiments and collecting specimens instead of studying Greek and Latin. But his boyhood interest in the natural world led him to make startling discoveries about life on Earth and the development of the planet. When he returned from sea in 1836, he married, settled in London, and wrote up the notes of his discoveries. These formed the basis of his famous theory of evolution.

The *Beagle*

Darwin made careful notes of everything he observed.

Galapagos finch

Galapagos tortoise

## VOYAGE OF THE *BEAGLE*

On the five-year voyage, HMS *Beagle* made many stops, during which Darwin studied plant and animal life, and land formation. On the outward-bound journey, the ship sailed to the Canaries, across the Atlantic (where Darwin realized that the Cape Verde islands had been made by volcanoes erupting under the sea), along South America's east coast, round Cape Horn, and up the west coast, where he witnessed an earthquake.

PACIFIC OCEAN

Galapagos Islands

NORTH PACIFIC OCEAN

SOUTH ATLANTIC OCEAN

Darwin studied the wildlife in the isolated Galapagos Islands.

The ship returned via New Zealand, New South Wales, and the Keeling Islands.

### ALFRED WALLACE
Welsh naturalist Alfred Wallace (1823-1923) carried out studies that led him to agree with Darwin's theories. He travelled to the Amazon and to Malaysia, where he began to think that nature encouraged the survival of the fittest. He sent Darwin an article, and friends encouraged them both to publish their views. On 1 July 1858, members of the scientific Linnaean Society heard papers by both men.

### CORAL
On the Keeling Islands, Darwin studied coral reefs, whose structure was not understood at the time. He thought they were formed by coral building up on the sea floor while the floor itself was gently subsiding. Modern deep-sea drillings have since proved that Darwin was right.

### THE ORIGIN OF SPECIES
As a result of his study of wildlife on the Galapagos Islands, Darwin began to believe that species (types of plants and animals) were not fixed forever, but that they evolved (changed) to suit their environment. In 1859, he published *On the Origin of Species*, a book in which he set out his evolutionary theory, suggesting that humans evolved from apes.

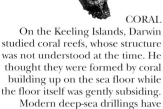

___Find out more___
CORALS, ANEMONES and jellyfish
EVOLUTION
FOSSILS
GEOLOGY

# DEEP-SEA WILDLIFE

THE DEPTHS OF THE SEA form the largest wildlife
habitat on Earth. In waters below about 1,000 m (3,000 ft)
no plants can grow because there is no sunlight. Yet here, in
the vast blackness, many extraordinary creatures live. These
animals are found nowhere else. They have adapted to
survive where the water pressure is up to 1,000 times that
at the surface. Some deep-sea fish feed on the bodies and
remains of plants and animals that sink down from the
water above. Some other fish have enormous mouths
and long, back-curved teeth for grabbing and swallowing
anything that swims by. These fish have huge stomachs
which stretch to hold prey that is even bigger than
themselves. On the deep-sea floor, sea anemones, worms,
sea cucumbers, brittlestars, crabs, prawns, and other
shellfish sieve the mud searching for tiny particles of
food. Many kinds of deep-sea squid, shrimps, and
jellyfish are also found here.

LANTERN FISH
The lantern fish lives in the dim water hundreds
of metres below the surface. With its large eyes
it watches for predators as it eats tiny floating
plants and animals. Scientists are not sure why
the spots along its body glow – perhaps to help
the fish recognize other lantern fish, see food,
or confuse enemies.

*Lateral line organs along sides
of body sense water currents
made by prey.*

*Mouth gapes
open to give
the best chance
of catching
small fish and
other prey.*

*This map shows the deep-sea areas of the world.*

■ Deep-sea areas

North
America

Asia

Africa

South
America

Australia

*Flexible spine
on back*

GULPER
EEL
Some kinds of
gulper eel grow to
more than 2 m (6.5 ft)
in length. Gulper eels
look as if they consist of a
mouth and a tail, unless they have
fed well, when the stomach bulges
hugely. Like many deep-sea fishes,
gulper eels are often black or dark
brown. The gulper eel shown
above is about 60 cm (24 in) long
and has tiny teeth. It feeds on
small prey, simply by swimming
along with its mouth open.

*Body has
a jelly-like
covering
containing
blood vessels
and light organs.*

*Thin body and long
fins typical of the
eel group*

VIPERFISH
The viperfish is only 30 cm (12 in) long,
but it is a fearsome hunter. It floats with
the spine on the dorsal (back) fin held over its
head. The tip of the spine glows, attracting curious fish.
The viperfish stabs its victim with its long lower fangs,
then swallows it, using its curved teeth to prevent the
victim from escaping.

## BIOLUMINESCENCE

Hundreds of deep-sea fish glow
in the dark, including anglerfish,
lantern fish, and slickheads.
They make their own light by a
process called bioluminescence.
The light is produced by a
chemical reaction in parts of
the body called photophores; it
may be a general glow or a pattern
of spots. The lights may be bright (as a
signal from a fish looking for a mate),
or they may be a pale glow, for
camouflage in the dull light.

*The lure may be shaped like
a blob, tassel, flap, or fringe,
depending on the species.*

ANGLERFISH
Dozens of
different anglerfish
patrol the ocean depths.
They are similar to their relatives, the
shallow-water anglerfish, in the way they fish
for food. They use a long, flexible spine on
their back as a fishing rod. A glowing lure
on the end of the spine acts as bait.

# CONSERVATION

Unlike other wildlife areas, such as the rain forests, the deep sea is not in great danger from habitat loss or pollution. However, harmful polluting chemicals have been found at great depths. Fishing boats have also overfished many shallow seas and are now fishing in deeper waters. Deep-sea fish such as these orange roughie fish (right) may soon be in danger because of overfishing.

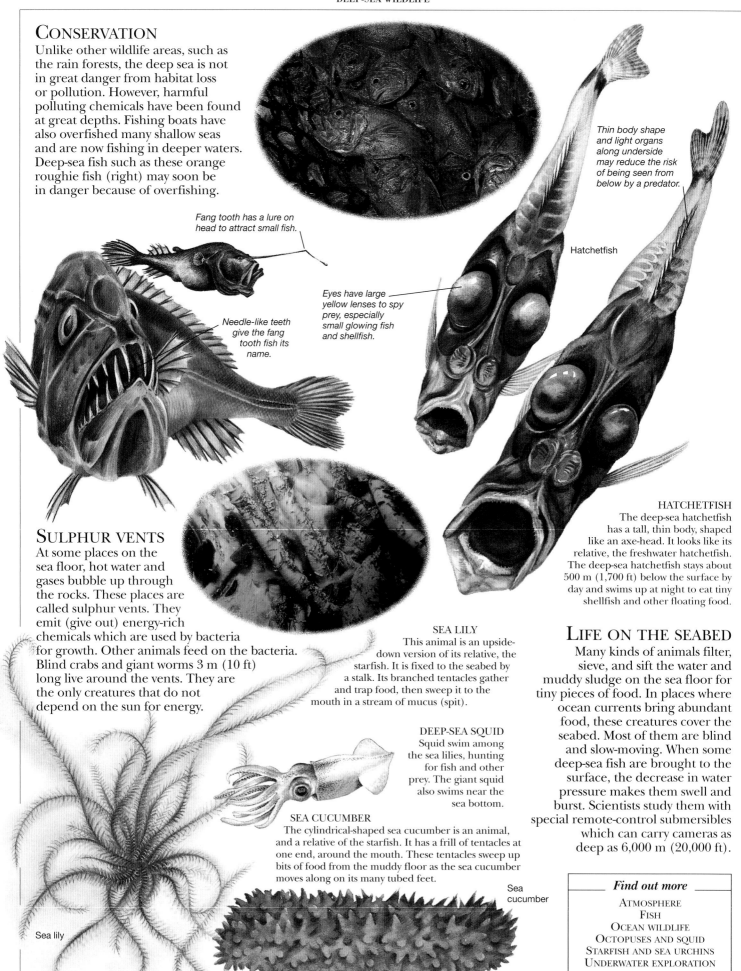

Fang tooth has a lure on head to attract small fish.

Needle-like teeth give the fang tooth fish its name.

Eyes have large yellow lenses to spy prey, especially small glowing fish and shellfish.

Thin body shape and light organs along underside may reduce the risk of being seen from below by a predator.

Hatchetfish

## SULPHUR VENTS

At some places on the sea floor, hot water and gases bubble up through the rocks. These places are called sulphur vents. They emit (give out) energy-rich chemicals which are used by bacteria for growth. Other animals feed on the bacteria. Blind crabs and giant worms 3 m (10 ft) long live around the vents. They are the only creatures that do not depend on the sun for energy.

### HATCHETFISH

The deep-sea hatchetfish has a tall, thin body, shaped like an axe-head. It looks like its relative, the freshwater hatchetfish. The deep-sea hatchetfish stays about 500 m (1,700 ft) below the surface by day and swims up at night to eat tiny shellfish and other floating food.

### SEA LILY

This animal is an upside-down version of its relative, the starfish. It is fixed to the seabed by a stalk. Its branched tentacles gather and trap food, then sweep it to the mouth in a stream of mucus (spit).

### DEEP-SEA SQUID

Squid swim among the sea lilies, hunting for fish and other prey. The giant squid also swims near the sea bottom.

### SEA CUCUMBER

The cylindrical-shaped sea cucumber is an animal, and a relative of the starfish. It has a frill of tentacles at one end, around the mouth. These tentacles sweep up bits of food from the muddy floor as the sea cucumber moves along on its many tubed feet.

## LIFE ON THE SEABED

Many kinds of animals filter, sieve, and sift the water and muddy sludge on the sea floor for tiny pieces of food. In places where ocean currents bring abundant food, these creatures cover the seabed. Most of them are blind and slow-moving. When some deep-sea fish are brought to the surface, the decrease in water pressure makes them swell and burst. Scientists study them with special remote-control submersibles which can carry cameras as deep as 6,000 m (20,000 ft).

Sea cucumber

Sea lily

| *Find out more* |
| --- |
| ATMOSPHERE |
| FISH |
| OCEAN WILDLIFE |
| OCTOPUSES AND SQUID |
| STARFISH AND SEA URCHINS |
| UNDERWATER EXPLORATION |

# DEER, ANTELOPES, AND GAZELLES

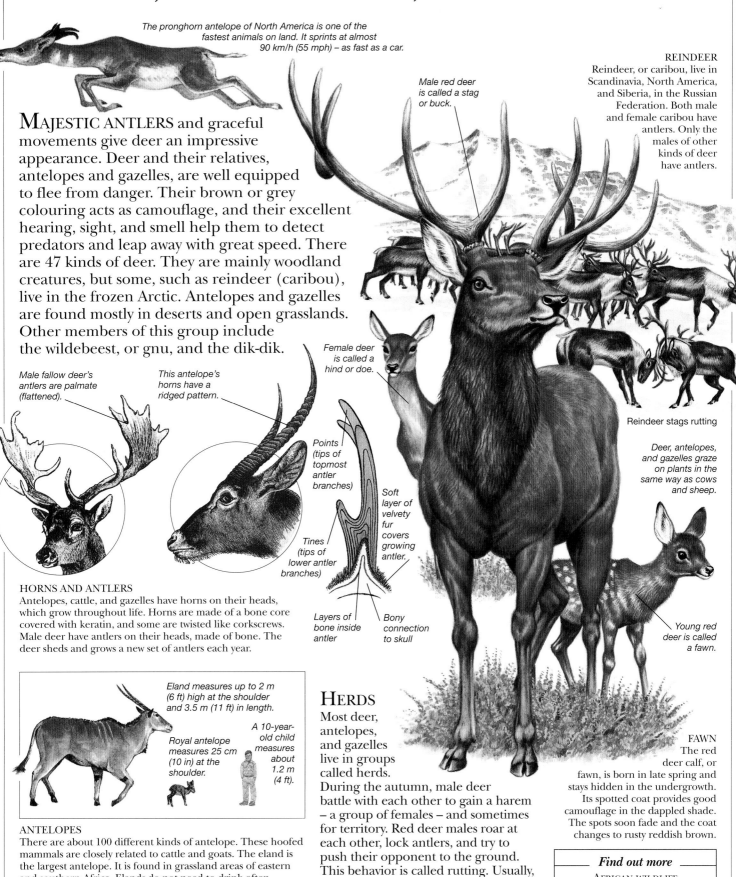

The pronghorn antelope of North America is one of the fastest animals on land. It sprints at almost 90 km/h (55 mph) – as fast as a car.

Male red deer is called a stag or buck.

REINDEER
Reindeer, or caribou, live in Scandinavia, North America, and Siberia, in the Russian Federation. Both male and female caribou have antlers. Only the males of other kinds of deer have antlers.

MAJESTIC ANTLERS and graceful movements give deer an impressive appearance. Deer and their relatives, antelopes and gazelles, are well equipped to flee from danger. Their brown or grey colouring acts as camouflage, and their excellent hearing, sight, and smell help them to detect predators and leap away with great speed. There are 47 kinds of deer. They are mainly woodland creatures, but some, such as reindeer (caribou), live in the frozen Arctic. Antelopes and gazelles are found mostly in deserts and open grasslands. Other members of this group include the wildebeest, or gnu, and the dik-dik.

Female deer is called a hind or doe.

Male fallow deer's antlers are palmate (flattened).

This antelope's horns have a ridged pattern.

Reindeer stags rutting

Deer, antelopes, and gazelles graze on plants in the same way as cows and sheep.

Points (tips of topmost antler branches)

Soft layer of velvety fur covers growing antler.

Tines (tips of lower antler branches)

Layers of bone inside antler

Bony connection to skull

## HORNS AND ANTLERS
Antelopes, cattle, and gazelles have horns on their heads, which grow throughout life. Horns are made of a bone core covered with keratin, and some are twisted like corkscrews. Male deer have antlers on their heads, made of bone. The deer sheds and grows a new set of antlers each year.

Young red deer is called a fawn.

Eland measures up to 2 m (6 ft) high at the shoulder and 3.5 m (11 ft) in length.

Royal antelope measures 25 cm (10 in) at the shoulder.

A 10-year-old child measures about 1.2 m (4 ft).

## HERDS
Most deer, antelopes, and gazelles live in groups called herds. During the autumn, male deer battle with each other to gain a harem – a group of females – and sometimes for territory. Red deer males roar at each other, lock antlers, and try to push their opponent to the ground. This behavior is called rutting. Usually, the largest, strongest males win. These large males then defend their group and its territory against other herds.

## ANTELOPES
There are about 100 different kinds of antelope. These hoofed mammals are closely related to cattle and goats. The eland is the largest antelope. It is found in grassland areas of eastern and southern Africa. Elands do not need to drink often because they absorb enough water from the plants they eat. Elands live for about 15 years. The royal antelope, from western Africa, is the smallest antelope.

FAWN
The red deer calf, or fawn, is born in late spring and stays hidden in the undergrowth. Its spotted coat provides good camouflage in the dappled shade. The spots soon fade and the coat changes to rusty reddish brown.

*Find out more*
AFRICAN WILDLIFE
FOREST WILDLIFE
NORTH AMERICAN WILDLIFE

# DEMOCRACY

THE WORD DEMOCRACY COMES FROM the ancient Greek words *demos,* which means "people", and *kratia,* which means "power". Democracy means "rule by the people". Within a democracy, all persons have the right to play a part in the government of their country. In most democracies, all persons over the age of 18 can elect a member of parliament to represent them in the national government; and a councillor – their representative in local government. Occasionally they vote about an issue in a referendum. Twenty-five hundred years ago the people of Athens, Greece, practised a form of democracy. Men met in one place to decide on laws for their community. Today, most democracy is representative. Because there are usually too many people in a country to be involved in making every decision, the people elect representatives to make decisions on their behalf.

**BALLOT BOX**
When people vote in an election, they mark their votes on a piece of paper which they then drop into a ballot box. Their vote is secret, because no one can tell who marked each piece of paper. Today, electronic voting booths are replacing ballot boxes.

*A French journal shows political parties campaigning for votes in the United States, 1908.*

**REPRESENTATIVE DEMOCRACY**
Representative democracy means that citizens vote for certain people to represent them. People form political parties and citizens vote for their favoured party in elections. The different parties compete with each other for votes in election campaigns. Getting the right to vote (suffrage) has been a dedicated struggle for both men and women. Today, adult men and women in most countries can vote.

*Indians queue to cast their vote at polling booths around the country.*

## MAJORITY RULE

Democracy means government by the people, but one group of people might want to do one thing and another group something completely different. In that case, the view of the majority (the larger group of people) rules. This could lead to the views of the minority being ignored, so many democratic countries and organizations have a constitution (a set of rules) that safeguards the rights of individuals and minorities. A few countries still do not have a democracy and are ruled by just one person, usually called a "dictator".

*Pro-democracy demonstrators in former Czechoslovakia light candles at a vigil.*

Minority vote

Majority vote

# VOTING

India is the biggest representative democracy in the world: more than 600 million people are able to vote. In the general election of 2004, close to 400 million people went to the polling stations to vote for their representatives in the national parliament. When so many people vote, it can take several days for all the votes to be counted.

**EASTERN EUROPE**
From 1989, people in Communist Eastern Europe demanded democratic governments. They felt they did not have enough say in how their countries were run. In 1990, what was then Czechoslovakia became the first of many Eastern European Communist countries to declare themselves a real democracy.

---

### *Find out more*
COMMUNISM
GOVERNMENTS AND POLITICS
GREECE, ANCIENT
LAW

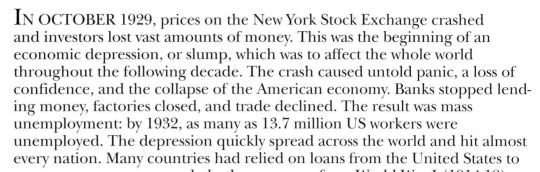

| 1929 :<br>1 billion | 1930 :<br>800<br>million | 1931 :<br>600<br>million | 1932 :<br>400<br>million |
|---|---|---|---|

# DEPRESSION
## OF THE 1930s

IN OCTOBER 1929, prices on the New York Stock Exchange crashed and investors lost vast amounts of money. This was the beginning of an economic depression, or slump, which was to affect the whole world throughout the following decade. The crash caused untold panic, a loss of confidence, and the collapse of the American economy. Banks stopped lending money, factories closed, and trade declined. The result was mass unemployment: by 1932, as many as 13.7 million US workers were unemployed. The depression quickly spread across the world and hit almost every nation. Many countries had relied on loans from the United States to help them recover from World War I (1914-18).

Now these loans stopped. Businesses collapsed, and millions of people were thrown out of work. Unemployment caused misery and poverty.

Disillusioned and frightened people turned to extreme right-wing political parties, such as the National Socialist German Workers' (Nazi) Party in Germany. The build-up to World War II ended the Depression, because increased production of arms created jobs.

## DUST BOWL

During the 1930s, a terrible drought turned the soil of the American Midwest into dust. High winds blew clouds of dust over fields and farms, which hid the sunlight. The region became known as the Dust Bowl. Many ruined farmers were forced to trek across the country to find work in the orchards and farms of California, United States.

## TENNESSEE VALLEY AUTHORITY

When Franklin D. Roosevelt became US President in 1932, he set up many programmes to improve the economy. The Tennessee Valley Authority was given money to employ people to build massive dams and hydroelectric power stations in southeastern United States.

*Amount of sales on the New York Stock Exchange 1929-32.*

## WALL STREET CRASH

On 24 October 1929, known as "Black Thursday", the boom years that had followed World War I came to an end. To get richer, people had been investing a lot of money in the New York Stock Exchange. When it crashed, people wildly tried to sell their shares. In two months, share values had declined by one third. Many people lost all their savings, and thousands of companies collapsed.

## JARROW MARCH

In Britain, mass unemployment led to "hunger marches". In 1936, some 200 out-of-work and hungry men marched 480 km (300 miles) from Jarrow, in the northeast of England, to the capital, London, in order to draw people's attention to their plight.

*Find out more*
GERMANY, HISTORY OF
ROOSEVELT, FRANKLIN DELANO
WORLD WAR I
WORLD WAR II

# DESERTS

A FIFTH OF THE EARTH'S LAND consists of dry, hostile regions called deserts, empty of all but a few plants, the hardiest of animals, and some wandering tribes. Life for desert dwellers, such as the Bedouin nomads who roam the Middle East, is a constant fight for survival, because food and water are scarce.

Little rain falls in deserts because the air is warm and no clouds can form. The clear skies make most deserts scorch with the sun's heat by day, but with no clouds to trap heat, the temperature may drop below freezing at night. Not all deserts are blazing hot and covered with vast stretches of sand; many are strewn with rocks, and deserts in some parts of Asia are often cold because they lie at high altitudes. New deserts can form in regions where droughts often occur and where people cut down all the trees, or allow their animals to eat all the plants, a process called overgrazing. During the 1970s, drought and overgrazing turned the Sahel region of central Africa into desert, and the problem still exists today.

**MONUMENT VALLEY**
Fantastic columns of rock adorn Monument Valley, a desert region in the United States. Sand carried by the wind wears away the rock to form pillars with extraordinary shapes.

## SAND

Desert temperatures soar by day and plunge by night. Rock continually expands and contracts as it warms and cools, and its surface breaks up into fragments. These fragments are blown by the wind and grind down other rocks. Eventually, millions of tiny pieces of rock cover the desert as sand. But the wind may also blow away the sand and leave bare rock or stony ground.

**SAND DUNES**
Many deserts contain huge mounds of sand called dunes. The wind heaps up sand to form the dunes, which slowly advance over the desert as the wind blows. The dunes are like waves of sand and can be 33 m (100 ft) high or more.

**SAND STORMS**
Strong winds blow sand and dust which sweep over the desert in swirling clouds. High winds can blow fine particles of dust across entire continents.

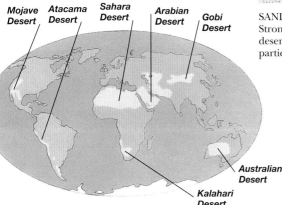

**DESERTS OF THE WORLD**
Mojave Desert · Atacama Desert · Sahara Desert · Arabian Desert · Gobi Desert · Australian Desert · Kalahari Desert

Two great belts of desert climate encircle the world on either side of the equator. Deserts also form in regions sheltered from rain by high mountains. The largest desert in the world is the Sahara in North Africa, covering an area of more than 9 million sq km (3.5 million sq miles). Some cold deserts lie in the hearts of continents where the winds are dry.

**OASES**
Desert travellers often seek an oasis, pockets of water in the desert. The water comes from a great distance and flows under the desert, reaching the surface in springs. This oasis is in the Tamerza Desert, Tunisia.

**IRRIGATION**
Irrigation can change desert regions into green and fertile land. The water may come from dams across nearby rivers, or it may be pumped up from wells in the ground.

---

*Find out more*

CAMELS AND LLAMAS
CLIMATES
DESERT WILDLIFE

# DESERT WILDLIFE

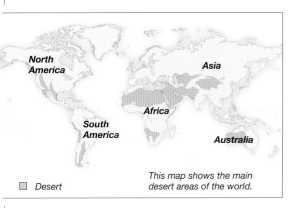

*Desert*

This map shows the main desert areas of the world.

THE VAST, DRY EXPANSE OF A DESERT may look uninhabited, but all kinds of plants and animals survive in these sandy regions – including insects, reptiles, mammals, and fish. Deserts are the driest places on Earth; some have less than 10 cm (4 in) of rainfall each year. Desert animals have adapted to the lack of water in various ways. Camels, for example, can survive for a long time without drinking. Other animals find enough water in the plants and insects they eat, so they never have to drink at all. Plants such as baobab trees have deep-growing roots to search for water underground.

Other problems for desert wildlife are the extremes of temperature and the lack of shelter. Some deserts are scorching hot; others are freezing cold. Desert mammals have thick fur to keep out heat as well as cold. Many find shelter from the sun and icy winds by digging burrows. In hot deserts, animals stay in their burrows by day and hunt at night when the temperature is lower.

## MONGOOSE
These adaptable mammals hunt by day for all kinds of small animals, including bees, spiders, scorpions, mice, and snakes. A mongoose has extremely quick reactions, so it can easily dodge an enemy such as a snake. The mongoose then leaps onto the snake and kills it with one bite.

## TAWNY EAGLE
The tawny eagle survives well in desert conditions. Its incredible eyesight enables it to spot a rabbit or lizard thousands of metres away. When it sees prey, the tawny eagle dives at great speed and grabs the victim in its powerful talons.

## COBRA
The hooded cobra kills small mammals, frogs, and lizards by biting them with its deadly fangs full of venom (poison). When this snake is in danger, it rears up its head and spreads out the ribs in the loose skin of its neck to form a hood. The hood makes the cobra look bigger and more threatening.

## COLD DESERTS
It is often bitterly cold at night and during the winter in deserts such as the Gobi Desert in Asia. This is partly because the Gobi is very high – about 1,000 m (3,500 ft) above sea level. Day temperatures rise as high as 50°C (122°F), then fall to -40°C (-40°F). For some creatures, a burrow is the only place that provides warmth. Some animals, such as the mongoose, dig their own burrow; others, such as snakes, take over an empty burrow or kill and eat the occupier.

Long-eared hedgehog

## LONG-EARED HEDGEHOG
The long-eared hedgehog shown here has large ears which give off excess warmth to keep the animal cool. Prickly spines protect it from predators. During the day, the long-eared hedgehog stays in its burrow; at night it hunts for insects and worms.

*Many lizards prowl across the dry sand, flicking their tongues in and out to taste the air. This monitor lizard eats eggs belonging to birds and other reptiles.*

## JERBOA
Many small mammals live in the desert, including various kinds of mice, gerbils, and jerboas. With its long back legs, the northern jerboa shown here can leap away from danger, keeping its large toes spread out to prevent it from sinking in the soft sand. Jerboas feed on seeds and other plant matter.

Northern jerboa

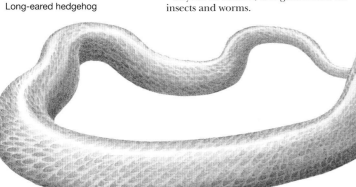

## CONSERVATION

Most desert wildlife is not in urgent need of conservation measures because deserts are not seriously threatened by habitat destruction. However, some deserts are being turned into farmland for growing cereals, fruit, and other crops, and this destroys the unique desert plant life.

## DORCAS GAZELLE

Dorcas gazelles are found across northern Africa, the Middle East, and India. They are an endangered species because they are being forced out of their natural habitat by farm animals and crops.

## DATE PALM

The date palm tree has many different uses. The nourishing date fruit is food for people and animals, the stringy bark and wood are made into matting and ropes, and the leaves are fashioned into roofs and sunshades.

Dorcas gazelle

## CACTUS

The cactus stores water in its swollen stem. Sharp prickles protect it from plant-eating animals. The cactus shown here is called the prickly pear cactus. The fruit is edible.

# HOT DESERTS

The Sahara in Africa is the world's largest and hottest desert. At midday in the Sahara, the scorching sand is so hot that it can burn through skin in seconds. The temperature in the shade soars to more than 55°C (130°F). Few animals are active. Yet as the sun sets and the air and sand cool, many creatures emerge from under rocks and out of burrows. Dew falls at night, providing the plants and animals with much-needed moisture.

## ROADRUNNER

The roadrunner can fly, but it usually races along the ground and runs into the undergrowth if it is disturbed. Roadrunners live in deserts and dry, open country in North America, feeding on all kinds of small animals, including grasshoppers and snakes, eggs, and certain fruits.

## ADDAX

This large grazing antelope from the Sahara never drinks – it obtains enough water from its food. Like other sandy desert dwellers, the addax's feet splay out widely to spread the animal's weight and keep it from sinking in the sand. The addax's horns have spiral ridges. The horns are used for defence and in contests for control of the herd.

## SIDEWINDER

A row of S-shaped marks in the sand at daybreak is a sign that a sidewinder snake passed during the night, probably on the trail of a mouse or a rat. This snake's wavelike way of moving means that only two small parts of its body touch the ground at any time, giving a better grip on the shifting sand.

## NAKED MOLE RAT

This hairless rat is virtually blind and lives in underground tunnels in groups called colonies. The colonies are organized in a similar way to an ant's nest, with one queen who gives birth to all the young. Naked mole rats feed only on tubers which they find in the soil.

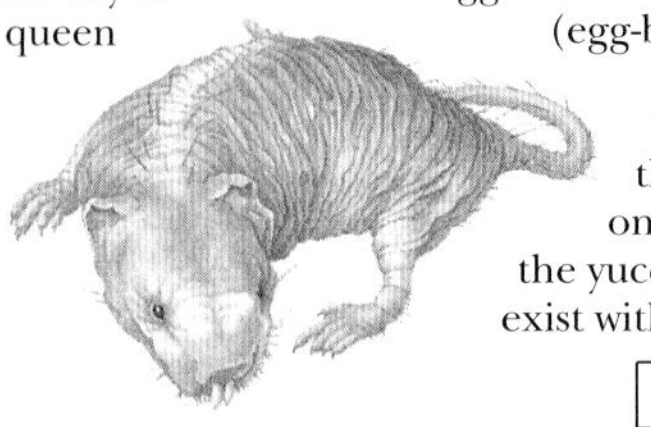

## YUCCA MOTH AND YUCCA PLANT

The yucca is a desert lily. It has pale, scented flowers which attract the tiny female yucca moth. The moth climbs into the flower and gathers pollen, then flies to another yucca. Here the yucca moth lays its egg in the flower's ovary (egg-bearing part), and transfers pollen. As the yucca's fruit ripens, the moth caterpillar feeds on it. The yucca moth and the yucca flower could not exist without each other.

## PINK FAIRY ARMADILLO

Measuring only 15 cm (6 in) long, the pink fairy armadillo lives in the deserts of South America. It leaves its tunnel at nightfall to dig up ants, worms, and other food.

### Find out more
BUTTERFLIES AND MOTHS
DEER, ANTELOPES, and gazelles
DESERTS
NORTH AMERICAN WILDLIFE
REPTILES
SNAKES

# DESIGN

THE OBJECTS AROUND US HAVE BEEN CAREFULLY shaped to do their jobs as well as possible. But before they are made, they have to be designed. Design is the process of planning and deciding the best way to make and style an object. Good design means that an object fits its purpose well. For instance, a chair that is stable and comfortable is well designed. A lamp that can be easily moved so light is cast all over a work surface is also good design. If the object is also attractive, inexpensive, and safe, its design is even better. To meet these needs, designers – people who work in design – have to understand the properties of the materials they work with. There are various different types of design, including garden, industrial, fashion, and graphic design. Today, computers are playing a greater role in design.

*Desk lamp is designed so light can be angled.*

*Designer working at drawing board*

## INDUSTRIAL DESIGN

The area of design that is concerned with developing practical products, such as cars, computers, office furniture, and lighting is known as industrial design. Industrial designers may also be involved in planning the layouts of buildings, or designing packaging or company logos.

*Designed in the 1960s by Alec Issigonis, the Mini looked good, was cheap to run, and easy to park.*

## DESIGN METHODS

Traditionally, designers worked at a drawing board, using paper and pens to produce two-dimensional plans. Today, most designers use computers to create three-dimensional models, or plans that can be rotated on screen, and looked at from every angle.

*Designer can create three-dimensional model on screen.*

*A Bauhaus tea set designed by Walter Gropius.*

## DESIGN PROCESS

The design process has a number of stages. Design also means to sketch, and a designer usually begins his or her work by doing a sketch of the object to be produced, for instance a vacuum cleaner. Working from the sketch, the designer then produces a prototype, or rough model. This is usually tested to make sure it works properly, and is safe. Finally, the object is made in a factory.

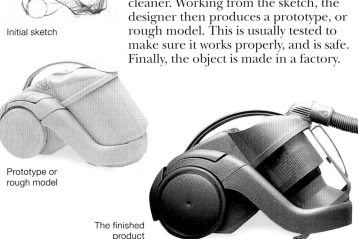

Initial sketch

Prototype or rough model

The finished product

## BAUHAUS

In Germany in 1919, architect Walter Gropius (1883-1969) founded an important school of design called the Bauhaus. It attracted great artists and architects, and revolutionized design by combining art and crafts to produce goods that were beautiful and useful. Its striking designs were famous worldwide.

*1970s' fabric designed in the style of the Bauhaus.*

In the late 19th century, fashionable outdoor wear for both sexes included a long cloak. Gentlemen wore shiny top hats and leaned elegantly on canes; ladies peered from beneath large decorative bonnets.

Most late 18th-century furniture was highly decorative.

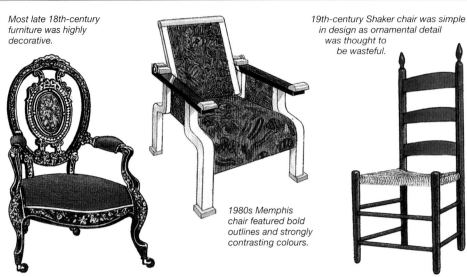

19th-century Shaker chair was simple in design as ornamental detail was thought to be wasteful.

1980s Memphis chair featured bold outlines and strongly contrasting colours.

## FASHION DESIGN

Nothing changes faster than the design of clothes. Each year designers create new garments that will appeal to the fashion-conscious public. Designers use new fabrics that are easy to care for and which keep out rain, wind, and cold. Some clothes are specially designed to suit the needs of mountaineers, sailors, athletes, and other people who work or play outdoors. Some are designed for comfort and durability. Even babies' nappies are designed for easy fitting and maximum absorption. But many clothes are made just to look colourful, appealing, or outrageous.

## CHANGING DESIGNS

Design evolves to suit changing tastes and the availability of new materials. Much of the furniture made in the 19th century was highly decorative, except for the simple items designed by the deeply religious Shaker sect. The Thonet chair of 1850 used wood that was shaped in a new way and cut manufacturing costs. The outline of a Bauhaus chair stressed its purpose of supporting the sitter's weight. Rethinking exactly how people sit produced the kneeling chair during the 1970s. Modern designers are again introducing ornamentation, as on the Memphis chair (above).

1970s kneeling chair helped office workers sit correctly.

1850s Thonet bentwood chair was mass-produced using new manufacturing techniques.

The severe lines of a 1920s Bauhaus reclining chair emphasized the shape of the human body.

## PRODUCT DESIGN

Product design should be functional and stylish: for example, a coffeepot must hold hot coffee but also look good on the table. The designer considers all sorts of factors – the shape, the materials to suit its purpose, its safety and durability, cost of manufacture, and the retail price to the customer.

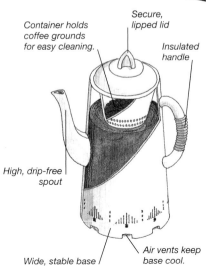

Container holds coffee grounds for easy cleaning.

Secure, lipped lid

Insulated handle

High, drip-free spout

Wide, stable base

Air vents keep base cool.

## INTERIOR DESIGN

Interior designers create the feel of a room through choice of colour and furnishings, making the best of the space available. For this bedroom, the designer has selected attractive items that are comfortable, safe, and easy to use. The bedroom features washable wallpaper and nontoxic toys, flameproof fabrics, and safety-tested lights. The storage areas have adjustable shelving.

### Find out more
ADVERTISING
ARCHITECTURE
CLOTHES
FURNITURE

# CHARLES
# DICKENS

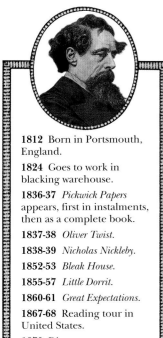

**1812** Born in Portsmouth, England.

**1824** Goes to work in blacking warehouse.

**1836-37** *Pickwick Papers* appears, first in instalments, then as a complete book.

**1837-38** *Oliver Twist.*

**1838-39** *Nicholas Nickleby.*

**1852-53** *Bleak House.*

**1855-57** *Little Dorrit.*

**1860-61** *Great Expectations.*

**1867-68** Reading tour in United States.

**1870** Dies.

IN 1836, A YOUNG ENGLISH JOURNALIST published his first novel. The book was called *Pickwick Papers,* and its unknown writer, Charles Dickens, quickly became famous. Pickwick was followed by many other novels, and made Dickens one of the best-loved of English writers. His books appealed to children and adults alike. They dealt with all levels of society, and included scenes of both touching emotion and hilarious comedy. As a journalist, Dickens was also good at tackling the important social problems of the time. In all his books, he brought to life poverty, bad schools, injustice, crime, and the poor working conditions in England's factories. His sympathy for the deprived, together with his entertaining stories, mean that his books are still very popular today. Many are made into films and television series.

## BLACKING FACTORY
When Dickens was 12 years old, his father was put in prison for debt. Charles had to go to work for a company that sold blacking – black polish that people used on shoes and iron fireplaces. He never forgot the poor conditions in the blacking factory, and his memories helped to make his descriptions of poverty both realistic and moving.

*GREAT EXPECTATIONS*
One of Dickens's most popular books, *Great Expectations* tells the story of Pip, a young boy who grows up expecting to become rich. In the end he learns to accept poverty and his poor friends.

## DICKENS THE WRITER
In the 19th century, novels often came out in instalments, and this was the way Dickens usually worked. He liked to end episodes on a cliff-hanger, or dramatic scene, which kept his readers interested. Dickens edited a series of weekly magazines, including *Household Words,* in which his books appeared. He also wrote articles about current issues.

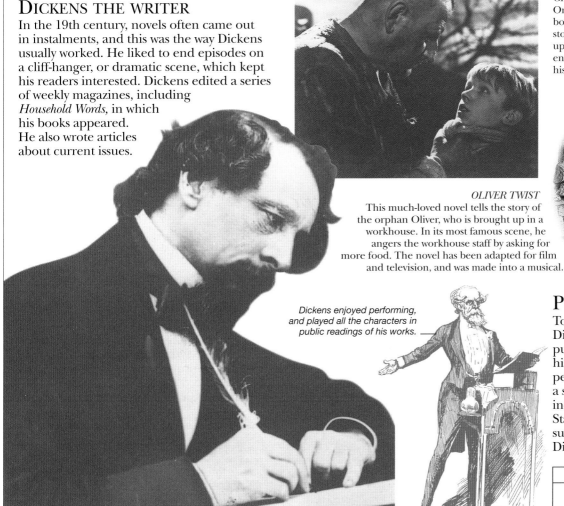

*OLIVER TWIST*
This much-loved novel tells the story of the orphan Oliver, who is brought up in a workhouse. In its most famous scene, he angers the workhouse staff by asking for more food. The novel has been adapted for film and television, and was made into a musical.

*Dickens enjoyed performing, and played all the characters in public readings of his works.*

## PUBLIC READINGS
Towards the end of his life, Dickens gave a series of public readings. He adapted his books specially for performing, and went on a series of reading tours, including one to the United States. The tours were hugely successful, but exhausted Dickens and made him ill.

---
***Find out more***
LITERATURE
VICTORIANS
WRITERS AND POETS
---

# DIGESTION

HUMANS MUST EAT TO LIVE. The body needs food to work properly and to grow and repair itself. Food contains water and five vital nutrients – proteins, carbohydrates, fats, vitamins, and minerals. For food to be useful, the body has to break it down, or digest it, and combine it with oxygen. The digestive system consists of a long tube called the alimentary canal which runs from the mouth to the anus. Each part does a particular job. The stomach is like a bag where chewed food is mixed with acids and digestive juices. The small intestine pushes the food along by a squeezing action called peristalsis. The tiny particles of digested food pass easily through the walls of the small intestine and into the bloodstream, to be used by the body. The large intestine absorbs water from the food and turns the waste products into semi-solid lumps called faeces.

## DIGESTION
Digestion begins in the mouth, as teeth crush the food. Watery saliva moistens the food and makes it easy to chew and swallow. The muscular walls of the stomach churn the food into a soup-like liquid and mix it with powerful digestive juices. The broken-down nutrients are small enough to seep through the lining of the small intestine and into the blood vessels in its wall.

## VILLI
Each fold of the lining of the small intestine has thousands of microscopic finger-shaped projections called villi. The villi allow the small intestine to absorb more nutrients.

Teeth chew, crunch, and grind food into a pulp.

Tongue tastes different flavours.

Salivary glands produce a watery liquid to mix with food and help with swallowing.

Oesophagus pushes swallowed food down through the chest, behind the windpipe and heart, into the stomach.

Liver

Stomach is where muscles crush food into a pulp and mix it with digestive juices.

Small intestine absorbs digested food into the body.

Large intestine absorbs water from undigested pieces of food.

Rectum is the last part of the large intestine.

## STOMACH
This bag is lined with a thick layer of slimy mucus. Tiny glands in the lining produce strong digestive juices, which contain substances such as enzymes and acids.

## EATING FOOD
When you swallow food, it enters your throat. A flap called the epiglottis folds over the entrance to the windpipe so that food goes into the oesophagus and not into the lungs, where it could cause choking.

## LIVER
The liver is the body's "chemical factory". It receives digested nutrients from the intestines and converts them into more easily used forms, such as glucose (blood sugar) for muscle fuel.

## SMALL INTESTINE
The small intestine is coiled into the lower part of the body. It is very long, measuring about 6 m (20 ft) in length. Its lining has many folds and ridges, so that it can absorb as many nutrients as possible.

Pancreas produces digestive juices.

## LARGE INTESTINE
The large intestine is much shorter than the small intestine, but three times as wide, measuring up to 7 cm (2.5 in) in width.

Anus is where waste products leave the body as faeces.

## TONGUE
The tongue is a flexible muscle. On its surface are tiny nodules called taste buds which sense different flavours. The tip of the tongue can taste sweet flavours, the part behind the tip tastes salty flavours, the sides taste sour flavours, and the back tastes bitter flavours.

Bitter

Sour

Salty

Sweet

## ENZYMES
Digestive juices contain proteins called enzymes which dissolve the food into tiny particles the body can absorb.

### Find out more
FOOD AND FOOD TECHNOLOGY
HEALTH AND FITNESS
HUMAN BODY
MUSCLES AND MOVEMENT

# DINOSAURS

WE HAVE KNOWN ABOUT DINOSAURS for only 150 years or so, but these great creatures roamed the Earth for 160 million years – long before humans appeared. Scientists first learned about dinosaurs in the 1820s, when they discovered the fossilized bones of unknown creatures. Today, these fossils show us where dinosaurs lived, what they looked like, and what they ate. Dinosaurs were reptiles and lived on land. Their name means "terrible lizard", and like lizards, many of them had tough, scaly skin. There were hundreds of different kinds of dinosaurs, divided into two main groups. The Ornithischians (bird-hipped dinosaurs), such as *Protoceratops*, had hipbones similar to birds; the Saurischians (lizard-hipped dinosaurs), such as *Diplodocus*, had hipbones similar to lizards. Not all dinosaurs were giants – *Compsognathus* was the size of a chicken and *Heterodontosaurus* was the size of a large dog. Some dinosaurs, such as *Tyrannosaurus rex*, were carnivores (meat eaters); others, such as *Stegosaurus*, were herbivores (plant eaters). About 65 million years ago, dinosaurs and the swimming and flying reptiles that lived at the same time died out. The reason for this is still a mystery.

REPTILES
Dinosaurs were reptiles, like crocodiles, alligators, and the lizard shown above. Like other reptiles, dinosaurs had scaly skin, and laid eggs. Unlike lizards and other reptiles, dinosaurs had long legs, so they could move faster on land.

*When dinosaurs lived on the land, flying reptiles called pterosaurs flew in the air, and reptiles called ichthyosaurs and plesiosaurs swam in the sea.*

*Criorhynchus was a fishing pterosaur – it swept low over the seas and caught fish in its beak.*

A lizard-type pelvis

Tyrannosaurus rex belonged to the group of lizard-hipped dinosaurs called Saurischians.

*Tyrannosaurus had tiny hands which did not reach its mouth. We do not know what the hands were used for.*

*Carnivorous dinosaurs often had large, strong claws for grabbing their prey. The claw shown here belonged to Baryonyx, which is nicknamed "Claws".*

## TYRANNOSAURUS REX
The gigantic *Tyrannosaurus* was the largest carnivorous dinosaur. It was also the largest known meat-eating land animal of all time. Scientists first discovered its fossils in North America. *Tyrannosaurus* measured 14 m (46 ft) in length and stood almost 6 m (20 ft) high. Its massive teeth were more than 15 cm (6 in) long. *Tyrannosaurus* weighed almost 7 tonnes (7 tons), so it was probably too heavy to run and hunt other dinosaurs. *Tyrannosaurus* fed on small creatures and dead dinosaurs.

*GORGOSAURUS*
Carnivorous dinosaurs, such as the *Gorgosaurus*, had huge teeth and powerful jaw muscles for a strong bite. Not all dinosaur teeth were this large, however; some were as small as human teeth.

Jaw bone of a *Gorgosaurus*

Protoceratops *was about 2 m (6 ft) long. It probably snipped at plants with its beak-like mouth.*

## DIPLODOCUS

The largest dinosaurs, including *Diplodocus*, belonged to the group of plant eaters called sauropods. At 27 m (88 ft) in length, *Diplodocus* was one of the longest dinosaurs. Its long, thin tail made up most of its length. With its slim body, it probably weighed only about 9 tonnes (9 tons).

Diplodocus *was a herbivore; all its teeth were at the front of its mouth for nibbling at tough leaves.*

## PROTOCERATOPS

Scientists discovered fossils of *Protoceratops* in the Gobi Desert, Mongolia, in the 1920s. The bones of adults and young were found, together with fossilized eggs. About 80 million years ago, this area was a nesting site for many families of *Protoceratops*.

### BREEDING

The fossils of *Protoceratops* show that the female scooped out a shallow hole in the sand and laid the eggs in a circular pattern. Scientists found many nests near each other, which shows that these dinosaurs bred in colonies, or groups, in the same way as some birds do today.

## TYPES OF DINOSAURS

Dinosaurs varied greatly in size and shape, and they did not all live at the same time. Some lived 200 million years ago; others lived 70 million years ago. This chart gives the sizes of some dinosaurs in comparison to the size of a 10-year-old child.

*m.y.a. = million years ago*

Coelophysis
210 m.y.a.

Diplodocus
140 m.y.a.

Iguanodon
120 m.y.a.

Ornithosuchus
210 m.y.a.

Triceratops
65 m.y.a.

Protoceratops
80 m.y.a.

Comp-
sognathus
140 m.y.a.

Baryonyx
120 m.y.a.

Euplocephalus
75 m.y.a.

Tyrannosaurus
70 m.y.a.

*Scientists have been able to reconstruct some dinosaur species, such as this Tuojiangosaurus.*

## THE END OF THE DINOSAURS

There are many ideas about the end of the dinosaurs. Some people believe they died out because a giant meteorite crashed into the Earth, throwing up a dust cloud and blotting out the sun. Without sunlight, the plants and the dinosaurs that fed on them could not survive.

### BARYONYX

In 1983, the fossilized claw and bones of a dinosaur were found in Surrey, England. This dinosaur is named *Baryonyx*. Fossilized scales of fish were found in this dinosaur's stomach, so it was probably a fish eater and may have used its claws to catch fish.

## IGUANODON

*Iguanodon* was a herbivore. As an adult it was about 10 m (33 ft) long, with small hooves on its hands and feet. Some scientists believe that *Iguanodon* lived in herds because, in some areas of Europe, they have found many fossilized skeletons of *Iguanodon* together in one place.

Iguanodon *had versatile hands – the three middle fingers acted like hooves, the little finger could grasp food, and the spiked thumb was a fearsome weapon.*

A bird-type pelvis

Iguanodon *belonged to the bird-hipped group of dinosaurs called Ornithischians.*

*Heavy tail balanced the rest of* Iguanodon's *body.*

*Find out more*

EVOLUTION
FOSSILS
PREHISTORIC LIFE
PREHISTORIC PEOPLES

# DISEASE

AT SOME POINT IN YOUR LIFE you may have a disease. It may be relatively harmless or it may be quite serious. Disease is a sickness of the body or mind. There are thousands of diseases that can strike almost any part of the body. They range from measles and the common cold to heart disease and emotional disorders such as depression. Some diseases are chronic (lasting for a long time); arthritis is a chronic disease that makes the joints swell painfully. Other diseases, which are called acute, occur in short, sharp attacks and include flu (influenza). There are many different causes of disease. Harmful micro-organisms (microscopic plants or animals) can invade the body and cause infectious diseases. Poor living conditions can also cause disease. Some diseases occur at birth; others may be passed from parent to child. The reasons for some diseases such as cancer are unclear. Scientists are constantly working to understand the causes of diseases and find possible cures.

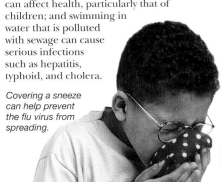

### ENVIRONMENTAL DISEASE
Living conditions affect people's health. Nuclear radiation in the atmosphere can cause cancer; pollution of the air from chemicals such as lead can affect health, particularly that of children; and swimming in water that is polluted with sewage can cause serious infections such as hepatitis, typhoid, and cholera.

*Covering a sneeze can help prevent the flu virus from spreading.*

*There are several different types of bacteria (below). Each consists of a single living cell. Some bacteria cause disease in humans and animals, but most are harmless.*

Causes boils

Causes typhoid

Causes sore throat

*Viruses are smaller than a living cell. Viruses cause disease when they enter healthy cells in order to reproduce. The flu virus (above) is spread from person to person by coughing and sneezing.*

## BACTERIA AND VIRUSES
Infectious diseases are the only diseases that can spread from person to person. Most are caused by microscopic organisms called bacteria and viruses that invade the body. Typhoid and cholera are examples of diseases caused by bacteria; chicken pox and measles are caused by viruses.

*Heart disease is often caused by blockage of blood vessels in the heart. It has been linked to a rich, fatty diet and smoking.*

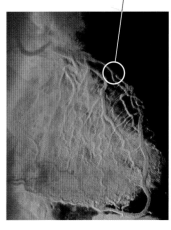

### AIDS
Our bodies have natural defences which help us fight disease. One is the immune system, which attacks diseases that invade our bodies. In the 1980s, a new disease began to spread. Known as acquired immunodeficiency syndrome (AIDS), it stops the immune system from working correctly and can result in death.

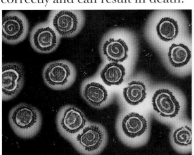

*AIDS virus particles under a microscope.*

### HEREDITARY AND CONGENITAL DISEASES
Parents can pass on certain diseases, called hereditary diseases, to their children. Sickle cell anaemia is a hereditary blood disease. Hereditary diseases do not usually affect all the children in a family, and may appear late in life. Diseases that appear at birth such as spina bifida, a defect of the spinal cord and nervous system, are called congenital diseases.

*Hereditary diseases are passed from parents to children in their genes.*

### NUTRITIONAL DISEASES
In parts of the world, particularly Africa and Asia, many people do not have enough to eat. Lack of food can cause many disorders, including anaemia, rickets, and scurvy. In places such as Europe and North America, many people eat too much. Overeating can also cause disorders, including obesity (fatness), diabetes, and heart disease.

### EPIDEMICS
When a disease affects many people at the same time, it is called an epidemic. Epidemics of AIDS and of malaria, a disease carried by mosquitoes, affect many parts of Africa. AIDS epidemics are also affecting industrialized countries. In Western countries, too, so many people suffer from heart disease and cancer that these diseases are sometimes described as epidemic.

---

***Find out more***
DOCTORS
DRUGS
GENETICS
HEALTH AND FITNESS
HOSPITALS
MEDICINE
MEDICINE, HISTORY OF

---

# DOCTORS

IF YOU ARE ILL, you may need to see a doctor. A doctor is someone who is trained to recognize what is wrong with sick people and know what will make them well. A general practitioner is usually the first doctor you see. These doctors, who are also called physicians, have a knowledge of many different types of illness. They also perform checkups and give vaccinations. Depending on your illness, the doctor may send you to a surgeon or some other specialist. Surgeons are doctors who carry out surgery or operations. They cut open the patient's body and take out or repair the sick organ. Other specialists include paediatricians, who specialize in treating children. To be licensed as a doctor takes five years of study at a medical school, and one year of internship (practical training) at a hospital.

HIPPOCRATIC OATH
Doctors have existed since ancient times. Hippocrates was a famous Greek doctor who lived 2,500 years ago. He swore an oath to preserve life and to work for the benefit of everyone. Today, doctors still swear the same oath when they complete their training.

The stethoscope enables the doctor to hear lung sounds and the flow of the blood.

DOCTOR'S TOOLS
Physicians use x-rays and a variety of special instruments to help them find out what is wrong with their patients.

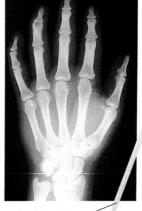

X-ray photographs reveal broken bones and some diseases, such as lung cancer.

The inflatable cuff of the sphygmomanometer temporarily stops the flow of blood, so that the doctor can measure its pressure.

With an otoscope the doctor can get a clear view inside the ears.

Doctors use an ophthalmoscope to examine the eyes.

A hammer tap below the knee tests the reflexes: a healthy patient's knee jerks.

## DOCTOR'S OFFICE
A family doctor sometimes visits sick patients in their homes; patients who are well enough visit the doctor in his or her office. There the doctor asks questions and examines the patient, then makes a diagnosis (decides what is wrong). Before giving any treatment, the doctor may also need to take x-rays or do blood tests.

TRAVELLING DOCTORS
In remote parts of the world, doctors travel from village to village to treat health problems. If there are not enough doctors, health workers can learn to treat common health problems. In Australia and Canada "flying doctors" reach isolated areas by aeroplane.

## MICROSURGERY
With the aid of microscopes, surgeons can see and operate on minute parts of the body. This technique, called microsurgery, makes it possible to repair or cut out damaged organs that are too small to work on without magnification. Microsurgeons can operate on delicate structures in the eye and the ear, and try to reconnect nerves and blood vessels of fingers or toes that have been cut off.

---

**Find out more**
DISEASE
HEALTH AND FITNESS
HOSPITALS

# DOGS
## WOLVES, AND FOXES

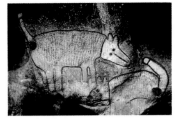

**EARLY DOGS**
The domestic dog is one of the 35 species of the dog family. As this early cave painting shows, it existed as long ago as the Stone Age.

WHEN A PET DOG BARKS at a stranger, or walks around in a circle before settling down to sleep, it is behaving in the same way that its wild wolf cousins did thousands of years ago. The dog family is made up of about 35 different species, one of which is the domestic dog. There are more than 300 breeds of domestic dog, from labradors to terriers. Others types of dog include the Asian dhole, the African wild dog, many kinds of foxes, and three species of jackals. These fast-running hunters are built for chasing prey; their elongated skulls are thought to be adaptations for seizing prey on the run. Many wild dogs, such as wolves and dingos, live in extended family groups called packs. Each pack has a leader, to whom all the other animals in the pack submit. A domestic dog sees its owner as a pack leader and is willing to obey that person's commands.

*Extremely sensitive nose for tracking animals and people*

*Reasonable eyesight in daylight; night vision weak.*

**GREY WOLF**
This wolf is believed to be the ancestor of our domestic dogs. It is the largest member of the dog family, measuring at least 2 m (6 ft) in length, including its tail. Where food is readily available, wolves may form a pack consisting of up to 20 wolves. When food is difficult to find, a large pack of wolves splits up into smaller groups of about seven animals.

*Good hearing, with ears that turn to locate the source of a sound*

*Dogs have four claws on each paw. The tough toe pads help them grip well when they run.*

*Long, strong legs for fast, sustained running*

**GERMAN SHEPHERD**
This dog has a long muzzle and large ears, and still resembles its wolf ancestors. It is a strong, agile, extremely intelligent breed of dog – popular both as a working dog and as a pet.

*Tail is used to give social signals, such as wagging when happy.*

*Fur coat keeps animal warm and dry.*

*Meat-eating teeth, with large, pointed canines for seizing and tearing at prey*

## DOMESTIC DOGS
Dogs have lived in harmony with humans for more than 10,000 years. It is quite possible that over thousands of years, humans have caught and tamed several members of the dog family, at first to help with hunting, herding, and guarding, and, much later, to keep as pets. Today, 203 breeds of domestic dogs are recognized in Britain, and more than 160 in the United States.

**WORKING DOGS**
Dogs are trained to do many jobs for humans. Some tasks, such as herding sheep or guarding property, involve the dog's natural instincts. Other jobs include guiding the blind, pulling sleds, and racing. Many dogs are trained by the police and the army to find people who are trapped or in hiding.

## RED FOX

Few animals are as adaptable as the red fox, which lives in almost every country north of the equator. Red foxes eat almost anything, including insects and fish. The fox springs up and pounces on its prey like a cat. This creature's legendary cunning helps it survive in suburban gardens and city dumps. In towns and cities, it feeds on scraps from dustbins and rubbish heaps.

*Mongrels are domestic dogs that are not pedigree – such as the three dogs shown here.*

*A female coyote usually has one litter of puppies each year.*

## COYOTE

The North American coyote is closely related to wolves, jackals, and domestic dogs. Like most dogs, the female is pregnant for nine weeks before giving birth to about five puppies. The puppies feed on their mother's milk for up to seven weeks. After the first four weeks they also eat food regurgitated, or brought up, by their parents. Coyotes were thought to live alone, but we now know that some form small packs.

**PANTING**
When a dog becomes hot, it cannot lose heat from its skin because it does not have sweat glands on its body. Instead, the dog opens its mouth and pants to give off heat from its mouth and tongue.

YORKSHIRE TERRIER
This small dog measures only 18 cm (7 in) in height. It is an agile runner, originally bred for catching rats.

MANED WOLF
The maned wolf is being bred in zoos and parks in an attempt to save it from extinction.

## TOY DOGS

Dog breeders have created dogs of all sizes and shapes by mating dogs with unusual features, such as short legs or small ears. The smallest breeds, known as toy dogs, have become quite different from their distant ancestors, the wolves. A chihuahua, one of the smallest recognized breeds, can weigh less than 1 kg (2 lbs).

CRAB-EATING FOX
The crab-eating fox, also called the common zorro, is from South America. It eats many kinds of food, including crabs, as it forages along the coast. Other common zorros live far inland in woods and grassland and never even see a crab.

## CONSERVATION

The long-legged, maned wolf from South America is one of many members of the dog family that are officially listed as in danger of extinction. Many wolves and foxes, including the grey wolf, have been hunted not only for their beautiful fur, but also because they sometimes attack farm animals. One of the greatest threats to the dog family is the loss of the natural areas where they live, which are now used for farmland, houses, and factories.

PUPPIES
Young dogs, such as the labrador puppy shown here, spend much of their time in play – tumbling, jumping, and biting and shaking things. These games help the young dog develop hunting skills for adult life.

***Find out more***
AFRICAN WILDLIFE
ANIMALS
ANIMAL SENSES
AUSTRALIAN WILDLIFE
CONSERVATION
and endangered species
MAMMALS
POLAR EXPLORATION

# DRAWING

EARLY PEOPLE MAY HAVE begun to draw by scratching images in the dirt with sticks or their fingers, possibly outlines copied from shadows. They then learned to use natural earth pigments and charcoal to draw on other surfaces. They may have started to draw in order to communicate ideas. Points of soft lead, tin, copper, and other metals were used from ancient times to the 18th century. Today, people draw with chalk, charcoal, crayon, pastel, pencil, or pen and ink. Paper is the most practical medium for drawing. Creative drawings are often done as preparations for paintings or sculptures; a painter may sketch out an idea in a drawing before starting to paint a picture. But many drawings are seen as finished works of art. Drawing has practical as well as artistic uses. An architect has to draw up detailed, accurate plans in order for a building to be constructed properly. Courtroom artists draw pictures of scenes during a trial where photographers are not allowed. And before photography was invented, artists drew battles and other events for newspapers.

ALBRECHT DÜRER
The German artist Albrecht Dürer (1471-1528) made many drawings of people, landscapes, and animals. His brush drawing *Praying Hands* (above) was a study for part of an altarpiece for a German church. Dürer also produced a variety of paintings, engravings, and woodcuts.

Pencils range from 7H, which gives a hard, fine line, to 8B, which gives a soft, dark line.

Charcoal sticks were used by early peoples to sketch on the walls of caves.

Pastels are powdered pigments bound together with gum or resin.

Drawing ink is generally water resistant.

Conté crayons are made by mixing chalk and pigment with fatty materials such as wax.

Metal nib pen

Coloured pencils

## PENS AND PENCILS

The "lead" pencil we use today is a mixture of graphite and clay fired at a high temperature and mixed with wax. This kind of pencil was not developed until the end of the 18th century. To get the best results, good-quality paper is necessary. Paper sometimes has a textured surface which adds to the character of the drawing.

TECHNICAL DRAWING
Architects, engineers, and designers make technical drawings of their designs with the aid of instruments such as T squares and compasses. Technical drawings show exactly how to construct things, from bridges to aeroplanes, so they must be very accurate. A technical artist needs to have a steady hand and pay great attention to detail. A mistake in the drawing could be disastrous.

SKETCH
Artists often make sketches – quick drawings – to record things that they see or to prepare for a finished work. The Italian artist Leonardo da Vinci (1452-1519) made thousands of sketches to record his observations. He filled notebooks with drawings of human anatomy, machines, plants, and plans of cities. Above is one of his sketches: a study for the *Head of Leda*.

### Find out more
ARCHITECTURE
CARTOONS
PAINTING

# DRUGS

**I**F YOU ARE ILL, the doctor might give you a drug. Drugs, or medicines, are substances used in the treatment of illnesses. They can relieve the symptoms (effects) of a disease, ease pain, and prevent or cure illnesses. Drugs are also used to treat a wide range of emotional disorders such as depression. There are thousands of different kinds of drugs in use today. Each drug has a specific function and often acts on a single part of the body, such as the stomach. There are many sources of drugs. They may be natural or synthetic (artificial). Medicinal plants and herbs yield natural drugs which have been in use for thousands of years. Scientists search constantly for new drugs and often make them from chemicals. In many cases, the discovery of a drug has eased suffering and saved many lives. Antibiotics such as penicillin, for example, cure infections that would have been fatal 50 years ago.

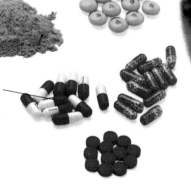

**ORAL MEDICINES**
Many drugs are taken orally (by mouth). The drug passes through the digestive system and into the bloodstream, which carries the drug to the relevant part of the body.

*Drugs can be dangerous. Today, many containers are made with specially designed tops that are difficult for children to remove.*

*Some drugs, such as antihistamines for treating allergies (sensitivity to certain substances), work more quickly if they are injected directly into the bloodstream through a needle and syringe.*

*The body can absorb creams and ointments through the skin. Medicinal creams are often used to treat skin disorders.*

*Some drugs, particularly those for small children, are dissolved in a sweet-tasting syrup. Special spoons that hold a fixed amount of liquid ensure that the patient receives the correct dose. Medicines can also be given by oral syringe.*

*Tablets containing drugs are made with a smooth shape so that they are easy to swallow.*

*Some powdered drugs dissolve in water, which helps them enter the bloodstream more rapidly than if they are taken as pills.*

## TYPES OF DRUG
Different drugs have different uses. They range from antibiotics (for treating infections) to painkillers, such as aspirin. Anaesthetics are used to put patients to sleep before surgery. There are different ways of taking drugs. They can be swallowed, injected, put on the skin, used in a spray, or inhaled.

*Tablets and capsules contain carefully measured amounts of drugs. When they are swallowed, the drugs slowly filter into the bloodstream via the digestive system. Some tablets have a coating which dissolves slowly, releasing the drug at a controlled rate.*

**DRUG ADDICTION**
Many drugs, including some of those recommended by doctors, are addictive. This means that the user becomes dependent on them. Drug addiction can lead to illness and death. The use of many dangerous drugs such as heroin, crack, and cocaine is illegal. However, other addictive drugs, such as alcohol and nicotine (in cigarettes), are not controlled by law.

## SOURCES OF DRUGS
In the past, all drugs used in treating illnesses came from natural sources, particularly herbs and plants. Today, most drugs are made from chemicals, and some are made by genetic engineering, a method in which the cells in bacteria or yeasts are altered to produce drugs.

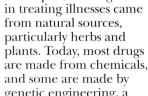

*Some drugs such as insulin (for treating diabetes) can be obtained from pigs and cattle.*

*The heart drug digitalis originally came from a flower called the foxglove.*

*Aspirin is made from chemicals originally found in willowtree bark.*

*The antibiotic penicillin first came from a mould called penicillium.*

# DUCKS, GEESE, AND SWANS

A swan weighs about 13 kg (28 lb).

To reach takeoff speed, it has to run over the water.

The swan has to flap its wings very hard.

Large, powerful wings lift the swan into the air.

During flight, the feet tuck under the body.

WATERFOWL IS THE NAME given to the ducks, geese, and swans that live on the lakes and rivers of the world. Many waterfowl have long, flexible necks that allow them to reach down into the water for food. They spend much of their time preening and spreading oils over their feathers with their beaks. The oils are made in special glands; they keep the plumage waterproof and help keep the bird warm. Most waterfowl live in flocks except in the breeding season; some, such as barnacle and brent geese, migrate long distances to their nesting grounds. Many waterfowl are kept by people for their eggs, meat, and feathers. Eiderdown, often used to stuff quilts, is the soft, downy under-feathers of the eider duck.

Canada

United States

## SWAN
The female black-necked swan carries her fluffy cygnets (young swans) on her back when she is swimming, to keep them warm and safe from predators. Cygnets can fly about three months after hatching.

## DIVING DUCKS AND DABBLING DUCKS
The two main groups of ducks are divers and dabblers. Dabblers, such as mallard ducks, pintail, widgeons, and teals, feed at the surface or stick their tails in the air and dabble just below the surface. They sweep their bills from side to side, sieving out seeds, flies, and other bits of food. Diving ducks, such as pochards and tufted ducks, swim down below the surface to peck at water plants, worms, shellfish, and other small water creatures.

Canada geese fly north in pairs to breed.

Legs are at the back of body, for efficient swimming.

## CANADA GEESE
Each spring, Canada geese fly from Mexico and the southern United States to breeding grounds in Canada. They fly in V-shaped formations and often change position so the leader of the flock does not get too tired. Canada geese nest in grass-lined hollows on islands and marshes. Like most geese and swans, Canada geese stay with their partners for many years. Both geese bring up the young goslings (baby geese), and the family stays together until the next breeding season.

## WEBBED FEET
Most waterfowl have short legs and webbed feet that work well as paddles but make it difficult to walk on land.

Webbed foot has claws on the toes for scratching in the earth.

## TUFTED DUCK
Tufted ducks eat zebra mussels, a type of freshwater shellfish, as well as small fish, tadpoles, and water insects.

## MALLARD
Most male dabbling ducks are more colourful than the females, with bright patches on both wings.

*Find out more*

BIRDS
FLIGHT, ANIMAL
LAKE AND RIVER WILDLIFE
MIGRATION, ANIMAL

# EAGLES
## AND OTHER BIRDS OF PREY

IN THE SAME WAY that sharks are hunters in the sea and lions are hunters on land, eagles are powerful hunters in the sky. Birds of prey, such as eagles, falcons, hawks, and vultures, are also called raptors. There are about 300 different kinds, and they all have extremely sharp eyesight. They can spy their prey on the ground from a great height. Raptors have long, strong legs with sharp claws, called talons, for grasping their victims, and a sharp, hooked beak for tearing flesh. One of the largest, most majestic eagles is the Australian wedge-tailed eagle, with a wingspan of 2.5 m (8 ft). The Eurasian kestrel is a common bird of prey, often seen hovering alongside roads watching for prey in the grass. Many birds of prey are rare because the countryside where they live has been turned into farmland, and pesticides poison their food.

## FISH EAGLE
The African fish eagle has long feathers on the tips of its wings to help it control its gliding. Its sharp eyes are always on the lookout for fish as it patrols the lakes, swamps, and rivers of Africa south of the Sahara Desert.

## HAWK
The sparrow hawk (above) is a nimble woodland hunter of smaller birds. It can swoop down on its prey with a surprise dive, or chase it with twists and turns among the trees.

## FALCONRY
For hundreds of years, falcons, hawks, and other birds of prey have been trained to hunt from a gloved hand. Birds such as this Eurasian kestrel are hooded before the hunt, to keep them calm. Falconry is especially popular in the Middle East.

*Huge, powerful wings for soaring and diving*

*Excellent eyesight for spying fish*

*Large, strong beak for tearing flesh*

*Long, sharp talons on toes for grasping prey*

## BALD EAGLE
Because of their size and strength, eagles are popular symbols and emblems. The American bald eagle (left), a type of fish eagle, is the national emblem of the United States. It is not really bald but looks that way because the white feathers on its head contrast with the dark body.

## SCAVENGERS
Vultures and condors feed mainly on dead and dying animals, known as carrion. They circle on high, watching for food. When one vulture sees a meal, it drops quickly, followed by other vultures nearby. Soon there may be 50 or more vultures pecking over the dead body.

## KING VULTURE
Like all vultures, the colourful South American king vulture has a bald head and neck. This vulture lives in rain forests, and soars over the treetops, marshes, and grasslands in search of dead animals to scavenge. The king vulture also hunts small reptiles and mammals.

## CONDOR
Condors are among the largest flying birds. Their huge wings measure 3 m (10 ft) from tip to tip. The South American Andean condor can glide for hours and hours high above remote mountains.

*A brilliant orange head and a grey feather collar make the king vulture look dressed to kill.*

*King vulture watches for prey.*

*Find out more*
ANIMALS
BIRDS
FLIGHT, ANIMAL
OWLS

# EARS

*Ultrasonic sound is above the human range of hearing.*

THE EARS ARE THE ORGANS of hearing and balance. They collect sound vibrations from the air and turn them into messages called nerve signals which are passed to the brain. Each ear has three main parts – the outer ear, the middle ear, and the inner ear. The outer ear includes the part you can see. It consists of the ear flap, or auricle, and the ear canal. The middle ear consists of the eardrum and three tiny bones called the ossicles. These three bones send sounds from the eardrum to the inner ear. The main part of the inner ear is the snail-shaped cochlea, which is full of fluid. The cochlea changes vibrations into nerve signals. The inner ear also makes sure that the body keeps its balance. Although we can hear many different sounds, we cannot hear as wide a range as most animals. Also, unlike rabbits and horses, we cannot swivel our ears towards the direction of a sound – we have to turn our heads.

Human   Dog   Dolphin   Bat

### RANGE OF HEARING
Humans can hear sounds that vary from a low growl to a piercing scream. Many animals, including dogs, can hear sounds which are far too high-pitched for us to detect. A human's range of hearing is 30–20,000 hertz (vibrations per second); a bat's range of hearing is up to 100,000 hertz.

**INSIDE THE EAR**
The ear canal is slightly curved. It measures about 2.5 cm (1 in) in length. The delicate parts of the middle and inner ear lie well protected deep inside the skull bone, just behind and below the level of the eye.

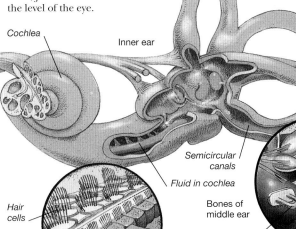

*Cochlea*

*Inner ear*

*Semicircular canals*

*Fluid in cochlea*

*Hair cells*

*Bones of middle ear*

*Stapes (stirrup)*

*Malleus (hammer)*

*Inside the cochlea*

*Inner ear*

### MIDDLE EAR BONES
The middle ear bones (ossicles) are called the malleus (hammer), incus (anvil), and the stapes (stirrup).

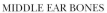

*Incus (anvil)*

*Middle ear*

*Outer ear canal*

*Ear flap (auricle)*

*Soundwaves*

*Eardrum (tympanum)*

*Ear canal*

*Bone*

## INNER EAR
The stirrup bone presses on a thin, flexible part of the cochlea's wall, called the oval window, and passes its vibrations to the fluid inside the cochlea. The vibrations shake microscopic hairs on cells along a thin membrane in the cochlea. This movement creates nerve signals which are sent along the cochlear nerve to the brain. There are more than 20,000 microscopic hair cells inside the cochlea. Sound vibrations make cochlear fluid flow over the hairs; this is how the hair cells receive sound vibrations to convert into nerve signals which travel to the brain.

## OUTER AND MIDDLE EAR
The ear flap on the side of the head funnels sound waves into the ear canal. The sound waves bounce off the eardrum at the end and make it vibrate. These vibrations pass along the ossicles, each of which is hardly bigger than a rice grain. The ossicles have a lever-like action that makes the vibrations louder.

### ANIMAL HEARING
Creatures such as fish and squid have sense organs to detect vibrations in the water. Fish have a lateral line – a narrow groove along each side of the body. Hair cells in the lateral line can sense the sound or movement of nearby animals. The catfish shown here also has whiskers called barbels which can sense vibrations.

### BALANCE
The ears help us keep our balance. The three semicircular canals inside the ear contain fluid. As you move your head, the fluid flows around. Tiny hair cells sense this movement and produce nerve signals to tell the brain which way "up" you are.

*Tight-rope walker*

---
***Find out more***
HUMAN BODY
SKELETONS
SOUND
---

# EARTH

A LARGE BALL OF ROCK spinning through space is our home in the universe. This is the Earth, one of the nine planets that circle around the Sun. The Earth is the only place we know of that supports life. It has oxygen in its atmosphere and water in its oceans, both of which are essential for life. And of all the planets in the solar system, the Earth is at just the right distance from the Sun to be neither too hot nor too cold. Land makes up less than a third of the surface of the Earth; more than two thirds is the water in the oceans. The Earth's interior consists of layers of rock that surround a core made of iron and nickel.

The processes that support life on Earth are in a natural balance. However, many people are worried that pollution, human over-population, and misuse of resources may destroy this balance and make the Earth unsafe for plants and animals.

## EARTH IN SPACE
When astronauts first saw the Earth from space, they were enthralled by the beauty of our blue planet. This picture shows the Earth rising over the Moon's horizon.

## ATMOSPHERE
A layer of air called the atmosphere surrounds the Earth. It is roughly 2,000 km (1,250 miles) deep and contains mainly the gases nitrogen and oxygen. The atmosphere shields the Earth from harmful ultraviolet rays coming from the Sun and prevents the Earth from becoming too hot or too cold.

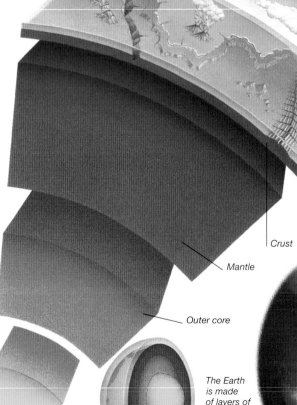

*Clouds containing tiny drops of water float low in the atmosphere, carrying water from the seas and land which falls as rain.*

*Atmosphere*

## OCEANS
The oceans are large water-filled hollows in the Earth's crust. Their average depth is 3.5 km (2.2 miles).

## MANTLE
Under the crust is the mantle, a layer of rock about 2,900 km (1,800 miles) thick. The temperature rises to 3,700°C (6,700°F) at the base of the mantle, but high pressure there keeps the rock solid.

## OUTER CORE
The core of the Earth consists of two layers – the outer core and the inner core. The outer core is about 2,000 km (1,240 miles) thick and is made of liquid iron. Its temperature is approximately 2,200°C (4,000°F).

## INNER CORE
A ball of solid iron and nickel about 2,740 km (1,712 miles) across lies at the center of the Earth. The temperature at the centre is about 4,500°C (8,100°F).

*Crust*

*Mantle*

*Outer core*

*Inner core*

*The Earth is made of layers of air, water, iron, nickel, and rock around a core of iron and nickel.*

## CRUST
The top layer of rock at the surface of the Earth is called the crust. It is up to 70 km (44 miles) deep beneath the continents, but as little as 6 km (4 miles) deep under the oceans. The temperature at the bottom of the crust is about 1,050°C (1,900°F).

## LIQUID ROCK
The interior of the Earth is very hot, heated by radioactive decay of the rocks inside the Earth. The temperature is so high that some rock inside the Earth is molten. This liquid rock rises to the surface at volcanoes, where it is called lava.

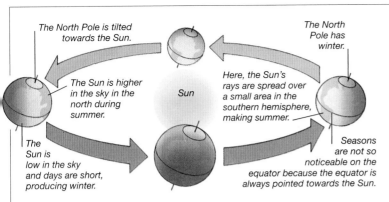

The North Pole is tilted towards the Sun.

The Sun is higher in the sky in the north during summer.

Sun

The North Pole has winter.

Here, the Sun's rays are spread over a small area in the southern hemisphere, making summer.

The Sun is low in the sky and days are short, producing winter.

Seasons are not so noticeable on the equator because the equator is always pointed towards the Sun.

## SEASONS

Seasons change as the Earth moves around the Sun. The Earth's axis is tilted at an angle of 23.5° to its orbit, which makes the Poles point toward or away from the Sun at different times of the year.

### EARTH FACTS

| | |
|---|---|
| **Diameter at equator** | 12,756 km (7,926 miles) |
| **Diameter at poles** | 12,714 km (7,900 miles) |
| **Circumference at equator** | 40,075 km (24,901 miles) |
| **Land area** | 29.2% of Earth's surface |
| **Ocean area** | 70.8% of Earth's surface |
| **Mass** | 6,000 billion billion tonnes (5,900 billion billion tons) |
| **Time for one spin** | 23 hours 56 minutes 4 seconds |
| **Time to orbit Sun** | 365 days 6 hours 9 minutes 9 seconds |
| **Distance from Sun** | 150 million km (93 million miles) |

The Earth spins around its axis, which passes through the North and South Poles. It also orbits the Sun at the same time.

**1** A cloud of gas and dust contracted (shrank) to form the Sun about 4,600 million years ago. The rest of the cloud then contracted further and broke up into large clumps of particles of ice and rock. After a short time, the particles stuck to each other and began to form the planets.

**2** The Earth may have taken about 100 million years to grow into a ball of rock. The new planet became hot as the rock particles crashed into one another. The surface was molten, and the young Earth glowed red-hot.

## FORMATION OF THE EARTH

Scientists have calculated that the Earth is nearly 4,600 million years old. Some Moon rocks and meteorites (pieces of rock that fall to Earth from space) are the same age, which suggests that the whole solar system formed at the same time. The Sun, Earth, and the other planets were formed from a huge cloud of gas and dust in space.

**3** Radioactivity in the rocks caused more heat, and the whole planet melted. Molten iron then sank to the centre of the Earth to form its core. Lighter rocks floated above the iron, and about 4,500 million years ago the surface cooled to form the crust. Volcanoes erupted and poured out gases, which formed the atmosphere, and water vapour, which condensed (changed into liquid) to fill the world's oceans.

## GEOTHERMAL ENERGY

The heat from the interior of the Earth provides a source of safe, clean energy, called geothermal energy. Hot rocks lie close to the surface in Iceland, Italy, and other parts of the world. The rocks heat underground water and often make it boil into steam. Wells dug down to these rocks bring up the steam and hot water, which are used to generate electricity and heat buildings.

Water that filled the oceans may have also come from comets that collided with the young Earth.

## THEORIES OF THE EARTH

People once believed that the Earth was flat. About 2,500 years ago, the Greeks found out that the Earth is round. Aristarchus, a Greek scientist, suggested in about 260 B.C. that the Earth moves around the Sun. It was not until 1543 that Polish astronomer Nicolaus Copernicus (1473-1543; right) reasserted this idea. New theories are still evolving. For instance, one idea called the Gaia theory suggests that the whole planet behaves as a living organism.

**4** Tiny living things began to grow at least 3,500 million years ago. Some produced oxygen, which began to build up in the atmosphere about 2,300 million years ago. The continents broke up and slowly moved into their present-day positions. They are still moving slowly today, a process called continental drift.

### Find out more

ATMOSPHERE
CLIMATES
CONTINENTS
GEOLOGY
OCEANS AND SEAS
RADIOACTIVITY
ROCKS AND MINERALS
UNIVERSE

# EARTHQUAKES

ONCE EVERY 30 SECONDS, somewhere in the world, the Earth shakes slightly. These earth tremors are strong enough to be felt, but cause no damage. However, every few months a major earthquake occurs. The land shakes so violently that roads break up, forming huge cracks, and buildings and bridges collapse, causing many deaths. Earthquakes are caused by the movements of huge plates of rock in the Earth's crust. They occur in places that lie on the boundaries where these plates meet, such as the San Andreas fault which runs 435 km (270 miles) through central California. In some cases, scientists can tell in advance that an earthquake is likely to occur. In 1974, for example, scientists predicted an earthquake in China, saving thousands of lives. But earthquake prediction is not always accurate. In 1989, a major earthquake struck San Francisco, United States, without warning, killing 67 people.

**INSTANT CHAOS**
Destruction can be so swift and sudden that people have no time to escape. Falling masonry crushes cars and blocks roads.

## CAUSES OF EARTHQUAKES
The Earth's crust consists of several vast plates of solid rock. These plates move very slowly and sometimes slide past each other. Most severe earthquakes occur where the plates meet. Sometimes the edges of the plates grip each other and cannot move, so pressure builds up. Suddenly the plates slip and lurch past each other, making the land shake violently.

The rocks suddenly slip along the fault; a movement of a few metres is enough to cause a severe earthquake.

**FAULT**
A deep crack, or fault, marks the boundary of two plates.

The earthquake is usually strongest at the epicentre, the point on the Earth's surface directly above the focus.

The place within the Earth where an earthquake occurs is the focus.

Rocks grip along the fault.

**RICHTER SCALE**
The severity of an earthquake is measured on the Richter scale, which runs from 0 to 9. An earthquake reaching 8 on the scale can flatten a city. The Richter scale measures the movement of the ground, rather than the damage an earthquake causes, which varies from place to place.

*An earthquake in the Indian Ocean on December 26, 2004, caused tsunamis that devastated the coasts of parts of South East Asia, India, and Africa. It was one of the worst natural disasters of recent times.*

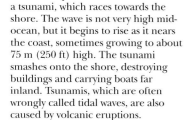

TSUNAMIS
Earthquakes that occur on the sea floor often produce a wave called a tsunami, which races towards the shore. The wave is not very high mid-ocean, but it begins to rise as it nears the coast, sometimes growing to about 75 m (250 ft) high. The tsunami smashes onto the shore, destroying buildings and carrying boats far inland. Tsunamis, which are often wrongly called tidal waves, are also caused by volcanic eruptions.

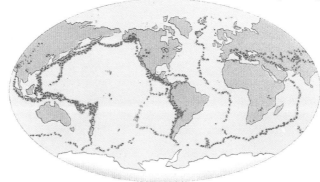

EARTHQUAKE BELTS
Earthquakes occur only in certain parts of the world. This map shows the world's earthquake belts, which also extend through the oceans. Most severe earthquakes happen near boundaries between plates in the Earth's crust, so the belts follow the edges of the plates.

## SEISMOLOGY
Sensitive equipment can pick up vibrations far from an earthquake. This is because the sudden slip of rocks produces shock waves which move through the Earth. The study of earthquakes and the shock waves they cause is called seismology.

---

*Find out more*
CONTINENTS
EARTH
GEOLOGY
VOLCANOES

# EAST AFRICA

EAST AFRICA IS A REGION of physical contrasts, ranging from the semi-desert of the north to the fertile highlands of Ethiopia and Kenya, and from the coastal lowlands to the forest-covered mountains of the west. Most people live off the land. Coffee, tea, and tobacco are grown as cash crops, while nomadic groups herd cattle in the savannah grassland which dominates much of the region. Four of the world's poorest countries – Ethiopia, Eritrea, Somalia, and Djibouti – lie along the Horn of Africa. Their traditional livelihoods of farming, herding, and fishing have been disrupted by drought, famine, and civil war between ethnic groups. Kenya, with its fertile land and warm, moist climate is by contrast, stable and prosperous, its income boosted by wildlife tourists. Ethnic conflict has brought chaos to Sudan, Rwanda, and Burundi, while Uganda is slowly recovering from civil war.

East Africa straddles the Horn of Africa, and is bordered by both the Red Sea and the Indian Ocean. It is dominated by the Great Rift Valley and, in the north, the upper reaches of the River Nile. Desert in the north gives way to savannah grasslands in much of the region.

## DINKA

The Dinka (above) are a nomadic people who live in the highlands of Sudan. They move their herds of cattle around according to the seasons, taking them to graze the savannah grasslands in spring, when the rivers flood and the land is fertile. Cattle are of supreme importance to the Dinka. They form part of a bride's wealth, and are offered as compensation, or payment, for marriage. Young men are presented with a special ox, and their adult name is inspired by the shape and colour of the animal.

### TEA CULTIVATION
The highlands of Ethiopia and Kenya are major tea-producing areas. The flavour of tea grown slowly in cool air at altitudes of 1,000-2,000 m (3,000-7,000 ft) is considered the finest. The leaves are dried, rolled, and blown with hot air, which ferments them, producing a rich black colour and strong flavour.

*Tea bushes are regularly clipped to stimulate the growth of tender young shoots and new leaves. They are harvested by hand.*

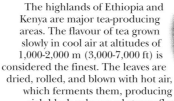

*The various styles of architecture in Mogadishu (right) reflect the city's history.*

### MOGADISHU
The capital of Somalia was one of the earliest Arab trading settlements in eastern Africa, dating to the 10th century. The city is dominated by a major port, and is a mixture of historic Islamic buildings and modern architecture. Civil war in the 1980s and 1990s has, however, destroyed much of the city.

### LALIBELA
The kings of Ethiopia converted to Christianity in the 4th century, but it was not until the 12th century that Christianity held sway over most of the population. King Lalibela built 11 remarkable churches, which were carved out of rock below ground level. They are still major pilgrimage centres for Ethiopian Christians today.

## KAMPALA
Since 1962, Kampala has been the capital of independent Uganda. It is located in the southern part of the country, on the hills overlooking Lake Victoria. It is an export centre for coffee, cotton, tea, sugar, and tobacco. Locally produced foods, such as cassava, millet, and sweet potatoes, are sold at lively street markets. Kampala has rainfall on nearly every day of the year, and violent thunderstorms 242 days a year.

## THE GREAT RIFT VALLEY

Stretching from Syria in Asia to Mozambique, the Rift Valley is a huge gash in the Earth's surface, formed where Africa and the Arabian peninsula are gradually moving apart. The Great Rift Valley, which was formed some 30 million years ago, is 6,400 km (4,000 miles) long, and up to 64 km (40 miles) wide. In Kenya and Tanzania, the valley is marked by deep fjord-like lakes. Elsewhere, volcanic peaks have erupted and wide plateaux, such as the Athi Plains in Kenya, have formed where lava has seeped through the Earth's surface.

### MASAI

The Masai people herd cattle in the grasslands of Kenya and Tanzania. The young men paint their bodies with ochre and have elaborate plaited hairstyles. Masai warriors wear beaded jewellery. Each man may take several wives, and is responsible for his own herd of cattle, which are driven to pasture far from the village during the dry season. Mothers pass on cattle to their sons. The staple diet of the Masai is cow's milk, supplemented by maize.

*The Masai keep their cattle for milk. They also drink blood drawn from the veins of living cows.*

*Tooled leather sandals from Uganda*

## WILDLIFE

The Great Plains of East Africa contain some of the world's most spectacular wildlife. In Kenya, ten per cent of all the land has been absorbed into more than 40 national parks. Tourists go on wildlife safaris to Kenya (below) to see herds of lions, antelopes, leopards, and elephants. Poaching animals, especially elephants for ivory, remains a major problem, and national parks are closely guarded by game wardens.

*Diseases such as cholera thrive in crowded refugee camps like the one pictured here.*

*A herd of elephants wander the savannah in Kenya in search of water. A number of lions monitor the elephants waiting to kill any weak animal.*

### GORILLAS

The forested mountains of Rwanda and Uganda are the last remaining refuge for gorillas, the world's rarest ape. Gorillas have long been targeted by poachers, hunters and collectors. The Albert National Park was established in 1925 for their protection, but civil war in the 1960s disrupted the gorilla population, while much of their forest habitat was cleared for agriculture, further reducing numbers.

Since the 1980s, national parks have been carefully guarded, and limited educational and tourist programmes put in place. Gorilla numbers in Rwanda have risen, but recent conflict now threatens their survival.

## REFUGEE CAMP

Many of the boundaries in central east Africa date back to colonial times and cut across ethnic borders. In Rwanda, the majority Hutus rebelled against the ruling Tutsis with terrible consequences. The country descended into violent chaos, and many people were forced to flee to refugee camps in Tanzania. There has also been conflict between Hutus and Tutsis in neighbouring Burundi.

### *Find out more*

AFRICA
AFRICAN WILDLIFE
ELEPHANTS
GRASSLAND WILDLIFE
LIONS

## Legend

|  |  |
|--------|-------------|
| Volcano | Volcano |
| Mountain | Mountain |
| Ancient monument | Ancient monument |
| Capital city | Capital city |
| Large city/town | Large city/town |
| Small city/town | Small city/town |

**NUBIAN DESERT**
*The Nubian Desert, the eastern extension of the Sahara, is located in northeastern Sudan between the River Nile and the Red Sea. This arid region is largely a sandstone plateau, with numerous seasonal rivers flowing through it.*

**KILIMANJARO**
Mt. Kibo in Tanzania is Africa's highest peak, at 5,895 m (19,341 ft). It is one of the Kilimanjaro group of three volcanoes. Mt Kibo's steaming crater indicates that it is still active. Mt Kibo rises from an arid plain, but has an annual average of 1,780 mm (70 in) of rain on its upper slopes.

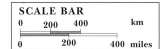

**SUDD**
*The north of Sudan is rocky desert, but in the south, the waters of the White Nile run into a swampy area called the Sudd, where much of its water disperses and evaporates.*

**LAKE VICTORIA**
*Lake Victoria is Africa's largest lake and the second largest freshwater lake in the world. It lies on the Equator, between Kenya, Tanzania, and Uganda, and covers 69,500 sq km (26,834 sq miles). Its only outlet is the River Nile in the north.*

**RIVER JUBA**
*This river rises in the highlands of Ethiopia and flows some 1,200 km (746 miles) southward to the Indian Ocean. The Juba, and the River Shebeli which joins it about 30 km (19 miles) from the coast, are the only permanent rivers in Somalia.*

### Map labels

LIBYA · EGYPT · SAUDI ARABIA · Libyan Desert · (administered by Egypt) · (administered by Sudan) · Nubian Desert · Red Sea · YEMEN · Gulf of Aden · Socotra (to Yemen)

Port Sudan · Dongola · Ed Damer · ERITREA · Omdurman · KHARTOUM · Kassala · ASMARA · Wad Medani · SUDAN · Darfur · El Fasher · Jebel Marra 3071m · Nyala · El Obeid · Gonder · Lake Tana · Bahir Dar · DJIBOUTI · DJIBOUTI · Danakil Desert · Shimbiris 2407m · Dire Dawa · Hargeysa · Abuye Meda 4000m · ADDIS ABABA · Harer · Burco · Garoowe · CHAD · White Nile · Blue Nile · Malakal · Ethiopian · ETHIOPIA · CENTRAL AFRICAN REPUBLIC · Wau · Gore · Jima · Highlands · Gaalkacyo · Rumbek · Sudd · Elemi Triangle (administered by Kenya) · Juba · Yabelo · Shebeli · Great Rift Valley · SOMALIA · Gulu · Lira · Lake Turkana · Baydhabo · Lake Albert · Wajir · MOGADISHU (MUQDISHO) · UGANDA · KENYA · Marka · KAMPALA · Jinja · Kisumu · Equator · Entebbe · Mbarara · Lake Victoria · Nakuru · Nyeri · Kismaayo · DEM. REP. CONGO · RWANDA · KIGALI · NAIROBI · BUJUMBURA · BURUNDI · Mwanza · Serengeti Plain · Kilimanjaro 5895m · Arusha · Malindi · Mombasa · TANZANIA · Tanga · DODOMA · Zanzibar · Lake Tanganyika · Morogoro · Dar es Salaam · ZAMBIA · Lake Rukwa · Iringa · Lindi · Mbeya · Songea · MALAWI · Lake Nyasa · MOZAMBIQUE · INDIAN OCEAN

### Country data

**BURUNDI**
**Area:** 27,830 sq km (10,750 sq miles)
**Population:** 6,800,000
**Capital:** Bujumbura

**DJIBOUTI**
**Area:** 23,200 sq km (8,958 sq miles)
**Population:** 703,000
**Capital:** Djibouti

**ERITREA**
**Area:** 93,680 sq km (36,170 sq miles)
**Population:** 4,100,000
**Capital:** Asmara

**ETHIOPIA**
**Area:** 1,128,221 sq km (435,605 sq miles)
**Population:** 70,700,000
**Capital:** Addis Ababa

**KENYA**
**Area:** 580,370 sq km (224,081 sq miles)
**Population:** 32,000,000
**Capital:** Nairobi

**RWANDA**
**Area:** 26,340 sq km (10,170 sq miles)
**Population:** 8,400,000
**Capital:** Kigali

**TANZANIA**
**Area:** 945,090 sq km (364,900 sq miles)
**Population:** 37,000,000
**Capital:** Dodoma

**UGANDA**
**Area:** 235,880 sq km (91,073 sq miles)
**Population:** 25,800,000
**Capital:** Kampala

**SOMALIA**
**Area:** 637,660 sq km (246,200 sq miles)
**Population:** 9,900,000
**Capital:** Mogadishu

**SUDAN**
**Area:** 2,505,815 sq km (967,493 sq miles)
**Population:** 33,600,000
**Capital:** Khartoum

**SCALE BAR**

| 0 | 200 | 400 | km |
| 0 | 200 | 400 | miles |

# ECOLOGY AND FOOD WEBS

WE CAN LOOK AT NATURE in the same way that we look at a complicated machine, to see how all the parts fit together. Every living thing has its place in nature, and ecology is the study of how things live in relation to their surroundings. It is a relatively new science and is of great importance today. It helps us understand how plants and animals depend on each other and their surroundings in order to survive. Ecology also helps us work towards saving animals and plants from extinction and solving the problems caused by pollution. Plants and animals can be divided into different groups, depending on their ecological function. Plants capture the Sun's light energy and use it to produce new growth, so they are called producers; animals consume (eat) plants and other animals, so they are called consumers. All the plants and animals that live in one area and feed off each other make up a community. The relationships between the plants and animals in a community is called a food web; energy passes through the community via these food webs.

## ECOSYSTEM
A community and its surroundings, including the soil, air, climate, and the other communities around it, make up an ecosystem. The Earth can be seen as one giant ecosystem spinning through space. It recycles its raw materials, such as leaves and other plant matter, and is powered by energy from the Sun.

*The European kingfisher has little to fear. Its brightly coloured plumage warns predators that it is foul-tasting. The kingfisher is well named – it is extremely skilful at fishing.*

## FOOD CHAINS AND FOOD WEBS
A plant uses the Sun's energy to grow. A herbivore (plant eater) eats the plant. A carnivore (meat eater) or an omnivore (plant and meat eater) then eats the herbivore. This series of events is called a food chain.

*A frog forms a link between two different food webs – the pond and the meadow food webs.*

*During spring, the frog is part of the pond food web. In autumn, it moves onto land and becomes involved in the meadow food web.*

Pond food web

Meadow food web

*The fox is a top carnivore in the meadow food chain.*

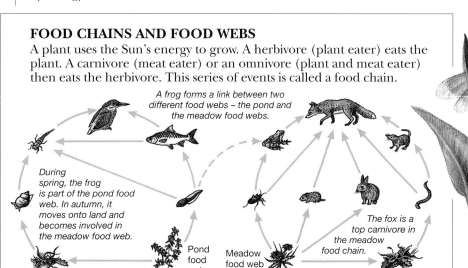

## CARNIVORE
The adult frog is carnivorous; it catches flies and other small creatures.

## OMNIVORE
Many small fish are omnivores, feeding on whatever they can find – from water weeds to tiny animals such as tadpoles.

*Plants form the beginning of the food chain in a pond, as they do on land.*

## KINGFISHER
Some carnivores are called top carnivores because they have almost no predators. Their usual fate is to die of sickness, injury, or old age, at which time they become food for scavengers. The European kingfisher shown here eats a wide variety of food, including small fish such as minnows and sticklebacks, water snails and beetles, dragonfly larvae, tadpoles, and small frogs. The kingfisher is therefore at the top of a complex food web.

## DETRITIVORE
Certain types of worms and snails are called detritivores because they eat detritus, or rotting matter, at the bottom of a pond or river. They help recycle the materials and energy in dead and dying plants and animals.

## HERBIVORE
As a young tadpole, the frog is a herbivore, eating water weeds.

# HABITAT

A habitat is a place where a certain animal or plant usually lives. There are several characteristic habitats, such as oak forests, mangrove swamps, and chalk cliffs. A habitat often has one or a few main plants, such as the pampas grass which grows in the grassland habitats of South America. Certain characteristic animals feed on these plants. Some animals live in only one or two habitats; the desman, for example, is a type of muskrat found only in fast-running mountain streams. Other animals, such as red foxes and brown rats, are able to survive in many different habitats. The coral reef shown here is one of the Earth's richest habitats. Its warm, shallow water is full of nutrients, and the sunlight encourages many different forms of life.

# BIOME

A biome is a huge habitat, such as a tropical rain forest or a desert. The deserts of Africa, central Asia, and North America each have distinct kinds of plants and animals, but their ecology is similar. Each of these large habitats, or biomes, has a big cat as a top predator – the caracal (a kind of lynx) in Africa, the bobcat in North America, and Pallas's cat in central Asia. The major types of plants that grow in a biome are determined by its climate. Areas near the equator with very high rainfall become tropical rain forests, and in cold regions near the Arctic and Antarctic, only tundra plants can survive.

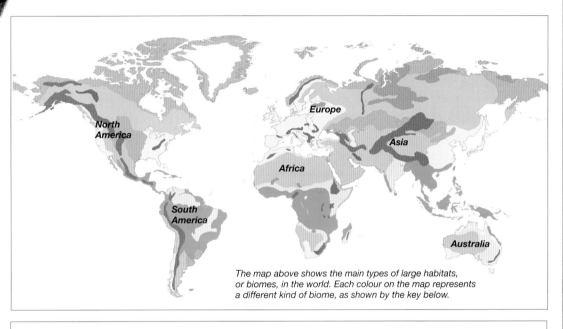

The map above shows the main types of large habitats, or biomes, in the world. Each colour on the map represents a different kind of biome, as shown by the key below.

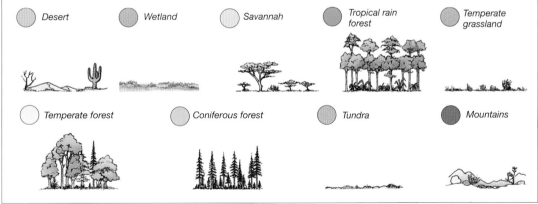

Desert · Wetland · Savannah · Tropical rain forest · Temperate grassland

Temperate forest · Coniferous forest · Tundra · Mountains

## PESTICIDES

Farmers and gardeners use pesticides to kill insects that are pests on vegetable and cereal crops. In 1972, the insecticide called DDT was banned in the United States because it caused great damage to wildlife. When DDT is sprayed on crops, some of it is eaten by herbivores such as mice and squirrels. The insecticide builds up inside the animal's body. A bird of prey such as a hawk eats the animal, and the DDT becomes concentrated (builds up) in the bird's body. The DDT causes the bird to make very thin or deformed eggshells, which break and kill the developing chicks inside. Since DDT was banned, the number of falcons has slowly risen.

Today, falcons and other birds of prey are rare. Many have died as a result of the pesticides used by farmers to kill insects on farm crops.

> ### Find out more
> ANIMALS
> CONSERVATION
> and endangered species
> EAGLES
> and other birds of prey
> LAKE AND RIVER WILDLIFE
> PLANTS
> POLLUTION

# EDUCATION

LEARNING DOES NOT ONLY take place at school. Education – the process of acquiring knowledge – begins when we are born and continues throughout life. Learning to speak, for instance, is a basic skill we acquire at an early age by imitating and repeating the sounds produced by our family and others around us. As we grow older, travelling, reading, and other pastimes also increase our knowledge. Formal education begins when we have learned certain basic skills, such as speech, and can benefit from going to school. Through nursery, primary and secondary school, we learn vital skills and valuable knowledge. At 16, some students go on to the sixth form or to tertiary college, where they widen their general knowledge and study one or more subjects in depth. School and college can also help us recognize and develop the individual talents and skills that each of us possesses, and show us how we can use this potential in a career and to benefit society as a whole. University and various other colleges provide education to match an individual's chosen career.

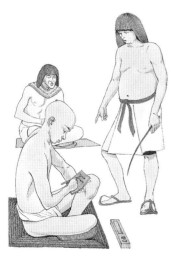

## SCRIBE SCHOOLS
In Ancient Egypt only educated scribes could read and write. Boys who trained to be scribes laboriously wrote and copied each day. At first they wrote on useless objects such as broken pottery; when their work improved they were allowed to write on papyrus, a precious kind of paper. Girls were educated at home, learning domestic skills from their mothers.

## CHOICES IN EDUCATION
No two people are the same. For this reason education offers students a wide choice. From the arts, or humanities, students may choose subjects such as fine art (painting and sculpture), languages, and law. From science subjects there is the choice of pure science, such as physics; applied science, such as engineering; and medicine.

Scientists in the 19th century believed that portions of the human brain were reserved for specific kinds of knowledge. Modern medicine has proved it wrong.

## UNIVERSITY
Many students continue their education at university, polytechnic, or college. Studies usually take three or four years. Students receive degrees – qualifications showing they have completed the course.

## EDUCATION FOR THE FEW
Free education for all has become available only during the last 100 years. Before then only the very wealthy could afford education. During the 13th century, Latin was the language of learning in Europe; it was essential for those who wanted to work in the church, the army, or in law.

## GREEK EDUCATION
The Ancient Greek philosopher Aristotle held strong views about education. He believed that, from the age of seven, children should learn gymnastics, music, reading, writing, and drawing. Later studies would include physics, philosophy, and politics. Aristotle's ideal was an active and enquiring mind in a healthy body.

## PRACTICAL LEARNING
Education is designed to meet society's needs. The children of tribes who live in tropical rainforests learn survival skills, such as building boats and hunting. But in developing societies the educational system must produce the scientists and engineers the country needs in order to industrialize.

## RAGGED SCHOOLS

During the early 1800s, few poor children received any education. In 1818, John Pounds (1766-1839), a shoemaker and teacher, set up a school in Portsmouth to teach deprived children. Within 50 years, there were 250 "Ragged Schools", as they were known, in London and more than 100 in other major cities. These schools were free and provided a basic education and some practical skills to as many as 70,000 children.

Frances Buss

## PRIMARY EDUCATION

In 1870, the British government set up elected school boards to provide new schools and, by 1880, education became compulsory up to the age of 10. Many primary schools were built. They provided separate classrooms for different age groups and a central assembly hall.

## WOMEN'S EDUCATION

Until the late 19th century, women received little education. Pioneer teachers Frances Buss (1827-94), founder of North London Collegiate School for Girls, and Dorothea Beale (1831-1906), of Cheltenham Ladies' College, raised the standard of women's education.

### EDUCATION

**1200s** First colleges set up at Oxford and Cambridge.

**1300s** First fee-paying public schools established.

**1870** Forster's Education Act: primary education introduced.

**1880** Education compulsory up to age 10.

**1902** Local councils gain control over schools.

**1944** Butler Education Act introduces free secondary education.

**1969** Open University set up.

**1973** Leaving age is 16.

**1989** National curriculum is introduced into schools.

## SECONDARY EDUCATION

As the school leaving age rose after 1880, many older children remained in primary schools as there were no secondary schools to go to: in 1938 one-third of all children over 11 were still at primary school. In 1944 a clear break was established between primary education up to the age of 11 and secondary education up to 15, with separate buildings for each school.

*A few secondary schools, called single-sex schools, teach only girls or boys.*

## ADULT EDUCATION

Many adults leave school with low grades or large gaps in their knowledge. Adult education classes provide a chance to acquire more qualifications and to gain new skills, such as learning a foreign language or how to use a computer. Some adults attend classes to learn English if it is not their main language, or to help them read and write.

## DISTANCE LEARNING

Not everyone can spare the money or the time to go to college or university. Distance learning uses television, radio, the Internet, and the post to bring education to people in their own homes. The Open University was set up in 1969 to help people study for a university degree in their own time.

---

### *Find out more*
COMPUTERS
MEDIEVAL EUROPE
SCHOOLS

# ANCIENT
# EGYPT

THE RICH, FERTILE SOIL of the Nile Valley gave birth to Egypt, a civilization that began over 5,000 years ago and lasted more than 3,000 years. The River Nile made the black soil around it productive, and the civilization of Egypt grew wealthy. For much of its history Egypt was stable. Its pharaohs ruled with the help of officials called viziers who collected taxes and acted as judges. The Egyptians worshipped many gods and believed that when they died they went to the Next World. Pharaohs built elaborate tombs for themselves; the best known are the magnificent pyramids. The Egyptians also made great advances in medicine. Gradually, however, the civilization broke down, leaving it open to foreign invasion. In 30 B.C. the Romans finally conquered the empire.

## PHARAOHS

The rulers of Ancient Egypt were called pharaohs, meaning "Great House". They were thought to be divine and had absolute power: all the land in Egypt belonged to them. People believed the pharaohs were the sons of Ra, the Sun god. Above is a famous pharaoh, Tutankhamun, who died when he was only 18.

The internal layout of the Great Pyramid

Grand Gallery

King's Chamber

Entrance

Escape shaft

Queen's Chamber

## PYRAMIDS

The Egyptians believed in an eternal life after death in a "perfect" version of Egypt. After their bodies had been preserved by embalming, pharaohs were buried in pyramid tombs. The earliest pyramids had steps. People believed the dead king's spirit climbed the steps to join the Sun god at the top. Later, the pyramids were built with smooth slanted sides. However, people could rob the pyramid tombs easily, so later pharaohs were buried in unmarked tombs in the Valley of the Kings and guarded day and night.

Scenes show gods judging if the dead person is worthy of travelling to the afterlife.

Painters decorated royal tombs with scenes of the gods and the Next World.

Painting of the time shows cattle being transported across the River Nile in special wide boats.

Royal tombs were filled with food, jewellery, clothing, weapons, tools, and statues of servants.

## TRANSPORT AND TRADE

The quickest way to travel in Egypt was by water. Barges carried goods along the Nile, and Egyptian traders travelled to ports around the eastern Mediterranean and the Red Sea in wooden reed ships. Using a system called bartering, they exchanged gold, grain, and papyrus sheets for silver, iron, horses, cedar wood, and ivory.

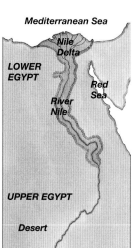

Mediterranean Sea

Nile Delta

LOWER EGYPT

Red Sea

River Nile

UPPER EGYPT

Desert

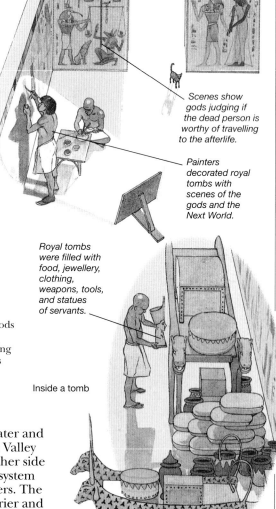

Inside a tomb

## RIVER NILE

Each year, the River Nile burst its banks and spread water and fertile silt over the land. This "inundation" of the Nile Valley made the land fertile for about 10 km (6 miles) on either side of the river. The Egyptians planned their agricultural system around this, farming the land by storing the floodwaters. The desert on either side provided a natural defensive barrier and a rich source of minerals and stone.

Water was drawn from ponds or lagoons with a shadoof.

People carried water to the land on their backs.

Seed was scattered by hand, then trodden in by animals and watered.

The Egyptians used wooden ploughs drawn by oxen.

The Egyptians fished from papyrus reed boats using baskets, nets, spears, and lines with hooks.

# FARMING AND FISHING

Most Egyptians were farmers who worked for priests, wealthy landowners, or the pharaoh. They were paid in crops. They watered the lands with floodwaters trapped in lagoons or with water-lifting machines called shadoofs. Crops grown included emmer for bread, barley for beer, beans, onions, dates, melons, and cucumbers. People also fished from the Nile.

The royal name of Tutankhamun

NEFERTITI

Nefertiti was the wife of the pharaoh Ikhnaton, who ruled from 1367 to 1355 B.C. She had great influence over her husband's policies. Usually, however, the only women who held important titles were priestesses.

## HIEROGLYPHICS

The Egyptians developed picture writing, or hieroglyphics, around 3000 B.C. At first each object was shown exactly by its picture, or pictograph. Gradually the pictures came to stand for sounds. Groups of "sound hieroglyphs", or phonograms, were used to spell words.

## MEDICINE AND MAGIC

Egyptian doctors were the first to study the body scientifically. They also carried out some effective dentistry. However, many "cures" were based on magic.

Scarab beetles were sacred to the Egyptians, who used them as charms to ward off illness.

Headrest amulet

Relief of the time showing Ancient Egyptian medical tools.

## ANCIENT EGYPT

**c. 10,000-5000 B.C.** First villages on the banks of the Nile. Slow growth of the two kingdoms of Upper and Lower Egypt.

**c. 2630 B.C.** First step pyramid built at Saqqara.

**c. 2575 B.C.** During Old Kingdom period, bronze replaces copper. Pyramids built at Giza. Dead bodies are embalmed.

**c. 2134 B.C.** Old Kingdom ends with power struggles.

**c. 2040 B.C.** Middle Kingdom begins. Nobles from Thebes reunite the country. Nubia conquered.

**c. 1640 B.C.** Middle Kingdom ends.

**1550 B.C.** New Kingdom begins. Permanent army.

**1400 B.C.** Egypt reaches height of its power.

**1070 B.C.** Egyptian power begins to decline.

**332 B.C.** Alexander the Great conquers Egypt.

**51 B.C.** Cleopatra rules.

**30 B.C.** Egypt becomes a Roman province.

## MUMMIES

The Egyptians thought that if they preserved their bodies after death, they would "live" forever. So they made "mummies" – corpses that did not decay. Embalmers removed the liver, lungs, and brain from the dead body, leaving the heart inside. They then coated the body with saltlike natron crystals to preserve it, and finally wrapped the whole package in bandages.

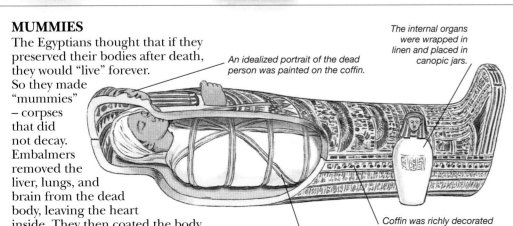

An idealized portrait of the dead person was painted on the coffin.

The internal organs were wrapped in linen and placed in canopic jars.

Linen protected the body.

Coffin was richly decorated with hieroglyphs of spells to help the dead person in the afterlife.

### Find out more

AFRICA, HISTORY OF
ALPHABETS
ARCHAEOLOGY
CATS

# ALBERT EINSTEIN

PHYSICIST ALBERT EINSTEIN was one of the greatest scientific thinkers of all time. His theories, or ideas, on matter, space, and time revolutionized our understanding of the universe, and have formed the basis for much of modern physics. He is probably best known for his work on relativity, first published in 1905, which astounded the scientific community. In this, Einstein showed that distance and time are relative, not fixed. The faster anything travels, the slower time seems to pass. His work on relativity led to other revolutionary ideas on energy and mass, and in 1921 he was awarded the Nobel Prize. From 1933 he lived in the United States. A scientific genius, he was also a pacifist, and deeply religious.

**1879** Born in Ulm, Germany.

**1900** Graduates in maths and physics, Switzerland.

**1902-09** Works in Patent Office, Switzerland.

**1905** Publishes Special Theory of Relativity.

**1916** Publishes General Theory of Relativity.

**1921** Awarded Nobel Prize for Physics.

**1933** Emigrates to USA.

**1955** Dies Princetown, USA.

**THE YOUNG EINSTEIN**
Einstein was born in Germany, and, as a small boy, was very curious about things around him. When he was 15, the family moved to Switzerland, where Einstein was educated. By the time he graduated, he was already pondering the nature of light. He worked in a Patent Office and at the age of 26, wrote his first paper on relativity.

*Someone in a descending lift drops a ball. The ball appears to travel further to someone watching from outside than it does to the person inside the lift, over the same amount of time. Is the ball going faster?*

*A visual puzzle helps to demonstrate the theory of relativity.*

*Albert Einstein working in his study in the United States.*

*Different relative viewpoints can alter our perceptions.*

*Einstein was famous for his untidiness.*

## RELATIVITY
The concept of relativity is very difficult to grasp. One of the central ideas is "time dilation", time seeming to slow down when things are moving in relation to an observer who is still. This effect increases at very high speeds approaching the speed of light. This increase is not easy to show, because we cannot notice it at the slow speeds we experience. Nothing can travel faster than light, which always travels at the same speed.

## SCIENTIST
Einstein developed his revolutionary theories by devising what he called "thought experiments". For example, he wondered what the world would look like if he rode on a beam of light. Such simple questions often had surprising answers, which Einstein confirmed with complex mathematics. At the time, many people did not believe Einstein's theories, but later research has proved him correct.

## ATOMIC ENERGY
Einstein produced the famous equation $E = mc^2$, where energy (E) = mass (m) multiplied by the square of the speed of light (c). It showed that an immense amount of energy could be released by splitting the nucleus of an atom. This contributed to the development of the atom bomb. From 1946, Einstein was opposed to atomic weapons.

---

***Find out more***
ATOMS AND MOLECULES
SCIENCE, HISTORY OF
TIME

# ELECTRICITY

A FLASH OF LIGHTNING that leaps through the sky during a thunderstorm is one of the most visible signs of electricity. At almost all other times, electricity is invisible but hard at work for us. Electricity is a form of energy. It consists of electrons – tiny particles that come from atoms. Each electron carries a tiny electric charge which is an amount of electricity. When you switch on a light, about one million billion electrons move through the bulb every second. Cables hidden in walls and ceilings carry electricity around houses and factories, providing energy at the flick of a switch. Electricity also provides portable power. Batteries produce electricity from chemicals, and solar cells provide electricity from the energy in sunlight. Lamps, motors, and dozens of other machines use electricity as their source of power. Electricity also provides signals which make telephones, radios, televisions, and computers work.

*Electricity flows into homes through cables that run either underground or above street level on poles.*

*Some power stations generate electricity by burning coal and oil. Other stations are powered by nuclear energy.*

*A transformer boosts the voltage (force) of the electricity to many thousands of volts.*

*Tall pylons support long cables that carry the electricity safely above the ground to all parts of an area.*

*Another transformer reduces the voltage of the electricity to levels suitable for domestic appliances.*

## CURRENT ELECTRICITY

Electricity comes in two forms: electricity that flows, and static electricity, which does not move. Flowing electricity is called current electricity. Billions of electrons flow along a wire to give an electric current. The electricity moves from a source such as a battery or power station to a machine. It then returns to the source along another wire. The flow of electric current is measured in amperes (A).

## CONDUCTORS AND INSULATORS

Electricity flows only through materials called conductors. These include copper and many other metals. Conductors can carry electricity because their own electrons are free to move. Other substances, called insulators, do not allow electricity to flow through them. This is because their electrons are held tightly inside their atoms.

*Electrons flow through copper conductor.*

*Most plastics are insulators.*

*Batteries produce direct current, which flows one way around a circuit.*

*Battery pushes electric current around the circuit.*

*Power stations produce alternating current, which flows first in one direction and then the other.*

*Wires connect battery and bulb to form a circuit.*

## ELECTRIC CIRCUITS

Electric current needs a continuous loop of wire to flow around. This is called a circuit. If the circuit is broken, the electricity can no longer flow.

*Bulb in bulb holder*

## SUPERCONDUCTORS

Ordinarily conductors, while letting most electricity flow through them, also resist it to some extent. So a measure of electricity is lost. However, some materials, lose their resistance when very cold. They become superconductors.

*A superconductor can produce a strong magnetic field which makes a small magnet hover above it.*

## STATIC ELECTRICITY

There are two types of electric charge, positive (+) and negative (−). Objects usually contain equal numbers of both charges so they cancel each other out. Rubbing a piece of amber (dried gum or resin from trees) against wool or fur makes it pick up extra electrons, which carry a negative charge. This charge is called static electricity. It produces an electric force which makes light objects, such as hair and feathers, cling to the amber.

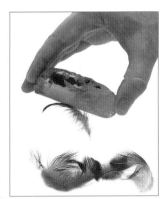

## GENERATOR

Generators produce electricity from the energy of movement. A coil of wire moves between the poles of a magnet. This produces an electric current in the coil. Small, simple generators that power bicycle lamps are called dynamos. Large generators in power stations produce huge amounts of electricity for homes and factories.

Basic generator

Coil of wire

Magnetic field produced by magnet.

*A simple generator (above) contains a coil of wire that spins between the poles of a magnet. A current flows in the coil when it moves through the magnetic field.*

*Instead of a simple magnet, there is a set of electromagnets – coils that use electricity to produce a strong magnetic field.*

*Electromagnets spin inside another set of coils. This produces electricity in the outer set of coils.*

*A shaft connected to the turbine (a set of vanes) drives the generator.*

*In a hydroelectric power station, water falling from a dam spins a turbine.*

## ELECTRICITY FROM CHEMICALS

Chemical energy from food changes into movement in your muscles. Chemical energy can also change into electrical energy. This is how a battery works. Chemicals react together inside a battery and produce an electric current. When there are no fresh chemicals left, the current stops. Fuel cells also produce electricity from chemicals in the form of gases.

### ELECTRIC EEL

The rivers of South America are the home of the electric eel. This eel has special organs in its long body that work like batteries to produce electricity. With a powerful electric shock, the electric eel can stun its prey.

Positive terminal

Powdered chemicals react together to release electrons.

Negative terminal

### BATTERY

Connecting a battery in a circuit makes the chemicals inside react to produce an electric current. The battery provides a force that pushes electrons around the circuit. The energy provided by this force is measured in units called volts.

*Inside the battery, the electrons flow from the positive terminal and back to the negative terminal.*

Shaft of motor

*The magnetic force pushes on the coil and makes it spin around.*

Gears connect motor to wheels of car.

Coil of wire

Magnet produces magnetic field.

Electric current flows from battery into coil, producing a magnetic field.

### ELECTRIC MOTOR

Many machines are powered by an electric motor, which contains a coil of wire placed between the poles of a magnet. The electric current fed to the motor flows through the coil, producing a magnetic field. The magnet pushes on the coil and makes it spin around and drive the shaft of the motor.

### ELECTRIC SHOCKS

Living things make use of electricity. Weak electric signals pass along the nerves to and from the brain. These signals operate the muscles, maintain the heartbeat, and control the way in which the body works. A strong electric current can give an electric shock that damages the human body and may even cause death. *Never* play with the main electricity supply because of the danger of electric shock.

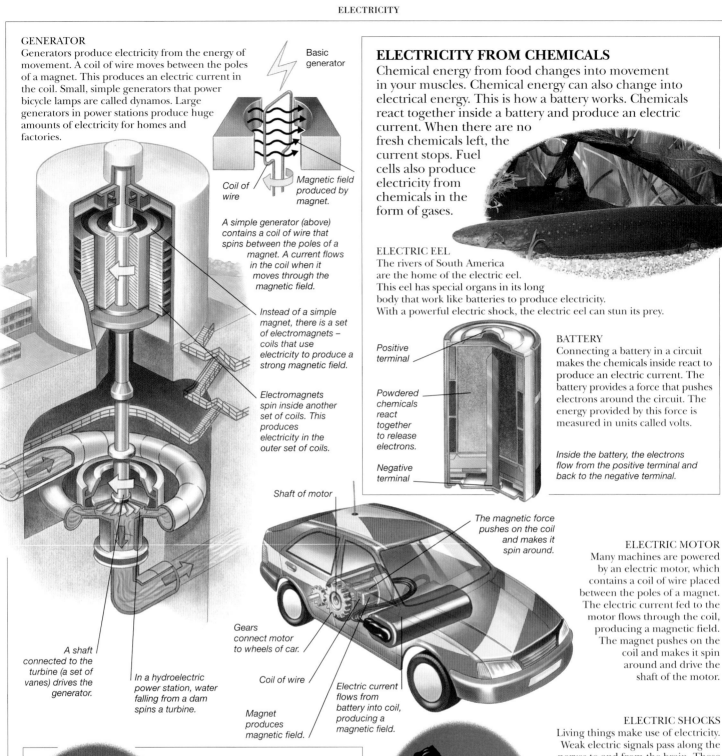

### DISCOVERY

About 2,500 years ago, the Ancient Greeks found that rubbing amber (a yellow solid) produces a charge of static electricity. The Greek for amber is *elektron*, which is how electricity got its name. Around 1750, American scientist Benjamin Franklin (left) discovered that lightning is electricity and explained what electric charges are. At the end of the 18th century, Italian scientists Luigi Galvani and Alessandro Volta produced the first electric battery.

*Benjamin Franklin (1706-90) studied the electrical nature of lightning by flying a kite during a thunderstorm.*

*A bird sitting on an electric cable does not get an electric shock. The electricity does not pass into its body because the bird is touching only one wire and does not complete an electric circuit.*

*Find out more*

ATOMS AND MOLECULES
ELECTRONICS
ENERGY
FISH
MAGNETISM

# ELECTRONICS

The semiconductor silicon comes from sand, which is a compound of silicon and oxygen.

A diode is made from the junction between pieces of n- and p-type semiconductors.

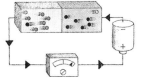

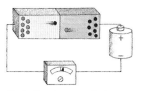

A diode allows current to flow through it in only one direction. The current is carried by the flow of holes and electrons.

If a battery is connected the other way around, holes and electrons cannot cross the junctions so current cannot flow.

**ELECTRICITY** is a source of power that drives machines and provides heat and light. Electricity is also used to produce signals that carry information and control devices. Using electricity in this way is called electronics. We are surrounded by thousands of electronic machines, including computers, CD players, telephones, and televisions. All these machines contain circuits through which electric currents flow. Tiny electronic components in the circuits control the flow of the current to produce signals. For instance, a varying current may represent sound in a telephone line, or a number in a computer. The most important electronic component is the transistor. A small radio receiver may contain a dozen transistors; a computer contains thousands of miniaturized transistors inside microchips.

## SEMICONDUCTORS
Most electronic components are made of materials such as silicon, which are called semiconductors. Semiconductors control the flow of current because they contain a variable number of charge carriers (particles that carry electricity). In n-type semiconductors, the charge carriers are negatively charged electrons; in p-type semiconductors, the charge carriers are positively charged "holes" – regions where electrons are absent.

Capacitor stores electric charge. In a radio circuit, capacitors help tune the circuit so that it picks up different radio frequencies.

Resistor reduces the amount of current flowing in the circuit.

## CIRCUIT BOARD
An electronic device such as a telephone contains an electronic circuit consisting of several components joined together on a circuit board. Every circuit is designed for a particular task. The circuit in a radio, for instance, picks up and amplifies (boosts) radio waves so they can be converted into sound.

Diode allows current to pass in only one direction.

Transistor boosts the strength of electrical signals.

Variable resistor allows the flow of current to be varied.

Wires are used to connect some components.

Microchip in plastic casing

Metal tracks on the underside of the board connect components.

## CONTROLLING CURRENT
Electronic circuits do several basic jobs. They may amplify current; they may produce an oscillating current – one that rapidly changes direction, essential for generating radio waves; or they may switch current on and off.

Oscillation: Some circuits convert a steady one-way current (direct current, or DC) into a varying alternating current (AC).

Amplification: An amplifier circuit generates a strong AC current that is an accurate copy of a weaker AC current.

Switching: In computers, electronic circuits rapidly switch current on and off in a code that represents data.

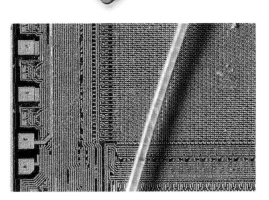

MICROCHIPS
Microchips, or silicon chips, contain circuits consisting of hundreds of thousands of microscopic components. These circuits are squeezed onto the surface of a semiconductor less than 25 mm (1 in) square.

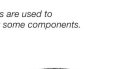

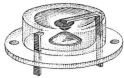

TRANSISTOR
Transistors lie at the heart of most electronic machines. They boost current and voltage in amplifier circuits, store information in computers, and perform many other tasks. Physicists William Shockley, John Bardeen, and Walter Brattain invented the transistor in 1947.

*Find out more*
COMPUTERS
ELECTRICITY
RADIO
SOUND RECORDING
TECHNOLOGY

# ELEPHANTS

**GREAT TUSKS**, huge ears, and a strong trunk make the elephant one of the most magnificent creatures on Earth. Elephants are the largest living land mammals and among the most ancient. They are extremely strong and highly intelligent, and have been trained to work for humans for thousands of years. There are three kinds of elephants – African Savannah, Forest, and Asian (Indian). African elephants are slightly bigger than Asian elephants, with much larger ears. A large male measures more than 3 m (10 ft) high at the shoulder and weighs more than 5.4 tonnes (5.3 tons). The elephant's trunk reaches to the ground and high into the trees to find food. It is also used for drinking, smelling, greeting other members of the herd, and as a snorkel in deep water.

## WOOLLY MAMMOTH
The prehistoric mammoth became extinct about 10,000 years ago. Frozen remains of mammoths have been found in Alaska and Siberia.

## TRUNK
The trunk is formed from the nose and the long upper lip. It is extremely sensitive to touch and smell. The elephant uses its trunk to grasp leaves, fruits, and shoots, and place them in its mouth. In order to drink, the elephant must squirt water into its mouth because it cannot drink through its trunk.

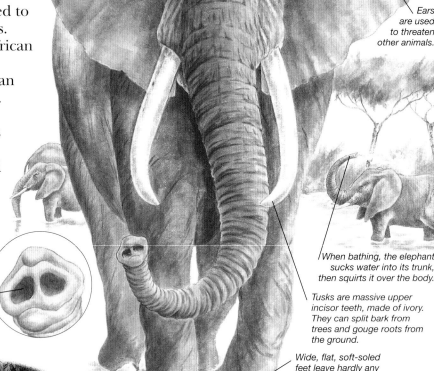

Head and jaws are huge, with wide, ridged teeth for chewing plant matter.

Huge ears help to cool elephant by allowing heat to escape.

Ears are used to threaten other animals.

Two nostrils at tip of the trunk

When bathing, the elephant sucks water into its trunk, then squirts it over the body.

Tusks are massive upper incisor teeth, made of ivory. They can split bark from trees and gouge roots from the ground.

Wide, flat, soft-soled feet leave hardly any tracks.

## ASIAN ELEPHANT
There are probably fewer than 50,000 Asian elephants left in the wild, in remote forests of India, China, and Southeast Asia. Female or cow elephants are quite easy to tame between the ages of about 10 and 20 years. They are caught and kept in captivity, and used for clearing forests and towing logs. Asian elephants are also dressed and decorated for ceremonies and processions.

## AFRICAN ELEPHANTS
In the late 1970s there were about 1.3 million elephants in Africa. Today there are half that number. Poachers kill them for their ivory, and farms are built on the land where they live. In reserves, however, where elephants are protected, their numbers have increased. Here, they are culled (killed in a controlled way) to prevent them from damaging the countryside. Today elephants are on the official list of endangered species, and the trade in elephants and ivory is controlled by international agreement.

A six-year-old male African elephant

## BREEDING
A newborn elephant calf weighs 100-120 kg (220-260 lb) at birth. It sucks milk from the teats between its mother's front legs until it is about four years old. A young elephant stays with its mother for the first 10 years of its life. By the age of six it weighs about one tonne, and at about 15 years of age it is ready to breed.

---

*Find out more*

AFRICAN WILDLIFE
ANIMALS
CONSERVATION
and endangered species
MAMMALS

---

# ELIZABETH I

**1533** Born, the daughter of Henry VIII and Anne Boleyn.

**1536** Mother is executed for treason.

**1554** Imprisoned in the Tower of London.

**1558** Crowned queen.

**1559** Establishes Protestant Church of England by the Act of Supremacy.

**1587** Orders execution of Mary, Queen of Scots.

**1588** Faces the Armada.

**1603** Dies.

MORE THAN 400 YEARS AGO, one woman brought 45 years of peace and prosperity to England through her determination and wisdom. Queen Elizabeth I began her life as a neglected princess, whose mother had been executed by her father. She was ignored and imprisoned as a girl, but upon the death of her half sister, Queen Mary, Elizabeth became a strong and popular queen. She tried to end years of religious conflict between Catholics and Protestants by insisting that the Church of England should be only moderately Protestant, so that it included as many people as possible. Elizabeth avoided expensive foreign wars for many years. Her most dangerous conflict was with Philip II, king of Spain, who sent the Armada (fleet of ships) against England. The queen's court was a centre for poets, musicians, and writers. Her reign is often called England's Golden Age.

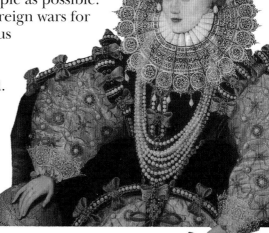

### SIR WALTER RALEIGH

One of Elizabeth's favourite courtiers was Sir Walter Raleigh (1552-1618). In 1584 she knighted him, and later made Raleigh her Captain of the Guard. He made several voyages across the Atlantic, set up an English colony in Virginia, and brought tobacco and potatoes from the Americas to Europe.

## ELIZABETHAN AGE

Elizabeth was the first monarch to give her name to an age. During her reign the arts of music, poetry, and drama flourished. Despite foreign threats and religious unrest at home, she won the loyalty and admiration of her subjects.

SPANISH ARMADA
In July 1588 Philip II, king of Spain, launched his Armada of nearly 150 ships to invade England and restore the Catholic religion. Sir Francis Drake (1540-96) sailed in command of a large group of warships to oppose the Armada. Aided by stormy weather, the English defeated the great fleet.

MARY, QUEEN OF SCOTS
Mary was Elizabeth's Catholic cousin and heir. Forced to abdicate her own throne in Scotland, she fled to England to seek Elizabeth's protection. Mary became involved in Catholic plots against Elizabeth, who reluctantly ordered her execution.

*Find out more*

HENRY VIII
STUARTS
TUDORS
UNITED KINGDOM, HISTORY OF

# EMIGRATION AND IMMIGRATION

WHEN YOU EMIGRATE, YOU LEAVE the country of your birth and settle elsewhere to live and work. When you arrive in a new country, you become an immigrant. Since the 17th century, many British people have left to start new lives elsewhere, in North America, Australia, New Zealand, or African and Asian countries that were once part of the British Empire. In the same way, people from all over the world have arrived to settle in Britain. Some came from countries of the Empire, and later the Commonwealth, to work, because they held British passports. After Britain joined the European Union, large numbers of Europeans came to work in Britain. Other immigrants – refugees of war or religious or political persecution – come to Britain to seek asylum (safety).

**EAST END OF LONDON**
Many immigrants to Britain first landed at London's docks and so settled in the nearby East End. Huguenots (French Protestants) fleeing persecution in the 1680s and Jews escaping massacres in Russia and Eastern Europe in the 1880s both settled there. Synagogues show where the Jewish communities were. More recently, people from Bengal and Bangladesh have come to the area.

## EMPIRE WINDRUSH

During World War II (1939-45), many islanders from the British West Indies fought in the British armed services. Their islands were poor, and, after the war, some decided to move to Britain in search of jobs. In June 1948, the first group arrived on a boat, the *Empire Windrush*. More followed, and a West Indian community was established.

**IMMIGRATION CONTROL**
When immigrants arrive at a port or airport they must fill in forms to apply for permission to stay. Britain has always had some form of restriction on immigration, although people from the Empire were allowed in. In 1962, the law was changed so that black Commonwealth citizens could only enter if they had a job to come to. Since then, the law has been tightened many times, making it harder to enter the country.

*Some of the first 510 Jamaicans to sail to Britain in search of work arrive at Tilbury Docks.*

## EMIGRATION

For at least 400 years, more people left Britain than have arrived. In 1620, a group known as the Pilgrim Fathers left for North America because of religious persecution, while many more left because of poverty. Today, there are thousands of people in Canada, Australia, and elsewhere who can trace their families back to Britain.

**EMIGRATION AND IMMIGRATION**

**1620** Pilgrims leave for New World.

**1685** Huguenots flee France.

**1880s** Jews flee Eastern Europe.

**1905** Aliens Act restricts entry of foreigners to Britain.

**1948** *Empire Windrush* brings 510 Jamaicans to Britain.

**1962** Commonwealth Immigration Act restricts immigration from Commonwealth.

**1971** Immigration Act allows entry to those with British-born parents or grandparents.

**2000s** Increasing numbers of asylum seekers come to Britain.

**RACE RELATIONS**
Racism is the belief that people of one culture or skin colour are superior to others. Many people who have settled in Britain have faced hostility and sometimes violence as a result of racism. In response, governments have made race discrimination illegal and have promoted equal opportunities for all Britons, black and white.

*Orphaned boys taken to Australia in the 1920s by Dr. Barnado's children's charity.*

**Find out more**
BRITISH EMPIRE
GOVERNMENT AND POLITICS
UNITED KINGDOM, HISTORY OF

# ENERGY

THE MOVEMENT OF A CAR, the sound of a trumpet, the light from a candle – all these things occur because of energy. Energy is the ability to make things happen. For example, when you throw a stone you give it energy of movement which shows itself when the stone smashes glass. All life on Earth depends on energy, almost all of which comes from the Sun. The Sun's energy makes plants grow, which provides the food that animals eat; the energy from food is stored in an animal's muscles, ready to be converted into movement. Although energy is not an object that you can see or touch, you can think of it as something that either flows from place to place, or is stored. For instance, energy is stored by water high at the top of a waterfall. As soon as the water starts to fall, the stored energy changes into moving energy which flows to the bottom of the waterfall.

### WORK, ENERGY, AND POWER
When a force moves an object, energy is transferred, or passed, to the object or its surroundings. This transfer of energy is called work. The amount of work done depends on the size of the force and how far it moves. For instance, this weightlifter does a lot of work lifting a heavy weight through a large distance. Power is the rate of doing work. The weightlifter produces more power the faster he lifts the weight.

### POTENTIAL ENERGY
Energy can be stored as potential energy until it turns into another form such as movement. Examples include water in a raised reservoir waiting to flow through turbines, chemical energy in a battery waiting to drive an electric current, and a coiled spring waiting to be released.

### KINETIC ENERGY
An object such as an aeroplane needs energy to make it move. Moving energy is called kinetic energy. When the plane stops, it loses kinetic energy. This often appears as heat – for instance, in the plane's brakes.

## TYPES OF ENERGY
Energy takes many forms, and it can change from one form into another. For example, power stations turn the chemical energy stored in coal or oil into heat energy which boils water. Turbines change the heat energy of the steam into electrical energy which flows to homes and factories.

Heat energy, such as the warmth of the Sun, is carried by invisible waves called infrared or heat radiation.

Light is one form of energy that travels in waves. Others include X-rays and radio waves.

Sound waves are vibrations of the air, so they carry kinetic energy.

Some power stations produce electricity from nuclear energy, which comes from the nuclei (centres) of atoms.

Electrical devices turn the energy of electric currents into many other forms of energy, including heat, light, and movement.

Oil and coal contain stored chemical energy which changes into heat and light when these fuels are burned.

A battery runs out when all its stored energy has been converted into heat in the wires, and heat and light in the bulb.

### ENERGY CYCLE
Energy cannot be created or destroyed; it can only change from one form into another. The only exception might seem to be when matter changes into energy in a nuclear reactor. However, the rule still applies because matter and energy are really the same and one can be converted into the other.

### ENERGY RESOURCES
The Earth's population uses a huge amount of energy. Most of this energy comes from coal, oil, gas, and the nuclear fuel uranium. However, these fuels are being used up and cannot be replaced. Today, scientists are experimenting with energy sources, called renewable resources, that will not run out. These include the Sun, wind, waves, and tides.

Rows of solar panels for producing electricity

| Find out more |
| --- |
| ELECTRICITY |
| HEAT |
| LIGHT |
| NUCLEAR ENERGY |
| SOUND |
| SUN |
| WATER |
| WIND |

# ENGINES

**FOUR-STROKE ENGINE**
Most car engines are four-stroke engines, which means that each piston makes a set of four movements.

*Piston 4 rises and pushes waste gases out through exhaust valve.*

*Piston 2 rises and compresses (squeezes) fuel-air mixture.*

*Piston 3 is pushed down by expanding gases when the mixture explodes.*

*Spark plug produces electrical spark that ignites fuel-air mixture.*

*Valves open and close to admit and expel the fuel-air mixture.*

*Piston 1 moves down and sucks fuel-air mixture in through inlet valve.*

*The piston moves up and down inside the cylinder.*

*Most engines have between four and eight cylinders. These work in sequence to produce continuous movement.*

*Crankshaft changes the up-and-down movement of the pistons into circular movement, which drives the wheels.*

WHEN PREHISTORIC PEOPLE discovered fire, they also found a way of obtaining energy; because burning releases heat and light. About one million years later, the steam engine was invented, and for the first time people could harness that energy and turn it into movement. Today, there are many different kinds of engines which drive the world's transport and industry. All engines serve one function – to use the energy stored in a fuel such as oil or coal, and change it into motion to drive machines. Before engines were invented, tasks such as building and lifting depended on the strength of people and their animals. Today, engines can produce enough power to lift the heaviest weights and drive the largest machines. The most powerful engine is the rocket engine; it can blast a spacecraft away from the pull of the Earth's gravity and out into space.

## INTERNAL-COMBUSTION ENGINE
The engine that powers almost all the world's cars is the internal-combustion engine. It uses the power of gases created by exploding fuel to produce movement. A mixture of air and tiny droplets of petrol enters the engine's cylinders, each of which contains a piston. An electrical spark ignites (sets alight) the fuel mixture, producing gases which thrust each piston down.

## ELECTRIC MOTORS
Petrol and diesel engines produce waste gases that pollute the air and contribute to the greenhouse effect (which causes the Earth's temperature to rise). Electric motors are clean, quiet, and produce no pollution. Several car manufacturers are developing cars powered by electric motors. Hybrid cars such as the Toyota Prius (below) use a combination of electric and petrol or gas power to provide good performance with low pollution.

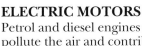

## DIESEL ENGINE
Many trains and lorries have powerful diesel engines, which are internal-combustion engines that burn diesel fuel instead of petrol. The engine works in the same way as a petrol-fuelled engine, but does not have spark plugs. Instead, each cylinder has an injector that squirts diesel fuel into the cylinder. The piston compresses the air, making it very hot. The hot air is all it needs to make the diesel fuel explode.

# JET ENGINE

The jet, or gas turbine, engine now powers most high-speed aircraft. The engine blasts a jet of hot, fast-moving air backward out of its exhaust; this pushes the engine forward. Fans at the front of the engine spin and suck air into it and squeeze it at high pressure into several combustion chambers. There, flames of burning kerosene heat the air, which expands and rushes towards the exhaust. As the air streams out, it spins a turbine, which drives the fans at the front of the engine.

## FRANK WHITTLE

In 1928, English pilot and engineer Frank Whittle (born 1907) suggested the idea of the jet engine. Whittle's engine powered an experimental aircraft for the first time in 1941. However, the first jet-powered flight was made during the 1930s in Germany, where engineer Hans von Ohain had developed his own jet engine.

Burning kerosene fuel inside the combustion chambers heats the air and makes it expand violently.

Some of the air that enters the engine flows through the bypass duct.

Large fan spins, sucking air into the engine.

Hot air and exhaust gases rush out of the engine, spinning the turbine as they go.

Fast-spinning fans called compressors increase the pressure of the air and push it into the combustion chambers.

## TURBOFAN ENGINE

A turbofan engine is a very efficient kind of gas turbine engine. Some of the air flows through a bypass duct around the main part of the engine. This increases the amount of air flowing through the engine, giving it more thrust. The duct also helps make the engine quieter.

## JAMES WATT

The first engine was a simple steam engine invented by the Greek scientist Hero in the 1st century A.D., but it was little more than a toy. In 1712, the British engineer Thomas Newcomen built the first real engine. It was a huge steam engine used to pump water out of mines. In 1769, another British engineer, James Watt (left), greatly improved the steam engine. The unit of power, the watt, is named after him.

## STEAM ENGINE

The steam engine was developed during the 18th century and greatly changed people's lives. It led to the development of industry and transport. People left the land to work in the new factories which contained steam-powered machines, and steam railways allowed people to travel further and faster than ever before.

Boiler burns wood or coal, producing heat.

Hot air and smoke pass through pipes that run through the water tank. The heat turns the water into steam.

Steam and smoke escape through a valve and pour out of the smokestack.

Steam passes through a pipe to a cylinder. The steam pushes a piston back and forth inside the cylinder.

The movement of the piston drives the wheels of the train.

---

### Find out more

AIRCRAFT
CARS
ELECTRICITY
ROCKETS AND MISSILES
TRAINS
TRANSPORT, HISTORY OF

# ENGLAND

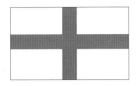

**ST. GEORGE'S FLAG**
The red cross of St. George of England is the national flag.

EIGHTY FIVE PER CENT of the population of the United Kingdom, more than 50 million people, live in England. The country has always been the largest, wealthiest, and most crowded region of Great Britain. The Industrial Revolution began in England in the late 1700s, causing a huge shift from agriculture to industry, and the emergence of industrial centres, such as Birmingham and Manchester. In the 19th and early 20th centuries, England was a major power as the centre of the British Empire. Today, England's manufacturing has declined but the country remains a centre for scientific research. Tourism based on England's heritage and traditions is also a major industry, employing thousands of people.

England stretches from Land's End in Cornwall, upwards to the border of Scotland. It covers 130,360 sq km (50,332 sq miles). It is divided into counties.

## LONDON
London is England's capital, and a leading international centre for finance, business, theatre, art, and music. One of the biggest cities in Europe, London is a popular destination for millions of tourists every year. The city was founded by the Romans on the banks of the River Thames in A.D. 43.

*The famous statue of Eros stands in busy Piccadilly Circus in London.*

**RURAL ENGLAND**
England is only a small country, but from the Yorkshire Moors in the north to the spectacular South Downs, it contains varied and beautiful countryside. Urbanization (the growth of towns) has destroyed much of England's rural areas. Preserving what remains has become an important issue.

**THE ENGLISH LANGUAGE**
Because the British Empire was so vast, English is spoken worldwide. More than 300 million people speak English as a first language, and it is the second or third language for another 600 million. It is the global language for air traffic control and science.

**ARCHITECTURE**
Most English people live in towns and cities, many of which are very crowded. Home ownership is valued, and town houses vary from from small terraced houses to apartment blocks. The most popular town houses include semi-detached houses, with their own gardens.

**ENGLISH BREAKFAST**
Traditional English cooking is variable, and not always liked by the people outside England. One popular speciality is the English breakfast with fried bread, eggs, bacon, sausages, tomatoes, and black pudding.

*Find out more*
INDUSTRIAL REVOLUTION
UNITED KINGDOM
UNITED KINGDOM, HISTORY OF

# ENGLISH CIVIL WAR

IN 1649 CHARLES I, king of England, was put on trial for treason and executed. His death marked the climax of the English Civil War, also called the English Revolution, a fierce struggle between king and Parliament (the law-making assembly) over the issue of who should govern England. The struggle had begun many years before. Charles I believed that kings were appointed by God and should rule alone; Parliament believed that it should have greater power. When the king called upon Parliament for funds to fight the Scots, it refused to co-operate, and in 1642 civil war broke out. England was divided into two factions – the Royalists (also called Cavaliers), who supported Charles, and the Roundheads, who supported Parliament. Charles was a poor leader, and the Roundheads had the support of the navy and were led by two great generals – Lord Fairfax and Oliver Cromwell. By 1649 Cromwell had defeated Charles and declared England a republic. Despite various reforms, Cromwell's rule was unpopular. In 1660 the army asked Charles's son, Charles II, to take the throne and the monarchy was restored.

CHARLES I
King Charles I (reigned 1625-49) was the only English monarch to be executed. He ignored the Parliament, and ruled alone from 1629 to 1640. After a disagreement with the Parliament in 1642, Charles raised an army and began the civil war which ended his reign. The picture above depicts the scene of his execution.

Parliamentary (New Model) army

Royalist cavalry

Royalist officers wore wide-brimmed hats.

Pikeman

## BATTLE OF NASEBY
At the Battle of Naseby in 1645 the heavily armed and well-organized pikemen and musketeers of Cromwell's "New Model Army" crushed the Royalists.

## DIGGERS
During the turbulent years new political groups emerged. Some, such as the Diggers, were very radical. They believed that ordinary people should have a say in government and wanted to end private property.

## OLIVER CROMWELL
The English Republic (1649-60) was organized and ruled mainly by Lord Protector Oliver Cromwell (1599-1658). Cromwell was an honest, moderate man and a brilliant army leader. But his attempts to enforce extreme purity upon England made him unpopular with many.

RUMP PARLIAMENT
At the end of the English Civil War, all that was left of King Charles's parliament was a "rump" parliament, whose members refused to leave. In 1653 Cromwell, determined to get rid of any remnant of the king, dismissed Parliament. He pointed at the mace, the speaker's symbol of office, and laughingly called it a bauble (left).

---

***Find out more***
CROMWELL, OLIVER
UNITED KINGDOM,
history of

# ESCALATORS AND LIFTS

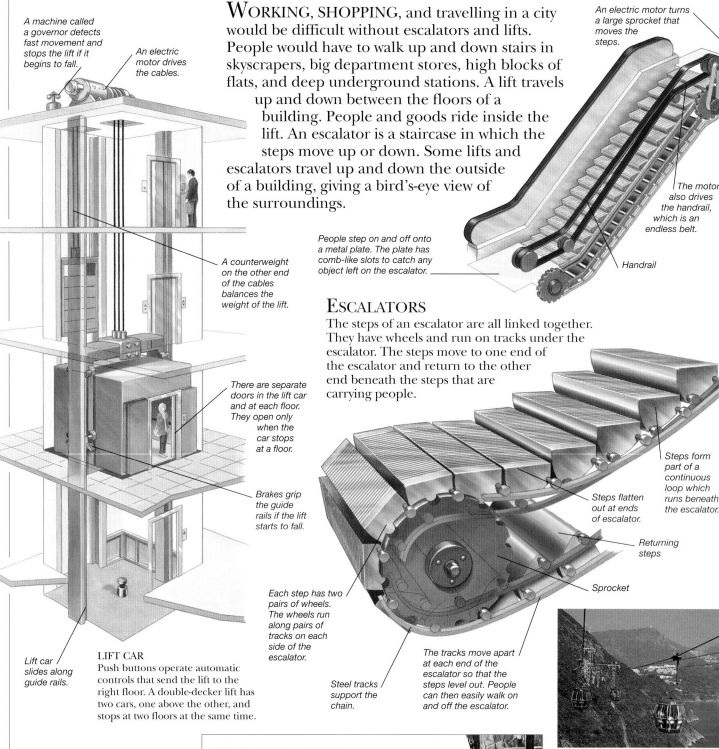

WORKING, SHOPPING, and travelling in a city would be difficult without escalators and lifts. People would have to walk up and down stairs in skyscrapers, big department stores, high blocks of flats, and deep underground stations. A lift travels up and down between the floors of a building. People and goods ride inside the lift. An escalator is a staircase in which the steps move up or down. Some lifts and escalators travel up and down the outside of a building, giving a bird's-eye view of the surroundings.

A machine called a governor detects fast movement and stops the lift if it begins to fall.

An electric motor drives the cables.

A counterweight on the other end of the cables balances the weight of the lift.

There are separate doors in the lift car and at each floor. They open only when the car stops at a floor.

Brakes grip the guide rails if the lift starts to fall.

Lift car slides along guide rails.

An electric motor turns a large sprocket that moves the steps.

The motor also drives the handrail, which is an endless belt.

Handrail

People step on and off onto a metal plate. The plate has comb-like slots to catch any object left on the escalator.

## ESCALATORS
The steps of an escalator are all linked together. They have wheels and run on tracks under the escalator. The steps move to one end of the escalator and return to the other end beneath the steps that are carrying people.

Steps form part of a continuous loop which runs beneath the escalator.

Steps flatten out at ends of escalator.

Returning steps

Sprocket

Each step has two pairs of wheels. The wheels run along pairs of tracks on each side of the escalator.

Steel tracks support the chain.

The tracks move apart at each end of the escalator so that the steps level out. People can then easily walk on and off the escalator.

## LIFT CAR
Push buttons operate automatic controls that send the lift to the right floor. A double-decker lift has two cars, one above the other, and stops at two floors at the same time.

## LIFTS
Most lifts have strong steel cables that support the car, which travels along guide rails up and down a shaft. Some lifts are pushed up from below by a long steel tube. The world's fastest lifts can rise about 17 m (56 ft) per second.

## THE OTIS SAFETY LIFT
In 1854, an engineer called Elisha Otis demonstrated his safety lift. While standing on the lift, he ordered the rope to be cut. A safety mechanism automatically gripped the guide rails and kept the lift from falling. Otis's invention made the building of skyscrapers possible. All lifts now have safety mechanisms of this kind.

## CABLE CARS
A moving cable pulls cable cars and ski lifts up mountain slopes and steep hills. These cable cars are in Hong Kong.

*Find out more*
ARCHITECTURE
BUILDING
MACHINES

# EUROPE

COMPARED TO ITS mighty eastern neighbour, Asia, Europe is a tiny continent. But the culture of Europe has extended far beyond its boundaries. Europe has a long history of wealth, industry, trading, and empire building. Much of its prosperity comes from its green and fertile land, which is watered by numerous rivers and plenty of rain. Yet the climate varies considerably across the continent. The countries of southern Europe border the Mediterranean Sea. Holiday-makers visit the coast of this enclosed sea to enjoy its long, hot summers. The far north, by contrast, reaches up into the icy Arctic Circle. There are also a number of high mountain ranges within Europe, including the Alps and the Pyrenees. The ethnic composition of Europe's 725 million people is as varied as the landscape. The continent is culturally diverse with a rich history. The Nordic people of the north have blond hair, fair skin, and blue eyes, while many Europeans in the south have darker skin and dark, curly hair.

Europe lies to the north of the Mediterranean Sea and overlooks the northern part of the Atlantic Ocean. It includes the surrounding islands, such as the British Isles and Iceland. The Ural Mountains in the Russian Federation mark the long eastern frontier with Asia.

**EURO**
The European Union made a major move towards monetary union when the Euro was introduced as a single European currency. Eleven EU countries, including Germany and France, formally adopted the currency in 1999, and the Euro replaced the national currencies of 12 countries at the start of 2002 (Greece joining in with the original 11). Other EU countries, such as Britain and Denmark, kept their national currencies.

*To meet increasing competition from abroad, particularly from Japan, European companies have modernized their factories.*

**INDUSTRY**
Large-scale industry began in Europe. Labor-saving inventions of the 18th and 19th centuries enabled workers in European factories to manufacture goods cheaply and in large numbers. The Industrial Revolution soon spread to other parts of the world, including the United States, India, and Japan. Manufacturing industries still play a vital role in most European countries.

*Old European buildings may look picturesque, but the architecture is more than decorative. The mellow brick and stone provide essential protection against the cool, damp weather.*

*Austrian composer Johann Strauss Jr. (1825-99) named his famous waltz tune* The Blue Danube *after the river.*

**DANUBE RIVER**
Europe's second-longest river is the Danube. The Danube flows from the Black Forest in Germany to the Black Sea and passes through nine European countries: Germany, Austria, Slovakia, Hungary, Croatia, Serbia, Romania, Bulgaria, and Ukraine.

**CITIES**
Most European cities pre-date those in Australia and America. Many are of ancient origin and have grown gradually over several centuries. As a result, they differ enormously in design and layout to their modern counterparts abroad. Originally designed to cope with small volumes of traffic, Europe's cities are composed of an irregular mixture of narrow winding streets, and wider boulevards. Modern cities, designed with current modes of transport in mind, are carefully planned and tend to follow a more uniform grid pattern.

## TRADE

Europeans have always been great traders. Between the 15th and 18th centuries, the countries of Europe were the most powerful in the world. They took their trade to all corners of the globe, and their settlers ruled parts of the Americas, Africa, India, Southeast Asia, and Australia. Almost all of these regions are now independent, but many still retain traces of European culture.

*European trade and money formed the basis of the world's banking system.*

*The people paint the houses white to reflect the heat of the sun.*

## SCANDINAVIA

A great hook-shaped peninsula encloses most of the Baltic Sea in northern Europe and extends into the Arctic Ocean. Sweden and Norway occupy this peninsula. Together with Denmark to the south, they make up Scandinavia. Finland, to the east of the Baltic, and the large island of Iceland in the North Atlantic, are often also included in the group.

*In the warm climate of the Mediterranean region olives, oranges, lemons, sunflowers, melons, tomatoes, and aubergines grow well.*

*Goats and sheep are more common than cattle, which require richer pasture.*

## MEDITERRANEAN

Ten European countries border the Mediterranean Sea: Spain, France, Monaco, Italy, Slovenia, Croatia, Bosnia and Herzegovina, Serbia, Albania, and Greece. A small part of Turkey is also in Europe. The Mediterranean people have traditionally lived by farming (above), but many of these countries now have thriving industries. Though the climate around the Mediterranean is much warmer than that of northern Europe, winters can still be quite chilly.

### ART AND CULTURE

Europe has its own traditions of art and culture which are quite distinct from those of other parts of the world. Oil painting, classical music, and ballet had their origins in Europe. The traditions of European theatre, music, literature, painting, and sculpture all began in ancient times.

*Tallinn (left), Estonia's capital city, is a major Baltic port.*

## BALTIC STATES

Lithuania, Latvia, and Estonia, low-lying agricultural countries on the eastern coast of the Baltic Sea, are together called the Baltic States. They were formed in 1918 and remained independent until 1940 when they were occupied by the Soviet Union. In 1991, Lithuania became one of the first of the former Soviet republics to achieve independence, followed a few months later by Estonia and Latvia.

---

### *Find out more*

FRANCE
GERMANY
ITALY
RUSSIAN FEDERATION
SCANDINAVIA
SPAIN
UNITED KINGDOM

---

## STATISTICS

**Area:** 10,498,000 sq km
(4,053,309 sq miles)
**Population:** 725,000,000
**Highest point:** El' brus,
Caucasus Mountains
(European Russia)
5,642 m (18,511 ft)
**Longest river:** Volga
(European Russia)
3,688 m (2,290 miles)
**Largest lake:** Ladoga
(European Russia)
18,300 sq km
(7,100 sq miles)
**Main occupations:**
Agriculture,
manufacturing, industry
**Main exports:**
Machinery and transport
equipment
**Main imports:** Oil and
other raw materials

### EUROPEAN UNION

In 1957, five European countries agreed to form the European Economic Community (EEC). They believed that economic and political co-operation would reduce the likelihood of wars between the member countries and would bring prosperity to the peoples of Europe. In December 1991, the Maastricht Treaty created the European Union (EU) and committed its member states to the introduction of a single currency. The EU flag (below) has 12 yellow stars on a blue background. The Union now has 25 members.

 **ALBANIA**
**Area:** 28,750 sq km
(11,100 sq miles)
**Population:** 3,200,000
**Capital:** Tirana

 **ANDORRA**
**Area:** 468 sq km
(181 sq miles)
**Population:** 69,000
**Capital:** Andorra la Vella

 **AUSTRIA**
**Area:** 83,850 sq km
(32,375 sq miles)
**Population:** 8,100,000
**Capital:** Vienna

**BELGIUM**
**Area:** 33,100 sq km
(12,780 sq miles)
**Population:** 10,300,000
**Capital:** Brussels

 **BELARUS**
**Area:** 207,600 sq km
(80,154 sq miles)
**Population:** 9,900,000
**Capital:** Minsk

 **BOSNIA AND HERZEGOVINA**
**Area:** 51,130 sq km
(19,741 sq miles)
**Population:** 4,200,000
**Capital:** Sarajevo

 **BULGARIA**
**Area:** 110,910 sq km
(42,822 sq miles)
**Population:** 7,900,000
**Capital:** Sofia

 **CROATIA**
**Area:** 56,540 sq km
(21,830 sq miles)
**Population:** 4,400,000
**Capital:** Zagreb

 **CZECH REPUBLIC**
**Area:** 78,370 sq km
(30,260 sq miles)
**Population:** 10,200,000
**Capital:** Prague

 **DENMARK**
**Area:** 43,069 sq km
(16,629 sq miles)
**Population:** 5,400,000
**Capital:** Copenhagen

 **ESTONIA**
**Area:** 45,125 sq km
(17,423 sq miles)
**Population:** 1,300,000
**Capital:** Tallinn

 **FINLAND**
**Area:** 338,130 sq km
(130,552 sq miles)
**Population:** 5,200,000
**Capital:** Helsinki

 **FRANCE**
**Area:** 551,500 sq km
(212,930 sq miles)
**Population:** 60,100,000
**Capital:** Paris

 **GERMANY**
**Area:** 356,910 sq km
(137,800 sq miles)
**Population:** 82,500,000
**Capital:** Berlin

 **GREECE**
**Area:** 131,990 sq km
(50,521 sq miles)
**Population:** 11,000,000
**Capital:** Athens

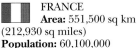 **HUNGARY**
**Area:** 93,030 sq km
(35,919 sq miles)
**Population:** 9,900,000
**Capital:** Budapest

 **ICELAND**
**Area:** 103,000 sq km
(39,770 sq miles)
**Population:** 290,000
**Capital:** Reykjavik

 **IRELAND**
**Area:** 70,280 sq km
(27,155 sq miles)
**Population:** 4,000,000
**Capital:** Dublin

 **ITALY**
**Area:** 301,270 sq km
(116,320 sq miles)
**Population:** 57,400,000
**Capital:** Rome

 **LATVIA**
**Area:** 64,589 sq km
(24,938 sq miles)
**Population:** 2,300,000
**Capital:** Riga

 **LIECHTENSTEIN**
**Area:** 160 sq km
(62 sq miles)
**Population:** 33,100
**Capital:** Vaduz

 **LITHUANIA**
**Area:** 65,200 sq km
(25,174 sq miles)
**Population:** 3,400,000
**Capital:** Vilnius

 **LUXEMBOURG**
**Area:** 2,586 sq km
(998 sq miles)
**Population:** 453,000
**Capital:** Luxembourg

 **MACEDONIA**
**Area:** 25,715 sq km
(9,929 sq miles)
**Population:** 2,020,000
**Capital:** Skopje

 **MALTA**
**Area:** 320 sq km
(124 sq miles)
**Population:** 394,000
**Capital:** Valletta

 **MOLDOVA**
**Area:** 33,700 sq km
(13,000 sq miles)
**Population:** 4,300,000
**Capital:** Chisinau

**MONACO**
**Area:** 1.95 sq km
(0.75 sq miles)
**Population:** 32,100
**Capital:** Monaco

**NETHERLANDS**
**Area:** 37,330 sq km
(14,410 sq miles)
**Population:** 16,100,000
**Capital:** Amsterdam, The Hague

**NORWAY**
**Area:** 323,900 sq km
(125,060 sq miles)
**Population:** 4,500,000
**Capital:** Oslo

**POLAND**
**Area:** 312,680 sq km
(120,720 sq miles)
**Population:** 38,600,000
**Capital:** Warsaw

**PORTUGAL**
**Area:** 92,390 sq km
(35,670 sq miles)
**Population:** 10,100,000
**Capital:** Lisbon

**ROMANIA**
**Area:** 237,500 sq km
(88,934 sq miles)
**Population:** 22,300,000
**Capital:** Bucharest

**RUSSIAN FED.**
**Area:** 17,075,400 sq km
(5,592,800 sq miles)
**Population:** 143,000,000
**Capital:** Moscow

**SAN MARINO**
**Area:** 61 sq km
(24 sq miles)
**Population:** 28,100
**Capital:** San Marino

**SERBIA AND MONTENEGRO**
**Area:** 102,173 sq km
(39,449 sq miles)
**Population:** 10,500,000
**Capital:** Belgrade

**SLOVAKIA**
**Area:** 49,500 sq km
(19,100 sq miles)
**Population:** 5,400,000
**Capital:** Bratislava

**SLOVENIA**
**Area:** 20,250 sq km
(7,820 sq miles)
**Population:** 2,000,000
**Capital:** Ljubljana

**SPAIN**
**Area:** 504,780 sq km
(194,900 sq miles)
**Population:** 41,100,000
**Capital:** Madrid

**SWEDEN**
**Area:** 449,960 sq km
(173,730 sq miles)
**Population:** 8,900,000
**Capital:** Stockholm

**SWITZERLAND**
**Area:** 41,290 sq km
(15,940 sq miles)
**Population:** 7,200,000
**Capital:** Bern

**UKRAINE**
**Area:** 603,700 sq km
(223,090 sq miles)
**Population:** 47,700,000
**Capital:** Kiev

**UNITED KINGDOM**
**Area:** 244,880 sq km
(94,550 sq miles)
**Population:** 59,800,000
**Capital:** London

 **VATICAN CITY**
**Area:** 0.44 sq km
(0.17 sq miles)
**Population:** 900
**Capital:** Vatican City

**Volcano** △ Mountain 🏛 Ancient monument ◻ Capital city ● Large city/town • Small city/town

**SCALE BAR**
0 300 600 km
0 300 600 miles

POPULATION
More than 700 million people live in Europe and its population is highly urbanized. In Belgium and the Netherlands, almost 90 per cent of people live in cities. In the south and east, more people still live in rural areas.

PYRENEES
The Pyrenees mountains lie on the border between France and Spain. The mountain range stretches from the Bay of Biscay to the Mediterranean Sea, a distance of 435 km (270 miles). The climate of the Pyrenees is mild and humid. The mountains offer fishing, sightseeing, and winter sports. There are also health spas with hot springs.

*The majestic Pyrenees (left) form a spectacular natural border between Spain and France.*

*In 1992 UN peacekeeping forces entered war-torn Sarajevo, capital of Bosnia.*

## EASTERN EUROPE

This refers to countries such as Hungary and Poland that came under Soviet control in 1945. It also refers to what was the western Soviet Union. From 1989, the Communist regimes in Eastern Europe collapsed and were replaced by more democratic governments. Some countries kept their boundaries; others changed. There was also communist rule in Yugoslavia, a country that broke up in the early 1990s. After much bitter fighting, the separate states of Serbia, Croatia, Slovenia, Macedonia, and Bosnia and Herzegovina were formed.

# EUROPEAN UNION

IN THE 75 YEARS BETWEEN 1870-1945, France and Germany fought each other three times. After the end of World War II in 1945, they decided to live together as friends, not enemies, by combining their industrial strength. Four other countries joined them, and by 1951 the European Steel and Coal Community was created. Seven years later, the six countries signed the Treaty of Rome to set up the European Economic Community. Since then, the Community has grown into a European Union (EU) of 25 countries, including Britain and Ireland. The EU has a huge impact on daily life in Europe, from the price of food to the colour of passports. Many Europeans, however, resist the idea of the EU becoming a "superstate" with its own army and constitution.

**JEAN MONNET**
French economist Jean Monnet (1888-1979) helped to set up the European Coal and Steel Community, and was its first president. He told the French government that this would prevent another war with Germany.

**THE FLAG**
The flag of the European Union was first used in 1955 and consists of 12 five-pointed stars on a blue background.

*Countries of Europe which do not form part of the EU.*

A meeting of the European Parliament in Strasbourg.

*MEPs sit in a semi-circle.*

**EU MEMBERSHIP**
The six original members of the EU were France, West Germany, Netherlands, Belgium, Luxembourg, and Italy. Britain, Ireland, and Denmark joined in 1973, Spain and Portugal in 1981, Greece in 1986, East Germany in 1990, and Finland, Sweden, and Austria in 1995. Cyprus, Czech Republic, Estonia, Hungary, Latvia, Lithuania, Malta, Poland, Slovakia, and Slovenia joined in 2004.

*Original members*

*Current members*

## EUROPEAN PARLIAMENT

Every five years, the voters of Europe elect 626 Members of the European Parliament (MEPs) to represent them in Strasbourg, France. MEPs have the power to approve or throw out the Commission (the EU government), reject the annual budget, and question the Commission on its policies. The European Parliament is not as powerful as a national parliament, but it plays an important part in deciding how the European Union will develop.

*Common passport allows holder to travel freely in the EU.*

**WHAT THE EU DOES**
The EU looks after farming, fishing, economic, industrial, and cultural affairs. It helps the poorer parts of Europe by building roads, and paying for education and training projects. Everybody in the EU holds a common European passport.

*The EU helps farmers to produce and sell food.*

**EUROPEAN UNION**

**1951** France, Germany, Italy, and the Benelux countries set up European Coal and Steel Community.

**1957** ECSC members sign Treaty of Rome to set up European Economic Community (EEC) and Euratom, the atomic energy authority.

**1967** ECSC, EEC, and Euratom merge to form the European Community.

**1979** European Monetary System begins operation.

**1993** Moves towards closer union result in the European Union (EU).

**2002** The Euro becomes the currency of 12 EU countries.

**2004** Ten more countries join the EU.

Euro coins

**EUROPEAN MONETARY UNION**
EU countries first linked their currencies together in 1979, and began to move towards full monetary and economic union. In 1999, 11 member countries joined the euro, or single currency. Euro bank notes and coins came into use in those countries in 2002, replacing national currencies such as the French franc and German mark.

*Find out more*
EUROPE
EUROPE, HISTORY OF
TRADE AND INDUSTRY

# HISTORY OF
# EUROPE

EUROPE IS THE SECOND SMALLESTcontinent, but it has played an important part in world history. The Ancient Greek and Roman empires stretched into North Africa and the Middle East, and their art, thinking, and science are still influential today. More than a thousand years later, Portuguese and Spanish explorers sailed to new continents, and even around the world. This marked the start of a period of European dominance of world affairs that lasted 400 years. Throughout its long history, however, Europe's countries have rarely been at peace, and in the 20th century, quarrels between European nations led to two world wars. Since 1945, with the rise of the United States as a world superpower, Europe's global political influence is less, but it remains culturally important.

## PREHISTORIC EUROPE
The first Europeans were primitive hunters who moved around in search of food and shelter. By about 5000 B.C., Europeans were growing crops, and domesticating animals. They settled in villages, and in northern Europe, they built large burial mounds for their dead.

## GREECE AND ROME
In about 900 B.C., the Greeks set up powerful city states, such as Athens and Sparta. Their merchants traded around the coast of the Mediterranean Sea, founding colonies from Spain to the Black Sea. The Roman Empire began in 753 B.C. and by A.D.117 controlled most of Europe, northern Africa, and the Middle East.

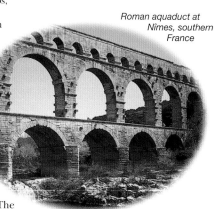

*Roman aquaduct at Nîmes, southern France*

*Rose window, Chartres Cathedral*

## CHRISTIANITY
In the 300s, Christianity became the major religion in the Roman Empire. Gradually, over the next 700 years, it spread throughout Europe. Headed by the pope in Rome, the Christian Church was very powerful. It unified the continent, and dominated all aspects of daily life, including education.

## MEDIEVAL TRADE
Trade prospered in medieval Europe. In the 13th century, a group of towns around the Baltic and North Sea formed the Hanseatic League, trading from ports such as Lübeck and Bruges, and monopolising trade until the 1600s. Cloth, spices, and gold were sold at great trade fairs.

## EUROPEAN DOMINATION
In mid-1400s, the Portuguese set out to explore the coast of Africa in a new, fast ship – the caravel. They set up trading stations, and were followed by other European explorers and traders, who moved outward from Europe to all parts of the globe. Europeans soon came to dominate world trade, setting up colonies in the Americas, Asia, and Africa, and building vast empires.

*Portuguese caravel*

# THE ENLIGHTENMENT

In the 18th century, European thinkers began to reject old beliefs based on religion and superstition, and developed new ideas based on reason and science. An intellectual revolution, called the Enlightenment, broke out across Europe. New ideas about government led to the French and American revolutions. Religious toleration increased, and economics, philosophy, and science prospered.

## WORLD WARS

In the 1900s, conflicts between European powers caused two devastating World Wars. World War I (1914-18) weakened Europe, but war broke out again in 1939. At its end in 1945, cities were in ruins, thousands were homeless, and two new "superpowers" – the USA and the Soviet Union – had emerged.

*Russian tanks in the streets of Budapest, Hungary in 1956.*

*Intellectuals gather to discuss new ideas in science.*

*Kemal Ataturk (1881–1939), "Father of the Turks"*

## BREAK-UP OF EMPIRES

After World War I, the multinational empires of Germany, Austro-Hungary, Ottoman Turkey, and Russia broke up as the different nationalities within them created independent countries, such as Czechoslovakia and Poland. Kemal Ataturk abolished the old Islamic government of the Ottoman Empire, and created the non-religious country of Turkey.

# COMMUNIST EUROPE

By 1945, Europe was effectively divided into Communist countries, dominated by the former Soviet Union, and non-communist nations influenced by the United States. Germany was split into two nations. Life was often harsh in Communist countries, and civil liberties were restricted. Revolts broke out in East Germany (1953), Hungary (1956), and Czechoslovakia (1968), but Russian troops put them down.

## THE COLLAPSE OF COMMUNISM

By the late 1980s, Communism was losing its hold, and the Soviet Union (USSR) withdrew its support from Eastern Europe. In 1989, East Germans demonstrated for union with West Germany, and pulled down the wall that divided their capital city, Berlin. Germany was reunited the following year. Popular protests then overthrew Communist governments throughout Eastern Europe.

### HISTORY OF EUROPE

**5000 B.C.** Stone Age peoples begin to settle in villages.

**900** Greek city states founded.

**753** Rome founded.

**A.D. 117** Roman Empire at its height.

**313** Christianity is tolerated throughout Roman Empire.

**1000s** Christianity spreads throughout Europe.

**c. 1241** Hanseatic League established between Hamburg and Lübeck merchants.

**1492** Columbus crosses Atlantic; leads to European dominance in the Americas.

**1498** European explorers reach India.

**1517** Reformation leads to emergence of Protestantism.

**1700s** Age of Enlightenment.

**1800s** European empires control most of Africa and Asia.

**1914-18** World War I devastates Europe.

**1939-45** World War II leads to division of European into Communist and non-communist sectors.

**1957** Treaty of Rome sets up European Economic Community (EEC).

**1989** Fall of Berlin Wall leads to end of Communism in Eastern Europe.

**1991** USSR divided into 15 separate countries.

**1991-99** Wars in the Balkans as Yugoslavia breaks up.

## YUGOSLAVIA

In the 1990s, Yugoslavia fell apart as Serbia, the largest and most powerful province, tried to take control. Slovenia, Croatia, and Bosnia and Herzegovina all declared independence, leading to terrible atrocities on all sides. Serbia pursued "ethnic cleansing" – killing or expelling all non-Serbs, notably in Bosnia and Kosovo. War between Serbia and NATO – a military alliance of Western Europe and the USA – led to an uneasy peace in 1999.

---

### *Find out more*

EUROPEAN UNION
MEDIEVAL EUROPE
WORLD WAR I
WORLD WAR II

# EVOLUTION

AROUND 150 YEARS AGO, an English naturalist named Charles Darwin shocked the world when he wrote a book suggesting that humans were related to apes. Today Darwin's idea still forms the basis of what we call the theory of evolution. The word evolution means unfolding, and it is used to describe the way that all living things evolve, or change with time. There are three main parts to the theory. The first is called variation. All living things vary in size, shape, colour, and strength. No two animals or plants are exactly the same. The second part of the theory is that these variations affect whether or not a living thing can survive and breed. Certain features, such as colour, may mean that one animal or plant has a better chance of surviving than another. Some animals and plants have features that suit their surroundings. In other words, they are better adapted, and these useful features are called adaptations. The third part of the theory is inheritance. The adaptations that help a living thing to survive, such as its colour or shape, may be passed on to its offspring. If the offspring inherit the adaptations, they too will have a better chance of survival. Gradually, over many generations, the better-adapted plants and animals flourish, and those that are less well adapted die out. Many people believe that this process of evolution has led to the millions of different species that inhabit the Earth today.

### NATURAL SELECTION
Charles Darwin wrote a book called *On the Origin of Species*, published in 1859, which explained his theory of evolution. Many people laughed at Darwin's idea that humans were related to animals. Above is a cartoon of the time, picturing Darwin as a monkey.

African elephant of today

Evolution of the elephant

Moenitherium *lived about 38 million years ago.*

Woolly mammoth *lived about two million years ago.*

Platybelodon *lived from 12 to 7 million years ago.*

Trilophodon *lived from 26 to three million years ago.*

## EVIDENCE FROM THE PAST
Fossils, the remains of animals and plants preserved in rocks, provide evidence for evolution. They show how animals and plants have gradually changed through time. For example, each of the elephants shown above lived for a certain amount of time, as we know by the age of their fossilized bones. Scientists cannot be certain that the first type of elephant gradually evolved into the next, but it is unlikely that each elephant appeared, completely separate from the others. It is far more likely that these elephants were related. As we find more fossils, the relationships between various kinds of animals and plants become clearer.

### EVIDENCE FROM THE PRESENT
Animals and plants alive today also provide evidence for evolution. In Hawaii, there are several kinds of honeycreepers that look similar. It is unlikely that this is by chance. More likely, these different honeycreeper birds all evolved from one kind of honeycreeper. This first honeycreeper flew to the islands five million years ago. Since that time, natural selection has produced several similar, but separate, species.

There are 28 species of honeycreepers on the Hawaiian Islands. Scientists believe they evolved from one species of bird.

Akiapolaau searches for insects with upper bill.

Iiwi beak and tubular tongue are suited to sipping nectar.

Apapane has useful all-round beak.

Maui parrotbill uses lower bill for chiselling into wood for insects.

Kona finch has strong bill for crushing seeds.

Original species of honeycreeper

Kauai akialoa has long beak for probing for insects.

# HOW EVOLUTION OCCURS

Imagine some green frogs, living and breeding in green surroundings. Most of the young inherit the green colouring of their parents. They are well camouflaged and predators do not notice them in the grass. Their green colour is an adaptation which helps them to survive. A few of the young have different colours, because of variation. Predators can see them in the grass and these frogs are soon eaten – this is natural selection at work. Then the environment slowly changes to yellow as the grass dies. Now the green frogs show up on the sand, and predators eat them. Gradually, the following generations of frogs change from mainly green to mainly yellow. A new species has evolved.

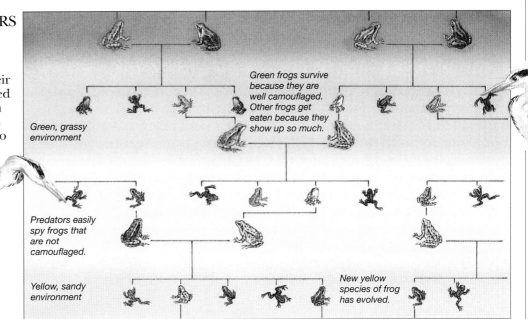

Green, grassy environment

Green frogs survive because they are well camouflaged. Other frogs get eaten because they show up so much.

Predators easily spy frogs that are not camouflaged.

Yellow, sandy environment

New yellow species of frog has evolved.

## CHANGING ENVIRONMENTS

As the environment changes, living things evolve. About 200 years ago in Britain, peppered moths had mostly light-coloured wings that matched the light-coloured tree trunks where they rested, so birds of prey could not see them easily. During the Industrial Revolution, smoke from factory chimneys made the tree trunks darker in some areas. Light-coloured moths became easier to see. Gradually, more dark-coloured moths evolved, which were better camouflaged on the dark tree trunks.

The ichthyosaur is an extinct reptile. Its paddle-like front limb had many small bones.

The dolphin is a mammal. Its paddle has the typical bones of the mammal arm and hand.

The penguin is a bird that cannot fly. It has the typical bird's wing bones in its paddle.

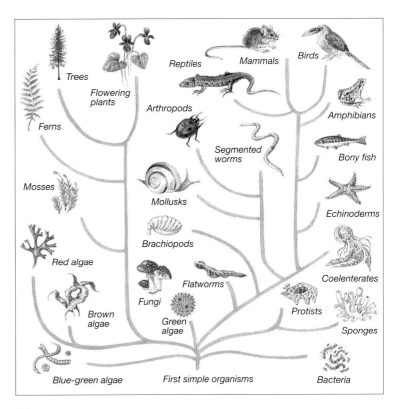

Trees

Flowering plants

Reptiles

Mammals

Birds

Ferns

Arthropods

Amphibians

Segmented worms

Bony fish

Mosses

Mollusks

Echinoderms

Red algae

Brachiopods

Coelenterates

Brown algae

Fungi

Flatworms

Green algae

Protists

Sponges

Blue-green algae

First simple organisms

Bacteria

# EVOLUTIONARY TREE

Scientists believe that all living things are related and that they have evolved from the same ancestors over millions of years. This chart is called an evolutionary tree. It has lines between the main groups of animals and plants alive today, showing which ones are most closely related.

# CONVERGENT EVOLUTION

Evolution sometimes makes different animals and plants look similar. This is called convergent evolution. It means that different animals or plants that live in the same environment, such as the sea, gradually take on the same adaptations, such as body shape. All the animals shown above have evolved, or developed, the same streamlined body form, because this is the best shape for moving speedily through water.

*Find out more*

ANIMALS
DARWIN, CHARLES
DINOSAURS
FOSSILS
GEOLOGY
PREHISTORIC LIFE
PREHISTORIC PEOPLES

# EXPLORERS

TODAY, PEOPLE ARE AWARE of the remotest corners of the world. But hundreds of years ago, many did not know that countries apart from their own even existed. In the 6th century, the Irish Saint Brendan is said to have sailed across the Atlantic in search of a land promised to saints. But it was not until the early 15th century that strong seaworthy ships were developed and Europeans such as Christopher Columbus were able to explore in earnest. Turkish Muslims had been controlling the overland trade route between Europe and the Indies (the Far East – now East Asia) since the 11th century. They charged such high prices for Eastern goods that European merchants became eager to find a direct sea route to the Far East which would bypass the Turks. The sailors who searched for these routes found the Americas and other lands previously unknown to Europeans. Of course, people already lived in most of these "newly discovered" lands, and the results of these explorations were often disastrous. All too often, the new arrivals exploited and enslaved the native peoples, destroying their cultures.

**VIKINGS**
The Vikings came from Norway, Sweden, and Denmark. Looking for new lands in which to settle, they sailed to Iceland, Greenland, and North America in their long ships, navigating by the sun and the stars.

**EARLY IDEAS**
The first explorers had few maps. Early ideas about the shape of the world were hopelessly inaccurate. Many scholars thought the world was flat and that those who went too far might fall off the edge. Some believed that the world was supported by a tortoise (above).

**PACIFIC ISLANDS**
Europeans exploring the Pacific Ocean in the 1500s were amazed to find that prehistoric peoples had found the Pacific Islands before them. In about 30,000 B.C., the original Polynesians moved from southeast Asia to the islands in the western Pacific, sailing in fragile canoes. By A.D. 1000, they had settled on hundreds of other islands.

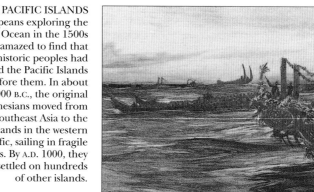

Maori ancestors leaving for New Zealand

**PERILS OF THE SEA**
Early sailors faced many natural dangers such as storms, reefs, icebergs, and fog. The sea was an alien territory, and rumours and legends spoke of huge sea monsters which swam in unknown waters. These stories were probably based on sightings of whales and other marine creatures. They were exaggerated by returning sailors telling tall tales of their adventures. Writers and artists added more gruesome details to these descriptions and so the myths grew.

**DISCOVERIES**
Explorers took gold, treasure, and exciting new vegetables from the Americas to Europe; they also carried silks, jewels, and spices from the East. People in Europe were eager to obtain these and wanted more. This led to a great increase in trade with both East and West.

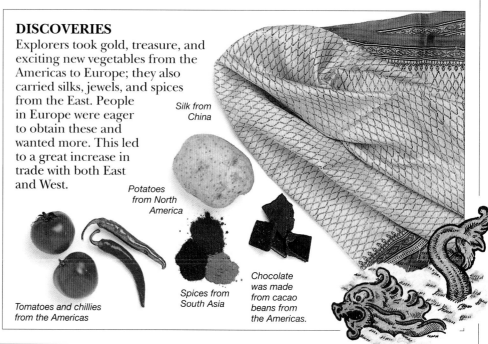

Silk from China

Potatoes from North America

Tomatoes and chillies from the Americas

Spices from South Asia

Chocolate was made from cacao beans from the Americas.

# INQUISITIVE EUROPEANS

Once Europeans had an idea of the correct shape of the world, they set out to explore it more thoroughly. Some were driven by curiosity, some by greed, and some by a desire to convert the peoples who lived in faraway places to Christianity. All faced hardships and dangers.

### SIR HENRY MORTON STANLEY (1841-1904)

Welshman Henry Stanley worked for a New York newspaper. He led an expedition into Africa to find the missing Scottish explorer David Livingstone. When he found him, he uttered the famous words "Dr. Livingstone, I presume?" Stanley later explored much of central Africa around Lake Victoria.

### MARY KINGSLEY (1862-1900)

A fearless and determined Englishwoman, Mary Kingsley travelled in West Africa, trading and making scientific studies. On her travels, she was entertained by cannibals. She was one of the first to demand fair treatment for the people of Africa by their colonial rulers.

### AMERIGO VESPUCCI (1451-1512)

The first European to explore the Brazilian coast, Italian-born Amerigo Vespucci gave his name to America. He was in charge of a school of navigation in Seville, Spain. Vespucci believed in a southwestern route to the Indies around South America.

### FERDINAND MAGELLAN (1480-1521)

Leader of the first European expedition to sail around the world, Portuguese explorer Magellan proved that there was a southwestern route to the Indies through the Pacific.

### VASCO DA GAMA (1469-1524)

Despite bad weather and hardships on the voyage, Portuguese-born Vasco da Gama reached the East African coast and proved that there was a southeastern route to India. He was the first European to sail around the southern tip of Africa.

*Marco Polo's journey from Italy to China lasted more than 24 years.*

Marco Polo leaving Venice

## WONDERS OF CHINA

On his travels, Marco Polo became a favourite of Kublai Khan, the Mongol ruler. Marco later published a detailed account of his journey and the wonders he had seen. Few believed the account and it was years before Europeans realized that he had experienced a great civilization – the empire of China.

## MARCO POLO

Marco Polo (1254-1324) was an Italian explorer. His father and uncle were merchants from Venice, Europe's greatest trading centre. They took the 17-year-old Marco with them on a journey from Italy to China.

---

***Find out more***

COLUMBUS, CHRISTOPHER
CONQUISTADORS
COOK, JAMES
POLAR EXPLORATION

# EYES

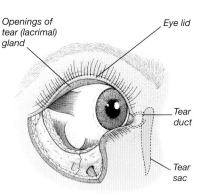

AS YOU READ THIS PAGE, you are using the two organs of sight – the eyes. Our eyes enable us to learn a great deal about the world around us. Each eyeball measures about 25 mm (1 in) across and sits in the front of the skull in the eye socket, or orbit. The eyes can swivel around in their sockets so that you can see things above, below, and to the side. Each eye has an adjustable lens and sees a slightly different view of the same scene. The eyes work together, controlled by the brain. This is called binocular vision. The lens of each eye allows rays of light to enter from the outside and project a picture onto the retina – the inner lining of the eye. The retina converts the light into nerve signals which travel along opticnerves to the brain, where images are formed.

**EAGLE SIGHT**
A golden eagle has the sharpest eyesight in the world. It can see rabbits and other prey from a distance of more than 1 km (half a mile).

Openings of tear (lacrimal) gland

Eye lid

Tear duct

Tear sac

**EYE SOCKETS**
The eyelid and eyelashes protect the front of the eye. When you blink, the eyelids sweep moisture over the eyeball, keeping it clean. The moisture is produced in the tear glands above the eyes. These glands also produce tears when you cry. Tiny holes called tear ducts drain the fluid into the tear sac, to the inside of the nose.

## OUTER EYE
Light rays enter the curved front of the eye called the cornea, where they are partly focused. They pass through the pupil, which enlarges in dim conditions to let in more light and shrinks in bright conditions to protect the inside of the eye from too much light. The rays are then focused onto the retina by the lens.

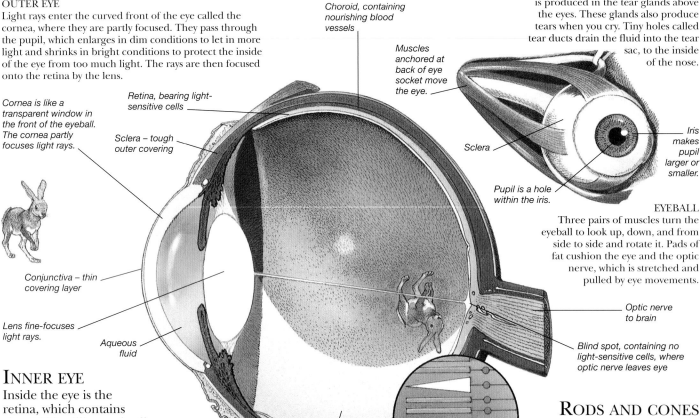

Choroid, containing nourishing blood vessels

Muscles anchored at back of eye socket move the eye.

Sclera

Pupil is a hole within the iris.

Iris makes pupil larger or smaller.

Cornea is like a transparent window in the front of the eyeball. The cornea partly focuses light rays.

Retina, bearing light-sensitive cells

Sclera – tough outer covering

Conjunctiva – thin covering layer

Lens fine-focuses light rays.

Aqueous fluid

Eye muscles

Vitreous fluid

**EYEBALL**
Three pairs of muscles turn the eyeball to look up, down, and from side to side and rotate it. Pads of fat cushion the eye and the optic nerve, which is stretched and pulled by eye movements.

Optic nerve to brain

Blind spot, containing no light-sensitive cells, where optic nerve leaves eye

## INNER EYE
Inside the eye is the retina, which contains about 120 million rod cells, mainly around the sides, and seven million cone cells, mainly at the back. When an image lands on the retina it is upside down, but nerve signals reaching the brain turn the image right side up.

## RODS AND CONES
The retina contains millions of light-sensitive cells called rods and cones. The rods are sensitive to black and white, and the cones are sensitive to different colours. Rods and cones produce nerve signals when light falls on them.

### CLEAR AND DEFECTIVE VISION
Clear vision depends on the lens bending light rays to the correct angle so that the rays form a sharp picture on the retina. In longsighted people, either the lens is too weak or the eyeball is too small for its focusing power. In the shortsighted, the lens is too strong, or the eyeball is too big. Glasses and artificial lenses, such as contact lenses, help the eye's own lens to focus the rays correctly, thus correcting defective vision.

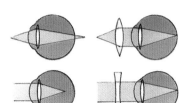

**LONGSIGHTEDNESS**
Rays are focused behind the retina. A convex lens corrects the focus.

**SHORTSIGHTEDNESS**
Rays are focused in front of retina. A concave lens corrects the focus.

---

***Find out more***
CAMERAS
COLOUR
EARS
HUMAN BODY
LIGHT

---

# FACTORIES

MILLIONS OF PEOPLE AROUND THE WORLD work in factories, making goods of all kinds from T-shirts to jumbo jets. Factories are buildings in which people work together on machines manufacturing, or producing, items for sale. The factory system began in Britain during the Industrial Revolution, when huge numbers of people moved from the country to towns to work in factories. Skilled craftworkers, who had produced handmade items in small workshops, were replaced by factory production lines of semi-skilled or unskilled workers, each performing a set task. One machine could do the work of many individuals, which greatly increased the number of goods that could be produced. Known as mass-production, this is the basis of modern manufacturing. Today, robots replace many factory workers.

VICTORIAN FACTORY
The first factories were noisy, unclean, and dangerous. Early factory workers included women and small children.

The car body travels down the assembly line between rows of robots, which weld it together.

Arm extends to car

HENRY FORD
US industrialist Henry Ford (1863-1947) pioneered assembly line mass-production. In 1913 he introduced assembly-line methods to make his new car, the Model T. The cars were pulled through the factory on trolleys. Workers stayed in the same place on the line, performing set tasks, as the vehicles moved past them.

## ROBOT ASSEMBLY LINE
In many car factories, computer-controlled machines, or robots, have replaced most of the workers on the assembly line. The machines can be programmed to perform a wide variety of tasks from painting to welding. They are expensive to buy, but, unlike human workers, can be set to work day and night with perfect accuracy.

FACTORY SHIP
Factory ships move to where the raw materials for their product – fish – can be found. Instead of having to come back to harbour to process the fish, they stay at sea for months at a time. Below decks, workers prepare and freeze the catch, which is then stored in the hold. Factory ships follow fish around the world's oceans.

CLEAN CHIP MANUFACTURE
While some factories are dirty and noisy, others need to be as clean as the operating theatre of a hospital. Computer chips are very delicate and are made in the cleanest conditions possible, to prevent them being damaged. Workers in computer chip factories wear protective clothes, and the whole building is sealed to prevent even dust getting in.

CHILD LABOUR
In the 1800s, politicians in Britain passed laws to protect women and children from exploitation by factory owners. Today, most indusrial nations have laws governing child labour. However, in some parts of the world, children still work in factories. They are employed because they provide very cheap labour.

### Find out more
FISHING INDUSTRY
INDUSTRIAL REVOLUTION
TRADE AND INDUSTRY

# FARM ANIMALS

Female sheep are called ewes, males are rams, and the young are called lambs.

Merino sheep have the best quality wool. The ancestor of today's Merino sheep is the Spanish Merino – a breed of sheep that is about 1,000 years old.

The Suffolk is an English breed that was first developed about 100 years ago.

Meat from adult sheep is called mutton.

Female chickens are called hens. Males, like the one shown here, are usually more colourful. They are called cocks, cockerels, or roosters.

HAMBURGERS, sausages, butter, and cheese are produced from animals that we keep on farms. Many other foods, including eggs, bacon, and yoghurt, also come from farm animals. Farm animals include pigs, cows, sheep, rabbits, goats, and chickens. People keep these animals for their meat, milk, fur, and skins. We use the skins, or hides, of cows, pigs, and sheep to make shoes, and the wool of sheep, goats, and rabbits to make clothes. People have been keeping animals on farms for at least 9,000 years. Many are kept in small enclosed areas called pens, others in fields, and still others in cages. The first farm animals were wild creatures that people captured and domesticated, or tamed. Today's chickens are descended from tropical forest birds of southeast Asia. Through the ages, farmers have bred (mated) the healthiest, most docile animals with the best milk, meat, or wool production, to produce the breeds that we know today.

The female pig is called a gilt before she has any young, and a sow once she has young. Male pigs are called boars.

AMERICAN HAMPSHIRE PIG
The American Hampshire pig has little fat on its body, so the pork and bacon from this pig are lean (that is, they have little fat).

The Rhode Island red is named after the state of Rhode Island in the United States. It is a good egg layer and is well known for its meat.

Chicks are sold for meat when they are about eight weeks old and weigh about 2 kg (4.5 lb).

## POULTRY

Many people keep chickens as a source of meat and eggs. These chickens scratch around in farmyards and fields, eating seeds, worms, insects, and scraps. They lay their eggs in a small chicken coop or any other secluded place. This is called free-range rearing – the chickens are able to wander freely. Most chickens are raised indoors, under controlled conditions.

PLYMOUTH ROCK
There are about 7,000 million chickens around the world, and about 500 breeds. The Leghorn is the most common egg-laying hen. The Plymouth rock shown here is a fast-growing chicken that produces tasty meat in a short time.

SHEEP
Wool comes from sheep, goats, rabbits, camels, alpacas, and vicunas. Young sheep, or lambs, produce the softest, finest wool. The largest flocks of sheep are in Australia, where there are about 140 million sheep. The sheep we farm for wool are sheared for their fleeces (coats) once a year. An expert shearer with electric clippers can shear one sheep every 40 seconds. The wool is washed and combed, then stretched and twisted into yarn for woollen fabric. Here, a woman in Nepal, Asia, is spinning wool by hand to make into carpets and rugs.

## INTENSIVE REARING

Some farm animals such as pigs and chickens are kept under controlled conditions in huge hangar-like buildings. Chickens are raised by the thousands in this way, for their meat or their eggs. These chickens sit in wire cages and cannot run around freely or scratch for their food. The food, temperature, and light in the building are controlled so that each chicken lays up to 300 eggs each year. Pigs are kept in pig units like the one shown here. They are fed an exact mixture of nutrients that makes them put on the most weight in the least time. Some kinds of pigs gain more than 0.7 kg (1.5 lb) in weight each day. A pig may be sold for pork when it is only three months old.

## PIG

There are about 400 million pigs in Asia, and another 400 million scattered around the rest of the world. Some pigs are allowed to roam freely to feed on roots, worms, and household scraps; others are kept inside buildings (see above). There are more than 80 breeds of pigs, and some of the largest weigh more than 200 kg (450 lb). Almost every part of a pig can be eaten, including the trotters, or feet. Pork is the name for fresh pig meat; cured or preserved pig meat is called bacon or ham.

### ZEBU

Cattle are the most numerous of farm animals, with 200 million in India and about 1,000 million in the rest of the world. They were first used to pull carts. Today some cattle are bred for their meat (beef breeds), others for their milk (dairy breeds), and some for both (dual-purpose breeds). There are about 200 breeds of cattle. The zebu cattle shown here have a hump at the shoulders, and a long, narrow face. They were originally from India and are suited to hot climates. Zebu are also used to pull ploughs.

## TURKEY

Today's most common breed of turkey is the White Holland, which was developed from the bronze turkey, shown here. Turkeys came originally from North America. When Europeans first travelled to North America in the 16th century, they domesticated (tamed) turkeys and took some back to Europe.

*Every year on 25 December, millions of turkeys are eaten in celebration of Christmas.*

### DUCKS AND GEESE

Waterfowl such as ducks and geese are kept mainly for their meat, especially in Southeast Asia. They also provide fluffy down (underfeathers) for stuffing mattresses, quilts, and clothing. Geese are good guards in the farmyard, as they hiss at strangers. The most common egg-laying waterfowl are Indian runner ducks, khaki campbell ducks, and Emden and Chinese geese.

*Male turkeys, or toms, are often twice the weight of the female hens. Young turkeys are called poults.*

*In many parts of the world, people keep goats for their milk, which is made into cheese and yoghurt.*

*The Toulouse goose, from France, looks like its wild ancestor, the greylag goose. Adult birds weigh more than 13 kg (28 lb).*

*The Indian runner duck is kept in large flocks and can move swiftly on its long legs.*

## GOAT

The goat was one of the first animals to be domesticated. Goats feed on thorny bushes, spiky grasses, and woody stems, and they can leap up easily into the branches of small trees to eat the leaves. Almost 500 million goats are kept worldwide, often in dry and mountainous regions. They are used for their milk, meat, skins, and wool. The main dairy breed is the Anglo-Nubian, which produces up to 660 litres (1,200 pints) of milk each year.

---

### Find out more

COWS, CATTLE,
and buffaloes
DUCKS, GEESE, AND SWANS
FARMING
FARMING, HISTORY OF
HORSES, ZEBRAS, AND ASSES
MOUNTAIN WILDLIFE

---

# FARMING

TO STOCK THE FOOD SHELVES of supermarkets in the world, farmers make nature and technology work in harmony. They use machinery to plough and reap great fields of wheat; they fertilize and irrigate greenhouses full of vegetables and orchards of fruit; and they rear animals indoors to fatten them quickly. Through this intensive agriculture, Western farmers feed up to ten people from land that once fed one. However, not all the world's farmers can be so productive. Those who have plots on hilly land cannot use machines. Instead they graze a few animals or cultivate the land with inefficient hand tools. Farmers in dry climates must be content with lower yields or choose less productive crops that will tolerate dry soil. And farmers who cannot afford machines and fertilizers are forced to use slower farming methods that have not changed for centuries.

## SUBSISTENCE FARMING

In some developing countries, most farming families grow only sufficient food for themselves. This is called subsistence farming. In a good year it provides enough food for all. But a drought or an increase in the population may lead to famine and starvation.

Superwheat

## CROPS

Almost all crops that are grown today are the descendants of wild plants. However, special breeding has created varieties that give high harvests. Grain crops such as wheat have especially benefitted. Modern varieties have much larger grains than traditional species. However, this new "superwheat" is not as resistant to disease as other varieties and must be grown carefully.

Ordinary wheat

Ploughing

Planting seeds

Harvesting

Spraying

## FARM MACHINERY

Modern grain farming requires special machinery at different times of the year. In spring a plough breaks the soil into furrows for planting. A seed drill puts a measured amount of seed into the prepared soil and covers the seed so that birds do not eat it. A sprayer covers crops with pesticides to kill harmful diseases and pests. Finally a combine harvester cuts the crop and prepares it for storage.

*A baler rolls up the straw – the cut stalks of wheat left after the grain has been harvested – and ties it into tight round bundles called bales.*

## ORGANIC FARMING

Some farmers in Western countries prefer to grow crops and raise animals in a natural or organic way. They do not use artificial pesticides or fertilizers. Organic food is more expensive, but it may be healthier to eat.

*Organic farmers use natural fertilizers such as seaweed or animal dung to make the soil more productive.*

## INTENSIVE FARMING

The purpose of intensive farming is to increase the production of crops and animals, and to cut food prices. Food animals such as chickens and pigs are kept indoors in tiny, overcrowded pens. Many people feel this is unnatural and cruel, and prefer to eat only "free-range" animals – animals that have been allowed to move freely in the farm.

*In intensive chicken houses conveyor belts carry food to the hens in the crowded cages, and take away the eggs.*

### Find out more
FARM ANIMALS
FARMING, HISTORY OF

# HISTORY OF
# FARMING

## EARLY FARMING

The first farmers domesticated (tamed) wild animals and kept them in herds to provide meat, milk, hides, and wool. Some people became nomadic herders rather than farmers; they moved their animals continuously in search of new pasture. The picture shown here was painted in a cave in the Sahara Desert in Africa about 8,000 years ago, at a time when the desert was grassland.

GROWING CROPS and breeding animals for food are among the most important steps ever taken by humankind. Before farming began, people fed themselves by gathering berries and other plant matter and hunting wild animals. People were nomadic – they had to move around to find food. About 12,000 years ago in the Middle East, people discovered they could grow cereal crops, such as wheat. These people were the first farmers. With the start of farming, people began to settle permanently in one place. Villages grew into towns and cities. Farmers produced enough food to support the population, so some people were free to do other jobs such as weaving, and making pottery and tools. Since everyone depended on farming for their food, however, many people died of starvation when the crops failed because of bad weather. Over the centuries people have tried many different ways of producing better crops. In the agricultural revolution of the 1700s, new scientific methods helped overcome the problem of crop failure. Today, farming is a huge international industry.

## CROP GROWING

In about 10,000 B.C., farmers in the Middle East began to plant crops to provide food. Cereals, such as wheat, barley, millet, and corn, were the main crops. In the Far East, people first grew rice in about 5,000 B.C.

*The huge Berkshire pig was first bred for meat in the 18th century.*

## IRRIGATION

Farmers need a good supply of water for their crops. In China and other Far Eastern countries, where rice is the main crop, water flows along channels on the terraced hillsides to make the paddies for growing rice.

## MEDIEVAL FARMING

In the 11th century the hard horse collar came to Europe from China. It allowed horses, rather than oxen, to pull ploughs. By the 13th century, European farms consisted of open fields and each peasant farmer had a piece of land. Later, much of the land was enclosed with ditches or hedges.

## MECHANIZATION

During the 19th century, the development of steam power and, in the 20th century, the combustion engine changed agriculture forever. Tractors replaced horses as the main source of power, and railroads and refrigerated ships meant that food could be transported all over the world.

Seed drill

Steam tractor

## AGRICULTURAL REVOLUTION

During the 18th century, new methods of agricultural production were developed and breeds of livestock were improved, such as the huge Berkshire pig (above). The invention of new machines, such as the seed drill, allowed farmers to produce more crops.

*Find out more*
ENGINES
FARM ANIMALS
FARMING

# FESTIVALS

ALL OVER THE WORLD people set aside special times during the year for festivals and feasts. Most of these celebrations are linked to a society's religious or other beliefs. Festivals also celebrate the changing seasons and special events in a country's history. Rituals such as singing or exchanging gifts often form part of annual festivals, and in many societies certain actions, pictures, and objects take on a special meaning at festival time. For instance, at Chinese New Year golden fish become symbols of wealth. Very different cultures sometimes share the same symbols in their festivals: Christians light candles at Christmas, and Hindus do the same at their festival of Diwali. Dressing up in elaborate costumes and sharing meals are festive activities common to many parts of the world.

**MAYPOLE**
In Britain, young people once celebrated the coming of spring by dancing around a maypole. This was usually a hawthorn or may tree decorated with blossoms and ribbons for the May Day festival.

*The procession is lit by lanterns.*

*People set off crackling fireworks.*

## CHINESE NEW YEAR
New Year in the Chinese calendar falls in late January or early February. Chinese people living in the rest of the world remember the customs of their homeland by holding processions led by huge dragons, and by exploding firecrackers.

**CARNIVALS**
Carnivals began in Roman Catholic countries such as Mexico as a way of using up foods that were forbidden during the fast of Lent, which precedes Easter. At the famous Mardi Gras in New Orleans, Louisiana, United States, the streets are filled with music, dancing, and long processions of people wearing colourful costumes.

## THANKSGIVING
In the autumn of 1621 a group of European settlers in North America celebrated their first harvest by inviting the Native Americans to join them in a thanksgiving feast because the Native Americans had taught them how to grow the native crops. Today families gather together on Thanksgiving Day, a national holiday celebrated in November, to share the traditional dinner of turkey and pumpkin pie.

**HALLOWEEN**
Lighting candles inside frightening pumpkin faces scares away evil spirits at Halloween, 31 October.

---

### *Find out more*
BUDDHISM
CHRISTIANITY
HINDUISM
ISLAM
JUDAISM
RELIGIONS

# FILMS

IN A PARIS café in December 1895, people sat down to watch the world's first motion picture. It was shown by two French brothers, Louis and Auguste Lumière, and though it consisted only of a few short, simple scenes, films have been popular ever since. The first films were silent, with titles on the screen to explain the story. A pianist accompanied the film with the right type of music – for example, fast and furious music during a chase scene. The United States took the lead in making films. Soon the public began to select its favourite actors and actresses, and the first film stars were created, such as Rudolph Valentino. In 1927, the first full-length "talkie" – film with sound – was shown, and from then on the public would settle for nothing less. Technical improvements continued. In the United States, Metro-Goldwyn-Mayer and a few other powerful studios made 95 per cent of the films. During the 1950s, television captured people's attention and the film industry went into decline. In recent years films have become popular again. Russia, Germany, France, and Japan have produced films that have influenced filmmaking throughout the world, and there are many national film industries.

CHARLIE CHAPLIN
The British actor Charles Chaplin (1889-1977) created a movie character that touched the hearts of millions: a silent little tramp with a funny walk.

HOLLYWOOD
Southern California, United States, had the ideal climate and scenery for making films. Between 1907 and 1913 a Los Angeles district called Hollywood became the centre of the American film industry. Not all stars were human: King Kong (above) was an animated model.

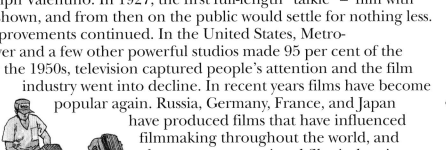
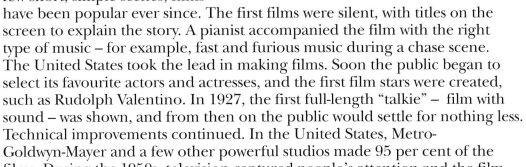

The senior electrician on the film set is called the gaffer.

Teams of expert makeup artists and dressers prepare an actress or actor for a day's shoot.

The art director designs the sets and chooses suitable locations for filming away from the studio.

A continuity worker makes sure that scenes shot out of order match each other. He or she notes the details of each shot, to ensure that there are no mistakes when the scenes are put in order.

Sound technicians follow the actors with microphones suspended from long poles (booms).

Lighting experts operate huge lamps, to ensure that the light looks as natural as possible in a film. Lighting is needed on location as well as in the studio.

The producer chooses the script, finds financial backing, picks the director and the technical teams, oversees the filming, and organizes publicity.

The director guides the actors' performances, the action, and the camera angles, and gives the film its style and character.

The cinematographer leads a team which also includes the camera operator and camera assistants, who help with focusing, load magazines, and operate the clapper board. Workers called grips move the camera down tracks or rails for the camera to run along smoothly.

## FILM SET

Set builders make film sets – from city streets to tropical jungles – inside huge buildings like aircraft hangars, or outdoors on studio grounds. Hundreds of people are involved in getting things ready for the first filming of the day. When all is satisfactory, a red warning light goes on, the studio is told to stand by for a take (an attempt at a scene), sound and cameras roll, and the director shouts "Action!"

Acting on the big screen is very different from the theatre. In close-ups, every movement can be seen, and actors have to play their part with subtle facial expressions. They must also be able to act the story out of sequence.

Stuntmen and stuntwomen take the place of actors in dangerous action. They risk their lives performing stunts, such as falling from a great height, crashing a car, or leaping from a moving train.

## SPECIAL EFFECTS

Special effects have created a vast new fantasy world in films. In a technique known as back projection, first used as early as 1913, the cinematographer projected a previously filmed background onto a screen from behind. Actors or models were then filmed in front of the screen, giving the impression that they were actually at that location. Glass screens painted with realistic backgrounds, studio sets wired up with controlled explosions, special smoke and wind machines, and stop-frame animation of models were all used to help bring make-believe scenes to life. As recently as the 1970s, life-like models were still being filmed in a studio to produce gruesome horror effects, such as the shark in *Jaws*, and convincing space battles, such as those in *Star Wars*. Today, almost all of these effects are created digitally using powerful computers.

*The actors are filmed against a background of solid blue or green colour.*

### "BULLET-TIME" SLOW MOTION EFFECT

Each small hole in the scene above conceals a still camera taking a picture of the scene from a different angle. The series of shots is put together in sequence on computer, along with thousands of extra "in-between" frames created in software. The effect is of the camera moving around the action in extreme slow motion.

*The actors are superimposed on a new background, and the wires supporting them are erased.*

*On computer, the coloured background is easily removed using a software filter – sometimes called "Chromakey".*

## SPIELBERG

Directors often become "stars" in their own right. Director Steven Spielberg was born in 1946. He shot his first film when he was 12 and won a contract with Universal Studios, Hollywood, after leaving college. He became the most successful American director of the 1970s, 1980s, and 1990s with blockbusters such as *Jaws* (1975) and *Jurassic Park* (1993), and Oscar winners such as *Schindler's List* (1993).

# DIGITAL TRICKERY

Digital video editing software allows moviemakers to insert actors into almost any environment imaginable. Actors are filmed in front of a green or blue "matte" background, which is later replaced with a new scene – one either filmed elsewhere or created on computer. Real people can also be combined with computer-generated characters and models, as in *Harry Potter*, and whole armies can be created that have an "artificial life" entirely of their own, as in *Lord of the Rings*.

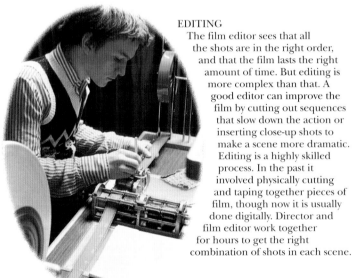

### EDITING

The film editor sees that all the shots are in the right order, and that the film lasts the right amount of time. But editing is more complex than that. A good editor can improve the film by cutting out sequences that slow down the action or inserting close-up shots to make a scene more dramatic. Editing is a highly skilled process. In the past it involved physically cutting and taping together pieces of film, though now it is usually done digitally. Director and film editor work together for hours to get the right combination of shots in each scene.

### DUBBING

The sound editor is responsible for assembling the soundtrack for the film. This consists of dozens of separate tracks, including all the dialogue, music, sound effects, and background sound. After editing, these sounds have to be balanced against each other and blended in a process called dubbing. Technicians known as mixers watch the film and operate controls on a sound console to get perfect timing and balance of sounds.

### FILMS

**1895** First public film show held in Paris.

**1905** In the United States the first nickelodeon film theatre opens.

**1907** Hollywood founded.

**1927** *The Jazz Singer* (USA) is the first full-length film with sound.

**1929** First Academy Awards.

**1928** American cartoonist Walt Disney (1901-66) launches his most popular cartoon character, Mickey Mouse, in the film *Steamboat Willie*.

**1935** First full-spectrum Technicolor feature, *Becky Sharp*, is released.

**1947-54** House Un-American Activities Committee investigates Communists in Hollywood.

**1953** First CinemaScope (wide screen) movie, *The Robe*, released.

**1995** *Toy Story*, first completely computer-animated feature film, released.

---

*Find out more*

CAMERAS
CARTOONS
TELEVISION AND VIDEO
THEATRE

# FIRE

A BOLT OF LIGHTNING hitting a tree, or the red-hot lava from a volcano, can start a fire in seconds. It was probably from natural events such as these that prehistoric people discovered fire about one million years ago. Later they learned how to make fire for themselves by rubbing sticks together or by striking certain stones, such as flint. Today, fire is useful to us in many ways. The heat from fire cooks food, warms homes, and provides energy in engines and power stations. Fire is the heat and light that are produced when something burns. Burning occurs when a substance rapidly combines with oxygen gas, which makes up about one fifth of the air around us. Each material has a certain temperature, called its ignition temperature, above which it will burst into flame. Once it is burning, it produces so much heat of its own that it continues to burn. When fire gets out of control, it can be very dangerous. Every year, fires kill and injure thousands of people and cause great damage to property.

A cage raised on a long motorized boom carries firefighters high in the air to rescue people and spray water or foam over the flames.

## MATCHES
Fire requires three things: fuel, heat, and oxygen. To produce fire we rub the match against the box to produce heat. The heat makes chemicals in the head of the match burst into flame as they combine with oxygen from the air.

## FIRE ENGINE
There are several kinds of fire engine. All contain powerful pumps that force water through hoses at high pressure.

*Fire engines carry ladders, oxygen tanks, lamps, crowbars, and many other items of equipment that the fire crew may need as they fight a fire.*

When people are trapped by fire, firemen use tools such as hatchets to break open windows and doors. Firefighters wear strong fireproof and waterproof clothing and breathe with the aid of oxygen tanks so they can work in smoke or fumes.

*Fire produces smoke, ash, and dangerous gases that can make people collapse or die.*

*Water tank contains a limited supply of water for the hoses.*

### FIRE HYDRANT
Fire hydrants, like large taps on the street, provide unlimited water from the city supply for fighting fires.

## HOW FIRES SPREAD
Fires are often the result of carelessness: a smouldering match or cigarette left on the ground has caused many huge forest fires. Once started, a fire can spread in three ways. Currents of hot air can carry burning fragments that start new fires. Heat radiation from the flames can set nearby objects alight. And metal objects can conduct the heat of a fire to another place, starting a new fire.

*In 1988, huge forest fires occurred in Yellowstone National Park, United States.*

## FIRE BRIGADE
Firefighters are specially trained to put out fires quickly and safely. They race to the scene of a fire as soon as the alarm is raised. The firefighters' first task is to rescue people who are trapped in a burning building. Then they pump water or foam over the flames to put out the fire.

*Squeezing the handle punctures a cylinder of compressed carbon dioxide gas. The gas expands and forces the water out of the nozzle.*

*Water should never be used on electrical fires because water conducts electricity.*

### FIRE EXTINGUISHER
There are different kinds of fire extinguisher for tackling different kinds of fire. A water extinguisher puts out wood and paper fires because it removes heat from the flames. Other types, such as foam extinguishers, kill fire by smothering it and depriving it of oxygen.

*Firefighters may give oxygen to people who have breathed in too much smoke.*

---

***Find out more***
HEAT
OXYGEN
PREHISTORIC PEOPLES

# FIRE OF LONDON

IN 1666, THE WORST FIRE IN LONDON'S HISTORY raged for five days. It destroyed most of the business part of the city, wiped out 13,200 houses, 87 churches, including St Paul's Cathedral, and dozens of important halls and public buildings. Surprisingly, only nine people were killed. King Charles II and his brother the Duke of York took charge of fighting the fire. They stopped it from spreading further by blowing up houses in its path. Thousands of people were made homeless and had to camp in fields outside the city. However, the fire did destroy the rats that spread the terrible bubonic plague and the unhealthy buildings where the disease thrived. After the fire, the architect Sir Christopher Wren suggested a new layout for the city, but it was rejected by business men. Wren was also responsible for rebuilding St Paul's and more than 50 other churches. Diarist Samuel Pepys left a vivid account of the fire.

A plague doctor

## THE GREAT PLAGUE
In 1664-65, bubonic plague, the Black Death, swept through London, killing nearly 70,000 people. Doctors wore leather clothing, gloves, and bird-like masks to protect themselves. The beaks were stuffed with medicinal herbs to prevent the doctors catching the plague.

### SAMUEL PEPYS
Pepys (1633-1703) was a civil servant at the Admiralty, and worked hard to make sure that England had a powerful navy. He is famous for his diary, which contains accounts of the Great Plague and the Great Fire. Pepys took the news of the fire to King Charles II, who acted quickly to fight it.

Old St Paul's Cathedral had been on the site since 1087.

Many people took to boats on the river to escape the flames.

Fire burned houses at the northern side of London Bridge.

## HOW IT STARTED
The fire began very early on 2 September 1666, in Farriner's baker's shop in Pudding Lane. In those days most of the houses in London were built of wood, and were huddled close together in narrow streets. This allowed the fire to spread quickly. The warehouses on the banks of the River Thames were full of oil, tar, and corn. They too were wooden, and flames soon engulfed them. A Frenchman, Robert Hubert, later confessed to starting the fire. He was hanged.

A flaming urn, made of gilt bronze, tops the Monument.

## THE MONUMENT
The government decided to build a memorial to remember the fire. Called the Monument, it was finished in 1677. It is nearly 62 m (203 ft) high, and stands the same distance west of the place where the fire started. It is the world's tallest free-standing stone column. People can climb the 311 steps to a viewing gallery.

The River Thames was a barrier that helped stop the spread of fire.

Houses and buildings on the south side of the river escaped fire.

The Monument

Old St. Paul's Cathedral

## OLD ST PAUL'S
Old St Paul's was the fourth cathedral built on the site. Fire and Viking invaders destroyed the others. By 1664, the cathedral was in a very bad state, and repairs had begun in 1666, supervised by Sir Christopher Wren (1632-1723). When the fire destroyed the old building, Wren designed a new one.

*Find out more*
ARCHITECTURE
BLACK DEATH
STUARTS

# FIRST AID

IN AN EMERGENCY, quick, calm help is vital. For example, someone who chokes on food cannot wait for a doctor. Instead, non-medical people close by must remove the obstruction immediately so that the choking person can breathe. This sort of rapid treatment is called first aid, and it varies depending on the injury. For slight injuries such as cuts, a doctor may not be needed. Instead, first aid consists of cleaning the wound and applying a bandage. Some accidents result in broken bones. Then first aid involves keeping the injured person calm and still, and getting him or her to a hospital. And in a major emergency, such as a traffic accident or a heart attack, first aid may involve re-starting the injured person's heart while waiting for an ambulance. Unskilled first aid can do more harm than good, but training is easy. A course lasting half a day is enough to learn skills that could help you save lives.

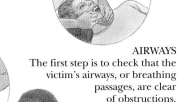

### AIRWAYS
The first step is to check that the victim's airways, or breathing passages, are clear of obstructions.

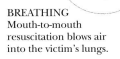

### BREATHING
Mouth-to-mouth resuscitation blows air into the victim's lungs.

### CIRCULATION
Checking circulation means making sure that the heart is pumping blood and that there is no bleeding. Cardiac massage (left) can help to restart the heart.

## FIRST-AID TECHNIQUES
Skilled first aid means learning basic skills and staying calm in an emergency. Important techniques involve helping an unconscious person whose heart or breathing has stopped, and preventing severe loss of blood. When treating someone who has lost consciousness, trained first aiders follow the ABC code, as shown above.

### PARAMEDICS
At the scene of an accident, paramedics give emergency treatment to the injured. Paramedics are highly trained first-aid professionals. Their emergency ambulances contain life-saving equipment such as defibrillator machines, which are used to restart the hearts of heart attack victims. Paramedics save many lives because treatment begins immediately, even before the patient reaches the hospital.

### RED CROSS
The sign of a red cross is recognized everywhere. The Red Cross organization began in Europe in the 19th century. Today, members of the Red Cross teach first aid, collect blood for transfusions, and carry out welfare work.

## FIRST-AID KIT
Every home and car should have a first-aid kit containing items needed for emergency treatment. Keep the box clean and dry and clearly labelled. Replace items as soon as you use them or if the protective seal is accidentally broken.

*Cotton wool is useful for cleaning wounds.*

*Tweezers for removing splinters*

*Scissors for cutting bandages*

*Different kinds of injuries require a variety of dressings and bandages.*

*Adhesive tape and safety pins hold dressings in place.*

*Adhesive dressings protect small cuts and scrapes while they heal.*

*Eye bath is useful for washing the eye clean of foreign bodies.*

*Elastic bandages stretch to provide support for sprained ankles.*

*Antiseptic cream guards minor cuts against infection.*

---

***Find out more***
DISEASE
HEALTH AND FITNESS
HOSPITALS
MEDICINE

# FISH

## FEATURES OF A FISH

The cod has all the features of a typical fish – a streamlined body for speed, a powerful tail, and fins for balance and steering. The lateral line along the body is a row of sense organs. These organs detect movements made by other creatures in the water.

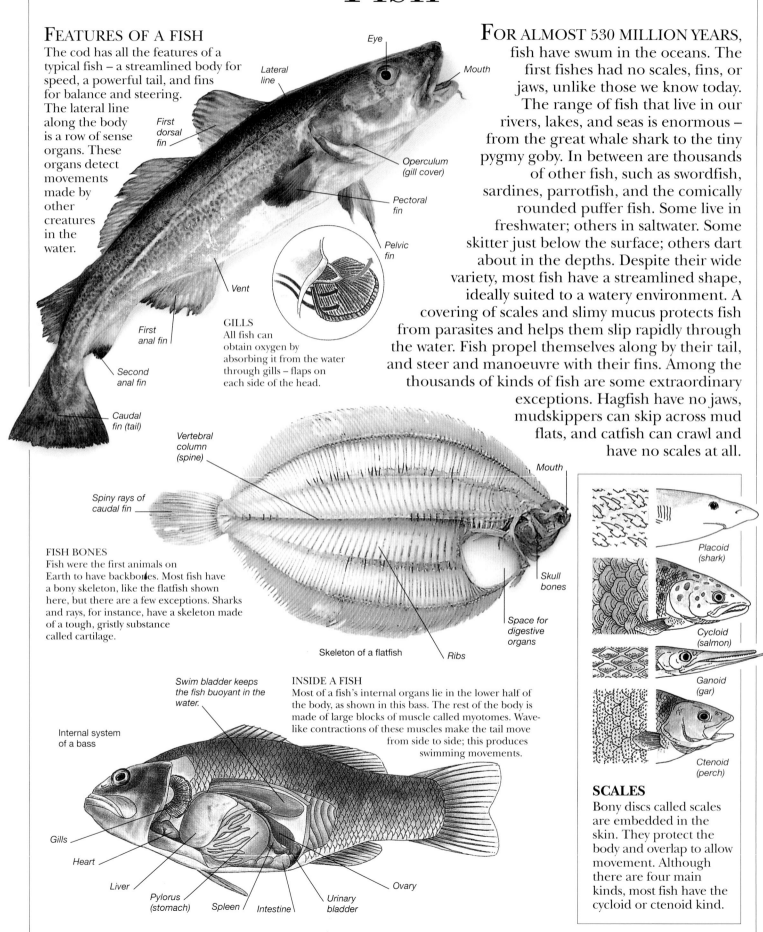

*Eye*

*Mouth*

*Lateral line*

*First dorsal fin*

*Operculum (gill cover)*

*Pectoral fin*

*Pelvic fin*

*Vent*

*First anal fin*

*Second anal fin*

*Caudal fin (tail)*

### GILLS
All fish can obtain oxygen by absorbing it from the water through gills – flaps on each side of the head.

FOR ALMOST 530 MILLION YEARS, fish have swum in the oceans. The first fishes had no scales, fins, or jaws, unlike those we know today. The range of fish that live in our rivers, lakes, and seas is enormous – from the great whale shark to the tiny pygmy goby. In between are thousands of other fish, such as swordfish, sardines, parrotfish, and the comically rounded puffer fish. Some live in freshwater; others in saltwater. Some skitter just below the surface; others dart about in the depths. Despite their wide variety, most fish have a streamlined shape, ideally suited to a watery environment. A covering of scales and slimy mucus protects fish from parasites and helps them slip rapidly through the water. Fish propel themselves along by their tail, and steer and manoeuvre with their fins. Among the thousands of kinds of fish are some extraordinary exceptions. Hagfish have no jaws, mudskippers can skip across mud flats, and catfish can crawl and have no scales at all.

*Vertebral column (spine)*

*Spiny rays of caudal fin*

*Mouth*

### FISH BONES
Fish were the first animals on Earth to have backbones. Most fish have a bony skeleton, like the flatfish shown here, but there are a few exceptions. Sharks and rays, for instance, have a skeleton made of a tough, gristly substance called cartilage.

*Skull bones*

*Space for digestive organs*

Skeleton of a flatfish

*Ribs*

*Placoid (shark)*

*Cycloid (salmon)*

*Ganoid (gar)*

*Ctenoid (perch)*

*Swim bladder keeps the fish buoyant in the water.*

### INSIDE A FISH
Most of a fish's internal organs lie in the lower half of the body, as shown in this bass. The rest of the body is made of large blocks of muscle called myotomes. Wave-like contractions of these muscles make the tail move from side to side; this produces swimming movements.

*Internal system of a bass*

*Gills*

*Heart*

*Liver*

*Pylorus (stomach)*

*Spleen*

*Intestine*

*Urinary bladder*

*Ovary*

### SCALES
Bony discs called scales are embedded in the skin. They protect the body and overlap to allow movement. Although there are four main kinds, most fish have the cycloid or ctenoid kind.

## STRANGELY SHAPED FISH

Each kind of fish is suited to its own way of life. The butterfly fish uses its long nose to pick food from crevices in rocks. Flying fish use their enlarged fins as "wings" for gliding as they leap out of the water. The bright colours on a lionfish warn other creatures of the deadly poison in its fin spines.

Lionfish

Flying fish

Long-nosed butterfly fish

## SCHOOL OF FISH

Small fish often live in large groups called schools, or shoals, twisting and turning together as they search for food. A predator is sometimes so confused by their numbers and quick, darting movements that it cannot single out a fish to attack.

School of sea goldfish on a Red Sea coral reef

## FEEDING

Fast predatory fish such as barracudas have long, slim, streamlined bodies and sharp teeth. Slower swimmers usually have more rounded bodies. Despite its shape, the parrotfish is an agile swimmer. It slips through cracks in the rock in search of food.

*Parrotfish eating algae on a coral reef*

Sea horses

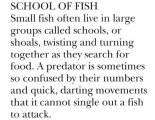

*Sea horses use their tails to cling to seaweed.*

## SEA HORSE

Sea horse eggs are deposited by the female into the male's front pouch, where they develop for about four weeks. When the eggs hatch, the young sea horses emerge from the pouch.

## BREEDING

Most fish reproduce by depositing their eggs and sperm in the water, then leave the fertilized eggs to develop into fish. Some fish, such as sticklebacks and bowfins, look after the eggs and the young (called fry) once they have hatched. Other fish, such as some types of sharks, give birth to fully formed young fish after the eggs have developed in the mother's body.

### MOUTHBREEDERS

The cichlid fish, found in African lakes, keeps its eggs safe inside its mouth. When the young hatch they swim out, then return to the parent's mouth for safety.

Cichlid fish and young

## EUROPEAN EELS

Adult eels lay eggs in the Sargasso Sea. The eggs hatch into larvae which swim north for the next three years. Upon reaching reach Europe they change into elvers and swim up streams. There, they grow into yellow eels, then adults.

*Yellow eels change into adult eels, then return to the Sargasso Sea to breed.*

*Larvae swim north and change into elvers.*

*Eggs develop into larvae.*

*Young elvers travel inland along rivers, where they change into yellow eels.*

Royal gramma fish

## TROPICAL OCEAN FISH

Fish, especially those from tropical waters, are among the brightest of all animals. Their dazzling colours and lively patterns have many different purposes. They help fish hide from predators among the coral, warn neighbouring fish to keep out of their territory, show other creatures that they are poisonous, or advertise for a mate.

---

*Find out more*

ANIMALS
DEEP-SEA WILDLIFE
MIGRATION, ANIMAL
OCEAN WILDLIFE
SEASHORE WILDLIFE

---

# FISHING INDUSTRY

THE WORLD'S RIVERS, seas, and oceans provide one of the most important of all foods. Fish are a rich source of protein and other vital nutrients. It is possible to catch a few fish using just a hook on the end of a piece of string. But to feed large numbers of people, a huge industry exists to catch millions of fish. Japanese fishing boats, for instance, catch more than 35,500 tonnes (35,000 tons) of fish each day. Fishing fleets use different methods to catch these vast numbers of fish, such as nets, traps, and hooks. Some nets are several miles long and can catch more than 100 million fish in one haul. Baskets, boxes, and other traps are left in the sea for shellfish, such as crabs, lobsters, and crayfish. Hooks are arranged in a longline – a single line carrying hundreds of hooks – that is attached to a fishing boat and can trap huge numbers of fish at one time.

### WHALING
For two centuries whaling has been a major industry and has made some species of whale almost extinct. As whales come to the surface to breathe, whale hunters shoot them with harpoons – huge explosive arrows fired from guns.

*Drift nets are up to 100 km (60 miles) long. They catch fish very effectively, but may also harm other marine life.*

### FISHING GROUNDS
Fishing boats catch most fish near the coast in the seas above the continental shelf (shown in the dark blue on the map). This shelf is an extension of the continents covered by shallow sea water. Deep-water currents rich in nutrients rise onto the shelf and create good feeding grounds for fish.

*At night lights attract fish into the dip nets.*

*The purse seiner tows its net in a huge circle to enclose the fish.*

### SEA FISHING
Seines are nets that float down from the surface. Drawing the net into a circle around a school, or group, of fish forms a huge bag which encloses the catch. Gill nets are long curtains of net which trap fish by the gills. Some gill nets float on the surface as drift nets; others are fixed to the sea bottom with anchors. A trawl is a large net bag towed behind a boat. Dip nets are hung over the side of the fishing boat on a frame. Lifting the frame catches the fish.

*Weights keep the mouth of the trawl net open.*

### FREEZING FISH
Once a fish is dead, its flesh quickly rots. Freezing, canning, drying, smoking, and pickling all slow the decay and preserve the fish. Freezing is the best method. Large fishing boats have freezing plants on board to preserve the catch – the harvest of fish – before returning to port.

### FISH FARMS
Not all fish are caught in the wild. Some fish, such as carp, salmon, trout, and shellfish, can be bred in controlled conditions on fish farms. In the United States, fish farmers raise catfish for food. Fish farmers build pens in lakes, ponds, or estuaries (river mouths). They hatch fish from eggs, then keep the fish until they are big enough to sell.

*Find out more*
FARMING
FISH
FOOD AND FOOD TECHNOLOGY
OCEAN WILDLIFE

# FLAGS

The cap provides a neat, decorative top to the flagpole.

Flags can be any shape, but most national flags are rectangular.

The edge of the flag is the part most exposed to the wind, so it will be the first to show wear and tear.

The sleeve or heading is made of tough material into which the hoist rope is sewn.

The halyard is the long rope used to raise the flag.

BRIGHTLY COLOURED FLAGS, flying in the wind, have special meanings. They are used to send messages, greet the winner of a race, or encourage people to fight for their country. Every nation now has its own flag, which is a symbol of that country. Most organizations, such as the International Red Cross, also have their own flags. A flag is a piece of cloth with an easily recognized pattern. One edge is fixed to a pole, and the rest flaps freely. Flags have always been important in battles. The leader of each warring army carried a flag. In the confusion of war, soldiers looked for their flag to see where their leader was. Capturing the enemy's flag often meant winning the battle. Before telephones or radio were invented, flags were a quick way to send messages. Today, signal flags are rarely used, but some flag codes have kept their meaning. Waving a white flag in war means that you want to surrender. And flying a flag halfway up the mast is a sign of respect for someone who has died.

## NATIONAL FLAGS

The flags of many nations have symbols to represent the qualities or traditions of the country and its people. The Australian flag has a Union Jack – the British flag – to show the country's historic connection with Great Britain. The small stars on the flag are in the shape of the constellation *Crux Australis* (Southern Cross), which is visible only in the Southern Hemisphere.

### CHECKERED FLAG

Waving a black and white checkered flag at the end of an auto race shows that the winner has crossed the finish line. Other flags are used as signals to drivers in car racing. A black flag indicates that the driver must make a pit stop. A yellow and red striped flag warns drivers that there is oil on the track. A red flag tells drivers to stop at once.

### FLYING FLAGS

Flags make impressive decorations when they fly in a group in front of a building. Important buildings belonging to international organizations, such as the United Nations, may fly the flags of all their different members. Similar rows of flags brighten up hotels, supermarkets, and factories.

### SIGNAL FLAGS

One of the earliest uses of flags was to send signals at sea. There was a flag for each letter of the alphabet and each number. Signalers spelled out words or used special combinations of flags to represent whole words. In the message above, for instance, "have" or "they have" is spelled with the flags for A, E, and L.

*End of message flag*

### SEMAPHORE

With just two flags a signaler can spell out messages. Each flag position represents a different letter of the alphabet or a number. This system is called semaphore. Using large, plain, but colourful flags, messages can be sent over long distances, as far as the eye can see.

C      E      X

N
D
Q

Sharks

A
E
L

Have

F
L
G

Eaten

R
K
D

My

C
T
W

Captain

Find out more

KNIGHTS AND HERALDRY
NAVIES
SHIPS AND BOATS

# FLIES AND MOSQUITOES

*Housefly can walk upside down.*

SOME OF THE SMALLEST creatures in the world are the most dangerous to humans. Flies and mosquitoes carry some of the world's most serious diseases. With their habit of sucking blood and scavenging on rubbish, many of these insects spread cholera, malaria, and yellow fever. There are about 120,000 kinds of fly, including bluebottles, horseflies, fruit flies, tiny gnats, and almost invisible midges. We call many small, winged insects flies, but the only true flies are those with two functional wings; they belong to the insect group *Diptera*. All flies lay eggs. The eggs hatch into larvae called grubs or maggots. The maggots feed and grow into pupae or chrysalises, from which the adult flies finally emerge. Despite their unpopularity with humans, flies play a vital role in nature. They pollinate flowers and recycle nutrients as they scavenge, and they are a source of food for many larger animals.

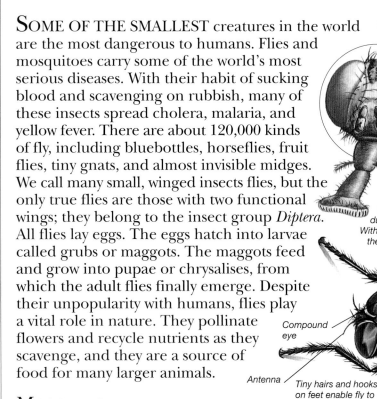

*Housefly has excellent eyesight and sponge-like mouthparts.*

*Eggs*

*Larva (maggot)*

*The bluebottle, or blowfly, lays thousands of eggs in dustbins and on meat. Within just a few weeks these eggs produce thousands more flies.*

*Housefly feeding on rotting meat*

*Compound eye*

*Antenna*

*Tiny hairs and hooks on feet enable fly to walk on the ceiling.*

*Wing*

## MOSQUITO

The mosquito has needle-shaped mouthparts that pierce the skin to suck the blood of humans, horses, and other animals. If a female *Anopheles* mosquito bites a person with malaria, it takes in blood infected with the microscopic organisms that cause this disease. When the mosquito goes on to bite another victim, the organisms pass into that person's blood, and so the disease spreads. The map below shows those parts of the world where malaria is most severe.

## FLIES AND DISEASE

Houseflies, bluebottles, and similar flies feed on and lay their eggs in rotting matter, including rubbish and excrement. Their mouthparts and feet pick up bacteria, or germs, which rub off when they settle on our food, dishes, and kitchen equipment. The illnesses which spread in this way range from minor stomach upsets to deadly infections such as typhoid.

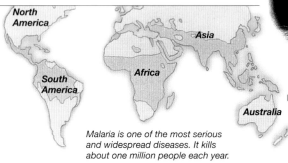

North America

Asia

Africa

South America

Australia

*Areas where malaria occurs*

*Malaria is one of the most serious and widespread diseases. It kills about one million people each year.*

*Hoverfly's wing tips make a figure-of-eight pattern with each wing beat.*

## HOVERFLY

The hoverfly is one of the most expert fliers. It can hover perfectly still, even in a wind, then dart straight up, down, sideways, or backwards. Tiny ball-and-stick structures behind the wings, called halteres, rotate rapidly and act as stabilizers during flight.

### LIFE CYCLE OF A DRONE FLY

The drone fly is a kind of hoverfly. It resembles a bee in appearance and makes a low droning sound in flight. After mating, the female lays her eggs near a puddle, a polluted pond, or other stagnant (non-moving) water. The larvae, known as rat-tailed maggots, live in the water, breathing through the long tail which acts like a snorkel. The rat-tailed maggots wriggle onto drier soil before pupating. When the adults emerge from the pupal cases, they fly off to feed on pollen and nectar from flowers.

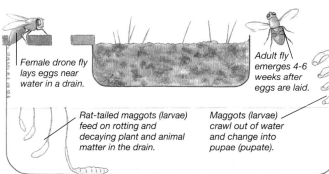

*Female drone fly lays eggs near water in a drain.*

*Adult fly emerges 4-6 weeks after eggs are laid.*

*Rat-tailed maggots (larvae) feed on rotting and decaying plant and animal matter in the drain.*

*Maggots (larvae) crawl out of water and change into pupae (pupate).*

### Find out more
ANIMALS
DISEASE
FLIGHT, ANIMAL
INSECTS

# ANIMAL
# FLIGHT

BIRDS, BATS, AND INSECTS are the only animals that truly fly. Other animals, such as flying squirrels, flying fish, and flying lizards, swoop or glide but cannot climb upwards into the air under their own power. Life in the air has several advantages for flying animals – some birds, such as hawks, can hunt their prey in midair; other birds can quickly escape from their predators. Birds are also able to migrate very long distances to find more suitable feeding areas in a cold season – the Arctic tern, for example, migrates about 18,000 km (11,000 miles) from the North Pole to the South Pole every year. Another bird, the swift, spends much of its life in the air, landing only to nest. A swift eats and drinks on the wing for nine months of the year. Birds, bats, and insects are also able to find food on land quickly and efficiently – a hummingbird hovers to gather nectar, a fruit bat flies into a tree to feed on fruit, and a dragonfly swoops over a pond to catch small flies. All flying animals from bees to buzzards need plenty of food to provide them with the energy to take to the air. Animals first began to fly about 300 million years ago, when Earth's prehistoric coal swamps were becoming overcrowded with all kinds of creatures. Through evolution, special features began to develop, such as a flap of skin on the body for gliding. In order to fly, an animal needs a lightweight body and strong muscles with which to flap its wings. Birds have hollow bones to save weight when they are in flight, so that a huge bird such as the golden eagle weighs less than 4 kg (9 lb).

*ARCHAEOPTERYX*
One of the first birds known to have existed is called *Archaeopteryx*. Fossil remains date back 150 million years. *Archaeopteryx* could glide and fly through the air.

*Elastic fibres allow the wings to shrink so the bat can fold them neatly.*

SOOTY TERN
The sooty tern lives on the wing for up to 10 years. It returns to the ground only to breed.

## WINGS
The wings of a flying animal are light so that they can be flapped easily. They are broad and flat, to push the air downwards and give lift. Wings must also be flexible for control in the air. An insect's wings are made of a thin membrane stiffened by tube-like veins. A bird's wings have bones and muscles at the front; feathers form the rest of the surface. A bat's wings consist of a thin layer of muscles and tough fibres sandwiched between two layers of skin that are supported by bones.

*Main bones in the wing*

*Wings stretch between the forearm and finger bones.*

*Powerful wing-flapping pectoral muscles are in the bat's chest.*

Bat

*Feathers near the wing root shape the wing smoothly into the body.*

*Flight feathers are light and stiff, with strong shafts and large, smooth vanes.*

*Covert feathers are at the front of the wing. They are small and packed closely together, to give a smooth edge.*

Wing of a kestrel

*Primary flight feathers help to reduce turbulence.*

# HOVERING

Only a few kinds of animals can hover. Staying still in midair requires great control and delicate balance as the animal adjusts its wingbeats to the slightest breeze. A few animals, such as some moths, hover as they gather food. Hummingbirds also hover expertly to feed. As they sip nectar from flowers, hummingbirds hover, go straight up and down, and fly backwards – just like helicopters. Hummingbirds beat their wings 20 to 50 times per second; this produces the humming sounds.

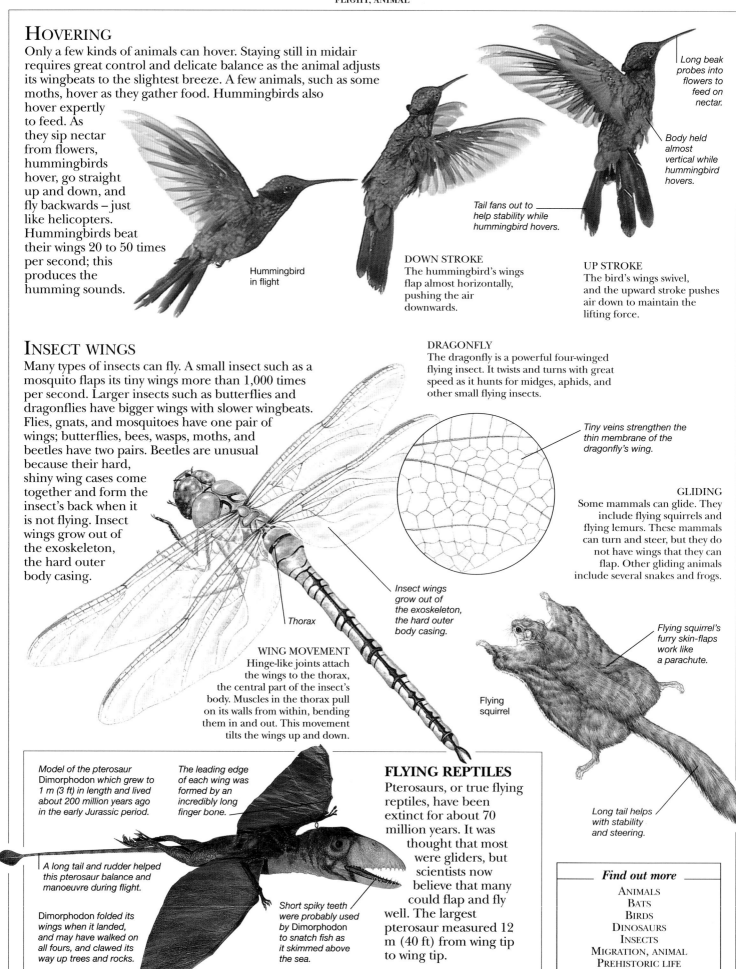

*Hummingbird in flight*

*Long beak probes into flowers to feed on nectar.*

*Body held almost vertical while hummingbird hovers.*

*Tail fans out to help stability while hummingbird hovers.*

### DOWN STROKE
The hummingbird's wings flap almost horizontally, pushing the air downwards.

### UP STROKE
The bird's wings swivel, and the upward stroke pushes air down to maintain the lifting force.

# INSECT WINGS

Many types of insects can fly. A small insect such as a mosquito flaps its tiny wings more than 1,000 times per second. Larger insects such as butterflies and dragonflies have bigger wings with slower wingbeats. Flies, gnats, and mosquitoes have one pair of wings; butterflies, bees, wasps, moths, and beetles have two pairs. Beetles are unusual because their hard, shiny wing cases come together and form the insect's back when it is not flying. Insect wings grow out of the exoskeleton, the hard outer body casing.

### DRAGONFLY
The dragonfly is a powerful four-winged flying insect. It twists and turns with great speed as it hunts for midges, aphids, and other small flying insects.

*Tiny veins strengthen the thin membrane of the dragonfly's wing.*

*Thorax*

*Insect wings grow out of the exoskeleton, the hard outer body casing.*

### WING MOVEMENT
Hinge-like joints attach the wings to the thorax, the central part of the insect's body. Muscles in the thorax pull on its walls from within, bending them in and out. This movement tilts the wings up and down.

### GLIDING
Some mammals can glide. They include flying squirrels and flying lemurs. These mammals can turn and steer, but they do not have wings that they can flap. Other gliding animals include several snakes and frogs.

*Flying squirrel's furry skin-flaps work like a parachute.*

*Flying squirrel*

*Long tail helps with stability and steering.*

*Model of the pterosaur Dimorphodon which grew to 1 m (3 ft) in length and lived about 200 million years ago in the early Jurassic period.*

*The leading edge of each wing was formed by an incredibly long finger bone.*

## FLYING REPTILES
Pterosaurs, or true flying reptiles, have been extinct for about 70 million years. It was thought that most were gliders, but scientists now believe that many could flap and fly well. The largest pterosaur measured 12 m (40 ft) from wing tip to wing tip.

*A long tail and rudder helped this pterosaur balance and manoeuvre during flight.*

*Dimorphodon folded its wings when it landed, and may have walked on all fours, and clawed its way up trees and rocks.*

*Short spiky teeth were probably used by Dimorphodon to snatch fish as it skimmed above the sea.*

### Find out more
ANIMALS
BATS
BIRDS
DINOSAURS
INSECTS
MIGRATION, ANIMAL
PREHISTORIC LIFE

# FLOWERS AND HERBS

THE EXQUISITE BEAUTY, colour, and perfume of flowers have inspired artists and poets for centuries. Flowers are among the most brightly coloured of all living things. They include sun-loving desert marigolds, hardy poppies in the snowy Arctic, tropical orchids, and cultivated garden roses, as well as some tiny inconspicuous flowers. Without the thousands of different flowers and herbs that grow on the Earth, bees could not make honey, butterflies and hummingbirds would have no food, we would have no flowerbeds, and perfume would have no fragrance. For most of us, the word "flower" describes any flowering plant that is particularly colourful or pretty. To the botanist, who studies plants, however, a flower refers strictly to the reproductive part of a plant – its bloom or blossom. The word "herb" is an everyday name we give to smaller, less colourful flowering plants whose leaves and blossoms have a strong, pleasant scent and taste.

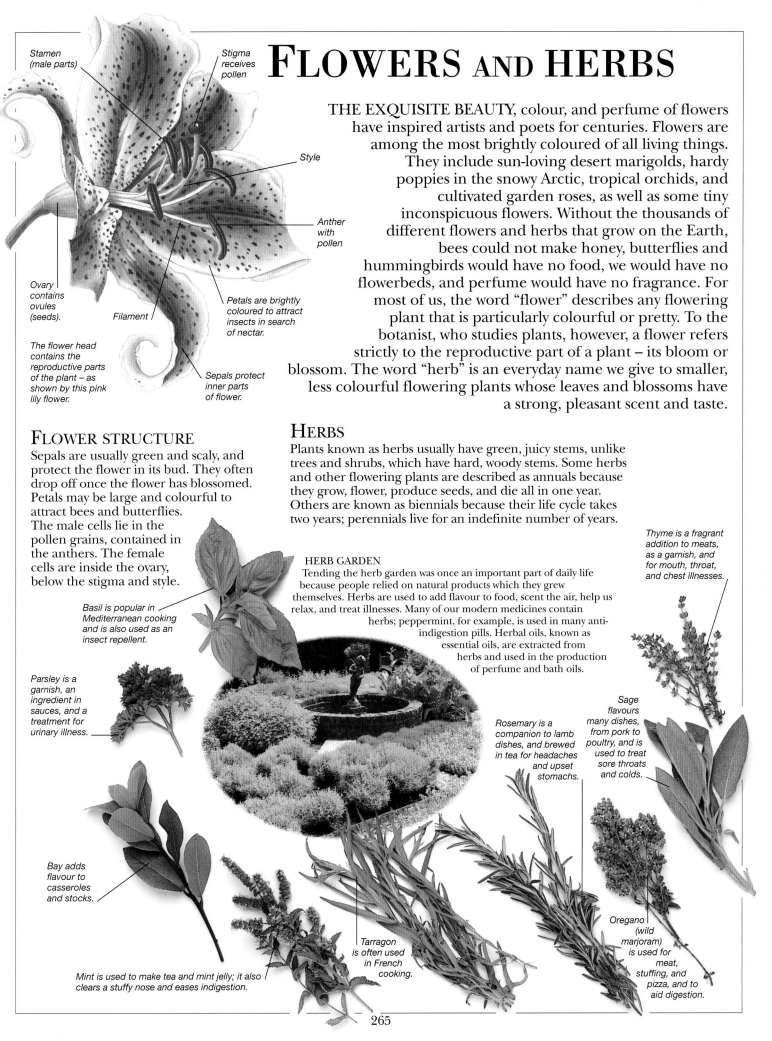

Stamen (male parts)

Stigma receives pollen

Style

Anther with pollen

Ovary contains ovules (seeds).

Filament

Petals are brightly coloured to attract insects in search of nectar.

The flower head contains the reproductive parts of the plant – as shown by this pink lily flower.

Sepals protect inner parts of flower.

## FLOWER STRUCTURE

Sepals are usually green and scaly, and protect the flower in its bud. They often drop off once the flower has blossomed. Petals may be large and colourful to attract bees and butterflies. The male cells lie in the pollen grains, contained in the anthers. The female cells are inside the ovary, below the stigma and style.

## HERBS

Plants known as herbs usually have green, juicy stems, unlike trees and shrubs, which have hard, woody stems. Some herbs and other flowering plants are described as annuals because they grow, flower, produce seeds, and die all in one year. Others are known as biennials because their life cycle takes two years; perennials live for an indefinite number of years.

### HERB GARDEN

Tending the herb garden was once an important part of daily life because people relied on natural products which they grew themselves. Herbs are used to add flavour to food, scent the air, help us relax, and treat illnesses. Many of our modern medicines contain herbs; peppermint, for example, is used in many anti-indigestion pills. Herbal oils, known as essential oils, are extracted from herbs and used in the production of perfume and bath oils.

Basil is popular in Mediterranean cooking and is also used as an insect repellent.

Parsley is a garnish, an ingredient in sauces, and a treatment for urinary illness.

Bay adds flavour to casseroles and stocks.

Mint is used to make tea and mint jelly; it also clears a stuffy nose and eases indigestion.

Tarragon is often used in French cooking.

Rosemary is a companion to lamb dishes, and brewed in tea for headaches and upset stomachs.

Thyme is a fragrant addition to meats, as a garnish, and for mouth, throat, and chest illnesses.

Sage flavours many dishes, from pork to poultry, and is used to treat sore throats and colds.

Oregano (wild marjoram) is used for meat, stuffing, and pizza, and to aid digestion.

Wild
dog rose

Cultivated
tea rose

# POLLINATION

To produce a seed, the male cell in a pollen grain must fertilize a female cell in the ovule. For this to happen the pollen must travel from its anther to the female stigma. In some flowers, the pollen is small and light, with wings, and is blown from one flower to another by the wind.

# HORTICULTURE

From the beginnings of civilization, people have cultivated flowers for their scent and colour. Today's garden roses have been bred from wild ancestors so that they have larger, more numerous, and more colourful petals, sweeter scents, and a longer flowering time. The art of gardening is called horticulture.

## BEES AND FLOWERS

Bees help pollination. As a bee feeds on nectar and pollen, more pollen inside the flower sticks to the bee's legs and body and is carried by the bee to the next flower, where it pollinates the female parts.

## NECTAR

Butterflies, moths, bats, and birds feed on the sweet, energy-rich nectar inside each flower. Bees convert nectar into honey in the beehive.

## BIRD-OF-PARADISE FLOWER

The bird-of-paradise plant comes originally from riverbanks in southern Africa and is now grown in many parks and gardens. Each plant has brilliant orange flowers which form a shape that looks like the head and beak of a bird of paradise. The bird-of-paradise flowers rise one after the other from a long, stiff, green-pink casing.

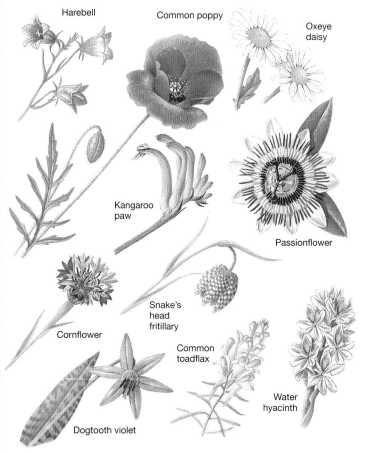

Harebell

Common poppy

Oxeye daisy

Kangaroo paw

Passionflower

Cornflower

Snake's head fritillary

Common toadflax

Water hyacinth

Dogtooth violet

## PERFUME

A flower's smell attracts butterflies, bees, and people too. Lily of the valley and rose are used in the manufacture of perfumes and soaps.

*Lily of the valley flowers have a sweet scent. Their leaves are scented too.*

# WILD FLOWERS AND CONSERVATION

Many wild flowers are in danger of extinction. Marshes are drained, and forests are felled for farmland and buildings, so the flowers that grow there are destroyed. Rare and beautiful blooms are at risk because they are dug up illegally by plant collectors. To save rare flowers, the places where they grow must be protected. As forests are cut down, thousands of flowers are disappearing even before they are known to science.

*Find out more*
BEES AND WASPS
CONSERVATION
and endangered species
FRUITS AND SEEDS
PLANTS

# FOOD AND FOOD TECHNOLOGY

## FOOD PRESERVATION
Food goes bad because of bacteria (harmful organisms) which can grow in it. Bacteria cannot thrive in salted, smoked, frozen, high-acid, or high-sugar foods. Tinned food has all the air drawn out and is heat-treated to stop decay from within. Irradiating foods with gamma rays to kill bacteria is the most modern method of preservation, but some doubt its safety.

ALL LIVING THINGS need food; it is the basic fuel of life. It keeps us warm, gives us energy, and helps us grow. Our daily pattern of eating and drinking is called our diet. Diets vary across the world according to the availability of food. Humans can digest a wide range of foods from both plant and animal sources, but some people, called vegetarians, choose not to eat meat for health, religious, or other reasons. Lack of the right kinds of food can lead to disease, inadequate growth, and eventually starvation. Eating too much of the wrong kinds of food can cause heart disease and other illnesses.

Fruit and vegetable market

## NUTRITION
A balanced diet is one that provides everything the body needs for health and growth. Energy-giving foods contain carbohydrates and fats, which are burned up slowly by the body. Energy in food is measured in calories. A 10-year-old needs about 2,000 calories a day. Body-building food is called protein and comes mainly from meat, fish, milk, eggs, nuts, and cereals. Vitamins are necessary to keep skin and eyes healthy and blood vessels strong. Water helps dissolve and digest food. Small quantities of minerals are needed for growth: calcium helps keep teeth strong, and iron is necessary for healthy blood. Fibre in food cannot be digested, but it enables our intestines to grip the food as it passes through.

### FAMINE AND PLENTY
The world's farms produce enough to feed everyone, but food does not reach the hungry. Western nations have mountains of foodgrain which is surplus for them. However, in various parts of the world more than 40 million people starve. Many even die of hunger.

Pasta and rice are basic or "staple" foods and provide bulk, energy, and protein. Grains, cereals, and legumes such as peas and beans are also staple foods. Their use varies from country to country.

Poultry and meat provide protein for body building and fat for energy.

Seaweed

Nuts are a good source of protein and fat.

### REGIONAL FOOD
Food varies across the world according to climate, local customs, and religious beliefs. In France, cooks use local seaweed, found around coastlines and snails in their recipes. The diet of some Aboriginal Australians and Africans includes insects and grubs.

Fruits and vegetables provide vitamins, fibre, and natural sugar. Some vegetables such as potatoes provide carbohydrates for energy.

Fungi provide small amounts of fibre and minerals.

Fish and shellfish are rich in body-building protein, minerals, and vitamins.

Eggs and milk products provide a great deal of fat. They are also high in protein, vitamins, and minerals.

Snail

*The closed cooking range, with an oven in which heat levels could be regulated, was invented by Benjamin Thompson in 1795.*

## TRADITIONAL COOKING

The oldest method of cooking is roasting over an open wood fire. Stewing or boiling, using a pot hanging over an open fire, came later. The first "modern" closed range, with top burners and an oven fuelled by wood or coal, was introduced in the 18th century. In the 1850s, gas became the new fuel, followed in the early 20th century by electricity.

*Modern stoves may run on gas or electricity or a mixture of both.*

## MICROWAVE OVEN

A microwave oven cooks with high-frequency electromagnetic waves (called microwaves) instead of radiated heat. Microwaves cause the water molecules in food to vibrate, which makes them become hot. The heat cooks the solid parts of the food. Metal blocks microwaves, which is why metal dishes cannot be used in a microwave oven.

*For safety the door cannot open when the oven is on.*

## FOOD PREPARATION

Many foods have to be cooked before we eat them to make them easier to digest and taste better. Boiling or steaming cooks food with water, frying or grilling uses fast heat, usually on top of the stove, and stewing, roasting, and baking need the slow heat of an oven. Uncooked foods, such as salad, also need to be prepared, by washing, chopping, and mixing.

## FOOD PROCESSOR

The electric food processor, or blender, has made it possible to do laborious jobs extremely quickly. Using different tools and attachments, processors can mix raw ingredients for cakes, make pastry dough, chop, slice, and grate raw vegetables, make breadcrumbs, blend pâtés, and turn cooked fruit and vegetables into a purée or soup. They can whip cream and beat eggs too.

*Mixing bowl*

*Wear a clean apron and keep hands and utensils clean.*

*Freshly ground pepper adds flavour to savoury foods.*

*Wooden spoon*

*Metal saucepan*

*Rolling pin for pastry*

*Measuring jug*

## KITCHEN SAFETY

Preparing and cooking food is fun, but must be done carefully to avoid accidents and prevent germs spreading. Wash your hands before you start and whenever you move on to different ingredients. Use oven gloves to move hot dishes in and out of the oven and protect yourself from splashes with a clean apron.

*Oven glove*

*Apron*

## EQUIPMENT

Most cooking pans are made of metal that can conduct heat to the food inside them without melting. Wooden spoons are used to stir hot food in a saucepan; as wood does not conduct heat, it therefore protects your hands as you work. Glass is used for measuring jugs so you can easily see the amount inside. Bowls can also be made of glass.

---

***Find out more***

DIGESTION
FRUITS AND SEEDS
HEALTH AND FITNESS

# FOOTBALL AND RUGBY

AT PACKED STADIUMS in almost every country, football and rugby fans cheer the skills of their favourite players. Association football (soccer) is the most popular spectator sport in the world, and more people play it than any other team sport. More than 169 countries play soccer at international level. Other forms of football are popular, but less widespread. Soccer is played with a round ball, but rugby football and American football is played with an oval ball. American football is the top US spectator sport, with professional and college-level games drawing huge crowds. Some European countries have taken up American football, and Canadians play a similar sport. Rugby players compete mainly in Britain, France, Australia, Italy, New Zealand, and South Africa. Other types of football include rugby league, Gaelic football, played in Ireland, and Australian Rules football, which is popular in Melbourne.

*A player dives for the ball in American football*

## ANCIENT FOOTBALL
Mob football was the ancestor of modern football. It was a violent game played in England, with few rules, and was banned in the 14th century. It was not until late in the 19th century that the modern form of the game was played.

## AMERICAN FOOTBALL
In American football, players score points by crossing the ball over their opponents' goal line for a touchdown (six points), or kicking it between the goalposts for a field goal (three points). Each team has 11 players, selected from a squad of up to 45.

## SOCCER
In soccer, the most popular form of football, two teams of 11 aim to send the ball into the opposing goal with their feet or head. Only one team player, the goalkeeper, is allowed to touch the ball with his or her hands.

## FOOTBALL AND RUGBY GROUNDS
The American football, rugby football, rugby league, and soccer fields are all rectangular in shape, while the Australian Rules field is oval. Each usually has a standard size for international competition, but may vary at other levels according to location or the level of competition being played.

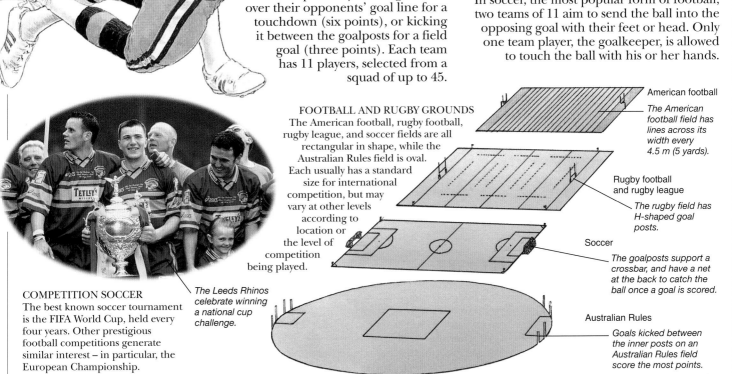

American football

*The American football field has lines across its width every 4.5 m (5 yards).*

Rugby football and rugby league

*The rugby field has H-shaped goal posts.*

Soccer

*The goalposts support a crossbar, and have a net at the back to catch the ball once a goal is scored.*

Australian Rules

*Goals kicked between the inner posts on an Australian Rules field score the most points.*

## COMPETITION SOCCER
The best known soccer tournament is the FIFA World Cup, held every four years. Other prestigious football competitions generate similar interest – in particular, the European Championship.

*The Leeds Rhinos celebrate winning a national cup challenge.*

Nou Camp, the home stadium of the Barcelona football team.

## STADIUMS

Important football and rugby games take place in stadiums. In recent years, stadiums have changed a lot. Fans used to stand on terraces, but these have now been replaced by seats, and stadiums have better facilities, access for disabled supporters, and restaurants. Some stadiums have roofs that can be pulled across.

## RULES OF THE GAME

Each type of rugby and football has different rules. A football game is ruled by a referee and two referee's assistants (linesmen). In rugby, the referee is supported by two touch judges. The referee has a whistle and the assistants and touch judges have flags to signal when a rule has been broken. A yellow card is shown as a warning; a red card means the player is sent off.

Red and yellow cards

## RUGBY

In 1823, schoolboy William Webb Ellis invented rugby when he picked up a football during a game and ran with it. Today, there are two forms of the game: Rugby Union, played between two teams of 15, and Rugby League, played between two teams of 13. Players run with the ball, kick it or use their hands, but must always pass backwards.

Rugby Union players form a scrum, each team trying to gain possession of the ball.

David Campesi

Football strip shows which team the player is on.

Goalkeeper's gloves

## SPORTING HEROES

Football and rugby stars are known around the world and are heroes to millions of fans. The legendary Brazilian player Pelé (b. 1940), considered the best footballer ever, was the star of four World Cup competitions. Australian Rugby Union player David Campese (b.1962) won 101 international caps in a 14-year career.

Rugby boot

Shin pads

Gum shield

Edson Arantes do Nascimento, better known to the world as Pelé.

Football

Rugby ball

Shin pads under socks protect from injury.

## EQUIPMENT

All you need to play a basic game of football or rugby is a ball, but modern equipment incorporates high-tech materials to help and protect players. Boots have studs to stop players slipping. Gloves with palm grips help football goalkeepers to catch the ball. Rugby balls have a non-slip covering to prevent players from dropping them during passing.

Players may wear trainers to practise.

*Find out more*

BALL GAMES
SPORTS
WALES

# FORCE AND MOTION

WHAT IS IT THAT MAKES objects move? Why does a boat float? How does a magnet work? Left to itself, any object would remain still, but when it is pushed or pulled, it begins to move. Something that pushes or pulls is called a force. Forces often produce motion, or movement. For example, an engine produces a force that pushes a car forward. There are several different kinds of forces. A magnet produces a magnetic force which pulls pieces of iron towards it, and a rubber band produces an elastic force when you stretch it. Liquids produce forces too. A boat floats because of the force of water pushing upwards on the hull. And a drop of water holds together because of a force called surface tension which makes all liquids seem as though they have an elastic skin around them. From the smallest particle inside an atom to the largest galaxy, the whole universe is held together by powerful forces. One of these forces is gravity, which holds us onto the surface of the Earth.

### CHANGING DIRECTION
When you move in a circle, on a fairground ride for example, a constant force is needed to change the direction of your motion. This force acts towards the centre of the circle. On the ride shown above, the force comes from the tension in the ropes that support the seats.

### ACCELERATION
The action of a force produces motion, making an object accelerate (speed up). For example, the force produced by the engine makes a ship accelerate. The stronger the force, the greater the acceleration.

### INERTIA
It takes a strong force to start a heavy object moving. In the same way, a strong force is needed to make it slow down and stop. This reluctance to start or stop moving is called inertia. The heavier the object, the greater its inertia.

### NEWTON'S LAWS OF MOTION
In 1687, the English scientist Isaac Newton (1642-1727) published his three laws of motion. The first law explains that an object stays at rest or moves at a constant speed unless a force pushes or pulls it. The second law explains how force overcomes inertia and causes acceleration. The third law explains that when a force (or action) pushes one way, an equal force (or reaction) always pushes in the opposite direction.

Water and air resist motion, producing a force called drag. A small boat accelerates easily and soon reaches its cruising speed. But, drag increases as speed increases. When drag force balances the driving force of the engines, speed stays constant.

### ACTION AND REACTION
A rowing boat moves by action and reaction. The force of the oars pushing on the water is the action. The moving water exerts an equal and opposite reaction on the oars. This reaction force pushes the boat forward.

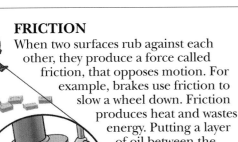

### FRICTION
When two surfaces rub against each other, they produce a force called friction, that opposes motion. For example, brakes use friction to slow a wheel down. Friction produces heat and wastes energy. Putting a layer of oil between the moving parts of a machine reduces friction and improves efficiency.

### STATIC FORCES
When two teams in a tug-of-war pull equally hard on the rope, neither team moves. This is because the forces produced by the teams balance exactly. Forces that balance and produce no movement are called static forces. A bridge stays up because of the balance of static forces. Its weight pushing down is balanced by parts of the structure pushing up.

*In an arch bridge, the piers (ends of the bridge) support the weight of the arch.*

___ *Find out more* ___
ATOMS AND MOLECULES
BRIDGES
GRAVITY
MAGNETISM
PHYSICS

# FOREST WILDLIFE

This map shows the main forest areas of the world.

North America

Asia

Africa

South America

Australia

☐ Temperate forest
☐ Coniferous forest
☐ Tropical forest

TREES ARE THE MOST IMPORTANT plants in a forest. They provide all kinds of animals, including monkeys, squirrels, and parrots, with food, homes, and escape routes from predators. The most common tree in any kind of forest often gives the forest its name, from the pine forests in the cold north, to the steamy teak forests in the tropical regions.

A forest consists of different layers of vegetation. The forest floor is covered with leaf litter. Here, parts of trees and other plants rot into the soil, helped by the millipedes, worms, and other small creatures that feed on them. The next layer of the forest is called the herb layer. It consists of small flowers and ferns that grow wherever enough sunlight filters through the trees. Bushes, shrubs, and young trees make up the under-storey of the forest. Next is a layer of tall tree trunks, laced with trailing vines and creepers. The uppermost part of the forest is called the canopy. Leaves grow in the sunlight; insects, birds, and bats pollinate the flowers; and fruit ripens to feed a host of creatures.

## LONG-EARED OWL
The long-eared owl swoops silently among the trees at twilight and during the night. These owls roost by day in a tree, and their mottled brown plumage provides good camouflage. The tufts on the feathers on this owl's head look like long ears – hence the name.

## WOLVERINE
The wolverine of northern forests is an exceptionally strong animal for its size. It tackles animal prey much larger than itself and also eats carrion (dead animals), fruit, and berries. The wolverine is nicknamed the "glutton" because of its large appetite.

## CONIFEROUS FORESTS
Pines and firs make up coniferous forests. These trees are evergreen – they keep their leaves all year, providing shelter for animals. The leaves are very tough, and only a few animals can eat and digest them. A few types of conifer, such as the larches, lose their leaves in autumn.

## BROAD-LEAVED FORESTS
The trees in a broad-leaved forest are called deciduous trees because their leaves drop off in the autumn, to be replaced by new leaves the next year. These trees blossom in the spring, which is the main animal breeding time. The new shoots provide food for animals. In the autumn, animals feed on the fruit, nuts, and berries of these trees, so they can survive the winter.

Ferns, such as bracken, grow quickly and rapidly cover clearings. Bracken is common on every continent except Antarctica. It spreads by sending out branching underground stems.

Bluebells are one of the spring woodland flowers. Some bluebells have pink flowers; others have white ones.

Wood anemone

## ROE DEER
The roe deer's reddish brown coat blends in well with the bracken where it lives. It lives alone for most of the year, feeding at twilight on the buds, shoots, and leaves of trees and shrubs.

Several heavy-bodied, strong-legged birds live in the forest, including pheasants such as the blue peacock shown here. These birds can fly but they often avoid danger by running into the dense forest undergrowth.

## CONSERVATION

As the forests are cut down or burned, animals lose their homes. Tree-living creatures such as this American uakari monkey are most at risk. These monkeys depend on the flowers and fruit from the large old trees in rain forests. Worldwide conservation organizations are trying to stop the destruction of the rain forests in order to save monkeys and thousands of other creatures.

## TANAGER

The paradise tanager is a noisy, active bird that lives high up in the rain forest canopy. Paradise tanagers keep their bright plumage all year and flutter from tree to tree in search of insects and ripe fruit.

# TROPICAL FORESTS

In tropical forests, the climate is much the same all year round. High temperatures and heavy rainfall make tropical rain forests some of the richest places for wildlife. There are many more species of trees than in any other kind of forest, and thousands more kinds of animals.

## SLOTH

Few animals move more slowly than the sloths of Central and South America. They hang from branches with their curved claws, eat leaves, and move so slowly that tiny green simple plants called algae grow on their coats. The algae help camouflage the sloths among the trees.

## PARROT

The male and female eclectus parrots shown here are so differently coloured that for many years people believed they were two different species of birds. These parrots live in the forests of New Guinea and Australia. Like all parrots, they have huge bills for cracking seeds.

*Several kinds of frogs, lizards, snakes, and squirrels have evolved, or developed, ways of gliding through the air from a high branch to escape from predators or to reach food. The gliding snake flattens its ribs as it leaps, to make a streamlined ribbon shape.*

## TOUCANET

With its large, light bill, the toucanet is an excellent berry picker. Its bright colours help it advertise for a mate in the breeding season. There are 42 kinds of toucanets, and they are all found in tropical South America. Toucanets nest in tree holes and eat birds' eggs and nestlings, fruit, insects, frogs, and lizards.

*Atlas moth resting on a bromeliad flower*

## POISON ARROW FROG

It is so damp in rain forests that frogs spend their lives in the trees and do not need to find water elsewhere. Frogs lay their eggs, or spawn, in pools of rain which collect on leaves, fungi, and in flowers such as bromeliads, which grow on trees. Poison Arrow frogs live in the rain forests of South America. Their bright colours warn predators of the deadly poison in their skin.

## ATLAS MOTH

The atlas moth is one of the largest moths in the world, with a wingspan of 30 cm (12 in). Today, atlas moths are rare. In the past, people killed thousands of them simply for their butterfly collections.

## LEMUR

There are 20 different kinds of lemur. These mammals are related to monkeys, and they live in trees in Madagascar, an island off the east coast of Africa. Mouse lemurs weigh only 60 gm (2 oz).

*Ground ginger is a spice made from the root of the ginger plant, which came originally from the forests of Asia.*

*Leaf roller ants curl up leaves on the forest floor and join the edges into a tube to make a nesting site.*

### *Find out more*
BIRDS
BUTTERFLIES AND MOTHS
CONSERVATION
and endangered species
FROGS AND OTHER AMPHIBIANS
OWLS

# FOSSILS

THE FIRST PLANTS, the earliest animals, the beginnings of human life – we know about prehistoric times because of fossils. Fossils are the remains of dead animals and plants that have been preserved for thousands or millions of years. A fossil might be the tooth of a dinosaur embedded in rock, or the outline of a leaf on a stone. By studying fossils, we can learn what ancient creatures and plants looked like and how they lived. Most fossils are of plants and animals that lived in water. When the living plant or animal died, its soft parts rotted away, leaving the hard pieces such as bones or leaf veins. Gradually, layers of mud piled up and squeezed the remains of the plant or animal at great pressure. Slowly the mud, bones, and other remains fossilized, or turned to rock, in the place where they lay underground. Over many thousands of years, the movements of the Earth twisted and buckled the rocks, lifting the fossils closer to the surface of the soil. Sun, rain, and wind wore away the rocks and exposed the fossil.

*Fossil collecting is a hobby that anyone can enjoy. You can find fossils in rocks, on beaches, and in quarries.*

## AMMONITE
Some of the most common fossils are the shells of sea creatures called ammonites. Ammonites were related to squid and octopuses. They were very widespread about 250 million years ago. The smallest ammonites measured less than 2 cm (1 in) across; the largest measured about 2.5 m (8 ft) across. Ammonites died out with the dinosaurs about 65 million years ago.

*Fossil of a fish called* Sparnodus – *an ancestor of the sea bream*

Fin on back for steering and stability

Backbone

Powerful two-lobed tail

Rear paddles

Long jaws and short, sharp teeth

Large eye socket

Ribs

Front paddle for steering

## TYPES OF FOSSILS
When rock-forming minerals slowly replace the original parts of a dead creature or plant, they make a mineralized fossil. Sometimes the parts of a creature or plant rot away after being buried, leaving a hole in the rock; this is called a mould fossil. If the hole fills up with rock minerals, it becomes a cast fossil. The fossilized signs of animals, such as footprints, droppings, and tracks, are called trace fossils.

*Mineralized fossil of a poplar leaf, 25 million years old*

*Cast fossil of a creature called a trilobite, which lived in the sea*

## ICHTHYOSAUR
Sometimes the outline of an animal's skin is preserved as well as its bones. This happened to the ichthyosaur shown above – a sea reptile from about 150 million years ago. The ichthyosaur looked like a dolphin, so it probably led a life similar to that of dolphins. The outline of this fossil shows a fin on the back and a two-lobed tail. The dozens of sharp teeth in the long jaws tell us that this animal grabbed fish and other slippery prey.

*The word* fossil *literally means "dug up". People who study fossils are called palaeontologists.*

### Find out more
DINOSAURS
EVOLUTION
PREHISTORIC LIFE
ROCKS AND MINERALS